Briefly,
ABOUT THE AUTHOR

Philip S. Foner, a native New Yorker, has a B.A. from the College of the City of New York, where he graduated with high honors, and an M.A. and a Ph.D. from Columbia University. He has taught history at City College, and lectured extensively at universities in the U.S.A. and abroad including Harvard, Yale, Columbia, University of Wisconsin, University of California, University of Moscow, University of Tokyo, and University of Havana. Dr. Foner is currently the Independence Foundation Professor at Lincoln University, Oxford, Pennsylvania, established in 1854 as the first black college in the United States. At Lincoln Dr. Foner teaches Black History. Dr. Foner is the author of many books including the four volume *Life and Writings of Frederick Douglass*, the four volume *History of the Labor Movement in the United States*, the two volume *Complete Writings of Thomas Paine*, a two volume collection of the Speeches of W. E. B. Du Bois, *Jack London: American Rebel*, and *Jews in American History, 1619–1865*. Besides his academic work, Dr. Foner is on the Board of Editors of *The Journal of Negro History*, and contributes regularly to the *Journal* as well as to *Labor History* and other scholarly publications.

"*The humorous writer professes to awaken and direct your love, your pity, your kindness — your scorn for untruth, pretension, imposture — your tenderness for the weak, the poor, the unhappy.... He comments on all the ordinary actions and passions of life about. He takes upon himself to be the week-day preacher.*"

— MARK TWAIN'S NOTES ON THACKERAY'S ESSAY ON SWIFT

INTERNATIONAL PUBLISHERS
381 Park Avenue South NEW YORK, N.Y. 10016

Mark Twain Social Critic
by Philip S. Foner

Mark Twain
Social Critic

by Philip S. Foner

International Publishers
New York

First published by International Publishers, New York, 1958
Second Edition, 1966. This edition is published
simultaneously by International Publishers, New York and
Seven Seas Books, Berlin, 1972
Second printing 1975.

To Moe and Henry

Copyright (c) by Philip S. Foner, 1958
ISBN: 0-7178-0356-2
Library of Congress Catalog Card Number 58-11505
Cover Design by Lothar Reher
Printed in the German Democratic Republic

Contents

Tributes to Clergymen, The Catholic Church, The Established Church, Was Twain an "Infidel"?

"In Defense of General Funston," "The War Prayer,"
King Leopold's Soliloquy, The Fruits of Imperialism.

PREFACE

The *New York Times* carried a report on April 7, 1956, from its correspondent in Ceylon, quoting the newly elected Prime Minister, S. W. R. D. Bandaranaike. Bandaranaike, who was also leader of the People's United Front which won the elections, pledged that his country no longer would tolerate foreign domination or interference. "But we are not wild men," he added. "We are not anti-Western and we are not hostile to the United States. How could I be hostile to a country that produced Mark Twain?"

The fact that Mark Twain, of all Americans, should personify for the leader of a country emerging from colonial oppression the best in American democratic tradition, must have come as a surprise to many who have regarded him either as a simple, happy humorist or a writer of books for children. Yet to men and women struggling for freedom the world over, he has long been, together with Jefferson, Lincoln, and Whitman, part of the great composite image of democratic America. Surely, it is time for a careful look at what Mark Twain had to say that makes him a powerful influence for freedom and democracy among peoples everywhere.

It is the purpose of this book to pursue such an examination. Towards this end, I have presented, as a background, a brief description of Mark Twain's life and personality and an analysis of the critical reception to his work during his lifetime and since his death. This is followed by a detailed examination of Mark Twain's thinking on a wide variety of social, political and economic issues. Throughout I have followed as a guiding principle Mark Twain's dictum that "in writing, it is usually stronger and more dramatic to have a man speak for himself than to have someone else relate a thing about him." Because they effectively reveal Mark Twain as a social critic and add color and vitality to the story, I have included a large number of quotations from Twain's own writings and speeches, many of them heretofore unpublished.

A full understanding of Mark Twain's social criticism is impossible without a study of the vast collection of Mark Twain Papers housed in the Bancroft Library at the University of California. Here, gathered under one roof, are thousands of unpublished writings of Mark Twain: notebooks, letters, autobiographical papers, manuscripts relating to many aspects of his social criticism, as well as letters to him. Thus I owe particular thanks to Clara Clemens Samossoud, Mark Twain's daughter, Mr. T. G. Chamberlain, and Professor Henry Nash Smith, trustees of the collection, who generously gave me the opportunity to do the necessary research in the papers and to quote from them.

Gratitude is also extended to the officials of Yale University Library, the Huntington Library at San Marino, California, the Widener Library of Harvard University, the New York Public Library, American Jewish Archives, and the Library of Congress for making available to me the Mark Twain Papers and other manuscripts in their collections.

I must also express my thanks to the following libraries for making available to me many magazines, newspapers, pamphlets and unpublished studies: The British Museum, Library of Congress, New York Public Library, Chicago Public Library, and the libraries of the Universities of Bucknell, California, Chicago, Columbia, Cincinnati, Harvard, Iowa, Louisiana, Michigan, Missouri, Oklahoma, Pennsylvania, Princeton, Stanford, Tennessee, Texas, and Wisconsin.

Excerpts from Mark Twain's published works have been reprinted here with the permission of the following publishers and holders of copyrights, to whom special thanks are due: Harper and Brothers; Charles Scribner's Sons; Harcourt, Brace and Co.; Harvard University Press; Stanford University Press; Houghton Mifflin Co.; University of California Press; University of Illinois Press. I wish to thank Miss Mildred Howells for permission to quote from her work, *Life and Letters of William Dean Howells*.

In closing I wish to thank Professors Henry Nash Smith and Arthur Laurence Vogelback for helpful suggestions and my wife, Roslyn Held Foner, for valuable assistance in reading the proofs.

PHILIP S. FONER

Croton-on-Hudson, New York
Summer, 1958

Chapter One
MARK TWAIN: A BRIEF PORTRAIT

Since 1910, the year of Mark Twain's death, there has been a steady flow of literature which has revealed many aspects of his life and character wholly unfamiliar to the readers of his books. The publication of his notebooks, autobiography, and many of his personal letters has provided an intimate self-portrait of the man. The reader who wishes to study Twain's career in detail will find no dearth of biographical information about America's greatest writer. The following discussion of Mark Twain's life and personality is devoted to the main highlights of his career. It is presented in the belief that, despite its briefness, it will make it easier for the reader to understand the evolution of Mark Twain's social criticism.

Background and Birth

Mark Twain chose to trace the continuity of what he called "the real turning-point of my life" to the Garden of Eden. "It was there," he wrote, "that the first link was forged of the chain that was ultimately to lead to the emptying of me into the literary guild." For a more limited purpose, however, the immediate forbears of Samuel Langhorne Clemens supply all that is needed in the quest for contributions of heredity to his make-up. The spirit of revolt against tyranny was imbedded in Mark Twain's background. There was Gregory Clemens — the English judge who signed the death warrant of Charles I, and who in so doing, Twain rejoiced, "did what he could toward reducing the list of crowned shams of his day." There were the Quaker ancestors in Twain's lineage who left a heritage of opposition to war, anti-clericalism, and "sympathy for all underdogs and minorities against cruelty and bullying in any form." One of his Quaker ancestors in

Virginia manumitted his thirty-three slaves, declaring himself "fully persuaded that freedom is the natural right of all mankind."

Mark Twain's father, John Marshall Clemens, was born on August 11, 1798, in Campbell County, Virginia. After migrating to the Western frontier across the Alleghenies, his father was killed, and his mother remarried. The family then moved to Kentucky. Here John M. Clemens studied law and was granted a license to practice in the courts. Here, too, in 1823, he married Jane Lampton, a Kentucky belle noted for her wit and beauty. The Lamptons claimed a connection with the Lamptons in England — the Earls of Durham — and a number of them devoted themselves almost exclusively to attempting to prove their claim to the earldom and the family's wealth. So deeply did he feel the futility of this that Twain wrote of James Lampton, one of the claimants: "'The earl' was a man of parts, and might have accomplished something for himself but for the calamitous accident of birth."

A year after his marriage, John Clemens started the series of moves that was eventually to bring him and a somewhat larger family to Missouri. One important stop was Jamestown, Tennessee, where he practiced law, became county commissioner, was elected circuit-court clerk of the county and acting Attorney General. So confident was he of the brilliant future of the section that he bought thousands of acres of land, thereby, as he thought, insuring financial security to the Clemenses. Bought at what he considered a bargain, the land proved to be so poor that it yielded nothing but potatoes and wild grass — and a harvest of alternating hope and despair for the family. "This land . . . influenced our life . . . during more than a generation. . . . It kept us hoping and hoping during forty years. . . . It put our energies to sleep and made visionaries of us — dreamers and indolent. We were always going to be rich next year. . . . To begin [life] poor and *prospectively* rich! The man who has not experienced it cannot imagine the curse of it."

The "curse" of this land took its toll early. From his envied position as "the most opulent citizen of Fentress County," reputedly worth at least $3,500, John Clemens gradually slipped into the comparatively menial posts of village storekeeper in Jamestown, and postmaster in a tiny village about nine miles north of that town.

In the spring of 1835, John Clemens sold everything but "the Tennessee land," the final symbol of hope for the poverty-ridden family, and turned his face westward. His destination was Florida, Missouri, where his brother-in-law, John Quarles, had been urging him to bring his family. In later years Twain explained that his father's "fortunes were wrecked" in "the great financial crash of '34. . . . He was a proud man, a silent, austere man, and not a person likely to abide among the scenes of his vanished grandeur and be the target for public commiseration." To such a man the West offered the promise of a fresh start.

After a harrowing journey by land and steamboat, the little band of Clemenses, seven in number, counting Jennie, the slave girl, last of the three Negroes John Clemens had inherited from his father's estate, reached Florida, Missouri. Here, on November 30, 1835, in a two-room clapboard house on South Mill Street, Mark Twain was born, increasing the population by one per cent, as he wrote later.

In Florida, John Clemens practiced law, served as Judge of the Monroe County Court, and ran a store, first in partnership with Quarles, and then on his own. He prospered sufficiently to build a better house for his family, and bought land in Monroe County. But his future in Florida received a devastating blow when the Salt River Navigation Project, which was to make Florida accessible to river boats, was rejected by Congress. In November, 1839, he moved his family to Hannibal, some thirty miles away, and "politically and socially the first town in northeast Missouri in the 1830's." Here he opened a general store, invested his remaining capital in rental properties, and loaned several thousand dollars to a land speculator named Ira Stout to whom he had already sold the most valuable of his holdings in Monroe County. Poor management and the Panic of 1837 brought the general store to the verge of bankruptcy. Clemens' tenants, crushed by the panic, could not pay, and Ira Stout defaulted on his debt. This last blow, Twain wrote later, ruined his father, and condemned him to "several years of grinding poverty and privation" before his death in 1847.

In later years, Mark Twain liked to remember Hannibal as a sleepy, peaceful village "drowsing in the sunshine of a summer morning." It was, indeed, a small community, but it was growing rapidly. In 1833, twenty-four years after its founding, Hannibal had only fifty inhabitants and three stores. By the end of the decade, however, it boasted 1,034 persons, a newspaper, a cigar factory, a whisky distillery, and several slaughter houses. The key to its growth and its promising future was the Mississippi River — "the great Mississippi, the magnificent Mississippi, rolling its mile-wide tide along." Three blocks from Twain's home, the big river steamers brought wheat, hemp, and tobacco to Hannibal's wharves.

Despite Mark Twain's impression very late in life that Hannibal epitomized small-town democracy "full of liberty, equality, and Fourth of July," he acknowledged that it had its own little aristocracy. "You perceived that the aristocratic taint was there," he noted. But the class division, he insisted, was not based on wealth. Ancestry was a prime factor in determining what families belonged to the aristocracy, and those from the South were looked up to. Hence the Clemenses, who were of Southern origin, and slaveholders, were accepted as people of "good family" despite their poverty. As Twain was later to emphasize, a major evil of slavery was that it fostered an aristocracy.

Aristocratic though he may have been according to the mores of Hannibal, John Clemens had "an unerring faculty of making business failures." Yet his lack of success as a businessman did not prevent him from occupying a distinguished place both in Florida and Hannibal. When the Missouri Legislature authorized the incorporation of the Salt River Navigation Company, his name headed the list of sixteen Commissioners from three counties to take subscription to its capital stock; when it was suggested that a railroad be substituted for a river channel, John Clemens' name appeared first among the six men appointed as Commissioners to create the Florida & Paris Railroad; when an act established the Florida Academy, John Clemens and John Quarles were listed as trustees. (The first of these two ventures never materialized.)

This public distinction continued in the larger town of Hannibal. John Clemens' name was included on committees chosen to appraise property, draft resolutions, report on roads, and found libraries. His obituary notice in the Hannibal *Gazette* of March 25, 1847, thus eulogized him: "He was noted for his good sense and a clear discriminating mind. These added to a high sense of justice and moral rectitude, made him a man of uncommon influence and usefulness. His public spirit was exercised zealously and with effect upon every occasion. His efforts to establish a library and institutions of learning in our city were such as to entitle him to all commendation, and his untimely death is felt . . . as a loss to the whole community."

Young Printer

In his *Autobiography*, written late in life, Twain recalls the difficulties the Clemens family faced following his father's death. "It was pretty hard sledding" for the family — the affairs of which fell largely on the shoulders of Jane Clemens, especially since her oldest son, Orion, was frequently away from home — and young Sam had to work to add to the family income. However, it is not true, as Twain recalls, that he "was taken from school at once upon my father's death," and began work as printer's devil on the Hannibal *Courier*, owned by Joseph Ament. He continued his education for at least a year following his father's death, meanwhile working after hours and during the summer as a newspaper delivery boy, grocer's clerk, blacksmith's helper, drugstore clerk, and bookseller's assistant.

In his twelfth year, Sam Clemens was projected into journalism, and it was to influence all phases of his later development. From the spring of 1848 until June, 1853, he was printer's devil, paper carrier, compositor, sub-editor, and reporter on two local papers: for two years on Ament's *Courier*, and for three years on a number of papers launched in Hannibal by his brother, Orion. By the time he joined his brother on the Missouri *Courier*, he was "swift and clean as a good journeyman," and by far a better compositor than the rest of his fellow apprentices. But these printing skills were not all that he learned during his five years' newspaper work in Hannibal. He found a world that he never would have discovered in its public schools. It was a world of the printed word, and it encompassed both the literature of the people and of the standard professional writers. The first group was represented by the local humorous writings. From these skits and tall tales which he set into type, Mark Twain learned much that went into his own writings. The second group was represented mostly by "fillers," anecdotes from Greek mythology, references to such classical writers as Cicero, allusions to contemporary British novelists, particularly Thackeray and Dickens, and many excerpts from American, English and Continental authors — Bryant, Milton, Theodore Hook, Franklin, Irving, Whittier, Horace Mann, Theodore Parker, Scott, Carlyle, Hood, Lamb, Dumas, and others. The pages of the exchanges which came to the office carried their own excerpts. With good reason the Hannibal *Gazette* could say in April, 1847: "There is something in the very atmosphere of a printing office, calculated to awaken the mind and inspire a thirst for knowledge."

Though much of the miscellaneous material that found

its way into the printing office was poor stuff, the great literature Twain encountered there stimulated his reading, and he learned also to distinguish the good from the bad. "One isn't a printer ten years without setting up acres of good and bad literature," he noted years later, "and learning ... to discriminate between the two."

Yet a stray leaf from a book that he picked up on the streets one afternoon on his way home from the printing shop seems to have influenced him most. It was from a book about Joan of Arc, and there was matter enough on the torn page describing the Maid's persecution by her English captors to make him feel her sufferings. It aroused in Sam a desire to read her entire history, especially after he learned that she was a real person. Thus was kindled a passion for history "which became the largest feature of his intellectual life." The event "crystallized suddenly within him sympathy for the oppressed, rebellion against tyranny and treachery, scorn for the divine right of kings. ... He read hungrily now everything he could find relating to the French Wars, and to Joan in particular. He acquired an appetite for history in general." The stray leaf, Twain maintained, opened to him the full world of literature.

Orion, Twain later recalled, "never was able to pay me a single penny as long as I was with him." But his elder brother gave him something that soon more than made up for lack of monetary reward — encouragement and the opportunity to publish his writings. In her study of Twain's formative years in Missouri, Miss Minnie May Brashear asserts that "it is probably no exaggeration to say that the greatest single influence in Mark Twain's life was his older brother, lasting through the publication of *Roughing It*." It is difficult, perhaps, to conceive of Mark Twain being influenced by Orion, except negatively, as a demonstration of what to avoid in order to succeed. This "gentle, kindly, plodding, inept soul of almost saintly humility and patience," alternated between fits of optimism and pessimism, attempted countless experiments and failed in all. Yet there is no doubt that Orion widened his younger brother's horizons. His "three hundred and sixty-five red-hot new eagernesses every year" acted as a whirring emery stone on which Sam whetted the blades of his intellect and interest. One could not be associated with Orion long without being drawn into a heated controversy over a moral, religious, or political issue. Sam loved Orion for his integrity, vitality, and generosity, though he could feel indulgent scorn for his ineptitude and failures. And Orion deserved this love, for he introduced his younger brother to the world of ideas, of issues and opinions, nourished in him the urge for writing, and welcomed his contributions, thus stimulating him to try his hand.

Twain's writings for his brother's newspaper in Hannibal have all been discovered, and several studies, analyzing them, have been made. Here we need merely note that his first writings consisted of humorous anecdotes, satirical sketches, local news reports, facetious squibs, and some verse. Among them, however, was what may be characterized as Mark Twain's first political satire, a feature story, "Blabbing Government Secrets," which was printed in the Hannibal *Journal* of September 23, 1852, under his then pen name, "W. Epaminondas Adrastus Blab." The article explained that an extra session of the State Legislature had been called by the Governor, expressly for the purpose of changing the writer's surname from Perkins to Blab. "My title was altered, shortened, and greatly beautified," the correspondent boasted, "and all at a cost of only a few thousand of dollars to the State." This first expression of Twain's contempt for corrupt legislators, also declared his contempt for monarchy and aristocracy in Blab's comment: "As for Queen Victoria and Lord Derby, they may cut up as much as they like (about the name-changing) — it's none of their business." It was feeble, naive political satire, to be sure, but it shows the young writer experimenting with a form he was to use so effectively in his mature work.

Sam Clemens found the limitations of life in Hannibal

more chafing with each passing year. The spring of 1853 found him in his eighteenth year, rich in experience and self-confidence, but with empty pockets. He had nothing to show for his work for Orion as printer and editorial assistant except "poor, shabby clothes." After a quarrel with Orion who turned down a request for a few dollars to buy a second-hand gun, Sam determined to leave Hannibal. He told his mother he was going to St. Louis to find work and be near his sister, Pamela. His real intention was to visit the fabulous Crystal Palace at the New York Fair. Sadly Jane Clemens gave her permission, first having made him promise not "to throw a card or drink a drop of liquor" while he was away. (With this and other "oppressive" influences of his mother, we shall deal later.)

Sam Clemens left Hannibal May 27, 1853. His last pieces for Orion's paper were written the day before. In the autograph album of one of his girl friends, he bade his farewell to Hannibal:

> Good-by, good-by,
> I bid you now, my friend;
> And though 'tis hard to say the word,
> To destiny I bend.

Sam Clemens was four years old when he was brought to Hannibal; he was eighteen when he left in 1853. Twain well understood the importance of these fourteen years, so lovingly recreated in his major works. Almost a half-century later he wrote in *Following the Equator*: "All that goes to make the *me* in me was in a Missourian village, on the other side of the globe." While one may attribute this sweeping statement in part to Mark Twain's nostalgia, one can also assert that much that went into the making of the social critic was derived from his experiences in Hannibal. This, as we shall see, was the source of his vigorous opposition to slavery, superstition and aristocracy. Through his Hannibal newspaper activity he became acquainted with the work of the great writers and with the "literature of the oral anecdote," as Bernard De Voto characterizes the humor of frontier journalism. This broadened his perspective and aroused his interest in the problems and controversies of the day. His Hannibal writings reflect little of the social critic. But when he reached maturity as a writer, the Hannibal experiences would influence to no small extent what he had to say to the world.

For four years, Sam Clemens traveled about America as a printer, setting type in composing rooms in St. Louis, New York, Philadelphia, Cincinnati, Keokuk and Muscatine, Iowa. During two of these years, December 1853 to March 1855, he furnished correspondence (five letters) to the Muscatine *Journal*, published by his brother, Orion. And between November 1856 and April 1857, he wrote three letters under the pseudonym, "Thomas Jefferson Snodgrass," for the Keokuk *Daily Post*.

Mark Twain's letters to his family during this period, his correspondence to the Muscatine *Journal*, and the Snodgrass letters reveal his social and political thinking at this stage, and we shall examine them later under the specific subjects they cover. Here we need only note those passages which reflect his eagerness for knowledge and his insatiable spirit of inquiry. As in Hannibal, his work as a printer kept him in touch with the literature that went into the newspapers as "fillers." But his interest in books could not be satisfied by excerpts, and in New York he spent his nights in the libraries. "You ask me where I spend my evenings," he wrote Pamela. "Where would you suppose, with a free printers' library containing more than 4,000 volumes within a quarter of a mile from me, and nobody at home to talk to."

Two friends of this period, Frank E. Burrough in St. Louis and a Scot named Macfarlane in Cincinnati, strengthened his interest in books. The former, a chairmaker, was especially fond of Dickens, and instilled a deep love for the English novelist in his young friend. (During his residence in Keokuk, Sam Clemens was often observed carrying a volume of Dickens with him.) Macfarlane, his boarding-house friend in Cincinnati, was an amateur philosopher and his personal library of three dozen books covered philosophy, history and science.

Tom Paine, Poe, Shakespeare, Goldsmith, Dickens, Cervantes, Lecky, and Voltaire were some of the authors Sam Clemens read during these years. One book picked up in a hotel in Muscatine, Iowa, also influenced him deeply. It was a study of the English kings and their reigns. The information contained in the volume, added to what he had already learned about Joan of Arc, deepened his antagonism toward vested authority in Church and State, later to find brilliant expression in *The Prince and the Pauper, A Connecticut Yankee in King Arthur's Court,* and *Joan of Arc.*

Pilot and Miner

On April 15, 1857, the *Paul Jones,* piloted by Horace Bixby, set off for New Orleans from Cincinnati. On board was young Sam Clemens. From the gulf port he planned to sail for the Amazon to make a fortune in cocoa. But when he walked up the gang plank, he was headed not for South America but for a new career — the profession of piloting.

To be a pilot on the great Mississippi River required untiring industry and perseverance. He had to guide his boat over twelve hundred miles of murky, swirling waters, along shifting channels, without the aid of markers or searchlights. Sam Clemens' packed notebooks reveal the detailed information he had to acquire. Yet in two years he had mastered the river. On April 9, 1859, he was granted his pilot's license, and became co-pilot with the veteran, Horace Bixby, on the *Crescent City.* Before long he was pointing with justifiable pride to his position on the *City of Memphis,* the "largest boat in the trade, and the hardest to pilot."

The influence of the greatest of American rivers permeates every phase of Mark Twain's development. "The

Mississippi," Dixon Wecter observes in his discussion of Twain's Hannibal years, "made him, even in his minority, a citizen of the world, added to his health and resourcefulness, and fostered that appreciation of natural beauty . . . whose stamp appears not only upon *Life on the Mississippi* but all of his travel books, from *The Innocents Abroad* to *Following the Equator*." All this and more was true of Mark Twain's years on the river. During these four years on the Mississippi, he widened and deepened his understanding of people. As he himself observed: "I got personally and familiarly acquainted with about all the different types of the human nature that are to be found in fiction, biography, or history. . . . The feature of it I value most is the zest which that early experience has given to my later reading. When I find a well-drawn character in fiction or biography, I generally take a warm personal interest in him, for the reason that I have met him before — met him on the river."

"Sam was always scribbling when not at the wheel," Horace Bixby, the man who taught him the river, recalled. These writings consisted of personal letters, river notebooks, a burlesque of Captain Isaiah Sellers and his river reports, published in the New Orleans *Daily Crescent* of May 17, 1859. This was the only piece of Twain's writing to find its way into public print during his years on the river.

The Civil War brought an end to Mark Twain's career as a pilot. His last trip up the river from New Orleans to St. Louis was on the *Uncle Sam*. He left the ship at St. Louis on April 19, 1861, one week after the firing on Fort Sumter, and hurried back to Hannibal. Here he joined the Confederate Marion Rangers, his service lasting between one and three weeks. (We will deal with Twain's attitude toward the Civil War and his experiences as a Confederate soldier later.) Apart from his exceedingly brief military service, he spent the war years far removed from the battlefronts. On July 26, 1861, he left St. Joseph, Missouri, with his brother, Orion, for the Nevada Territory. Orion had been appointed by President Lincoln Secretary of the Territory, an appointment maneuvered by Edward Bates, a St. Louis lawyer who was Attorney General in Lincoln's cabinet. Sam Clemens went along as the Secretary's secretary, planning to stay three months.

On August 14, the Overland Stage carried Orion and Sam into Carson City, the capital of Nevada. Orion went to work at once as Secretary to Governor James Warren Nye. Sam, finding his duties as secretary to the Secretary hardly time-consuming, set about adjusting himself to the exciting life of the frontier. It was "the d - - dest country under the sun," he wrote to his mother. All about him he saw men digging for gold and silver, and seeking diversion from the backbreaking labor in "gambling, drinking and murder. . . ."

Sam Clemens did not, at first, succumb to the Nevada mining craze. Instead, he was going to make his fortune in timber claims. But in the winter of 1861, after a fire had destroyed his claim, he went with three companions to Unionville in Humboldt County to look for silver. Nothing turning up in Humboldt County, he went to Esmeralda County where he and Orion had acquired a camp. He settled at Aurora in February, 1862, and from there, for half a year, he prospected for gold and silver.

"I expected to see it glittering in the sun on the mountain summit," he confessed later. But he was soon working harder than he had ever done before or ever would again. He was driven along by the sight of cartloads of silver bricks, as large as pigs of lead, arriving from the mill every day. "I succumbed," he wrote, "and grew as frenzied as the craziest." And he was determined to prove that what others could do, he could. Writing to his sister, Pamela, he quoted:

> *In the bright lexicon of youth,*
> *There's no such word as Fail —*

"And I'll prove it," he added. All he did prove was that

he could work hard. But his failure as a miner forced him to the one field of activity which was, in the not too distant future, to give him more wealth than he could have extracted from the richest vein — the field of writing. In August, 1862, he reluctantly began work on the *Territorial Enterprise* of Virginia City as local reporter and feature writer at a salary of six dollars a day.

Washoe Reporter

In two years the *Territorial Enterprise,* under Joe Goodman, its aggressive and astute editor-in-chief, had become an influential organ, "the most remarkable paper on the frontier . . . the brainiest sheet on the coast." Goodman demanded of his reporters that they have convictions and the courage to back them.

Sam Clemens took seriously Goodman's insistence that a reporter for the *Enterprise* have the courage to "speak out." As a reporter of the legislative sessions at Carson City, he might have appeared to be a bored observer who wasted his time doodling comic cartoons. But his was actually an "astute watchfulness," and some of his earliest social criticism, as we shall see, is contained in his reporting of the legislative sessions, where he exposed and ridiculed crooked legislators, executives and judges.

The *Territorial Enterprise* for February 2, 1863, carried a legislative article of special historical importance, more for the name underneath it than for its contents. It was the first piece of Samuel L. Clemens' writings to appear over the signature "Mark Twain." "By the mark, twain," the leadsman on the River called out when he sunk his line to the two-fathom knot, a cry which meant that the boat was safe with twelve feet of water under her. Soon these two words were to cover the entire globe as "the greatest *nom de plume* ever chosen." It was not the first time, however, that the words had been so used. Twain himself wrote in 1874: " 'Mark Twain' was the nom de plume of one Capt. Isaiah Sellers, who used to write river news over it for the

New Orleans *Picayune*. He died in 1863, & as he could no longer need that signature I laid violent hands upon it without asking permission of the proprietor's remains. That is the history of the nom de plume I bear."

Many of Mark Twain's contributions to the *Territorial Enterprise* were reprinted in San Francisco papers, thereby establishing his journalistic reputation along the Coast. This made him an influential figure in the Territory. His witty articles and shrewd jibes at the politicians caused the members of the Territorial Legislature to think twice before taking any action that might invite Mark Twain's caustic attention.

Yet the name "Mark Twain" became more widely known during the years when he was a Washoe reporter as an inventor of preposterous hoaxes than as an astute critic of territorial political life. His first hoax "A Washoe Joke," which came to be popularly known as "The Petrified Man," contained an hilarious sketch of a local coroner who allegedly held an inquest over a body turned to rock centuries ago. The hoax, published in the *Enterprise* in October, 1862, was reprinted in Cincinnati, St. Louis, New Orleans, and San Francisco papers.

Then on October 28, 1863, the *Enterprise* carried an item captioned "The Latest Sensation," and signed "Mark Twain," which spread that name from coast to coast and even in Europe as newspapers, including the London *Lancet*, reprinted it either as "The Empire City Massacre" or "The Dutch Nick Massacre." Related on the authority of "Abram" Curry, the article told with gruesome detail of the multiple murder committed by P. Hopkins, a resident of "the old log-house just at the edge of the great pine forest which lies between Empire City and Dutch Nick's." Hopkins killed his wife with an ax, clubbed out the brains of six of his children, knocked insensible his two other children, cut his own throat from ear to ear, and dashed on horseback to Carson City, bearing in his hand the "reeking scalp" of his red-headed spouse. The final paragraph explained that, influenced by the San Francisco papers,

Hopkins had sold his valuable Gold Hill and Virginia City mining stocks and bought worthless Spring Valley stocks. Brooding over this, he had become "subject to fits of violence."

The story was reprinted as straight reporting, but the newspapers soon discovered that they had been hoaxed. Needless to say, the editors were more than a bit piqued. Twain was not at all dismayed by the howls of dismay from gullible editors. He had become quite adept at the give-and-take abuse characteristic of frontier journalism.

It was his penchant for personal abuse which eventually forced his departure from Virginia City. During Goodman's absence from the editorial chair of the *Enterprise*, Twain took it upon himself to accuse the staff of the rival paper, the *Union*, of failing to pay their pledges to the Sanitary Fund for the relief of Union soldiers and sailors. The upshot of the controversy, which we will consider in greater detail later, was the arrangement of a duel between Twain and Laird, the rival editor. Whether or not the pair ever met on the field of honor is debatable — students today question the versions of purported witnesses to the duel — but it ended with Twain leaving Virginia City at the end of May, 1864, for San Francisco. His sudden departure was made necessary by a warrant for his arrest under the new law which made it a felony even to send or to accept a challenge to a duel.

Thus his Nevada experience came to an end for Mark Twain. He had spent almost three years in the West where he had at first planned to remain only three months. He had tried mining and speculation in timber land, and finally he had become a reporter on the most influential paper in the intermountain region. Now, at thirty years of age, he was established in the profession in which he would gain fame and fortune. His editorials and articles had been printed in the leading papers on the Pacific Coast and received some notice in the Eastern journals. Here he adopted the pen name that was to become famous the world over.

From May, 1864, until December, 1866, San Francisco was the hub of Mark Twain's activities. Already well known to the journalists on the Coast, he joined the staff of the San Francisco *Morning Call*. He was at once brought into association with such California literary figures as Bret Harte, Orpheus C. Kerr, Joaquin Miller, Artemus Ward, and Charles H. ("Ingo") Webb. The city's literary lights gathered in the offices of the *Golden Era*, California's first literary publication. Fraternizing with this group, Twain's craftsmanship improved under their stimulus, and the range of his satire broadened. Soon he became a leading figure in the San Francisco literary world, and like the other young writers, a contributor to the *Golden Era* and the *Californian*.

Twain's writings during these two and a half years reached the Coast public through the *Morning Call*, the *Golden Era*, the *Californian*, the Sacramento *Union*, the San Francisco *Bulletin*; and many other publications reprinted his pieces. He also continued to write for the *Territorial Enterprise*; indeed, he resorted increasingly to his old paper, for as his humor became more and more impregnated with social criticism, a number of the California papers stopped printing it. When the *Morning Call* refused his articles criticizing the San Francisco police and city officials, Twain severed his connections with it, and almost immediately arranged with Joe Goodman to write a daily letter to the *Enterprise*. This gave him the freedom to concentrate his fire on widespread abuses in San Francisco. He assailed a whole series of evils in the corrupt city, where, Twain wrote, "the air is full of lechery, and rumors of lechery."

For a long time, students of Twain's writings could only guess at the contents of these later contributions to the *Enterprise*, the files of the paper having disappeared. Based on hearsay, however, Albert Bigelow Paine wrote: "Those who remember Mark Twain's *Enterprise* letters . . .

declare them to have been the greatest series of daily philippics ever written.... San Francisco was fairly weltering in corruption, official and private. He assailed whatever came first to hand with all the fierceness of a flaming indignation long restrained." Later critics have echoed Paine's judgment, generally agreeing that the *Enterprise* contributions already revealed Twain as "social critic" and "an accomplished social satirist."

Now that long and diligent research has uncovered thirty of the letters and dispatches that originally appeared in the *Territorial Enterprise* as well as reprints of others in various San Francisco papers of that day, it is apparent that, while Paine's comment is an overstatement, the conclusion that Twain was already functioning as a social critic is accurate. What he said in these letters and dispatches will be discussed later. But it is worth noting here his attacks on the San Francisco police for brutality towards the poor, especially the cruel treatment of the Chinese immigrants, while they ignored the crimes of the wealthy and let "many offenders of importance go unpunished." These articles so incensed the authorities that Martin G. Burke, then Chief of Police, sued the *Enterprise* for libel, an action which only served to swell the paper's circulation and Twain's reputation.

As we shall see, during his California period, Twain also produced essays satirizing religious hypocrisy, attacking the clergy for putting monetary considerations ahead of ethical precepts, and criticizing other aspects of contemporary society. He had become a sort of general censor, earning for himself the dual title of "Moralist of the Main" and "The Wild Humorist of the Sage Brush Hills." The juxtaposition of these titles is quite logical, if somewhat surprising, for the truth is that he was now accepted on the Pacific Coast first as a moralist and second as a humorist.

In the East and Middle West, however, he was still hardly known at all. Throughout 1864, the circulation of material signed "Mark Twain," with the exception of a letter in the New York *Sunday Mercury* of February 2,

1864, and a review of the play *Ingomar* in *Yankee Notions* of April, 1864, was still limited to Western and Southwestern audiences. Then, from an anecdote related by an ex-miner innkeeper in the faraway foothills of the California Sierras, Mark Twain spun a yarn, and, against his own misgivings but at the insistence of a friend, published it in the eastern press. It appeared in the New York *Saturday Press* of November 18, 1865.

The "villainous backwoods sketch," which the world knows as "The Celebrated Jumping Frog of Calaveras County," delighted the whole country, and spreading abroad, amused readers and listeners, highborn and low, from England to Australia and India. Mark Twain awoke (as Byron had awakened) to find himself famous. No less an authority than James Russell Lowell pronounced it "the finest piece of humorous writing yet produced in America." This recognition enhanced Twain's prestige on the Coast, and placed him at the head of what he characterized as "my breed of scribblers in this part of the country." But it did not bring him proportionate returns in the way of money or interesting work; therefore, he made an agreement with the Sacramento *Union*, by which it was to send him as its special correspondent to the Sandwich Islands, as Hawaii was then known. The commission, as we shall see, gave him an opportunity to do serious reporting and to direct his attention to matters of importance, such as the government and economy of the Islands, the functions of the missionaries, and the intrigues of foreign powers. It also provided him with lecture material upon his return.

On December 15, 1866, Mark Twain left San Francisco under contract with the *Alta California* to publish travel letters describing his experiences during a trip around the world. The newspaper noted his departure in a lead article, concluding:

"Mark Twain" goes off on his journey over the world as the Travelling Correspondent of the *Alta California*, not stinted as to time, place or direction — writing his weekly letters on such subjects and from such places as will best suit him. . . . That his letters will be read with interest needs no assurance from us — his reputation has been made here in California, and his great ability is well known; but he has been known principally as a humorist, while he really has no superior as a descriptive writer — a keen observer of men and their surroundings — and we feel confident his letters to the *Alta*, from his new field of observation, will give him a world-wide reputation.

As the *Alta California* predicted, Mark Twain's greatest work still lay ahead. But by the time he left California, he had already experienced most of what was to go into *Tom Sawyer, Huckleberry Finn, The Gilded Age, Life on the Mississippi, Roughing It*, and many of his sketches and stories. "Washoe and California," notes Bernard De Voto, "had finished what the mid-western frontier and the Mississippi had begun. . . . The rest is only development."

Travels, Books and Lectures

During the first five months of 1867, except for a visit to St. Louis to see his family, Mark Twain stayed in New York as correspondent for the *Alta California*. He worked hard at his job, and the seventeen articles he sent from New York contain invaluable descriptions of life in the metropolis immediately after the Civil War. In April, 1867, Twain booked passage with a shipload of pilgrims bound for the Holy Land on the *Quaker City*, to begin the journey made famous by *The Innocents Abroad*. While awaiting its departure — the ship was scheduled to set sail on June 8, 1867 — Twain witnessed the publication of his book, *The Celebrated Jumping Frog of Calaveras County, and Other Sketches*, on May 1, 1867 — an important date in American literature — the date of Mark Twain's first book, published in New York by C. H. Webb.

In late November, 1867, Twain returned to New York from his Mediterranean cruise with "those venerable fossils," the pilgrim passengers. His letters from foreign lands had been printed not only in the San Francisco *Alta Cali-*

fornia but also in Horace Greeley's New York *Tribune* and James Gordon Bennett's New York *Herald.* As the *Alta California* had predicted, his reports from abroad had made him famous. Now, in his thirty-second year, the leading newspapers of New York and California solicited contributions from him, and the lecture circuits competed for his services. He wrote his family that he had "18 invitations to lecture, at $100 each, in various parts of the Union," which he had declined because he was "for business now." The "business" was in Washington where he took a job briefly as private secretary to William M. Stewart, Senator from Nevada. But they soon quarreled, and he returned to New York to prepare for the publication of his travel book.

Several publishers had approached Twain for such a book, but he finally accepted the offer of the American Publishing Company of Hartford, which published books by subscription. The contract provided for a royalty percentage "a fifth more than they have paid any author, except Greeley." Since the company required a book of two volumes for the house-to-house canvassing by which it distributed its publications, Twain had to fill out his correspondence with additional material.

While he was preparing this additional material, he was also drawing on his travels for lectures for the Redpath Lyceum Bureau to be delivered during the season of 1868-69. *The Lyceum,* published by James Redpath, announced that Mark Twain was available for lectures at $100, with modifications: "This celebrated humorist has been a very successful lecturer in the West.... Lyceums must apply for him at an early date, unless they can secure their hall for any evening."

Twain's title for the lectures was "The American Vandal Abroad." This description of his platform appearance and manner was published in the Chicago *Tribune* early in 1869:

Mr. Twain is a gentleman of some notoriety, and his effusions are constantly making the rounds of the press. The following sketch will be interesting to those who have not the pleasure of his acquaintance: Blessed with long legs, he is tall, reaching five feet ten inches in his boots; weight 167 pounds, body lithe and muscular; head round and well set on considerable neck, and feet of no size within the ken of a shoemaker, so he gets his boots and stockings always made to order. Next to Grant, he wears the belt for smoking. He smokes tobacco. Drink never crosses the threshold of his humorous mouth. Fun lurks in the corner of it. The eyes are deep-set and twinkle like stars in a dark night. The brow overhangs the eyes, and the head is protected from the weather by dark and curling locks. The face is eminently a good one, a laughing face, beaming with humor and genuine good-nature. He looks as if he would make a good husband and a jolly father. . . . His manner is peculiar; he hangs round loose, leaning on the desk or flirting round the corners of it; then marching and counter-marching in the rear of it, marking off ground by the yard with his tremendous boots. He would laugh at his own jokes, but that his doing so would detract from the fun of his hearers so he contents himself by refusing to explode, and swallows his risibility until the lecture is over, when he feels easier and blows off steam. His voice is a long monotonous drawl, well adapted to his style of speaking. The fun invariably comes in at the end of a sentence, after a pause. When the audience least expects it, some dry remark drops and tickles the ribs, and endangers the waist buttons of the "laughists" . . .

The Innocents Abroad, published July 20, 1869, was an immediate success. "It has met with a greater sale than any book ever published except 'Uncle Tom's Cabin'," Twain wrote joyfully in January, 1870, to Captain Horace Bixby, his old mentor on the River. "Not so bad, for a scrub-pilot, is it?"

In writing *The Innocents Abroad*, Twain had turned down the chance of becoming postmaster of San Francisco which offered what was then a substantial income. "I have thrown away that office," he wrote on February 6, 1868, "when I had it in my grasp, because it was plain enough that I could not be postmaster & write the book too. . . .

But it was worth from ten to twelve thousand a year." But he expected to make a good deal more money out of the book. He had written his mother and sister, upon signing the contract, that he was not "going to touch a book unless there was money in it, and a good deal of it." Actually, Twain did not then take himself seriously as a writer of books, considering it a side line to his profession as a journalist. Indeed, he had even hesitated to sign a contract for the book, doubtful of "the propriety of interfering with good newspaper engagements," and his ambition "lay in the direction of retirement in some newspaper enterprise."

Marriage and More Journalism

The realization of that ambition became imperative after February, 1869, when Olivia Langdon and Mark Twain became engaged. Olivia, called Livy by family and friends, was the only daughter of a wealthy but liberal coal dealer and mine owner of Elmira, New York. Her brother, Charles Langdon, had been one of Twain's fellow passengers on the *Quaker City*. In his cabin Twain had seen a miniature of Livy, and became interested in meeting the original. This took place in New York on December 27, 1867. From that moment all other women were driven from his mind. In a letter to "Mother," Mary Mason Fairbanks, a warm friend whom he had met on board the *Quaker City*, Twain wrote: "There isn't much of her, but what there is assays as high as any bullion that ever I saw."

Mark Twain was ten years older than Olivia Langdon when the two met during Christmas week of 1867. But age was the least of the differences between them. He was a vigorous-looking man: piercing blue-gray eyes under bushy brows, russet hair and mustache, a hawk nose. Behind him was a rough and adventurous career as steamboat pilot, gold prospector, and frontier newspaper man. Livy was the sheltered, semi-invalid daughter of a wealthy family — a girl of shy but appealing beauty, with her black hair combed back severely from a high, white forehead.

These startlingly different personalities fell deeply and permanently in love, and their love letters, withheld from publication for nearly half a century, demonstrate the depth and warmth of their relationship. "I do not regret that I have loved you, still love & shall always love you," he wrote in his first note to Livy in September, 1868, and this was a theme that was to run through all of his letters to her until the spring of 1904 when she lay dying.

The courtship culminated in an engagement on February 4, 1869. The Langdons had shown no enthusiasm over Twain as a son-in-law, but when Twain decided to marry her, they capitulated, even ignoring the dire predictions of Twain's own character witnesses, and gave their parental blessings. Jervis Langdon's token of acceptance was particularly generous and opportune. He insisted on advancing money required to buy an interest in the Buffalo *Express*.

After some hesitation, Twain accepted his father-in-law's help, and with the $25,000 advanced by Jervis Langdon, he bought a third interest in the Buffalo *Express* on August 14, 1869, and assumed his editorial duties. As literary editor of the *Express*, he usually avoided political comment because J. N. Larned, his co-worker, handled the paper's political policy. But he continued the role of social critic and his contributions were in much the same vein as his earlier San Francisco pieces. His writings for the *Express* revealed that he was still champion of the oppressed.

Ranging beyond the columns of his own paper, in the New York *Tribune*, the New York *Herald*, and magazines like *Galaxy* and *Packard's Monthly*, Twain published "savage assaults upon some human abuse, or fierce espousals of the weak." He continued, of course, to contribute his usual share of burlesque and ancedotes of a lighter nature to newspapers and magazines. But his journalistic writings show that he took his role as a social critic· seriously.

Twain ended the Buffalo period in April, 1871, when he sold his share in the *Express* and moved to Hartford, Connecticut. There he and his family immediately became part of the Nook Farm Circle which included Harriet Beecher Stowe, Charles Dudley Warner and his brother, George Warner, Mrs. Francis Gillette and her son, William, Thomas Hooker and his wife, Isabella, a strong advocate of woman's rights, and Reverend Joseph T. Twichell.

In the same month, Twain submitted his "Valedictory" to the *Galaxy*, announcing that he planned to devote himself to "writing a book." The book was *Roughing It* (originally entitled *Innocents At Home*). He had started writing it even before leaving Buffalo at the suggestion of Bliss of the American Publishing Company. He welcomed the suggestion, for he was beginning to look more and more to the past for inspiration. Writing to Olivia in 1870, he revealed that "down in my heart of hearts I yearn for the days that are gone and the phantoms of olden time. . . ."

Once established in Hartford among such acknowledged authors as Harriet Beecher Stowe and Charles Dudley Warner, Twain set about finishing *Roughing It*, and uncovering other means of making money. He was in debt for a portion of his share in the *Express* and he wanted to build a house in Hartford. He turned to the lecture platform, the most reliable source of immediate income. "I *do* hate lecturing," he wrote to his wife after four rigorous months on the road, "& I shall try hard to have as little as possible of it to do hereafter." But he would return to the circuit time and again, and each time, after he had earned enough to pay his obligations of the moment, he would quit the platform, insisting that it was his last appearance on the boards. He was to know this necessity oftener than one would have suspected of an author whose books proved so popular; but, then, Mark Twain was never satisfied to be just an author. He aspired to be a successful businessman, a publisher and a promoter of inventions too, and these aspirations cost him leisure and peace of mind.

With the publication of *Roughing It* early in 1872, Mark Twain began to think of himself as a writer of books rather than a journalist. Although he continued to contribute to periodicals and newspapers for the rest of his life, and even tried his hand at drama, he was thereafter primarily concerned with writing books. This progress from journalism to book authorship was hastened by the admission of the ex-sagebrush reporter into the *Atlantic Monthly* circle in November, 1874. For that more discriminating audience, he soon produced his great work on the river country, "Old Times on the Mississippi," published serially from January to July, 1875. The articles formed the first twenty chapters of *Life on the Mississippi*. It was William Dean Howells, then *Atlantic* editor and one of the country's foremost critics, who had accepted Twain's first piece for the *Atlantic*, "A True Story," a narrative of slavery. Soon Howells became Twain's literary mentor, and, as we shall see, defended him as a serious and important writer at a time when most critics regarded him merely as a "funny man."

The busy and productive years between 1874 and 1885 embraced Mark Twain's happiest period. They marked the publication of his greatest books, *The Gilded Age* (co-authored with Charles Dudley Warner and published in December, 1874), *The Adventures of Tom Sawyer* (published in December, 1876), *A Tramp Abroad* (published in March, 1880), *The Prince and the Pauper* (published in 1881), and *Adventures of Huckleberry Finn* (published in 1884). He was, contrary to the theory of later critics, happily married, and even though he traveled often — in quest of material for books, or to secure copyrights, or give a lecture here and there — absences from home were usually not prolonged. He returned to Nook Farm as quickly as he could, eager to join his wife and daughters in the family's amusements. Here he was the king, worshipped by wife and daughters, and free to indulge his love for whisky, cigars and even an occasional excursion into profanity. Livy had tried to "cure" him of these minor vices, but, like her attempt to get him to say grace at meals, her victory was temporary.

Twain spent many happy hours with his friends in Nook Farm. After a visit to the Twain and Warner families in 1874, Howells wrote: "It seems to me quite an ideal life. They live very near each other, in a sort of suburban grove, and their neighbors are the Stowes and Hookers, and a great many delightful people. They go in and out of each other's house without ringing, and nobody gets more than the first syllable of his first name — they call their minister *Joe* Twichell."

For writing, the best time for Twain was the summer, which he spent at his sister-in-law's farm near Elmira. Here on a hillside by an old quarry, a study shaped like a pilot-house had been built for him. In the quiet and "cool luxury of Quarry Farm he set himself to spin the fabric of his youth."

Businessman

By 1885 Twain was convinced that he was Fortune's darling. His name (or rather his pseudonym) was known everywhere. ("He is one of the few living persons with a truly world-wide reputation," wrote an admirer in the *Critic* in January, 1885. "There is no living writer whose books are so widely read as Mark Twain's.") His prosperity was phenomenal. From 1874, the family had lived in affluence and enjoyed all the benefits and luxuries that came with it. During the early 'eighties, Twain discovered he had spent $100,000 in one year. Still the money from books, articles and lectures came pouring in.

Ever since the success of *The Innocents Abroad,* Twain had felt that he was getting the short end of the profits from his books, the major part going to the publishers. His suspicion of commercial publishers, reflected in his letters and comments in his notebooks, led him to start his own publishing firm early in 1885.

Twain's publishing firm, with his nephew, Charles L. Webster, as nominal head, was remarkably successful with its first two books, *Huckleberry Finn* and the *Memoirs* of Ulysses S. Grant. Grant's *Memoirs*, published in 1885 and one of the truly phenomenal undertakings in American publishing annals, was an immediate best-seller. In February, 1886, the publisher and Grant's family divided a profit of nearly $600,000.

"I am frightened at the proportions of my prosperity," Twain is then said to have told a friend. "It seems to me that whatever I touch turns to gold." The success of the publishing venture so satisfied Twain that for the next five years he devoted most of his time and energy to issuing books instead of writing them. With considerable truth the *Literary World* observed in March, 1886: "Mr. Clemens is now so busy publishing other people's books, that we can hardly expect to see very soon two new ones of his own which he holds still in manuscript."

One of the two new ones was *A Connecticut Yankee in King Arthur's Court*. Twain had worked on it desultorily since he conceived the idea of an Arthurian satire in the fall of 1884 when the liberal Southern novelist, George Washington Cable, with whom he was on a lecture tour, gave him a copy of Malory's *Morte d'Arthur*. The *Yankee* was not published until 1889 and was his first book to appear in print since *Huckleberry Finn* in 1884.

The failure of several of his publishing firm's ventures — notably the disastrous sales of the *Life of Pope Leo XIII*, published in 1887 in six languages — and the drain on the business' treasury and his family's purse from his inclination to pour his money into any new invention which showed the slightest possibility of "making millions," forced Twain back to the writing of books.

Among the inventions Twain speculated on were a patent steam generator that was supposed to conserve practically all of the steam energy, a patent steam pulley into which he sank $32,000, an envelope-making machine, a marine telegraph, an engraving process, a carpet-pattern machine, a device for seeing at a distance, a synthetic food called plasmon, and a new type of cash register. In addition, he himself invented a history game, a self-pasting scrapbook, a spiral hatpin, a calendar watchfob, and a self-adjusting vest strap. None of these inventions produced the fortunes he anticipated — least of all the Paige type-setting machine which Twain thought to be "the most marvelous invention ever contrived by man," and to march "alone and far in the lead of human inventions." His support of this typesetting enterprise began in 1885, and by the end of the decade he was shoveling from $3,000 to $4,000 a month into the "*almost* perfected" machine.

Huckleberry Finn brought a good income, but it could not supply funds as fast as the "infernal machine" could absorb them, and Twain had pledged himself not only to see the machine through to completion but also to finance its promotion and marketing. Into the machine went his earnings from *A Connecticut Yankee, The American Claimant* (published in 1892), and *Pudd'nhead Wilson* (published in 1893), as well as those from stories and articles he wrote for well-paying magazines like *Cosmopolitan.*

Bankruptcy and Recovery

In May, 1890, an article in the *Book Buyer* said of Mark Twain: "His success is one of the romances of American life and letters." On the surface this seemed perfectly true. Bernard De Voto describes Twain at the beginning of the 'nineties as "the most widely known and admired writer in America, very likely in the world. He was at the summit of his personal happiness. His books had won him not only world-wide fame but a fortune as well." Twain was convinced that the Paige typesetter, whose market value he estimated a $150,000, would soon make him "one of the wealthiest grandees in America." The summer of 1890, which the family spent in the Catskills, was a happy one. But the storm clouds were rapidly gathering. In October, Twain's mother died, and in the following month, his wife's mother died. In the beginning of 1891, his finances became strained owing to the machine's voracious appetite and the dwindling fortunes of his publishing firm. In June, the family left for Europe, to reduce their living expenses. While they wandered about the continent for two years, Twain traveled back and forth to the United States, trying unsuccessfully to salvage something from the wreck of the fortune — close to $200,000 — sunk into the Paige machine.

Twain was in Europe when he learned that the project was about to be abandoned as a failure, and that "my dream of ten years was in desperate peril." He learned, too, of the imminent collapse of Webster & Co. whose treasury he had raided to feed the mechanical monster. He rushed back to New York, but was too late. The Panic of 1893 killed any hope of his raising money for his sinking enterprises.

Thus in 1894 Twain's Great Hope collapsed, and his vision of great wealth was transformed into a nightmare of bankruptcy. On April 18, the Webster concern went under, carrying to ruin the remnants of Twain's fortune and his wife's. A little later, all hope was abandoned for the Paige typesetting machine. The final failure of his "dear project" hit Twain, in his own words, "like a thunder-clap," and made him go "flying here and there and yonder, not knowing what I was doing." He confessed: "I never felt so desperate in all my life — and good reason, for I haven't got a penny to my name."

The news of Mark Twain's bankruptcy spread around the world, but so too did the news that he would repay every cent to his creditors. This he set out to do when he was almost sixty and nearly an invalid. Yet he must have felt confident of achieving this and other goals, for he wrote to his wife on July 24, 1894: "Dear Sweetheart, to-morrow Jean will be 14! My land, how times flies! Give the child my deep strong love — I am a bankrupt & haven't any other present. But we are rich, although we haven't any money, & by & by we will make up to the children all the lacking presents."

In 1889, Twain had announced his intention to quit authorship as a career. Of *A Connecticut Yankee* he wrote Howells: "It's my swan song, my retirement from literature permanently." Five years later, he wrote to his wife: "Farewell — a long farewell — to business! I'll never touch it again! I will live in literature, I will wallow in it, revel in it, I will swim in ink."

Mark Twain had returned to his first love.

Relieved of the unremitting cares of business, Twain put his heart into the writing of *Joan of Arc*. The novel was published in 1896, but Twain was not in the country when the book came off the press. He was in the midst of a world-wide lecture tour by which he hoped to repay his creditors. It was work which he dreaded, but it was the quickest way to pay off his debts.

Twain, his wife and his daughter, Clara, sailed for Australia on August 23, 1895. In his notebook, he recorded the departure as follows: "Two members of my family elected to go with me. Also a carbuncle." A year later, after triumphs in Australia, New Zealand, India, and South Africa, Twain closed the tour on the following note:

Our trip around the earth ended at the Southampton pier [in London] where we embarked thirteen months before. It seems a fine and large thing to have accomplished — the circumnavigation of this great globe in that little time, and I was privately proud of it. For a moment. Then came one of those vanity-snubbing astronomical reports from the Observatory-people, whereby it appeared that another great body of light had lately flamed up in the remoteness of space which was traveling at a gait which would enable it to do all that I had done in a *minute and a half*. Human pride is not worth while; there is always something lying in wait to take the wind out of it.

On August 18, 1896, Twain was alone in London, his wife and daughter having left for home. He was standing in the dining room of a house he had rented at Guilford, when a cablegram was placed in his hands. It read: "Susy was peacefully released today." That same day the press carried the story in headlines: "Mark Twain's Eldest Daughter Dies of Spinal Meningitis."

There was no ship to take Twain home in time for the funeral; he could do nothing but sit down and pour out his feelings in heartbreaking letters to his afflicted wife. "I know what misery is, at last, my darling," he wrote a week after he had received the shattering news. He sought consolation in the fact that Susy was now spared from pain, and that she had died in her own home. But it did not come easily, for Susy had been his favorite child, and the loss was irreparable.

Twain spent the fall and winter of 1896 in London. He plunged into his writing as an outlet for his grief; he told Howells that incessant work was absolutely essential "because of the deadness which invaded me when Susy died." Living a secluded life during these months, Twain worked on the account of his trip around the world and completed it in the spring of 1897. *Following the Equator*, was published in the autumn of that year.

Meanwhile, rumors about Twain flew thick and fast. Although his family was with him in London, the rumormongers deduced from his secluded life that his wife and children had deserted him and that he was living alone in an obscure corner of Chelsea, ill and in poverty. The New York *Herald* even sponsored a public benefit for the purpose of paying Twain's debts. The *Herald* itself subscribed $1,000 and Andrew Carnegie matched it with another thousand. On hearing of the project, Twain wrote to the *Herald* that he would almost welcome the offer since he was tired of debt, but his family wished him to refuse aid as long as he was able to take care of them through his own efforts. And this he succeeded in doing. The lecture tour had proved lucrative, and this, together with the success of *Joan of Arc* and *Following the Equator*, enabled him to pay off his debt of $190,000. Early in 1898 he made the last payment to his creditors. And the family could breathe again the more easily since they learned that Twain had forborne to sink another fortune in an Austrian carpet-pattern machine. It was a narrow escape, though, for Twain believed for a while that he was on the road to untold riches through the new "marvelous machine."

Once *Following the Equator* was finished, Twain and his family had moved to Vienna so that Clara could study the piano with the greatest teacher of the day, Theodore Leschetizky. Until five in the afternoon, Twain spent his time writing — he finished "The Man that Corrupted Hadleyburg" and other stories and essays which were published in 1900, and worked on drafts of *The Mysterious Stranger*. After five, Twain received callers. So many people clamored to meet him that his drawingroom became a second U.S. Embassy. In this respect, Vienna was merely repeating a general pattern. Twain wrote in his notebook in 1898: "During 8 years now, I have filled the post — with some credit, I trust — of self-appointed Ambassador at Large of the U.S. of America — without pay."

National and International Honors

On October 15, 1900, Twain and his family returned to the United States after nine years of wandering. He was greeted "literally as a conquering hero." "Twain Reaches New York," the headlines in the American press announced on October 16. "Doesn't Owe A Dollar," went a typical subheading. He settled in New York, took a house at 14 West Tenth Street, where hundreds of people sought him out as the city's reigning celebrity. He was excellent newspaper "copy," and his every utterance was rushed into print. He had become the grand old man of American letters, and his opinions on the crucial issues of the day, expressed with profound earnestness and wisdom, influenced large segments of the population. As we shall see, his writings and speeches against imperialism, against the oppression of the Boers in South Africa, the murder of Filipino rebels and the subjection of the islands, the slaughter of Chinese, and the massacre of the Negroes in the Congo, were a great force in the cause of freedom. *The Nation* paid him a special tribute for his fight against imperialism — especially praiseworthy, it emphasized, in view of the reluctance of men of letters to risk angering the men of wealth, putting Twain "as much morally above the mob of literary time-servers as his writings place him artistically."

Throughout the world, Twain, already beloved for his robust humor, was now also hailed as "the sturdy foe of oppression and injustice." His old friend, Howells, wrote: "You are the greatest man of your sort that ever lived, and there is no use saying anything else.... You have pervaded your century almost more than any other man of letters, if not more, and it is astonishing how you keep spreading...."

Although honors poured in on Twain — he was awarded an honorary Doctor of Letters degree by Yale University in 1901 and the degree of LL.D. by the University of Missouri in 1902 — his pleasure was diminished by successive personal tragedies. Not long after the death of Susy, his daughter Jean developed epileptic symptoms. The best physicians were consulted to no advantage, and the family lived for years in alternate moods of hope and discouragement.

In August, 1902, Livy fell gravely ill. For almost two years, she was bedridden, "a pallid, shrunken shadow." Twain's visits to his wife were restricted to a few minutes each day, "and it almost killed him." The end came on June 5, 1904, in Florence whence the family had gone in the hope that the Italian sun would help her. That evening, Livy had actually seemed much improved, so much so that Twain was moved to do a thing he had not felt like doing since the death of Susy. He went to the piano and sang some of his favorite Negro spirituals — "Go Chain the Lion Down," "Swing Low, Sweet Chariot," and "My Lord He Calls Me." His wife told the nurse, "He is singing a good-night carol to me." Later in the night she died.

Twain and his two daughters returned from Italy in June, and, after the funeral, he took up residence in New York at 21 Fifth Avenue. For a time his social and public appearances were restricted; instead, he worked incessantly, turning out 31,500 words in three weeks during May and June, 1905. He spent these months revising *Adam's Diary* and *Eve's Diary*, and writing *3,000 Years Among the Microbes*.

On November 30, 1905, Mark Twain celebrated his seventieth birthday, which occasioned a burst of enthusiastic acclaim in most of the newspapers and magazines of the country. *Harper's Weekly* published a souvenir supplement to serve as a record of a giant, celebrity-crowded banquet given in Twain's honor at Delmonico's. After all the tributes, Twain delivered his famous Pier 70 speech, which closed with these words: "... but I am seventy; seventy, and would nestle in the chimney-corner, and smoke my pipe, and read my book, and take my rest, wishing you well in all affection, and that when you in your turn shall arrive at Pier 70 you may step aboard your waiting ship with a reconciled spirit, and lay your course toward the sinking sun with a contented heart."

Of all the editorial tributes, *The Nation's* was best fitted to the occasion. It read: "He has not devoted himself to carving cherry-stones according to academic rules, but to the best of his ability he has written books to be read."

Twain was now at the height of his popularity. No American could avoid reading accounts of his smoking twenty-five cigars a day and playing billiards all night, and everyone had seen his picture in the Sunday press — in white linen even in winter and in full evening wear of white broadcloth.

By far the most important event of Twain's career during this period was the awarding of the degree of Doctor of Letters by Oxford University. In May, 1907, Lord Curzon, Chancellor of Oxford, wrote to him: "In persuading you to accept the degree I feel that in reality the honors will be paid to us, by one who has always set before himself the highest standard of literary work, and for nearly half a century has made an incomparable addition to the pleasure of the English-speaking race." Twain accepted. Although he always prided himself on being "unliterary," he felt that he had earned the honorary degree.

Early in June, he traveled once again across the ocean to be met with an "almost unheard of demonstration of affection and honor." George Bernard Shaw acclaimed him as "by far the greatest American writer." After the Oxford honors, which he acknowledged as the proudest moment of his life, he remained in England for a month, followed everywhere by reporters.

Back in the United States, Twain continued working on his autobiography, excerpts from which began appearing in the *North American Review* with the issue of September, 1906, and continued for twenty-five installments. His other writings were, in the main, potboilers: in 1907 he published an unimportant piece called "A Horse's Tale"; in 1908 he published no books nor any articles of importance. But just when the critics were asking, "Is Mark Twain Dead?" and observing that he had become "merely a public character," a particularly effective section of his autobiography would appear or a brilliant magazine article like "Captain Stormfield's Visit to Heaven" to remind them that he was still "the greatest and the sincerest writer in America."

Last Years

In June, 1908, Twain moved into Stormfield, his new home at Redding, Connecticut. "We soon saw Mark Twain about," Coley B. Taylor, who was a boy at the time, recalls, "in his famous white clothes, the great and witty man who was a friend of all the famous people in the world. . . .

The remarks he made to one neighbor or another went through the town like wildfire, and were talked of for days."

As the year 1909 drew to a close, it was apparent that the end was not far off for the great American. He had suffered his first heart attack on June 8, 1909, but was still able to joke about it several months later: "I hear the newspapers say I am dying. The charge is not true. I would not do such a thing at my time of life. I am behaving as good as I can. Merry Christmas to everybody!"

Then, without warning, his daughter Jean was found dead the morning of Christmas Eve. He poured out his grief in a tender tribute, and escaped the scene of the tragedy to Bermuda. There he spent a winter in an effort to regain his failing strength, and there he received from his old friend, Howells, a letter complimenting him on his most recent publication, "The Turning Point in My Life," which appeared in *Harper's Bazaar* for February, 1910. Howells wrote: "I want to tell you ... that you never wrote anything greater, finer, than that turning-point paper of yours. I shall feel it honor enough if they put on my tombstone, 'He was born in the same Century and general Section of the middle western country with Dr. S. L. Clemens, Oxon., and had his Degree three years before him through a Mistake of the University."

Twain was contented in Bermuda, but his "breast pains" became more and more frequent. Still he joked about his health. A New York newspaper sent a query to which Twain replied: "Dear Sir: In answer, I am able to say that while I am not ruggedly well, I am not ill enough to excite an undertaker."

By the first of April, Albert Bigelow Paine, who had begun his biography of Twain in the fall of 1905, had received reports that Twain was subject to frequent attacks. He sailed for Bermuda at once to bring the ailing man home.

On April 14, Twain was back at Stormfield. One week later, on April 21, 1910, he was dead.

Dressed in white, Twain's body lay in state in the Brick Church of New York where thousands came to pay him homage. A simple service was performed by Dr. Henry Van Dyke and Reverend Joseph T. Twichell. Then Mark Twain's body was carried to Elmira and laid to rest beside those he loved.

Chapter Two

JESTER OR SOCIAL SATIRIST?

In the extensive obituaries following Mark Twain's death
the issue was debated: to what degree was Mark Twain
merely an ephemeral humorist, and to what degree did he
transcend the limitations of the "professional humorist" by
serious undercurrents in his humor which gave body and
point to it.

The Debate Opens

It was not a new issue. It had been stated bluntly as early
as 1867 by the publisher of Twain's first book, Charles
Henry Webb, who insisted that the author was primarily a
moralist and only secondarily a *humorist*: "By his story of
the Frog, he scaled the heights of popularity at a single
jump, and won for himself the *sobriquet* of the Wild
Humorist of the Pacific Slope. He is also known to fame
as The Moralist of the Main: and it is not unlikely that as
such he will go down to posterity."

As editor of the *Californian*, Webb had more than once
pointed out that Twain's infectious fun only half-con-
cealed "his real character of a thoughtful and discriminating observer — a quality which underlies his love of fun
and humor — and gives it a peculiar force." Bret Harte,
another of Twain's close associates on the *Californian*, was
one of the first to recognize qualities in Twain's humor
which were not generally acknowledged until many years
later. In an article in the Springfield (Mass.) *Daily Republican* of November 10, 1866, Harte emphasized Twain's
hatred of shams and his capacity for serious writing which,
he predicted "will make his faculty serviceable to mankind. His talent is so well based that he can write seriously
and well when he chooses, which is perhaps the best test of
true humor."

Webb's and Harte's appreciation of Mark Twain's

genius — his dual quality of humorist and moralist — was a minority report. With rare exceptions, the critics tagged Twain as a professional funny man, one with Josh Billings, Sut Lovingood, Orpheus C. Kerr, Artemus Ward, and their like. His first book was little reviewed, and generally as a "collection of harmless drollery and mirth." The outstanding dissenting voice was Harte's. In his review in the *Californian*, he again emphasized the dual quality of Twain's humor: "One of the characteristic features of Mark Twain's humor is the basis of shrewd observation, good hard sense, and keen ... perception of the foibles of character that underlies it, giving it a certain value and significance quite independent of its power to excite the risibilities."

In *The Innocents Abroad*, published in 1869, Bret Harte felt that his earlier estimate of Twain was more than justified. Reviewing the book in the *Overland Monthly*, Harte praised it not only for its power, originality, and humor, but also for its "really admirable rhetoric, vigorous and picturesque." He concluded, "after a perusal of this volume, we see no reason for withholding the opinion we entertained before taking it up, that Mr. Clemens deserves to rank foremost among Western humorists; and in California, above his only rival, 'John Phoenix,' whose fun, though more cultivated and spontaneous, lacked the sincere purpose and larger intent of Mark Twain."

Now, however, Harte was not the only critic to regard Twain as more than a humorist pure and simple. *The Innocents Abroad* was reviewed in only three periodicals, though it became an immediate best-seller, and had, even before book publication, aroused nation-wide attention as a letter-serial in the San Francisco *Alta California* and the New York *Tribune*. William Dean Howells, reviewing the book in the *Atlantic Monthly*, was the second leading American critic to recognize that Twain's talents reached beyond burlesque humor. Like Harte, he paid tribute to those traits of Twain's writings which were to win gradual recognition over the years:

It is out of the bounty and abundance of his own nature that he is as amusing in the execution as in the conception of his work. And it is always good-humored humor, too, that he lavishes on his reader, and even in its impudence it is charming; we do not remember where it is indulged at the cost of the weak or helpless side, or where it is insolent, with all its sauciness and irreverence. . . .

. . . this book ought to secure him something better than the uncertain standing of a popular favorite. It is no business of ours to fix his rank among the humorists California has given us, but we think he is, in an entirely different way from all the others, quite worthy of the company of the best.

Thus Twain did not lack for critical appreciation even in the earliest stages of his career. Yet it would be incorrect to regard these comments as typical. Few critics shared their view. Most continued to see him as "the court jester." The *Nation* listed him in December 1870, a year and a half after the publication of *The Innocents Abroad,* among America's "several professed jesters" in the class of Artemus Ward, Josh Billings, and Petroleum V. Nasby. Twain's major distinction, in the eyes of *The Nation,* was that he gave "on the whole, harmless amusement to a large number of people."

The publication of *Roughing It* early in 1872 did nothing to alter the picture. For one thing, it was largely ignored, being reviewed only in the *Atlantic Monthly* and the *Overland Monthly.* Both reviews were favorable. Howells in the *Atlantic Monthly* pointed out that while the book could not be praised "for all the literary virtues . . . it is singularly entertaining and its humor is always amiable, manly, and generous." The *Overland Monthly's* reviewer (probably Bret Harte) emphasized: "Its specific character is its spontaneity and naturalness, together with an underlying element of sturdy honesty and rugged sense, antagonistic to sentimentality and shams." Thus the score stood as before: clear-visioned critics like Harte and Howells noted qualities in Twain's humor that set it apart from the general run of comic writers, but these were still solitary voices. Typical of the general critical attitude is his treatment in N. K. Royce's *A Manual of American Literature*, published in 1872. Twain's name was merely listed in a footnote as one of a group of "writers of funny sketches, depending perhaps, more upon a grotesqueness of style and orthography than upon any other element of the ludicrous."

Reasons for Critical Disapproval

What kept most critics from considering Twain an important writer? Samuel L. Clemens had introduced "Mark Twain" to the world as a professional humorist from the West. To the upholders of the genteel tradition, the keepers of the cherished flame of Eastern culture, a humorist was a jester and buffoon, *not* of the same breed of men as the gentle Whittier, the scholarly Longfellow, the urbane Lowell, the cultured Emerson, the polished Holmes. Even after Twain had become a figure of world renown, the genteel critics looked down their noses at him as simply a good practitioner of an ungenteel and inconsequential type of writing. To them Twain remained synonymous with California gold fields, jumping frogs, bucking Mexican plugs, farcical duels, mild buffoonery, and practical jokes. The jokes were good, it was conceded, but not even good jokes should be confused with good literature.

The critics considered themselves confirmed in this view by Twain's comic lecturing, the appearance of his works in subscription books, and the publication of many of his sketches in "funny books."

Mark Twain made his public bow to an Eastern audience as a comic lecturer. The handbills advertising his debut on the platform at New York's Cooper Union in 1867, showed him flying in mid-air on the back of a saddled frog. And he played up to the billing: "When I first began to lecture... my sole idea was to make comic capital of everything I saw and heard. My object was not to tell the truth, but to make people laugh." A good example of his audacious fun was his offer, during a lecture on the Sandwich (Hawaiian) Islands, "to show his audience how the cannibals consume their food — if only some lady will lend him a live baby." More startling even than this were his audacious and widely reported remarks at the *Atlantic* dinner to John Greenleaf Whittier in 1877 where he pictured Emerson, Longfellow, and Holmes as "three deadbeats, visiting a California mining-camp, and imposing themselves upon the innocent miners." Even though Twain publicly apologized for the offense to the three dignitaries, the genteel critics never forgave him for his remarks. To the Brahmins, the episode was conclusive proof of Twain's coarseness and lack of good taste.

Twain speedily became and remained one of the most phenomenally popular platform speakers America has produced, but he was early typed by the serious critics as just another popular showman, like Ward, Billings, Nasby and others, practicing what, during the ascendancy of the genteel tradition, was considered an inferior art form. An occasional critic sought to isolate Twain from other comic lecturers. The critic for the Cleveland *Morning Herald,* hearing him on November 17, 1868, complimented him on "having conclusively proved that a man may be a humorist without being a clown." But more typical was the comment by an editor that among the attractions of the approaching lecture season, "Billings and Twain will contribute the seasoning for the intellectual entertainments." Other lecturers (Emerson and Beecher among them) would furnish the intellectual fare.

If the critics of the East were alienated by Mark Twain as a comic lecturer, they were equally antagonized by the appearance of his works in subscription editions. On the title page of *The Innocents Abroad* appeared the following notation: "Issued by Subscription Only, and Not for Sale in the Book-Stores. Residents of Any State Desiring a copy Should Address the Publishers, and an Agent Will Call Upon Them." With one or two minor exceptions, all of Mark Twain's books for the first thirty years of his writing career were sold by subscription. Under the subscription system, complimentary review copies were not distributed; furthermore, the writer published in this way suffered a loss of prestige, and the critics tended to ignore him. The editor of the *Literary World* pointed out:

> Subscription books are in bad odor, and cannot possibly circulate among the better class of readers, owing to the general and not unfounded prejudice against them as a class.
>
> Consequently an author of established reputation, who resorts to the subscription plan for the sake of making money, descends to a constituency of a lower grade and inevitably loses caste.... For this loss no money could compensate.

During the years 1869-1873, as an editorial writer for the Buffalo *Express* and as correspondent for the *Packard's Monthly*, *Wood's* and *Galaxy* magazines, Twain produced both a body of social satirical writings and a mass of comicalities in the guise of editorials, letters, sketches and stories. While the serious writings were generally ignored, the comicalities were reprinted in many newspapers all over the United States and crossed the Atlantic to England, where they found a place in the "Variety" or "Notabilia" column of almost every journal in that country. In reviews of such pieces, Twain's name was again linked primarily with comical writings while his social satire was neglected.

We must add one other reason for the failure of most contemporary critics to acknowledge Twain's importance — namely, his immense popularity. "There has never been any doubt," Bernard De Voto points out, "of Mark Twain's greatness in that court of appeal whose jurisdiction over literature is final, the reading public. The verdict of that court has been a universal and sustained acclaim never equaled by any other American, and equaled by only a few writers in the history of literature." Yet it is one of the ironies of the history of literature that to the literary critics the very fact that the general public admired

Twain's writings was proof of its lack of real worth. As one of them put it: "Whatever is widely liked must . . . appeal to the general public, which is a vulgar body with crude tastes, and, generally speaking, anything which satisfies it is bad." In time, Twain was able to eradicate other causes of critical disdain, but never the last. He remained immensely popular with the people who recognized his literary eminence long before the critics did.

Reception of THE GILDED AGE and TOM SAWYER

Up to 1874 the name "Mark Twain" was generally associated in the minds of most critics with such "risible" collections as the *Burlesque Autobiography, Eye-Openers, Practical Jokes, Screamers,* and *American Drolleries.* The publication, early in 1874, of *The Gilded Age* (co-authored with Charles Dudley Warner) brought an important change in critical evaluation of Twain's literary standing. For one thing, the book was more widely reviewed than any previous Twain volume. Even though this may have been due to the standing among critics of the co-author (some reviewers felt that Warner was prostituting his talent by collaborating with a mere comic like Mark Twain), the fact that most critics, for the first time, acknowledged that Twain could write on a serious subject like politics and society was in itself significant. In *Appleton's Journal* of July, 1874, George T. Ferris still spoke of him in terms of his contribution to American humor rather than to literature, and as a "professional funny man." But he acknowledged that *The Gilded Age* revealed Twain's ability to write "bitter satire, true and honest to the core." He concluded on a note of prophecy: "Some of the best detached descriptions which have ever emanated from Mark Twain's pen may be found in this book. They show that the author's powers are at their best working capacity, and that the world has a right to look for liberal fruits from them."

In the next eighteen months, a number of other distinguished critics noted similarly that Twain was far more than a funny man. Reviewing *Sketches New and Old*, published in the autumn of 1875, Howells delighted in its humor, its burlesque, its "extravagance of statement," its "rightmindedness," and its "breadth." "But," he continued, "there is another quality in this book which we fancy we shall hereafter associate more and more with our familiar impressions of him, and that is a growing seriousness of meaning in the apparently unmoralized drooling, which must result from the humorist's second thought of political and social absurdities."

It was not news, of course, when Howells emphasized that Twain was no mere comic artist; but it was news when the distinguished New England critic, Edwin P. Whipple, praised Twain as a literary artist. In *Harper's Monthly* of March, 1876, Whipple called Mark Twain "a man of wide experience, keen intellect, and literary culture," and added the highly significant (and for that time) surprising comment: "The serious portions of his writings, indicate that he could win a reputation in literature even if he had not been blessed with a humorous fancy inexhaustible in resource."

One would expect that after such praise from a man whom John Lothrop Motley described as "one of the most brilliant writers of the country, as well as one of the most experienced reviewers," Twain's next book would be widely discussed — especially when this book was the first of his acknowledged masterpieces, *The Adventures of Tom Sawyer*, published in December, 1876. But the sole critical notice in the literary journals of the day appeared in the *Atlantic Monthly* where the ever-appreciative Howells characterized it as "full of entertaining characters, and of the greatest artistic sincerity." Among newspapers, only the *New York Times* reviewed the book, singling out the realism of the novel for special comment: "There is no cant about Mr. Clemens. . . . Matters are not told as they are fancied to be, but as they actually are." The absence of reviewers did not hurt the sales of the book which, as

Howells predicted, immediately became an "immense success." By March, 1877, the American Publishing Company, in advertising for agents to sell "Mark Twain's New Book," announced "30,000 copies sold in two months."

In general, critics continued to show little interest in America's best-selling author. A decade after his first book was published, the literary journals excluded Twain's works from the realm of "Literature." Despite Howells, Harte and Whipple, most literary critics still found little or no literary worth in Twain's writings or considered it useless to look for it there since he was a mere humorist. "We read Mr. Clemens solely for the humor of Mark Twain," a critic in the *Atlantic Monthly* wrote in 1873. This remained for many years the standard by which most critics measured Twain's work. When he failed as a humorist, he was regarded as having failed as an author. "Mark Twain can be so very funny," wrote a critic in 1874, criticizing "A True Story," a poignant portrayal of the evils of Negro slavery, "that we are naturally as dissatisfied with him, when he is not funny at all, as we should be with a parrot that could not talk, or a rose that had no odor."

"New Departure"?

With the publication of *The Prince and the Pauper* in December, 1881, most of the major critics, for the first time, acknowledged the existence of what Howells called "that unappreciated serious side of Clemens' curious genius." In an *Atlantic Monthly* review entitled, "Mark Twain's New Departure," a critic hailed the new Mark Twain, commenting that the book was "certainly not by the Twain we have known for a dozen or more years as the boisterous and rollicking humorist, whose chief function has been to diffuse hilarity with mirth in its most demonstrative forms."

Several reviewers, including Howells, took issue with the idea that *The Prince and the Pauper* marked a "new departure" for Twain. The reviewer for the *Century* argued that it was not necessary for Twain to prove that he was a serious writer: "His most humorous writings abound in passages of great excellence and serious compositions, and his serious, nervous style is the natural expression of an acute mind, that in its most fanciful moods is seldom superficial in its views. Indeed, it is because Mark Twain is a satirist, and in a measure a true philosopher, that his broadly humorous books and speeches have met with wide and permanent popular favor."

Many of the critical defenders of the genteel tradition, who had heretofore been actively hostile to Twain, now acknowledged that he was far more than a mere humorist. But others refused to be convinced, and insisted that there could be only one side to Twain — the buffoon. "The successful writer of burlesque seldom succeeds in anything else. Mr. Clemens' most ardent admirers cannot read his *Prince and Pauper*," wrote John Nichol in his *American Literature: An Historical Sketch*, published in Edinburgh, Scotland, in 1882. Dr. Nichol, Professor of English Literature at the University of Glasgow, blamed Twain, as the chief representative of "American prose," for having "done perhaps more than any other living writer to lower the literary tone of English-speaking people." The Scottish critic's views widely reprinted in American literary journals, and the only criticism voiced was that he was too lenient in his condemnation of Twain's influence. To call Twain's writing representative of American prose was an insult to our literary tradition: "It seems incredible that he [Dr. Nichol] should not see that this class of American humor is comparable only to the dreary Joe Millerisms that have served their terms for so many generations of Englishmen, and with the comic weeklies that die with commendable punctuality in English railway stalls."

Because of such sneers, Howells determined to declare himself, "in a large, free way, concerning his own personal estimate of Mark Twain." He chose for this purpose the *Century* magazine which, at the time, enjoyed the largest circulation of any American periodicals. Howells' essay, complete with a full-page portrait of Twain as frontispiece, appeared in the September, 1882, issue. It included a biographical sketch, an analysis of Twain's contribution to American humor, and an evaluation of Twain as a serious literary artist. It was this last characteristic, Howells emphasized, that set Twain apart from all other American humorists. Twain's humor was "at its best the foamy beak of the strong tide of earnestness in him"; hence those who regarded him as just a humorist or read him only because they wanted to laugh, missed the quality that made him a truly great literary artist. "I shall not insist here upon Mark Twain as a moralist; though I warn the reader that if he leaves out of account an indignant sense of right and wrong, a scorn of all affectation and pretense, an ardent hate of meanness and injustice, he will come indefinitely short of knowing Mark Twain."

Howells did not ignore the chief difficulty in establishing Twain's stature as a serious writer — the fact that most readers looked for humor even in his serious work: "He has made them laugh too long; they will not believe him serious; they think some joke is always intended. This is the penalty . . . of making one's first success as a humorist."

Other critics also raised this question. In its review of *A Tramp Abroad,* the Chicago *Tribune* observed in 1880: "The author is unfortunate in one respect. Every time he opens his mouth and puts his pen to paper he is credited with the intention of making you laugh. That is his avowed object in life. For that he exists. That is his profession. When he fails to make laughter — no matter how much useful information he may convey, or whatever else he may accomplish — his work is apt to be regarded as a failure." Three years later, reviewing *Life on the Mississippi, The Nation* stressed the same point: "Mark Twain labors under the disadvantage which attach to the position of the professional humorist. When he writes a serious book, the public receives it with a predisposition to laugh which interferes with its appreciation of what the author has to say."

Of the Mississippi volume itself, *The Nation* noted that it was "only secondarily the work of a funny man," and primarily an important "descriptive and historical work." Nearly all the other critics concurred, hailing Twain's departure from his "usual practice" of composing just a humorous compilation. Ignoring the fact that Howells had made the same point about Twain's previous books — and numbers of other critics had done so in their reviews of *The Prince and the Pauper* for the critics *Life on the Mississippi* marked a new dimension in Mark Twain's writings: "a good deal of grimness and soberness — underlying the surface of fun."

Reception of HUCKLEBERRY FINN

Twain's re-creation of the past in *Life on the Mississippi* was looked upon with such favor by the critics that he must have expected a similar reaction to *The Adventures of Huckleberry Finn*, with its realistic picture of pre-war life along the great river. Since the end of the Civil War, the critics had been searching for the "Great American Novel," calling upon American writers to stop imitating English and French authors and look into American life and history for their settings. Here at last in *Huckleberry Finn* they had what they had been demanding: its setting was native, its flavor was American, its language colloquial, its characterization based on first-hand knowledge, and its theme was universal. Naturally, Twain expected his novel to win critical acclaim.

But when the book appeared in the spring of 1885, most American critics received it very coldly. The guardians of the genteel tradition fumed over Twain's satirical handling of the bigots and hypocrites of the ante-bellum South and his audacious elevation of the rowdyish Huck Finn and the Negro runaway slave, Jim, into heroes. Louisa May Alcott, author of *Little Men,* among whom Huck Finn definitely would not fit, wrote indignantly: "If Mr. Clemens cannot think of something better to tell our pure-minded lads and lassies, he had better stop writing for them." The overall American critical reaction was summed up in one word: "trash."

Huckleberry Finn did find some defenders among contemporary American critics and literary figures. Thomas Sergeant Perry, one of the outstanding critics and scholars of the day, rated it better than *Tom Sawyer*, "a most valuable record of an important part of our motley American civilization." On the occasion of Twain's fiftieth birthday, Joel Chandler Harris (creator of Uncle Remus) sent a testimonial letter to the editors of the *Critic*, "there is not in our fictive literature a more wholesome book than 'Huckleberry Finn.' It is history, it is romance, it is life. Here we behold human character stripped of all tiresome details; we see people growing and living; we laugh at their humor, share their griefs; and, in the midst of it all, behold we are taught the lesson of honesty, justice and mercy."

But such approbations were rare; most critics vied with each other heaping abuse on the novel and its author. The most vitriolic comments came from New England, seat of the genteel tradition, and were sparked by the action of the Public Library Committee of Concord, Massachusetts, which excluded the book as "a dangerous moral influence on the young." The *Literary World* of Boston hailed the committee's stand: "We are glad to see that the commendation given to this sort of literature by its publication in the *Century* has received a check by this action at Concord." So did the Springfield *Republican*, attacking the "Huckleberry Finn stories" as being "no better in tone than the dime novels which flood the blood-and-thunder reading population. . . . Their moral level is low, and their perusal cannot be anything less than harmful." And the Boston *Advertiser* solemnly editorialized: "The burlesque of the stage and the burlesque in literature have their common root in that spirit of irreverence, which, as we are often and truly told, is the great fault in American character. In the cultivation of that spirit, Mark Twain has shown talents and industry which, now that his last effort has failed so ignominiously, we trust he will employ in some manner more creditable to himself and more beneficent to the country."

Critical reaction to *Huckleberry Finn* all over the country followed this pattern. A Western Superintendent of Public Schools charged that the book proved once again that the writings of Mark Twain were "hardly worth a place in the columns of the average country newspaper which never assumes any literary airs." The reviewer in the Arkansas *Traveler* announced smugly: "This book is condemned, American critics say, because it is vulgar and coarse. The days of vulgar humor are over in this country. There was a time when a semi-obscene joke would find admirers, but the reading public is becoming more refined. Exaggerated humor will also pass away. The humor of the future must be chaste and truthful."

British critics and writers proved quicker to appreciate the merits of *Huckleberry Finn*. The London *Saturday Review* defended Twain's novel, commenting that some passages had "poetry and pathos blended in their humor." "In Mark Twain," it continued, "the world has a humorist who is yearly ripening and mellowing." Robert Louis Stevenson said: "It is a book that I have read four times, and am quite ready to begin again tomorrow." Andrew Lang called *Huckleberry Finn* a masterpiece, "a nearly flawless gem of romance and humor," and criticized the "cultured critics" in the United States not only for refusing to recognize "its singular value," but failing to see that "the great American novel" they had been seeking, had finally arrived. Reprinting a typical denunciation of Twain and his book in the United States and contrasting it with an appreciative comment in a British journal, the *Critic* summed up the situation in its heading: "Not Without Honor, Save In His Own Country."

Changing Critical Attitudes

The British critics, as we shall see, lost a good deal of their enthusiasm for Mark Twain when he criticized the English monarchial system in *A Connecticut Yankee in King Arthur's Court*. Nevertheless, he remained for many years more popular in England than in the United States. While most American critics continued to see only a jester in him, in England he was thought worthy of the highest academic distinction. American critics expressed both amazement and concern over Twain's popularity abroad: amazement because as one critic put it, "he is only funny, after all," and concern because it would give Europeans a false picture of real American literary values. In his two-volume work, *American Literature*, 1607-1885, published in the late 'eighties, Professor Charles F. Richardson did not deem fit to mention Twain in his second volume dealing with "American Poetry and Fiction," but in the first volume, in a chapter headed "Borderlands of American Literature," he thus disposed of him:

Crude and repulsive writing, sometimes adorned with appropriate pictures, is read with delight in parts of Europe, and deemed not only amusing but national, characteristic, representative. . . . Bret Harte, Mark Twain, Artemus Ward, Nasby and the various professional newspaper "wits" have been put, by the half-educated, into the representative seats that belong to Emerson and Hawthorne. . . .

The reigning favorites of the day are Frank R. Stockton, Joel Chandler Harris, the various newspaper jokers, and "Mark Twain." But the creators of "Pomona" and "Rudder Grange," of "Uncle Remus and his Folklore Stories," and of "Innocents Abroad," clever as they are, must make hay while the sun shines. Twenty years hence, unless they chance to enshrine their wit in some higher literary achievement, their unknown successors will be the privileged comedians of the republic.

A half dozen or so articles about Twain, published during the 'nineties, furnished increasing evidence that Professor

Richardson's viewpoint was not the prevailing trend. A writer in the *Atlantic* commented in October, 1892: "One of the attractions in reading Mark Twain is that one never knows when he may be coming upon something serious. Though laughter rules, for the most part, now and then the jester puts aside his bells, and the tragic passage comes upon one with striking force." In August, 1893, Frank R. Stockton, the noted editor, novelist and "principal humorist of the genteel tradition," published an analysis of Twain's literary technique in *Forum*. "[His] most notable characteristic is courage," the essay opened, and Stockton went on to explain that few other men, even if they could think of them, "would dare to say the things that Mark Twain says." He cited "pure and unadulterated fun" as another of Twain's characteristics, but quickly noted: "It must be remembered, however, that Mark Twain does not depend entirely upon the humor of his situations and conditions to make his points. His faculty and range of expression are wonderful, and it is his courage which gives to his expressions as well as his inventions, their force and unique effect." Stockton observed that those who remembered Twain at the beginning of his writing career could not "help thinking of him as a humorist above everything," but soon other qualities became apparent, especially philosophic depth and narrative talent. "His philosophy of course, came in with his humor and although the fact was not always noticed, it often formed part of it. Later this philosophic spirit grew and strengthened until it was able to stand alone, and in some of his more recent writings it not only stands up very steadily but it does some bold fighting."

Among other critics stressing the same theme, Henry C. Vedder, in 1894, compared Twain with Carlyle, but put the American above the British satirist for not only sharing Carlyle's "hatred of sham," but adding something Carlyle lacked — "a hearty and genuine love of liberty." "Mark Twain's love of liberty is shown unostentatiously, incidentally as it were, in his sympathy for, and championship of the downtrodden and oppressed." "The world is beginning, by degrees, to realize that Mark Twain is a good deal more than a humorist," wrote the critic for *Harper's* in May, 1897, noting the republication of *Tom Sawyer Abroad* and *The American Claimant*. Brander Matthews of Columbia University, hailing Twain as more than a "professional humorist," wrote of *Huckleberry Finn*: "I do not think it will be a century ... before we Americans generally discover how great a book 'Huckleberry Finn' really is, how keen its vision of character, how close its observation of life, how sound its philosophy, and how it records for us once and for all certain phases of Southwestern society which it is very important for us to perceive and to understand." Writing a few months later in the *Atlantic*, Charles Miner Thompson reiterated what Matthews had said:

Under the humorist in Mark Twain lies the keen observer, the serious man, the ardent reformer, and he took note of all that was evil in the life he knew and proclaimed it indignantly to the world. His tenacious memory for detail, his microscopic imagination, and his real interest in the serious side of life make his pictures of the crude society in which he was born both absolutely accurate and surprisingly comprehensive. His writings cannot be neglected by anyone who wishes to know that life, and it is one which is in many respects highly important for us to understand.

Like Matthews, Thompson predicted that it would not be long before *Huckleberry Finn* was acknowledged in America, as it had already been in England, as "the great American novel." And both were correct! In 1901, Professor Berrett Wendell of Harvard University described Twain's novel as "the most admirable work of literary art as yet produced in this continent." Eight years later, H. L. Mencken wrote that *Huckleberry Finn* was "worth, I believe, the complete works of Poe, Hawthorne, Cooper, Holmes, Howells and James, with the entire literary output to date of Indiana, Pennsylvania, and all the States south of the Potomac thrown in."

Clearly it was no longer necessary for Howells to continue to remind critics of Twain's deeper meanings. Indeed, few even spoke now, as Howells had once done, of the humorist who disguised his serious observations under a cloak of comicality. The only issue dividing the critics was whether this was a "new Mark Twain."

Presenting the case for the affirmative, the *Critic* said in its review of *The Man That Corrupted Hadleyburg and Other Stories and Essays*, published in 1900: "We find here the old Mark, with a difference. The years that bring the philosophic mind have made of the inimitable humorist a writer of stories with a purpose." The review in *The Academy* was entitled, "Mark's New Way," and concluded: "Mark Twain, censor and critic, is rapidly taking the place of Mark Twain, fun maker. But the change need not to be deplored, for the new Mark Twain — the Mark Twain of this book in particular — is not a whit less readable than the old, and he is more provocative of thought." William Archer, however, denied that there was anything new in Twain's latest book: "Perhaps you wonder to find Mark Twain among the moralists at all? If so, you have read his previous books to little purpose. They are full of ethical suggestions. Sometimes, it is true, his moral decisions are a little summary. Often, nay, generally his serious meaning is lightly veiled in paradox, exaggeration, irony. But his humor is seldom entirely irresponsible for many pages together, and it often goes very deep into human nature."

Not even Twain's strictures on imperialism were "new," declared a number of critics. An editorial in the Louisville *Courier-Journal*, at the turn of the century, entitled "Mark Twain Reformer," pointed out the link between *Huckleberry Finn* and *A Connecticut Yankee* and Twain's anti-imperialist writings which, it noted, were almost as widely read as his greatest books:

A remarkable transformation, or rather a development, has taken place in Mark Twain. The genial humorist of the earlier day is now a reformer of a vigorous kind, a sort of knight errant who does not hesitate to break a lance with either church or State if he thinks them interposing on that broad highway over which he believes not a part but the whole of mankind has the privilege of passing in the onward march of the ages. . . .

Mr. Clemens' present conduct is only the evolution to be expected from the man who wrote the story of "Nigger Jim" and that inimitable romance of "A Connecticut Yankee at King Arthur's Court." Evidence in plenty abound in Mark Twain's writings of his consideration for the poor and the lowly and his disposition to go out and battle with their oppressors. If this was continually manifest in those rollicking productions of his earlier years, in which the saving grace of humor made him tolerant of all faults, even those of the ruling classes, how natural it is that this characteristic should become stronger with the seriousness of advancing age in such a determined personality.

The dissenting voices came now, interestingly and ironically enough, from many of the very critics who had been unable to perceive in Twain's writings anything more than "the contortions of the professional buffoon," and had argued that he could make no real contribution to literature as long as he confined himself to humor. Now they argued that his greatness rested only in his humor, that he became dull when he wandered off into politics and economics, and they urged him to return speedily to dispensing laughter. "As a Humorist Mark Twain is a success," went the refrain, "as a Moralist he is clearly a failure, and his friends should advise him quietly to withdraw from the fold." Again: "Mark Twain the humorist is a bull in the china-shop of ideas. He attempts to destroy what he could never build up, and assumes that his experiment is eminently meritorious." The editor of *Bookman* argued that critics like Howells had done Twain a disservice by having "proclaimed him a great philosopher" thus encouraging him to wander off into fields where he did not properly belong — such as war and imperialism. "It must be embarrassing to a humorist to be put down so much deeper than he really is."

It is significant, however, that these were now the minority voices. The majority of the critics gladly accepted the fact that Mark Twain was a philosopher as well as a humorist, and dwelt on his profundity, his strong philosophic vein, and his serious moral purpose. Perhaps the Oxford award of the degree of Doctor of Letters to Twain in 1907 forced even the reluctant American critics to reexamine the writer in their midst. At any rate, William Lyon Phelps summed up the picture at the height of the resulting enthusiasm: "During the last twenty years, a profound change has taken place in the attiude of the reading public toward Mark Twain. I can remember very well when he was regarded merely as a humorist and one opened his books with an anticipatory grin. Very few supposed that he belonged to literature; and a complete uniform edition of his 'Works' would perhaps have been received with something of the mockery that greeted Ben Jonson's folio in 1616." "He is much more than a humorist," Phelps emphasized. "He has shown himself to be a genuine artist."

The new critical trend culminated in Archibald Henderson's appreciation in *Harper's* of May, 1909. Henderson praised the "universality and humanity" of Twain's humor, and said, "he has been a factor of high ethical influence in our civilization; and the philosopher and humanitarian look out from the twinkling eyes of the humorist." He quoted George Bernard Shaw as having told him that he "thought of Mark Twain primarily, not as a humorist, but as a sociologist." Agreeing, Henderson concluded: "There is a 'sort of contemporaneous posterity' which has registered its verdict that Mark Twain is the world's greatest living humorist; but there is yet to come that greater posterity of the future which will, I dare say, class Mark Twain as America's greatest sociologist in letters."

The cycle had been completed. In 1867 Charles Henry Webb had predicted that Mark Twain "will go down to posterity" as "The Moralist of the Main," and forty-two years later, on the eve of Twain's death, Archibald Henderson went further to predict that he would go down to posterity as "America's greatest sociologist in letters." While most critics were not prepared to go as far as Henderson, they now accepted Webb's verdict. It was also widely recognized that it was not Twain but the critics who had changed. As Augustine Birrell put it in introducing Twain to members of London's Pilgrim Club in 1907, forty years after Webb had first referred to him as both humorist and moralist, Twain was "still the humorist, still the moralist. His humor enlivens and enlightens his morality, and his morality is all the better for his humor."

Reputation at Time of Death and Soon After

The obituaries following Mark Twain's death contained a number of disparaging comments which were pretty well summed up by Barry Pain who wrote in the London *Bookman*: "Mark Twain's artistic endowment was very slight but he was a successful funmaker." But Twain's disparagers were in the minority. Few indeed were the obituarists who considered him merely a public jester. A contributor to the *Dial,* which once had harshly criticized Twain, traced his progress from humorist to serious commentator, sage and moralist. Twain came to be considered no longer "a 'funny man' of the kin of Josh Billings and Artemus Ward," but "one of our foremost men of letters." The writer concluded by placing Twain with Irving, Swift and Carlyle — humorists who were also "creative artists and critics of life in the deepest sense, and social philosophers whose judgments are of weight and importance."

Samuel Gompers, President of the American Federation of Labor, asserted that "Mark Twain was more than a humorist. He was a deep student of men and events, a profound philosopher." Hamlin Garland expressed the same opinion — "He was much more than humorous" — and William Lyon Phelps wrote: "The funniest man in the world, he was at the same time a profoundly serious artist, a faithful servant of his literary ideals." Archibald Henderson bracketed Twain's name with that of Whitman as "the two great interpreters and embodiments of America," who represented "the supreme contribution of democracy to universal literature."

The most rapturous comment came from William Dean Howells who, shortly after Twain's death, published his little book, *My Mark Twain: Reminiscences and Criticism.* Howells concluded that Twain was "without a rival since Cervantes and Shakespeare," and by far the greatest figure in American letters: "Emerson, Longfellow, Lowell, Holmes — I knew them all and all the rest of our sages, poets, seers, critics, humorists; they were like one another and like other literary men; but Clemens was sole, incomparable, the Lincoln of our literature."

The eulogies at Twain's death continued during the years immediately following, and were echoed even by the academic critics. In 1911, Reuben Post Halleck's *History of American Literature* devoted ten pages to Twain's enduring traits as a philosopher and historian of phases of our national culture not otherwise recorded. Two years later, John Macy's *The Spirit of American Literature,* assigned Twain a high place among American writers on similar grounds. Fred Lewis Pattee's *A History of American Literature Since 1870,* published in 1915, hailed Twain as the first author to make American literature national rather than "the voice of a narrow strip of Atlantic seaboard." All three agreed that Twain was more than a humorist. But it was Archibald Henderson who made this the center of Twain's significance as a writer, devoting a section of his biography to this aspect of his work. "Beneath that humour," wrote Henderson, "underlying it and informing it, is a fund of human concern, a wealth of seriousness and pathos, and a universality of interests which argue real power and greatness. These qualities ... reveal Mark Twain as serious enough to be regarded as a real moralist and philosopher, humane enough to be regarded as, in spirit, a true sociologist and reformer."

72

Henderson's biography was published in 1911. The following year witnessed the appearance of Albert Bigelow Paine's official, elaborate, and eulogistic biography in three volumes running to more than 1,700 pages. Paine noted the importance of the serious aspects of Twain's writings, pointing out that his humor overlay "some deep revealment of human truth or injustice." But he dwelt on it only in passing. Primarily Paine, Twain's "appointed Boswell," romanticized his subject, picturing him as "not only human, but superhuman; not only a man, but a superman." Paine stood in such awe of his subject that the essence of Twain's genius remains elusive. In the interest of an idealized hero, a model for all Americans, Paine minimized Twain's searing criticism of institutionalized religion and other aspects of contemporary society.

Meanwhile, the posthumous publication of a number of Twain's books, most of which had been barely mentioned or ignored by Paine, revealed that he was more of a social critic than even his most fervent admirers had suspected. As Carl Van Doren remarked in an article entitled "Posthumous Thunder": "Gradually his accomplishments as a humorist are being reduced in the ratio they bear to his accomplishments as a commentator. The world which knew him in the flesh too often failed to distinguish him at many points from its favorite clown. . . . The more reflective world, which alone keeps alive the fame of a writer after his death, finds more and more in Mark Twain to remember him by, as more and more of his posthumous work sees the light."

The Mysterious Stranger, published in the fall of 1916, was immediately hailed as a masterpiece. *The Dial* said: "Shocking to all the conventionalities are his freely expressed opinions on many themes. Not a few of his bitterly satirical utterances are peculiarly appropriate to the present time." George Soule, writing in the *New Republic*, regarded it as "a satire from the courageous heart of a lover of mankind." H. E. Woodbridge wrote in the *Nation* that it was "a biting arraignment of the folly and brutality of mankind" in which Twain's hatred of oppression was never more vigorously presented, and that it was "the book which the future may perhaps regard as Mark Twain's greatest work. If he had written nothing else it would have given him an assured fame. No American writer, not Hawthorne or Poe, has surpassed *The Mysterious Stranger* in imaginative intensity; in breadth and virile sweep it is beyond the range of those masters of exquisite miniature. . . . As a satire it is more terrible than *Gulliver's Travels*."

What is Man? and Other Essays, published in 1917, stimulated another outburst of enthusiasm for the keenness of Twain's social criticism. "The truth about Mark Twain," wrote H. L. Mencken in the *Smart Set*, "is that he was a colossus, that he stood head and shoulders above his country and his time, that even the combined pull of Puritanism without and philistinism within could not bring him down to the national level." Although Stuart P. Sherman then disagreed with Mencken on almost everything else, on his evaluation of Twain's stature he did agree. Writing in 1917, Sherman said: "he [Twain] is one of those great men of letters whom we shall always revisit and about whom the 'last word' will never be uttered."

Three years later, Sherman's prediction was borne out when Van Wyck Brooks hurled a critical bombshell with the *Ordeal of Mark Twain*.

Van Wyck Brooks' THE ORDEAL OF MARK TWAIN

In *America's Coming of Age*, published in 1915, Van Wyck Brooks had advanced the thesis that America's great democratic experiment had taken a false turn just after the Civil War when an acquisitive and corrupt business civilization had destroyed all that was worthwhile in the American tradition. This vulgar, money-grabbing, oppressive environment had proved fatal to creative talent, especially to writers who, except for Walt Whitman, had either compromised with the stultifying environment, conforming to its tastes and sharing its material rewards, or had sought escape in Europe.

The first critic to apply Brooks' general theory to specific cases was Waldo Frank who, in *Our America*, published in 1919, used Twain as one of two significant examples. First he dealt with Jack London, "corporeally mature, innerly a child," then more important, with Mark Twain whose life he considered a failure. Though Twain was a greater writer capable of producing works of genius, he had capitulated to the mores of his time, and with one exception, *Huckleberry Finn*, published nothing of value. "His one great work was the result of a burst of spirit over the dikes of social inhibition and intellectual fears." Frank split Twain into two parts — a tendency of much modern criticism. There was the real, deeper Twain, the potentially great writer, and the clownish Twain who truckled to the standards of his time, produced worthless writings, and lost his soul in the process.

Waldo Frank devoted only a few pages to this thesis, but Van Wyck Brooks gave it a whole book: *The Ordeal of Mark Twain*, published in 1920. As the title itself indicates, Brooks rejected Paine's presentation of Twain's life as an unbroken success story, and contended, instead, that it had been a prolonged agony which had turned him into an embittered cynic: "That bitterness of his was the effect of a certain miscarriage in his creative life, a balked personality, an arrested development of which he was himself wholly unaware, but which for him destroyed the meaning of life."

Brooks' analysis of the reasons for Twain's "arrested development" was fundamentally simple. He claimed that there was in Twain the making of a great satirist — "the great purifying force with which nature had endowed him, but of the use of which his life deprived him." He could have been a Voltaire, a Swift, a Cervantes; indeed, "If anything is certain ... it is that Mark Twain was intended to be a sort of American Rabelais who would have done, as regards the puritanical commercialism of the Gilded

Age, very much what the author of *Pantagruel* did as regards the obsolescent medievalism of sixteenth-century France." But Twain's genius had been diverted from its true path into the production of humor by several factors — psychological and social: (1) his Calvinistic upbringing (mainly exemplified by his mother), which tended to inhibit all artistic creation; (2) his life on the frontier, beginning at Hannibal, a "desert of human sand," and continuing through his Nevada and California years, which forced him into the common mold of the pioneer, compelled him to repress all standards of individuality, and further stifled his creative impulses; (3) the softening influence of Olivia Langdon Clemens, a product of the narrow, provincial Elmira horizon, and of William Dean Howells, and the other representatives of the genteel tradition. These three forces produced Mark Twain's bitter duality — the artist unsuccessfully striving to emerge through the clown, the resulting frustration manifesting itself in his pessimism.

From his philosophy alone . . . we can see that Mark Twain was a frustrated spirit, a victim of arrested development, and beyond this fact, as we know from innumerable instances the psychologists have placed before us, we need not look for an explanation of the chagrin of his old age. He had been balked, he had been divided, he had even been turned, as we shall see, against himself; the poet, the artist in him, consequently, had withered into the cynic and the whole man had become a spiritual valetudinarian.

"As we know from innumerable instances the psychologists have placed before us." In these words on page 2 of his book, Brooks announced his intention of applying psychoanalysis to literary criticism. The rest of the book is replete with Freudian interpretations of the details of Twain's life. For example, take the famous deathbed incident related by Paine — there is no other evidence that the incident ever took place. When Twain's father died, writes Paine, his mother led him to the coffin and there extracted the promise that he would be a good boy. The fact that the twelve-year-old boy walked in his sleep for several nights after the event, leads Brooks to conclude that Twain was from then on a dual personality. In Brooks' opinion, the incident set the pattern for Twain's subsequent career:

His "wish" to be an artist, which had been so frowned upon and had encountered such an insurmountable obstacle in the disapproval of his mother, was now repressed, more or less definitely, and another wish, that of winning approval, which inclines him to conform with public opinion, has supplanted it. The individual, in short, has given way to the type. The struggle between these two selves, these two tendencies, these two wishes or groups of wishes, was to continue throughout Mark Twain's life, and the poet, the artist, the individual, was to make a brave effort to survive. From the death of his father onward, however, his will was definitely enlisted on the side opposed to his essential instinct.

Twain's reluctance to become a reporter for the *Territorial Enterprise,* his choice of a pen name, his dreams, even his drawl, are also interpreted in psychoanalytic terms, to prove the disintegration of the artist. So complete was that disintegration, in Brooks' eyes, that he regards nothing that Twain wrote as in any way approaching his potentialities — not even *Huckleberry Finn* and *Tom Sawyer,* about which he shared Arnold Bennett's opinion that they are "episodically magnificent," but "as complete works . . . of quite inferior quality."

In his conclusion, Brooks cited the tragic fate of Mark Twain as an example of what happens to a writer who betrayed his vocation and his country — for "if any country ever needed satire it is, and was, America" — and he pleaded with the writing fraternity to avoid the path of compromise Twain had followed: "Read, writers of America, the driven, disenchanted, anxious faces of your sensitive countrymen; remember the splendid parts your confrères have played in the human drama of other times and other peoples, and ask yourselves whether the hour has not come to put away childish things and walk the stage as poets do."

The Ordeal of Mark Twain has had a tremendous effect on Mark Twain criticism. Every book or article written about Twain since 1920 has had, as a matter of course, to weigh Brooks' thesis. As Edward Wagenknecht put it: "One may agree with Mr. Brooks or one may disagree with him. One may even disagree with him acrimoniously. The only thing that one cannot do with Mr. Brooks is to ignore him."

Brooks' interpretation created a literary sensation, and started a controversy which raged for almost a decade, and was revived in 1933, with the second "revised" edition of his work. (While there are some changes in details, there are few in viewpoint, the most significant being the toning down of derogatory references to Mrs. Clemens and the admission that Twain "accomplished a great deal.") Every literary magazine in the 'twenties carried articles and reviews (sometimes entire issues) which praised or condemned Brooks' thesis.

To the now familiar charges against Twain, the followers of Brooks added new ones such as that he was a man of "immeasurable conceit," a Philistine, and an exponent of Victorian sentimentality. (Brooks' followers included such critics as Lewis Mumford, Alfred Kreymborg, Vernon L. Parrington, Carl Van Doren, Fred Lewis Pattee, Granville Hicks, V. F. Calverton, Upton Sinclair, Edgar Lee Masters, Frank Harris.) But their central thesis was a restatement of Brooks': namely, that Mark Twain had failed to fulfill his promise, or to grow to his full stature, because he had sold out to the idols of the Gilded Age. Some of them carried Brooks' psychoanalytic method to further extremes. Thus Alfred Kreymborg, writing in the London *Spectator*, said: "Mark Twain remained throughout his career a 'fumbling, frantic child,' with Howells as 'his father confessor in literature,' and with his family, led by that arch-Puritan, Mrs. Clemens, and his multitudes of friends and millions of readers serving as the unconscious ranks upon ranks of enemies who secretly crippled and killed the creator of at least one masterpiece: *Huck Finn*.

Puritanism hemmed him in; he had to conform to innumerable taboos, religious, moral and social."

Not all of Brooks' followers, however, accepted his thesis uncritically. Some, like Carl Van Doren, agreeing that "the picture ... drawn of our great humorist is substantially accurate as well as brilliant," disagreed with Brooks' method, and regarded suspiciously "a good many of the details of his psychoanalyzing." Others felt that Brooks did not go far enough in analyzing the extent to which the social and economic changes in Twain's lifetime and his inability to understand them were responsible for his failure and his pessimism.

If several of Brooks' followers criticized some of his conclusions and methods, those who rejected his thesis were often violent in their reaction. They questioned both his "pseudo-Freudian method," and his derogatory evaluations of Twain's works; accused him of lacking a sense of humor and thus being temperamentally unfit to appraise Twain's achievements; charged that he devoted more space to what Twain might have been than to what he actually was, and claimed that his real target was not Twain but America and its institutions, and that these were never as hopelessly corrupt as Brooks assumed. Some critics insisted that, contrary to Brooks' opinion, Twain had never been repressed by his mother, his wife or Howells, and that the proof was that he expressed the boldest social views. Writing in the *Saturday Review of Literature* in 1924, an anonymous critic exclaimed: "Mark Twain was a radical. . . . His attack upon vested injustice, intolerance, and obscurantism in *A Yankee at King Arthur's Court* and *The Prince and the Pauper* is quite as indignant as Samuel Butler's *The Way of All Flesh*. Critics forget the social courage of his anti-imperialism and the commercial courage of his onslaught upon Christian Science."

Bernard De Voto's MARK TWAIN'S AMERICA

By far the most significant answer to Brooks was Bernard De Voto's *Mark Twain's America*, published in 1932.

De Voto attacked Brooks' thesis mercilessly, and rejected all his conclusions. He charged Brooks with choosing only that evidence which bore out the "frustration" theory, and he proved that some of Brooks' most impressive psychoanalytical conclusions, like the famous oath which Twain is supposed to have taken in front of his father's coffin and which Brooks held to be the key to his subsequent ordeal, were based on the most fragile evidence. Going further, he pointed out factual errors in Brooks' book, and took Brooks to task for knowing nothing about Twain's background. He insisted that it was nonsense to assume, as Brooks did, that Twain's humor involved some surrender of his real desires. He denied Brooks' thesis that Twain really wanted to be a satirist, asserting that his "earliest impulses led to the production of humor and nothing whatever suggests any literary impulse or desire of any other kind." At the same time, De Voto denied that the production of humor was for Twain a safe retreat from social satire. In a scorching paragraph, he wrote:

Criticism has said that he directed no humor against the abuses of his time: the fact is that research can find few elements of the age that Mark Twain did not burlesque, satirize, or deride. The whole obscene spectacle of government is passed in review — the presidency, the disintegration of power, the corruption of the electorate — bribery, depravity, subornation, the farce of the people's justice. Criticism has said that he assented in the social monstrosities of his period: yet the epithet with which criticism batters corrupt America, *The Gilded Age*, is his creation, and in the wide expanse of his books, there are few social ulcers that he does not probe. Criticism has said that he was incapable of ideas and all but anaesthetized against the intellectual ferment of the age: yet an idea is no less an idea because it is utilized for comedy, and whether you explore the descent of man, the rejection of progress, or the advances of feminism or the development of the insanity plea or the coalescence of labor, you will find it in that wide expanse.

De Voto flatly rejected a major contention of Brooks — that Olivia Clemens and William Dean Howells were guilty of suppressing Twain's real genius. Their revisions of Twain's manuscripts consisted of the deletion of a few slang words and the softening of statements likely to offend. Basically, the change in his writings wrought by these censors was purely verbal and in no way affected the content.

Many of the points De Voto raised to demolish the Brooks thesis had already been advanced by previous critics, though none had done the job so thoroughly and offered so much evidence to refute Brooks. What De Voto presented that was entirely new was an illuminating analysis of American frontier life, a contribution which he was singularly equipped to make, having experienced life in a frontier society himself.

Whereas Brooks and most of his followers argued that the frontier had thwarted Twain's creative impulses, De Voto demonstrated that it had actually shaped his genius. Indeed, he insisted that Twain was born at the right time and place to inherit and fulfill the tradition of back-country humor — especially since his appearance before the public had been well prepared by a generation of lesser Southwestern comic writers. Nor was this inheritance a barren one, as the Brooks' school contended. The frontier had a life of its own that was freer and more joyful than that on the seaboard, with a culture whose ballad, stories, tall-tales, and folk-tales combined Negro, white, and Indian elements. All of this Twain absorbed and later embodied in his novels and stories. In short, Mark Twain's America — nineteenth century frontier life — laid the foundations for the fullest expression of his genius.

The reviews by Brooks' champions, of De Voto's *Mark Twain's America*, were bitter counter-counter-attacks. The

De Voto thesis was ridiculed as "a shallow and romantic theory," his conception of Western society as "infantile," and his assertion that Twain had never "sold out" to the upper classes, as mere wishful thinking. Most critics, however, treated *Mark Twain's America* as a significant contribution to American literary criticism, though many felt that De Voto, carried away by his desire to demolish the Brooks thesis, had unreasonably painted everything white that Brooks had described as black. Furthermore, his book, in its overbalanced emphasis on Twain's Western surroundings, did not do full justice to the complete man and his career.

Recent Critical Opinion

By 1935, the centenary of Mark Twain's birth, the critics were divided into four camps. There were the Brooks forces who reiterated or extended the Brooks thesis that Twain had not fulfilled his potentialities as a great social satirist, but became a mere buffoon, and that if he saw the evils corrupting American life, he lacked the courage effectively to combat them. The opposed, followers of De Voto, among whom were John Macy, Max Eastman, C. Hartley Grattan, Minnie M. Brashear, and Cyril Clemens, while not accepting certain of De Voto's interpretations, agreed that there was no basis for the charge that Twain had allowed himself to be twisted out of the proper path of his genius. A third group, represented best by Edward Wagenknecht, whose *Mark Twain — The Man and His Work* was published in 1935, held aloof from the Brooks-De Voto controversy, and sought the truth somewhere between these two camps. The fourth group condemned both the Brooks and De Voto schools for devoting so much energy to analyzing and psychoanalyzing Mark Twain that they had none left for reading and studying his works. Fortunately, the people, who had never paid much attention to the critics, did what the analysis failed to do — they continued to read and to enjoy Mark Twain. "Mark

Twain," wrote Charles H. Crompton in the *American Mercury*, after announcing that Brooks' and De Voto's books had bored him, "is today the most widely read American author, living or dead.... Do we need to feel concerned about what the critics say about Mark Twain? He has the same place that he always had in the hearts of the people, and in that place, he is secure." The London *Times* (Literary Supplement) concurred, declaring in 1935 that it was time to end the prolonged critical post-mortem and to turn instead to an appreciation of Twain's work: "Since Mark Twain died, twenty-five and a half years ago, there has been inquest enough.... Surely little more can remain to be either revealed or remarked!... The analysts have had him long enough; it seems time for the plain reader to re-enter into what may remain of his heritage."

The *Times* was incorrect in assuming that nothing new about Twain remained to be revealed. To be sure, there has been only one full-length biography produced since the *Times* article — that by De Lancey Ferguson, published in 1943 — but much new information on all aspects of Twain's career, thought and work has been brought to light through the publication of hitherto unpublished manuscripts and letters, in specialized articles in learned journals, and in carefully documented doctoral dissertations (few of them as yet published), the product of post-graduate research at American universities. Despite this mass of scholarship, the argument that the critics were so engrossed in what Twain was or might have been that they paid little attention to what he said remains valid. In the continuing controversy over whether Twain was a jester or a social satirist, few critics bothered to examine what Twain himself had to say.

Twain's Concept of Humor

In his copy of Thackeray's essay on Swift, Twain underlined the plea for the recognition of the innate seriousness of the true humorist:

Harlequin without his mask is known to present a very sober countenance, and was himself . . . *a man full of cares and perplexities like the rest whose Self must always be serious to him, under whatever mask or disguise or uniform he presents it to the public. . . . The humorous writer professes to awaken and direct your love, your pity, your kindness — your scorn for untruth, pretension, imposture — your tenderness for the weak, the poor, the unhappy.* . . . He comments on all the ordinary actions and passions of life about. He takes upon himself to be the week-day preacher.

That Thackeray expressed Twain's own concept of humor is abundantly clear in his writings. Though he frequently voiced impatience at being typed as a humorist and complained about "demeaning" himself as a buffoon, he was not basically a split personality, for he never thought that humor and social criticism were separate and apart. "When an honest writer discovers an imposition," he wrote in *A Tramp Abroad*, "it is his simple duty to strip it bare and hurl it down from its place of honor, no matter who suffers by it; any other course would render him unworthy of the public confidence." Twain was convinced that he could achieve this goal as a writer through humor, and that this accounted for his success. "I succeeded in the long run," he told Archibald Henderson, "where Shillaber, Doesticks, and Billings failed, because they never had any ideal higher than that of merely being funny." What distinguished his humor from these others and gave it staying power, he declared, was "the gravity which is the foundation, and of real value." This was his great contribution, he felt; on this he was ready to rest his reputation. For as he expressed it so effectively in *The Mysterious Stranger*:

[The human race] in its poverty, has unquestionably one really effective weapon — laughter. Power, money, persuasion, supplication, persecution — these can lift at a colossal humbug — push it a little, weaken it a little, century by century; but only laughter can blow it to rags and atoms at a blast. Against the assault of laughter nothing can stand.

The degree to which Mark Twain succeeded in his purpose will best be determined as we proceed with the examination of his point of view on a variety of social issues.

Chapter Three
POLITICS AND GOVERNMENT

"Loyalty to petrified opinions never yet broke a chain or freed a human soul in *this* world — and never will." (From speech, "Consistency," 1885.)

"I always did hate politics," Mark Twain wrote in 1869 to Mrs. Fairbanks. He had received his first direct impressions of politics as a reporter for the Nevada *Territorial Enterprise*, and the experience had left him angry and disgusted. He saw elections manipulated by agents of commercial concerns; legislators serving as their tools; the courts of law as inept and corrupt; jury verdicts purchased; public officials from the highest to the lowest "for sale or rent on the mildest possible terms."

The rhetoric of stump oratory — "the voice of the people," "the tide of public opinion," "the welfare of the community," etc. — sounded hypocritical to Twain in the mouths of politicians serving the business interests. Each party charged the other with "hellish designs upon the freedom of our beloved country," but there was no difference to be seen between them for the interest of both was to serve the business groups that dominated the rival political machines. He observed how William Stewart, soon to become a millionaire and first U.S. Senator from Nevada, after having appealed to "the honest miner" in election campaigns, spent the rest of the year representing the big mining companies in legal battles against independent miners. He saw the elected mouthpieces of the big mining corporations being rewarded with higher office, while his brother Orion, then secretary to the territorial governor and doing an honest job, went unrewarded. "The government of my country shuns honest simplicity, but fondles artistic villainy," he concluded, "and I think I might have developed into a very capable pickpocket if I had remained in public service a year or two."

The lack of intelligent members in legislative bodies, Twain was convinced, made them easy prey to corruption. While reporting the proceedings of the Nevada Constitutional Conventions, Twain first made the acquaintance, as he wrote later, of "the small minds and the selfishest souls and the cowardliest hearts that God makes." This low estimate of legislators settled into a conviction. "The Story of the Bad Little Boy," written in 1865, ends with the boy grown up, becoming "wealthy by all manner of cheating and rascality, and now he is the infernalest wickedest scoundrel in his native village, and is universally respected, *and belongs to the legislature.*"

His short residence in Washington during 1868, as secretary to Senator Stewart, deepened Twain's contempt. He found the Capitol, "the place to get a low opinion of everybody in," and having "seen every Senator," concluded that Congress was made up of a host of pitiful intellects. He was so disgusted that he refused the offer of a postmastership in San Francisco. Although it was an influential post, it seemed to him "a falling from Grace. . . . Government pap must be nauseating food for a *man*," he wrote to Orion.

Corruption in Government

Twain left the Capitol convinced that "there are lots of folk in Washington who need vilifying." The events of the next few years only strengthened this feeling. It was during these years that, what Vernon L. Parrington has aptly called the "great barbecue" of corruption and greed reached its climax. National, state and municipal governments were the tools of the Robber Barons, who corrupted the nation, crushed smaller rivals by unscrupulous methods, and produced rule by a plutocracy. Jay Gould, the most notorious of the Robber Barons, told a New York State Legislative Committee how these men operated in politics: "It was the custom when men received nominations to come to me for contributions, and I made them, and considered them good paying investments for the [Erie Railroad] company. In a Republican district, I was a strong Republican; in a Democratic district, I was Democratic; and in doubtful districts, I was doubtful. In politics, I was an Erie Railroad man every time."

By 1873 Congress had given away nearly two hundred million acres of the public lands to railroad corporations of which nine million acres went to the Union Pacific. Oakes Ames, a Massachusetts Congressman, whose brother was president of the Union Pacific, prepared the way for the Crédit Mobilier swindle by offering stock at inside prices to other members of Congress. Those who would not buy were given their shares. The American Minister to England sold his name to a fraudulent mining scheme for $50,000 in stock. Senator James G. Blaine became involved in railroad stock manipulations, and lied repeatedly to save himself before a Congressional Committee. President Grant's Vice-President, Schuyler Colfax, was implicated in the Crédit Mobilier; his private secretary in the Whisky Ring; his brother-in-law in Jay Gould's infamous attempt to corner gold; his Secretary of War in a deal for the sale of his office; and his Secretary of the Treasury allowed his friends fifty percent commissions for collecting internal revenue.

Meanwhile, in the cities, bosses like Tweed of New York looted the public treasuries. The Tweed Ring robbed New York City of approximately $200 million (which would have a value of billions today) through huge sums paid for the rental of armories that did not exist, for repairs never made, for court houses built for four times the actual cost, for monumental bills for plumbing and carpentry work, and through other forms of wholesale graft, fraud, blackmail and extortion. The Tweed Ring owned every public official from the governor of the state, the courts, the grand jury, the district attorney, the police — from the highest city employee to the lowliest. The Ring sold immunity from prosecution to gamblers, dive-keepers, and also to "respectable" businessmen who wished to evade the law. Indeed, among the Ring's most enthusiastic supporters were businessmen who battened on contracts, favors and other forms of patronage. Jay Gould and James Fisk, Jr. were closely allied with Tweed, and, in return for legislative favors, made it possible for Tweed to share in the stupendous Erie Railroad thefts.

Indignant over the widespread corruption in government, Twain sought by use of his satirical powers to communicate his feeling to the people and arouse them to action. In ironic sketches, he exposed the corruption of the Nevada legislative and judicial process by the business interests. In San Francisco, he added the police to the list of "the dust-licking pimps and slaves" of the commercial groups, and marked how their "constant vigilance" was directed only against poverty-stricken, petty thieves while "many offenders of importance go unpunished." In articles in the *Galaxy* of 1870, he satirized political jobbery, corruption and red tape. His *Burlesque Autobiography,* published in the spring of 1871, contained a series of picture cartoons of the Erie Railroad Ring, presented in an adapted version of "The House That Jack Built." Jay Gould, James Fisk, Jr., and John T. Hoffman, Governor of New York, were portrayed in "The House," which was the Erie headquarters, and were depicted as engaged in swindling the people and bribing the legislature.

In a sketch entitled, "Running for Governor," Twain humorously depicted how he was defeated by his opponent, the same John T. Hoffman of the Erie Railroad Ring, simply because the newspapers did not regard him as properly equipped to run the governorship corruptly. He developed the same theme more seriously at a meeting of the Monday Evening Club of Hartford, accusing the newspapers of having sold out repeatedly to the politicians by protecting their grafting enterprises and supporting their candidates for office. The press had defended so many official criminals on party pretexts that it had "created a United States Senate whose members are incapable of determining what crime against law *is,* they are so morally

89

blind, and it has made light of dishonesty till we have . . . a Congress which contracts to work for a certain sum and then deliberately steals additional wages out of the public pocket."

In the New York *Tribune* of September 27, 1871, Twain presented in "The Revised Catechism" a scathing denunciation of Boss Tweed and his associates, and, at the same time, an indictment of the age that permitted such men to thrive. It consisted of questions and answers in a class of "modern Moral Philosophy," a section of which follows:

Q. What is the chief end of man?

A. To get rich.

Q. In what way?

A. Dishonestly if we can, honestly if we must.

Q. Who is God, the only one and true?

A. Money is God. Gold and greenbacks and stocks — father, son, and the ghost of the same — three persons in one: these are the true and only God, mighty and supreme; and William Tweed is his prophet.

Q. How shall a man attain the chief end of life?

A. By furnishing imaginary carpets to the Court-House; apocryphal chairs to the armories, and invisible printing to the city. . . .

Q. Who were the models the young were taught to emulate in former days?

A. Washington and Franklin.

Q. Whom do they and should they emulate now in this era of enlightenment?

A. Tweed, Hall, Connolly, Camochon, Fisk, Gould, Barnard, and Winans.

Q. What works were chiefly prized for the training of the young in former days?

A. Poor Richard's Almanac, the Pilgrim's Progress, and the Declaration of Independence.

Q. What are the best prized Sunday-school books in this more enlightened age?

A. St. Hall's Garbled Reports, St. Fisk's Ingenious Robberies, St. Camochan's Guide to Corruption, St. Gould on the Watering of Stock, St. Barnard's Injunctions, St. Tweed's Handbook of Morals, and the Court-House edition of the Holy Crusade of the Forty Thieves.

Q. Do we progress?
A. You bet your life.

In the first three questions and answers Twain sums up the speculators' spirit of the age. This brief, sardonic commentary on an era, revealing gold as the new divinity and money as the dominant standard of the country, anticipates the novel, *The Gilded Age*, in which Twain fired a barrage against the lust for gold and its rotting of the national morals and politics.

THE GILDED AGE

On April 23, 1873, the New York *Tribune* announced the forthcoming publication of a new novel by Mark Twain and Charles Dudley Warner: "It is called *The Gilded Age* — a name which gives the best promise of the wealth of satire and observation which it is easy to expect from two such authors."

It was a name, too, which described the epoch with such conciseness that it came to symbolize an entire era in American history. It was an age with no other than dollar values; an age marked by the feverish desire for sudden wealth; the incubation period of the great trusts; the age of speculation. "It was not 'business'; it was frenzy," writes Elias P. Oberholtzer. "The transactions of brokers in Wall Street for the year ending June 30, 1865, reached a total of six billion dollars." This is a commanding figure even for today. The new plutocracy had only one divinity — the golden calf. It was an age in which the *nouveau riche* lived in diamond-studded lavishness, spending its money on banquets for pet dogs, and ostentatiously handing out cigars wrapped in hundred-dollar bills. It was an age in which the buccaneers of industry and finance crushed the legitimate aspirations of an underpaid, overworked, miserably housed and miserably clothed working class with brutal force.

It was also an age in which literature, with few exceptions, was completely uncritical of the period or made a virtue of commercial success. Such books as Louisa May Alcott's *Little Women* (1869) and *Little Men* (1871), Horatio Alger's *Ragged Dick or Street Life in New York with the Bootblacks* (1868), and its almost identical predecessor, Edward S. Ellis' *Seth Jones, or the Captives of the Frontier* (1860), John Esten Cooke's *Surry of Eagle's Nest* (1866), Harriet Beecher Stowe's *Old-town Folks* (1869) are typical of American literature of the period. In the main, they dealt with romantic love, rural tranquility, pleasing descriptions of nature, and the rewards of go-ahead virtue. Even William Dean Howells' *A Chance Acquaintance,* published in 1873, was little more than a love story with a Boston setting. None of these books showed any awareness of the degrading demoralization of the entire national life. Most writers echoed in their novels the widely quoted line in American verse, published in 1866 in Elizabeth Akers' *Poems:* "Backward, turn backward, O Time in your flight."

Into this soporific literary scene burst the first indictment of the era — *The Gilded Age,* published late in 1873. The novel grew out of a conversation in the early winter of 1872-73 during which Warner and Twain were challenged by their wives to "write a better book than the current novels they had been discussing with some severity." We can assume that the discussion was critical of the failure of contemporary novelists to portray American realities during the Grant administration when the government itself served as an agency of the Robber Barons. That *The Gilded Age* was written to fill this gap is intimated in the Preface: "In a state where there is no fever of speculation, no inflamed desire for sudden wealth, where the poor are all simple-minded and contented, and the rich are all honest and generous, where society is a condition of primitive purity, and politics is the occupation of only the capable and patriotic, there are necessarily no materials for such a history as we have constructed out of an ideal commonwealth."

"Hatching the plot day by day," Twain and Warner completed the novel in about three months. The collaborators, after a discussion, would each write his version of the chapters under consideration. They would then call their wives into consultation, read their respective chapters, select the better version, and destroy the other.

We know today that the collaboration between the two men was much more closely interwoven than was formerly supposed. Yet, at the time of publication, a number of reviewers insisted that the book was really written by Warner it being impossible for "a mere comic like Mark Twain" to master the mechanics of serious novel-writing. The charge infuriated Twain. He exploded in a letter to Dr. John Brown:

We are all delighted with your commendations of the Gilded Age — & the more so, because some of our newspapers have set forth the opinion that *Warner* really wrote the book & I only added my name to the title-page in order to give it a large sale. It is a shameful charge to make. I wrote the first eleven chapters — every word & every line — Warner never retouched a sentence in them, I believe. I also wrote Chapters 24, 25, 27, 28, 30, 32, 33, 34, 36, 37, 42, 43, 45, 51, 52, 53, 57, 59, 60, 61, 62 & *portions* of 35, 49, 56. So I wrote 32 of the 63 chapters *entirely* & part of 3 others besides.

According to this division of work — and there is no reason to doubt its accuracy — Twain was responsible for the chapters elaborating the main plot and portraying those two remarkable characters, Colonel Sellers and Senator Dilworthy, while Warner was responsible for the sub-plot involving Philip Sterling and Ruth Bolton, and for advancing the conventional "love interest." Essentially, then, Twain was responsible for the social criticism and Warner for the romance. As Twain himself put it: "[Warner] has worked up the fiction, and I have hurled in the facts."

It is, of course, for its social criticism that *The Gilded Age* remains interesting and valuable today. These chapters can still be read with undiminished pleasure. They present truer history than appears in many textbooks in American history. Warner's part of the book, with its naïveté and old-fashioned melodrama, and its polite essayist style, is frankly dreary conception. The two plots are simply not woven together, a fact which Twain himself later admitted.

The main plot revolves about the effort to build the "City of Napoleon" on a God-forsaken prairie mud-flat, thirty miles from nowhere. (The sub-plot largely concerns Philip Sterling's search for a coal mine.) Colonel Sellers, initiator of the project, rhapsodizes: "All we want is capital to develop it. Slap down the rails and bring the land into market. The richest land on God Almighty's footstool is lying right out there. If I had my capital free I could plant it for millions." The fact was, however, that the capital for this development, like all speculative projects for "turning cross-road hamlets into great cities," had to come from Wall Street, and its agents in Congress. Sellers' scheme of transforming mud-flats into a metropolis was no more fantastic than the projects of other back-country speculators who sought financial backing in Wall Street, and federal aid from Senators like the sanctimonious Dilworthy. "It was a plan that the Senator could understand without a great deal of explanation, for he seemed to be familiar with like improvements elsewhere." Experienced in looting the government, Dilworthy tells Sellers: "You'd better begin by asking only for two or three hundred thousand, the usual way." Then he adds: "You can begin to sell lots on that appropriation, you know."

As the story shifts from the Missouri frontier to the commercial and financial center of the East and to the nation's Capitol in Washington, the novel tells how Eastern corporations successfully lobbied federal grants for backcountry developments. Congressional legislation was for sale to the biggest promoters. The lobbyists for the "paper city" of Napoleon found that: "You can't get a thing like this through Congress without buying committees for straight-out cash on delivery."

In Washington, highly "moral" Senators, mouthing pieties about acting "in the public interest" and for the welfare of the newly emancipated Negroes, sponsor only such legislative appropriations as enrich them personally. The services of beautiful women, like Laura Hawkins, are enlisted to win votes for corrupt appropriations. Every one is out to rob the government and fleece on a grand scale. Washington, the novel points out, was filled with a fat-salaried "invisible government," the lobbyists of big corporations, with headquarters in Wall Street, engaged in "large operations for the public good, men who in the slang of the day understood the virtues of addition, division and silence." With corporation funds, they could work with "friends" in Congress, paying sumptuous prices for an initial appropriation to insure subsequent "friendship" for follow-up grants. The first handout was "never intended for anything but a mere nest egg for the future and *real* appropriations."

The broad canvas of the novel covers many features of the Gilded Age which most deserved satire. Several major themes emerge — not in a consistent pattern, to be sure, but clearly enough to enable the reader to follow them through the shifting scenes and the crowding characters — frontiersmen, speculators, wealthy merchants, bankers and brokers, contractors, politicians, ministers, society women, etc.

1. *The corrupting influence of the speculative spirit and the greed for sudden wealth.*

This is reflected in Colonel Sellers' remark early in the book: "Speculation — my! the whole atmosphere's full of money. I wouldn't take three fortunes for one little operation I've got on hand now." Again, in the gleeful statement of a speculator in lands and mines: "I wasn't worth a cent two years ago, and now I owe two millions of dollars." Laura Hawkins sounds it in her feverish desire "to be rich; she wanted luxury, she wanted men at her feet, her slaves." Philip Sterling finds his training has not prepared him for the times:

It was not altogether Philip's fault, let us own, that he was in this position. There are many young men like him in American society, of his age, opportunities, education, and abilities, who have really been educated for nothing and have let themselves drift, in the hope that they will find somehow, and by some sudden turn of good luck, the golden road to fortune. He was not idle or lazy; he had energy and a disposition to carve his own way. But he was born into a time when all young men of his age caught the fever of speculation, and expected to get on in the world by the omission of the regular processes which have been appointed from of old. And examples were not wanting to encourage him. He saw people, all around him, poor yesterday, rich to-day, who had come into sudden opulence by some means which they could not have classified among any of the regular occupations of life.

No wonder Philip says to himself again and again: "Am I a visionary? I *must* be a visionary; everybody is these days; everybody chases butterflies; everybody seeks sudden fortune and will not lay one up by slow toil."

2. *The three-cornered alliance of western speculators, eastern capitalists in Wall Street, and a corrupt government.*

Harry Brierly represents the connection among all three groups: "A land operator, engaged in vast speculations, a favorite in the select circles of New York, in correspondence with brokers and bankers, intimate with public men at Washington. . . ." Colonel Sellers pins his hopes on Harry; he had "entire confidence in Harry's influence with Wall Street, and with Congressmen, to bring about the consummation of their scheme." He knew, however, that it was on Wall Street that everything really depended, and he advised Harry to go easy in paying off Congress — "give 'em a small interest; a lot apiece in the suburbs of the Landing ought to do a Congressman" — but to be more generous with the bankers and brokers in Wall Street — ". . . I reckon you'll have to mortgage part of the city itself to the brokers."

The President of the "Columbus River Slackwater Navigation Company," with headquarters at No. — Wall Street, tells Harry how the brokers and bankers function in obtaining a Congressional appropriation:

A Congressional appropriation costs money. Just reflect, for instance. A majority of the House committee, say $10,000 apiece — $40,000; a majority of the Senate committee, the same each — say $40,000; a little extra to one or two chairmen of one or two such committees, say $10,000 each — $20,000; and there's $100,000 of the money gone, to begin with. Then, seven male lobbyists, at $3,000 each — $21,000; one female lobbyist, $10,000; a high moral Congressman or Senator here and there — the high moral ones cost more, because they give tone to a measure — say ten of these at $3,000 each, is $30,000. Then a lot of small-fry country members who won't vote for anything whatever without pay — say twenty at $500 apiece, is $10,000 altogether; lot of jimcracks for Congressmen's wives and children — these go a long way — you can't spend too much money in that line — well, those things cost in a lump, say $10,000 — along there somewhere.

After hearing this explanation, Harry "reflected profoundly" and commented: "We send many missionaries to lift up the benighted races of other lands. How much cheaper and better it would be if those people could only come here and drink of our civilization at its fountain head." "I perfectly agree with you, Mr. Brierly," the Wall Street banker remarks.

Railroad companies are shown to be the chief agencies of corruption. Many are "merely kept on foot for speculative purposes in Wall Street," and to wangle huge government subsidies, with no plan in mind save profit for the planners.

One promoter describes his "plan of operations":

We'll buy the lands ... on long time, backed by the notes of good men; and then mortgage them for money enough to get the road well on. Then get the towns on the line to issue their bonds for stock, and sell the bonds for enough to complete the roads, and partly stock it, especially if we mortgage each section as we complete it. We can then sell the rest of the stock on the prospect of the business of the road through an improved country, and also sell the lands at a big advance on the strength of the road. All we want ... is a few thousand dollars to start the surveys, and arrange things in the legislature. There is some parties will have to be seen who might make us trouble.

The railroad, it becomes clear, is to end up nowhere, and when the promoter is asked "what would become of the poor people who had been led to put their little money into the speculation, when you got out of it and left it half way?" the reply is that "there's so many poor in the legislature to be looked after.... Yes ... an uncommon poor lot this year, uncommon. Consequently an expensive lot. The fact is ... that the price is raised so high on United States Senators now, that it affects the whole market; you can't get any public improvement through on reasonable terms."

It is not surprising that engineers who are to build such railroads know nothing about engineering. Their function is to help the small-time speculators in the frontier and the big-time speculators in Wall Street fleece the government and the public.

3. *Government in the United States had degenerated into a grand agency of corruption.*

A town in the wilderness is named "Corruptionville" after Congress itself. Twain's description of Congress in session is masterly:

Below, a few Senators lounged upon the sofas set apart for visitors, and talked with idle Congressmen. A dreary member was speaking; the presiding officer was nodding; here and there little knots of members stood in the aisles, whispering together; all about the House others sat in the various attitudes that express weariness; some, tilted back, had one or more legs disposed upon their desks; some sharpened pencils indolently; some scribbled aimlessly; some yawned and stretched; a great many lay upon their breasts upon the desks, sound asleep and gently snoring. The flooding gaslight from the fancifully wrought roof poured down upon the tranquil scene. Hardly a sound disturbed the stillness, save the monotonous eloquence of the gentleman who occupied the floor. Now and then a warrior of the opposition broke down under the pressure, gave it up and went home.

Among the tourist sights in Washington was the Capitol building which, by original estimate, "was to cost $12,000,000 and ... the government did come within $27,200,000 of building it for that sum." The tourists undoubtedly met many government officials like the Hon. Higgins. He had "not come to serve his country in Washington for nothing. The appropriation which he had engineered through Congress for the maintenance of the Indians in his Territory would have made all those savages rich if it had ever got to them."

To the graver charges of such wholesale robbery, leveled against the government's "misrepresentatives," the book adds their petty frauds and malfeasance — passing extra-pay bills for themselves, abuse of the franking privilege, vote-selling and other prerequisites of the spoils system. Public employment, from the highest bureau chief to the boy "who purifies department spitoons," is secured only through the wonder-working power of political influence. "Mere merit, fitness, and capability are useless baggage without 'influence.'" "There is something good and motherly about Washington, the grand old benevolent National Asylum for the Helpless."

In the rare event that the elected representatives of the people are publicly exposed for having sold their votes for cash, and the protests become too loud even for Congress to ignore, an investigation takes place — a farce which would not convict the devil himself. The following paragraphs are devastating in their evaluation of such investigations:

The statement of Senator Dilworthy naturally carried conviction to the minds of the [investigating] committee. It was close, logical, unanswerable; it bore many internal evidences of its truth. For instance, it is customary in all countries for business men to loan large sums of money in bank bills instead of checks. It is customary for the lender to make no memorandum of the transaction. It is customary for the borrower to receive the money without making a memorandum of it, or giving a note or a receipt for it — because the borrower is not likely to die or forget about it. It is customary to lend nearly anybody money to start a bank with, especially if you have not the money in bank bills about your person or in your trunk. It is customary to hand a large sum in bank bills to a man you have just been introduced to (if he asks you to do it) to be conveyed to a distant town and delivered to another party. It is not customary to make a memorandum of this transaction; it is not customary for the conveyor to give a note or a receipt for the money; it is not customary to require that he shall get a note or a receipt from the man he is to convey it to in the distant town. It would be at least singular in you to say to the proposed conveyor, "You might be robbed; I will deposit the money in the bank and send a check for it to my friend through the mail."

Very well. It being plain that Senator Dilworthy's statement was rigidly true, and this fact being strengthened by his adding to it the support of "his honor as a Senator," the committee rendered a verdict of "Not proven that a bribe had been offered and accepted."

One good thing, the novel ironically notes, came out of all this plundering of the government: it had caused Confederates and Unionists to bury the hatchet, for "Confederate are just as eager to get at the Treasury as Unionists!"

4. *The moral decay of the Gilded Age.*

This is also established in merciless descriptions of vulgar newly-rich, the "loud aristocrats," transformed overnight into the élite by speculations and fleecing the government and the public.

Official position, "no matter how obtained," opened the doors to the new aristocracy, but "great wealth gave a man a still higher and nobler place in it than did official position. If this wealth had been acquired by conspicuous ingenuity, with just a pleasant little spice of illegality about it, all the better." This new aristocracy of wealth exposed its coarseness in accoutrements overloaded with detail, jigsawed and embellished without rhyme or reason:

The three carriages arrived at the same moment from different directions. They were new and wonderfully shiny, and the brasses on the harness were highly polished and bore complicated monograms. There were showy coats of arms, too, with Latin mottoes. The coachmen and footmen were clad in bright new livery, of striking colors, and they had black rosettes with shaving-brushes projecting above them, on the sides of their stove-pipe hats.

When the visitors swept into the drawing-room they filled the place with a suffocating sweetness procured at the perfumer's. Their costumes, as to architecture, were the latest fashion intensified; they were rainbow-hued; they were hung with jewels — chiefly diamonds. It would have been plain to any eye that it had cost something to upholster these women.

The social conversation of these women is reproduced in documentary fashion, and reflects the ethics of the rich. Typical is the comment of Mrs. Oreille (formerly Mrs. O'Reilly) who complains, "there are people in society here that have really no more money to live on than what some of us pay for servant hire. Still, I won't say but what some of them are very good people — and respectable too."

The authors find it necessary to add in a footnote: "As impossible and exasperating as this conversation may sound to a person who is not an idiot, it is scarcely in any respect any exaggeration of one which one of us actually listened to in an American drawing-room; otherwise we could not venture to put such a chapter into a book which professes to deal with social possibilities."

5. *The continual evoking of Christian piety by the Robber Barons and politicos of the Gilded Age to advance and justify their operations.*

This theme runs throughout the novel. Wall Street, it is

made clear, can depend on the clergy to support its whole-sale robbery of the government and the public, for it does many favors for these ministers: "It was astonishing how many New England clergymen, in the time of the petro-leum excitement, took chances in oil. The Wall Street brokers are said to do a good deal of small business for country clergymen, who are moved, no doubt, with the laudable desire of purifying the New York stock-board."

The President of the "Columbus River Slackwater Navigation Company" reveals how Wall Street uses the religious press to put through a corrupt appropriation bill:

Your religious paper is by far the best vehicle for a thing of this kind, because they'll "lead" your article and put it right in the middle of the reading matter; and if it's got a few Scripture quota-tions in it, and some temperance platitudes, and a bit of gush here and there about Sunday-schools, and a sentimental snuffle now and then about "God's precious ones, the honest hard-handed poor," it works the nation like a charm, my dear sir, and never a man suspects that it is an advertisement; but your secular paper sticks you right into the advertising columns and of course you don't take a trick. Give me a religious paper to advertise in, every time; and if you'll just look at their advertising pages, you'll observe that other people think a good deal as I do — especially people who have got little financial schemes to make everybody rich with. Of course, I mean your great big metropolitan religious papers that know how to serve God and make money at the same time — that's your sort, sir, that's your sort — a religious paper that isn't run to make money is no use to *us*, sir, as an advertising medium — no use to anybody in our line of business.

"The high moral ones cost more, but are worth the extra expenditure." It is through the career of Senator Dil-worthy, who, for public consumption, "glibly links the name of God Almighty with his purposes," while privately he will touch no bill until a fat retainer's fee is guaranteed, that Twain most effectively exposes the hypocrisy of so many wealthy, deeply religious men of the Gilded Age. The Senator is described as a man who has only been in Congress a few years, and he must be worth a million. First thing in the morning when he stayed with me he asked about family prayers, whether we had 'em before or after breakfast. I hated to disappoint the Senator, but I had to out with it, tell him we didn't have 'em, not steady. He said he understood, business interruptions and all that, some men were well enough without, but as for him he never neglected the ordinances of religion. *He doubted if the Columbus River appropriation* would succeed if we did not invoke the Divine Blessing on it.

With high-sounding motives — "the good of the country, and religion, and the poor, and temperance" — Dilworthy sponsors Sellers' scheme to unload the Tennessee land on the government, ostensibly as the site of Knob Hill University for the emancipated Negro. He coaches Laura Hawkins in the use of her feminine charms to win votes for the scheme, and tells her in the same breath: "I never push a private interest if it is not justified and ennobled by some large public good. I doubt if a Christian would be justified in working for his own salvation if it was not to aid in the salvation of his fellow-men."

Dilworthy's most consummate stroke was his parade before the Hawk-eye voters as a Sunday-School hero, who had succeeded in the world by virtue of following the good-little-boy formula:

Temptations lay all about him, and sometimes he was about to yield, but he would think of some precious lesson he learned in his Sunday-school a long time ago, and that would save him. By and by he was elected to the legislature. . . .

And by and by the people made him governor — and he said it was all owing to the Sunday-school.

After a while the people elected him a Representative to the Congress of the United States, and he grew very famous. Now temptations assailed him on every hand. People tried to get him to drink wine, to dance, to go to theatres; they even tried to buy his vote; but no, the memory of his Sunday-school saved him from all harm. . . .

Well, at last, what do you think happened? Why the people gave him a towering illustrious position, a grand, imposing position. And what do you think it was? What should you say it was, children? It was Senator of the United States! That poor little boy that loved his Sunday-school became that man. *That man stands before you!* All that he is, he owes to the Sunday-school.

Dilworthy's sermon, of course, not only exposed his cynical depravity, but the flagrant dishonesty of Sunday-school tales circulated in that period. Dilworthy was modeled after Samuel C. Pomeroy, the corrupt Kansas Senator. Indeed, every important episode in *The Gilded Age*, outside of the love-plot, can be paralleled in the history of post-Civil War America. The William M. Weed of the novel, whose "bosom friend" sells shingle nails for the New York courthouse at $3,000 a keg, is a thin disguise for Boss William M. Tweed. The operation of railroad speculators is based on Crédit Mobilier and similar scandals of the period. Its women lobbyists were to be seen everywhere in Washington, "making the streets and hotels disreputably gay." Laura Hawkins's murder of Col. Selby, her trial and her acquittal on the ground of temporary insanity, closely parallel the case of Mrs. Laura D. Fair of San Francisco.

6. *The mass of the citizens are themselves to blame for the plunder of their government, for, either through stupidity or indifference, they allow unscrupulous politicians to gain office and sell their influence to the highest bidders.*

While the ignorant are shepherded to the polls by the bosses, and through their votes put into office men who loot the public treasury, the more intelligent sit at home. Thereby they leave the source of political power (the primaries) "in the hands of saloon-keepers, dog-fanciers, and hod-carriers," such as Patrick O'Reily, an immigrant hod-carrier who achieved wealth and power as a political leader in New York and a "bosom friend" of "Boss" Weed. The ward organizations sent their hand-picked delegates to the nominating conventions "where the publicans and their retainers rule," and where they made up a list of "incorruptibles" to submit to the electorate. "Then the great meek public come forward at the proper time and make unhampered choice and bless Heaven that they live in a free land where no form of despotism can ever intrude."

"The great putty-hearted public," is the way the novel sums up the electorate. Senator Dilworthy welcomes editorial denunciation of his thieving appropriation bill. "Persecution," he tells a companion, "changes the tide of public opinion. The great public is weak-minded . . . sentimental. . . . The great putty-hearted public loves to gush, and there is no such darling opportunity to gush as a case of persecution affords." He is proved correct. Although he is clearly guilty of selling his vote to the highest bidder, he received "a grand ovation" when he returned home. He is told that the citizens' "affection for him and their confidence in him were in no wise impaired by the persecutions that had pursued him, and that he was still good enough for them."

Occasionally, legislators are even brought to trial for irregularities. They are saved from jail by "our admirable jury system" which allows incompetents, mentally unbalanced individuals, and others who are "only stupid" to serve. The "inevitable American verdict" in such cases is "Not Guilty," and the corrupt legislators walk forth "with characters vindicated."

These, then, are the main themes that run through *The Gilded Age*. The novel thus concerned itself, mainly satirically and often seriously, with the influence of business groups over the government; their bribery of elected representations; the breakdown of morality; the vulgarity of the newly-rich; speculation and shady finance; the domination of society by a single impulse — greed; the hypocrisy of the professional Christians; the failure of the citizens to attend properly to their political duties. In short, the novel covered most of the features of the age which merited social criticism.

Published in December, 1873, *The Gilded Age* ran to three editions within a month. In two months, 40,000 copies had been sold. Twain claimed this was "the largest two-months' sale which any American book has ever achieved (unless one excepts the cheap edition of *Uncle Tom's Cabin*)." A year after publication, it was reported that 58,000 copies had been sold, and Twain's income from the book was estimated at nearly $25,000. *Colonel Sellers*, the play which Twain fashioned hurriedly from the novel and which was made up wholly of the chapters he had written, was also very profitable.

The Gilded Age was more widely reviewed than any previous Twain volume. The unfavorable reviews — and these were the majority — fell into two categories. One group expressed disappointment at not finding another of Twain's funny books, but a serious satire instead. The St. Louis *Democrat* considered the book simply "a gigantic practical joke." Other critics condemned the novel for dwelling on the seamier side of life in America instead of showing "the pleasanter features of American life." The Chicago *Tribune* snarled: "They have wilfully degraded their craft, abused the people's trust, and provoked a stern condemnation." The Boston *Literary World* expressed "wonder as to how a man of Mr. Warner's literary reputation could lend his name to such cheap and feeble stuff."

The Independent accused the authors of "selecting from real life what is worst and most repulsive. ... We should blush to see the book republished in Europe." The majority of the British critics shared this feeling. The *Athenaeum* reviewer frowned upon "the spirit which brings to light all the *'linge sale'* [dirty linen] of American speculation for the benefit of foreign readers."

Yet the book had its defenders precisely because of its pronouncements on social and political problems, and won for Twain high commendation as an interpreter of American life. The reviewer for *Appleton's Journal* was delighted that Twain did not allow his humor to blind him to existing evils in society, and that he had used his satirical powers, "acuteness ... (and) genius" to expose them. The novel had given "most of the falsities of the time a sound thrashing that will be appreciated in quarters to which no one of the Olympian bolts of the thunderers in daily press or Sunday pulpit could ever penetrate." In general, the authors had "achieved a success such as no less trenchant pens could have gained." The noted critic, F. B. Perkins, reviewing the novel in *Old and New,* commented: "The book is a story with a purpose as much as 'The Pilgrim's Progress.'" While Perkins found much to criticize in the novel's structure, he described it as a "remarkably well-executed work ... a book of real and high purpose, much graphic and portrait power, much knowledge of men and things, and uncommon swiftness and force of action."

The critic for the British *Spectator* concurred in Perkins' favorable evaluation. It was gratifying that the authors were Americans and not English, since those in the United States who read "its bitter exposure of American folly and cupidity" would not be able to chalk it up "as one proof more of the malignant persistence with which British writers misconceive and misrepresent Americans." Basically, he felt that the authors had made a real contribution to their country by calling attention to the need for vital reforms.

There were, in short, those who rejected the charge that the book was a slur on the nation, and pointed out, in the words of the Boston *Transcript,* that it "can hardly fail to help on the reforming tendency in the politics of the day."

On one point most critics were in agreement; the title of the novel and the character, Colonel Sellers, were destined to become part of American folk-lore. The New York *Tribune* even devoted a full editorial to "The Tribe of Sellers," noting that, though Twain's character was a fictional creation, he was "nevertheless a living and distinctive type of real American and peculiarly American character. He is no dramatic myth. American society is full of these interesting wrecks stranded on the shoals of misfortune, yet always basking in the sun."

Like contemporary critics, modern commentators on *The Gilded Age* are divided in their evaluation of the book. But unlike many of the former, they are not shocked by its exposure of evils in the body politic. On the contrary, the dividing point in modern criticism revolves about the question: did the book delve deeply enough into the basic evils of the period?

Van Wyck Brooks heads the negative critics. He concedes some "acid glances at the actual face of reality," but argues that "the total effect of the book is idyllic; the mirage of the American myth lies over it like a rosy veil." Twain, he insists, was anxious "to redeem himself" for even the small amount of realism in the book, and this he did by making the romantic story of Philip Sterling the "main thread." Vernon L. Parrington says bluntly: "The analysis is not penetrating. The real sources of political corruption — the rapacious railway lobbyists that camped in brigades about the capitol building — are passed over, and attention is fastened on small steals — the Knobs University Bill and the Columbus River Navigation Schemes — that do not touch the real rascals of the day. ... The portraits, one suspects, need not be taken seriously as pictures of the chief apostles of pre-emption and exploitation. To have sketched the real leaders of the great barbecue might have involved too many unpleasantries." Granville Hicks asks rhetorically: "How did it happen that so many Congressmen were venal and so many business men untrustworthy?" And then he says: "Such questions Clemens and Warner were not prepared to answer. It was easier to turn the most obvious kind of satire on the jury system ... to preach a sermon against speculation." Hicks contends that since Twain had no quarrel with the capitalist system, he could not understand the real causes for the corruption described in the book. Paul Carter, Jr. regards the satire as "thin. ... The more obvious, superficial evils were attacked, usually, in the humorous manner of Twain's, which removed much of the sting, and the reasons for their existence ignored." Kenneth R. Andrews maintains that the book "satirizes not the system so much as the self-delusion, the dishonesty, or the frontier crudity of individuals taking advantage of it."

On the opposite side, Lucy Lockwood Hazard points out that Van Wyck Brooks' discussion of the novel is based "almost entirely" on the story of Philip Sterling, the very sections of the book which Twain did not write, and "devotes a few casual and superficial sentences to Colonel Sellers and makes no mention at all of Senator Dilworthy. Yet it is these two who form a composite picture of the character produced by the Gilded Age as seen by one who regarded it with both fascination and contempt." For Charles and Mary Beard the novel "portrayed the social structure from top to bottom." Bernard De Voto agrees, writing: "The whole obscene spectacle of government is passed in review — the presidency, the Congress, the basis of politics, the nature of democracy, the disintegration of power, the corruption of the electorate — bribery, depravity, subornation, the farce of the people's justice." He points out that "the incredible Era of Grant" produced no other literary portrayal except Henry Adams' *Democracy* which is "just squeamish, a mere phobia of crowds." *The Gilded Age*, however, is "lively with the stench and tumult of the era ... [and] its creatures — the profiteers, politicians, and parasites — exist in three dimensions and the north light of contempt illuminates them." Walter F. Taylor makes much the same point. He concedes that Twain failed to "look deep enough into the orgy of avarice to discern the causes that produced it," but praises the novel for having succeeded "brilliantly in exhibiting ... an important stage in our American experience." Its "outspoken realism ... would be noteworthy at any period; when considered in reference to the early seventies, the sentimental era of Augusta Evans Wilson and E. P. Roe, it is astonishing. In daringly original, realistic portraiture and exposure, shot through with satire, and vigorously done on broad scale, *The Gilded Age* is unique among American novels of its time." Robert Alonzo Wiggins in his unpublished study, "Mark Twain's Novels: Principles and Practice of Realism," says of *The Gilded Age*: "The virtue of the book is that it strips away all the gilt and gets to the evil heart of the society it depicts...." And Thomas Bond Burnham in the unpublished work, "Mark Twain and the Gilded Age," concludes that, while the book "does not appear to question the fundamental precepts of capitalism ... it does portray acidly the glaring vulgarities and injustices which are so frequently the outgrowth of these precepts." He denies that the novel "sidesteps the real issues of the day," insisting that "a reading of the book, in my opinion, does not support such a view."

I would agree that a reading of the book should convince most readers that the criticism of Brooks, Parrington, Hicks, Carter and others is not fully justified. Indeed, the excerpts from the novel included in our discussion of *The Gilded Age* testify to its penetration into the sources of deep decay in American life. The book reveals the three related forces behind the corruption in government: Wall Street, the frontier speculators, and the politicos. This immoral trinity is set forth in considerable detail, with Wall Street shown as the central depository of power. How anyone who reads the section dealing with the passage of appropriation bills can argue that *The Gilded Age* purposely avoids sketching "the real leaders of the great barbecue," is beyond comprehension. If the "real leaders" were not the bankers, brokers, and presidents of Wall Street corporations, who were they? That the "Columbus River Slackwater Navigation Company" was not some mightier corporation does not detract from the validity of the portrayal. Twain was not, after all, writing a tract. He was performing the novelist's classic task — that of placing before us a group of characters and bringing them to life, causing the reader to say as he read, "Yes. This is right. This is the way the corporations buy legislators."

Though the role of the railroads is not dwelt upon in too great detail, it is by no means ignored. There is a precise exposé of the orgy of speculation associated with railroad promotions, and the description of senatorial investigations is obviously patterned upon the aftermath of the Crédit Mobilier-Union Pacific scandals. Readers of the period could not fail to identify the actual events upon which the description was based.

The novel certainly does not accept the idea, so prevalent in the literature of the period, that the rich are heroes to be emulated. On the contrary, it is filled with sardonic attacks on their social, personal, and political immorality. In powerful and unequivocal language, it makes clear the deep moral decay in the nation caused by the coarseness, hypocrisy, greed and lustfulness of the rich and their lackeys in government — the press, the church, the colleges, and other agencies of influence in America. Where in contemporary literature are there such acute and devastating descriptions of the way in which religion, journalism, education, the cause of the newly emancipated freedmen, even sex, are employed for one end — the profits of a small group of greedy men? True, the novel is by no means a complete mirror of the social and political history of the Gilded Age. That the mass of Americans were not involved in the speculative fever of "making money," but rather were concerned in making ends meet, was not touched on by the authors. The book glosses over many real problems of millions of Americans, leaving unmentioned the ferment of discontent in the rural sections and industrial cities. While it does expose how Northern capitalists made use of the Negro issue for profits, it fails to show that important sections of the Negro population were themselves aware of this and sought to disassociate themselves from their corrupt allies. Related to this, is the book's tendency to make the moral corruption of the period universal. Clearly, the authors believed that the debased values of the bankers, brokers, speculators, and corrupt politicians — get rich as fast as you can, even if you do it illegally and at every one else's expense — had become the moral values of all Americans. Yet this was a period when labor leaders, Negro leaders and agrarian leaders were upholding with passion entirely different values which emphasized the welfare and fraternity of all men.

It is true that at one point in the novel, Twain observes that, in contrast to the newly-rich, the common people were basically "honest and straightforward.... Their patriotism was strong, their pride in the flag was of the old-fashioned pattern, their love of country amounted to idolatry." Unfortunately, this appears early in the book, and is never followed through. Moreover, since the rest of the novel leaves an entirely opposite impression, the effect of the earlier statement is lost. In its place is the oft-repeated concept of a population either indifferent to the control of their government by wealthy corporations and corrupt politicians or actually abetting them. It is true that the descriptions of how political bosses gained power because of the ignorance or indifference of the voters had a basis in reality. (In spite of the already notorious corruption of his first administration, Grant was reelected.) But profound interest in ending governmental rule by wealth and corruption did exist and found expression in the formation of independent political parties of farmers, workers, small businessmen, and intellectual liberal reformers. These developments proved that the people were neither indifferent, politically idiotic, nor powerless, but were beginning to assert their power. Certainly the fact that the major political parties were forced to incorporate into their platforms many of the reforms called for by the independent parties demonstrated that important sections of the electorate were exerting influence on political events. None of this comes through in the novel.

In the end, we must return to the point we made at the outset of our discussion of *The Gilded Age*, namely, that it alone of all the novels published in the 'sixties and 'seventies dared to deal with real problems of the era, to expose widespread corruption and the forces responsible for it, and to alert the people to a spreading decay in society. It established that the idyllic America pictured in the novels of the period was simply a fairy tale. *The Gilded Age* is one of the few important novels produced in America in the last quarter of the nineteenth century. Despite limitations both as a literary form and as a social mirror, it will enhance any reader's comprehension of the social order of that period. Eight decades after it was written, it still makes thought-provoking reading.

Proposal for Suffrage Reform

For a book that exposes so many evils *The Gilded Age* is surprisingly lacking in proposals for reforms, other than a suggestion that perhaps the only way to get "decent members of Congress" was to give women the vote. But two years after the book was published, Twain advanced a specific reform plan in an article entitled, "The Curious Republic of Gondour," which appeared in the *Atlantic* for October, 1857. The Republic, a Utopia, had adopted a new law which had far-reaching effects:

Under it every citizen, howsoever poor or ignorant, possessed one vote, so universal suffrage still reigned; but if a man possessed a good common-school education and no money, he had two votes; a high-school education gave him four; if he had property likewise, to the value of three thousand *sacos*, he wielded one more vote; for every fifty thousand *sacos* a man added to his property, he was entitled to another vote; a university education entitled a man to nine votes, even though he owned no property. Therefore, learning becoming more prevalent and more easily acquired than riches, educated men became a wholesome check upon wealthy men, since they could outvote them. . . .

Votes based upon capital were commonly called "mortal" votes, because they could be lost; those based upon learning were called "immortal," because they were permanent, and because of their customarily imperishable character they were naturally more valued than the other sort. I say "customarily" for the reason that these votes were not absolutely imperishable, since insanity could suspend them.

Under this system, gambling and speculation almost ceased in the republic. A man honoured in the possession of great voting power could not afford to risk the loss of it upon a doubtful chance.

Twain went on to demonstrate other benefits. People ceased to bow "to mere moneyed grandeur" but only to learned people since they had so many more votes: "I heard mammas speak of certain men as good 'catches' because they possessed such-and-such a number of votes." There was no need for compulsory education in the schools and colleges: "When a man's child is able to make himself powerful and honoured according to the amount of education he acquires, don't you suppose that that parent will apply the compulsion himself? Our free schools and free colleges require no law to fill them."

Thereafter the republic functioned in the interest of all its citizens and not merely for a minority of wealthy plutocrats and their henchmen. Officials no longer stole, because liberal salaries obviated the need and additional wealth would not sufficiently increase their political influence; the country was governed intelligently, for at last education, rather than wealth, had come to mean power.

Certainly Twain was naive to believe that education by itself, regardless of the social and economic philosophy of the educated, would solve the basic problems facing America. But at least his plan was an advance over his earlier view that a government elected by the propertied interests offered the best solution. While in Hawaii, in the mid-'sixties, he had written approvingly of the abolition of universal suffrage in the islands and the imposition of property qualifications for voting. While in England, in the late 'sixties, he was impressed by the British plan for limiting the franchise to taxpayers. "There is no law here," he wrote from London, "which gives a useless idlery the privilege of disposing of public moneys furnished by other people." When Twain reached Washington and saw the bribery and corruption of the people's representatives by wealthy property-holders, saw politicians manipulated by businessmen, he revised his views of both the Hawaiian and the British plans. "It is too late now," he concluded, "to restrict the suffrage; we must increase it." Increasing an individual's vote on the basis of his education was the method he hit upon.

Twain had not signed his contribution to the *Atlantic*, fearing that the public would refuse to accept it seriously over his name. But he expected his proposal to be seriously considered, and was bitterly disappointed that it drew no response. Even Howells' requests for more reports from the model land did nothing to lessen his disappointment. He told Mrs. James Field that the article's failure to arouse a favorable response in influential quarters had caused him to lose "all faith in our government . . . where the vote of a man who knew nothing was as good as the vote of a man of education and industry. . . . He only hoped to live long enough to see such a wrong and such a government overthrown." A year later, in August, 1877, he wrote to Mollie Fairbanks that republican government based on universal suffrage "ought to perish because it is founded on wrong & is weak & bad & tyrannical."

Woman Suffrage

In his distress, Twain returned to the proposal he had merely touched upon in *The Gilded Age*, and advocated woman suffrage as a potential savior of American democracy. "I have been a woman suffragist for years," Twain told a meeting of the Hebrew Technical School for Girls in January, 1901. "For twenty-five years I have been a woman's rights man." This statement would place Twain's conversion to the cause in the early 1870's. We speak of "conversion" advisedly, for prior to the 'seventies he was an outspoken opponent whose articles ridiculing the woman's rights movement won the applause and laughter of male supremacists from coast to coast.

While in New York in the spring of 1867, Twain heard Miss Anna Dickinson, popular lecturer on woman's rights, deliver a plea at Cooper Institute "that the number of avenues to an honest livelihood that were open to women be increased." He wrote to the San Francisco *Alta California*:

"She keeps close to her subject, reasons well, and makes every point without fail. Her prose poetry often moves to tears, her satire cuts to the quick. ... She made a speech worth listening to." But he was not converted to her cause, noting that "she used arguments that would not stand analysis." That same spring, Twain published a series of articles on female suffrage, the agitation for which, he declared, made it "time for all good men to tremble for their country." Moreover, lest any reader dismiss Twain's contribution as mere farcical satire, the editors of the newspaper took pains to point out that its argument should be taken seriously.

In one article, Twain pictured a legislature after women had been enfranchised. An act for amending the Common School System is transformed, by the female legislators, into one "for remodeling and establishing fashions for ladies' bonnets."

Other proposed bills were likewise altered to deal with women's styles. In another article, Twain coupled farcical satire with a serious avowal of his opinions. He acknowledged that justice was on the side of the agitators for female suffrage, but insisted that the vote in the hands of women would only increase mediocrity and corruption in government, and, at the same time lower woman's real status in society. On the first point, he argued that, like the intelligent, educated male voter, the "educated American woman voter" would stay at home and refuse to vote, while the female rascal, like her male counterpart, would "work, bribe and vote with all her might." On the second point, he advanced an argument common in all literature opposing woman's rights — the debasement of woman's cherished place in society if she were to be seen "voting, and gabbing about politics, and electioneering." He did not want to take "the High Priestess we reverence at the sacred fireside and send her forth to electioneer for votes among a mangy mob who are unworthy to touch the hem of her garment."

Although Twain's articles reflected current prejudices, he did, unlike the other critics of the woman's rights cause, concede that justice was on its side. Moreover, when his satires brought forth a reply from a woman who defended woman's suffrage, Twain's humorous retort was exceedingly weak. He conceded privately "that his task would have been easier if she hadn't all the arguments on her side." It did not require too much prodding, therefore, for Twain to reverse himself, become a staunch advocate of woman's suffrage, and condemn as spurious the very arguments he himself had advanced. It is probable that this process was hastened by his friendship with Isabella Beecher Hooker, who was his neighbor in Hartford. Years later, in an unpublished portion of his autobiography, Twain wrote glowingly of her and the cause she championed:

Isabella Beecher Hooker threw herself into the woman's rights movement among the earliest, some sixty years ago, and she labored with all her splendid energies in that great cause all the rest of her life; as an able and efficient worker she ranks immediately after those great chiefs, Susan B. Anthony, Elizabeth Cady Stanton, and Mrs. Livermore. When these powerful sisters entered the field in 1848 woman was what she had always been in all countries and under all religions, all savageries, all civilizations — a slave, and under contempt. The laws affecting women were a disgrace to our statute-book. Those brave women besieged the legislatures of the land, year after year, suffering and enduring all manner of reproach, rebuke, scorn and obloquy, yet never surrendering, never sounding a retreat; their wonderful campaign lasted a great many years, and is the most wonderful in history, for it achieved a revolution — the only one achieved in history for the emancipation of half a nation that cost not a drop of blood. They broke the chains of their sex and set it free.

At Miss Beecher's request, Twain spoke frequently at public meetings for the cause, inveighing against the stupid prejudice which set up the requirement that the voter "wear pantaloons instead of petticoats," and which kept women from voting in a land which boasted of absolute equality: "We brag of our universal suffrage; but we are shams after all for we restrict when we come to the women." Civilized people considered the suppression of one sex by the other a mark of savagery; yet here, in the freest country in the world, the ballot was refused to women. Democracy was being sacrificed to bigotry, for how was it possible to have real democracy when half the nation was "voiceless in the making of laws and the election of officers to execute them. Born with brains, born in the country, educated, having large interests at stake they find their tongues tied and their hands fettered." Twain now argued that the influence of women in politics would reduce corruption and increase the caliber of elected officeholders: "I think it will suggest to more than one man that if women could vote they would vote on the side of morality ... would not sit indolently at home as their husbands and brothers do now, but would ... set up some candidates fit for decent human beings to vote for. ... It is our last chance. ... Both the great parties have failed. I wish we might have a woman's party now." He cherished this belief in the great benefits to be derived from woman's suffrage for the rest of his life. "I don't care who makes the laws," he declared in 1901, "so long as I can see the whip lash of the ballot in woman's hand. ... She is the source of morals. States are founded on morals not on intellect. If woman could occasionally vote, depend on it, it would be exercised righteously."

Although Twain was obviously idealizing the role that women could play in politics, this does not mean that he regarded all women as above criticism. In an unpublished comment in his notebook for 1891, he condemned the women of Illinois whose protest against a woman suffrage bill in the legislature had defeated the measure. "It was a narrow escape," he commented scornfully, "for the ballot, which is useful only when it is in the hand of the intelligent, could have gone into the hands of those very women." The incident did not alter Twain's belief in the vital importance to American democracy of enfranchising women. While in Melbourne, during his world-wide tour, he jotted down in his notebook on October 5, 1895: "A strong movement for woman's rights is in progress. Inquire into this." That the information was to be used in behalf of the crusade for woman's suffrage in the United States is indicated by his published report of the performance of New Zealand women after having been granted the vote. Referring to the arguments raised in his own country against woman's suffrage, he cited as proof of their active interest in politics and their right to have a place in government the fact that of eligible women in New Zealand, 85.18 per cent had voted and none of the prophesied disturbances occurred.

There was one prophecy which Twain approved of — that women in the United States would sooner or later be enfranchised. "If I live for twenty-five years more," he himself predicted in 1901, "I expect to see women armed with the ballot." He did not live to see it achieved on a national scale — although several states did grant woman the suffrage during his lifetime — and he did not live to see that woman suffrage would not accomplish for American democracy all that he had foretold. But he did make a notable contribution in his speeches and writings to the achievement of a more democratic America in which discrimination at the ballot-box because of sex was ended.

"Casting Vote Party"

In calling for a "woman's party," Twain indicated his loss of faith in the two major parties. Yet he saw little hope that a third party could triumph over the Democratic and Republican machines. Hence, in presenting his third and final plan for the effective use of the franchise, he proposed a scheme for independent political action that would not threaten the existence of the two major parties. Its object was to compel them "to nominate their *best men always*," on the theory that once all offices were filled with the parties' "best men ... we shall have good government."

The new political organization was to be called the "Casting Vote Party." Its members would not seek office, appointive or elective, nor vote for any but one of the regular party nominees. Once the candidate had been selected, the new organization would cast its *"entire vote* for that nominee." The "Casting Vote Party" would be formed on a nationwide basis through ward, township, town, city, congressional, state and national organizations. "The party should work wherever there is an elective office, from the lowest up to the presidency." Its membership need not be large — quality not quantity should be the watchword. In the main, the new party would be composed of workers, farmers, merchants, shopkeepers, professional people, and all others "who are disgusted with the prevailing political methods, the low ambitions and ideals of the politicians; dishonesty in office; corruption, and frank distribution of appointments among characterless and incompetent men as pay for party service; the evasion and sometimes straight-out violation of the civil-service laws." The party would appeal particularly to those who, while "ashamed of this condition of things ... have despaired of seeing it bettered; *who stay away from the polls and do not vote*; who do not attend primaries, and would be insulted there if they did."

The "Casting Vote Party" would obtain and keep the balance of power by securing enough members to nullify the majority of the winner of the last contest. It would act through lodges which would elect delegates to meet in secondary lodges, there to decide which candidate of the two parties to support. Then the party would cast a unanimous vote, which would swing the election as desired. Splits within the group itself would be impossible, since acceptance of the decision of the delegates was a condition of membership.

The plan was conceived in 1901 but was not printed during Twain's lifetime. (Part of it, as we shall see, was presented by Twain early in 1901 in a speech before New York's City Club.) It was projected in the hope of ending control of government by the boss and the machine. The need was desperate, Twain warned; action was necessary if democracy was to survive: "If in the hands of men who regard their citizenship as a high trust this scheme shall fail upon trial, a better must be sought, a better must be invented; for it cannot be well or safe to let the present political conditions continue indefinitely. They can be improved, and American citizenship should rouse up from its disheartenment and see that it is done."

Twain's plan resembled the political program of the American Federation of Labor at the time, which applied Samuel Gompers' principle of supporting the major parties' candidates most friendly to labor under the slogan, "Reward your friend and punish your enemy." But the plan was basically unworkable in the American scene. Its fundamental flaw was its concept that the mere election of good men would solve the political problem facing the nation.

Too often, as Lincoln Steffens so effectively demonstrated, these good men, themselves corporation lawyers or executives, used the government in behalf of corporations more efficiently than the ignorant candidates of political bosses. They simply carried over into government the practices they employed in private business. Twain never understood the significance of what Samuel Freeman Miller, Associate Justice of the Supreme Court, said of many of his colleagues in that Court — all of whom qualified for Twain's role as "good" men in politics: "It is in vain to contend with Judges who have been at the bar advocates for forty years, of railroad companies and all forms of associated capital, when they are called upon to decide cases where such interests are in contest. All their training, all their feelings are from the start in favor of those who need no such influence."

But regardless of its workability, the plan reveals Twain's strong desire to purge democracy's ranks of the elements threatening to destroy it.

Twain in Politics

Whatever the merits of Twain's plan for a "Casting Vote Party," it reveals that while he may still have hated "politics," as he had informed Mrs. Fairbanks in 1869, he was certainly no longer uninterested.

Twain had served several weeks as a volunteer in the Confederate Army, but he became a Republican when he went to Nevada with Orion, a Lincoln appointee. Whenever he voted in the ensuing years he voted Republican. Before 1876, however, he stayed aloof from political campaigns and was indifferent to the results. He saw no real distinction between the Republicans and Democrats on the issue that was to him most significant: the elimination of corruption in government. In *The Gilded Age,* he made no party distinctions in attacking corrupt politicians, pointing out the readiness of Northern Republicans and Southern Democrats to cooperate in plundering the government. As he explained in a letter to Orion in 1875, the era of corruption was neither Republican nor Democratic but national, and would not be ended by a victory of either party. *"Politics* are not going to cure moral ulcers like these nor the decaying body they fester on." A year later, in a letter read at a dinner of the Knights of St. Patrick, Twain returned to this theme. He called for an American patriot to do for the United States what St. Patrick had done for Ireland. For this, however, he would have to forget party labels. "St. Patrick had no politics. . . . When he came across a reptile, he forgot to inquire whether he was a democrat or a republican. . . . I wish we had him here to trim us up."

So little was Twain's political affiliation known at this

time that in the presidential election of 1876 he was invited by the Hartford Democrats to give a Tilden Club some counsel at a flag-raising. His refusal was sharp: "In view of Mr. [Samuel J.] Tilden's Civil War record my advice is not to raise the flag." The reference was to the fact that the Democratic presidential candidate had "disapproved of the war from the beginning," and encouraged opposition to Lincoln's policies.

The presidential campaign of 1876 brought a marked change in Twain's position. "It seems odd," he confessed to Howells during the campaign, "to find myself interested in an election. I never was before." It was Rutherford B. Hayes' letter of acceptance which caused this change. In it the Republican candidate had declared himself for civil service reform and for the prosecution of dishonest government officials. Twain was not interested, he informed Howells, in Hayes' party affiliation; what had influenced him was his advocacy of clean government. It expressed "my own political convictions." Twain was so impressed by Hayes' stand on what he considered the main issue in the campaign that he delivered an address in behalf of the Republican candidate. This Howells declared, "put civil service reform in a nutshell." It was doubly significant, he added, because the speaker was "the only Republican orator quoted without distinction of party by all newspapers." The *New York Times* published the entire text of the speech on page 1 under a banner headline:

MARK TWAIN IN POLITICS

He presides at a Great Republican meeting at Hartford — He thinks it a time for Literary Men to come out from their studies and work for Hayes and Wheeler.

Twain expressed gratitude for having been chosen to preside at the meeting. "The employment is new to me," he admitted. "I never have taken part in a political canvass before except to vote. The tribe of which I am the humblest member — the literary tribe — is one which is not given to bothering about politics, but there are times when even the strangest departures are justifiable, and such a season, I take it, is the present canvass." He called upon all writers to campaign for Hayes: "at last [we have] a chance to make this Government a good Government . . . a chance to institute an honest and sensible system of civil service which shall so amply prove its worth and worthiness that no succeeding President can ever venture to put his foot upon it." Twain castigated the current system of civil service, calling it "so idiotic, so contemptible, so grotesque, that it would make the very savages of Dahomey jeer and the very gods of solemnity laugh."

In an editorial entitled, "Mark Twain on Civil Service Reform," the *New York Times* commented: "It is a cheering sign of the times that many literary men are beginning to recognize the obligations resting upon them as citizens, and are endeavoring to elevate the tone of political discussion. It is natural, too, that when they emerge from their privacy, the condition of the public service should be one of the first subjects to command their attention. Men of culture and training, on whatever other points they may disagree, cannot fail to be of one mind regarding the evils of the spoils system."

Four years later, Twain spoke at a big Republican rally in Hartford in favor of the election of James A. Garfield. The Republican presidential candidate "suits me thoroughly and exactly," he said. But this was his last public appearance as a Republican. In the campaign of 1884 he spoke before another Hartford mass meeting — but this time he called for the defeat of the Republican ticket.

Twain's bolt from the Republican Party was caused by the nomination of James G. Blaine as its presidential candidate. Blaine's record in Congress had been questionable. A Democratic committee of Congress investigating railroad graft revealed, in the "Mulligan Letters," that Blaine, as Speaker of the House, had saved a land grant for the Little Rock and Fort Smith Railroad in 1869. In return, he had asked and received from the railroad the privilege of selling its bonds on a generous commission. In 1876 and again in 1880, Blaine had been rejected by the Republican Convention; but in the Convention of 1884, he was nominated on the first ballot. Thereupon, a group of reformers, led by Carl Schurz, which up to this time had cooperated mainly with the Republicans, seceded from the Republican Party to support Grover Cleveland, the Democratic candidate. Popularly they were known as mugwumps.

Five years before, in a satirical piece, entitled "Let's Look at the Record," published in the Kansas City *Journal* of June 15, 1879, Twain had poked fun at the defenders of Blaine who claimed that his record did not disqualify him for the highest office in the country:

I have pretty much made up my mind to run for President. What the country wants is a candidate who cannot be injured by investigation of his past history so that the enemies of the party will be unable to rake up anything against him that nobody ever heard of before. If you know the worst about a candidate to begin with, every attempt to spring things on him will be checkmated. Now I am going to own up in advance to all the wickedness I have done, and if any Congressional committee is disposed to prowl around my biography in the hope of discovering any dark and deadly deed I have secreted, why — let it prowl.

He then listed a whole series of outrages he had committed including the burying of a dead aunt under his grapevine:

The vine needed fertilizing, my aunt had to be buried, and I dedicated her to this high purpose. Does that unfit me for the Presidency?

The Constitution of our country does not say so. No other citizen was ever considered unworthy of this office because he enriched his grapevines with his dead relatives. Why should I be selected as the first victim of an absurd prejudice?

In 1884, there was nothing of comedy in Twain's reaction to the news that Blaine had been nominated. At once he proclaimed himself a mugwump, and urged his friends to follow him. Few did; the reaction in Hartford to his stand was one of such deep hostility that Twichell almost lost his pastorate by siding with Twain. To all appeals that he put party allegiance above everything else, Twain turned a deaf ear. "No party holds the privilege of dictating to me how I shall vote," he told one and all. He delivered a paper to the Hartford Monday Evening Club in which he attacked the community's loyalty to the Republican Party, charging that "the atrocious doctrine of allegiance to *party* plays directly into the hands of politicians of the baser sort." Although Twain respected Cleveland for the "enemies he made in the Democratic Party" and for his courageous rejection of Tammany Hall's terms for election support, he was actually against Blaine rather than for Cleveland. (He worked desperately, up to the eve of the election, for a movement to put an acceptable Independent candidate in the field.)

Twain presided at mugwump rallies and called for Blaine's defeat. He was one of fifty Hartford Republicans who signed an "Appeal to the Republican voters of Connecticut," which asserted, after citing five charges against Blaine: "His defeat may save our party by freeing it from the camp followers and office-seekers, who have too often dictated its policy." On election day he voted for Cleveland, and rejoiced the next morning in Blaine's defeat.

After the election of Cleveland, criticism of Twain's role in the campaign mounted in Hartford. He met the attacks head-on in a speech in which he condemned those who, like his critics, betrayed the people by teaching them "that the only true freedom of thought is to think as the party thinks . . . that patriotism, duty, citizenship, devotion to country, loyalty to the flag, are all summed up in loyalty to the party." He summed up his own position in a paper on "Consistency" which was read before the Monday Evening Club. Consistency was illogical, since growth was the basic law of life. Party allegiance was a practice borrowed from the monarchial system to enable base politicians to force corrupt men on their parties and get them elected by appealing to party loyalty. Twain ripped to shreds the "atrocious doctrine of allegiance to party" of the political old guards. He accused the Republican Party, in particular, of insisting on being put first, above the country's good, of branding one who bolts the party as a shameful traitor or deserter: "There you have the just measure of that freedom of opinion, freedom of speech and action, which we hear so much inflated foolishness about, as being the precious possession of the Republic. Whereas, in *truth*, the surest way for a man to make of himself a target for almost universal scorn, obloquy, slander, and insult is to stop twaddling about these priceless independences, and attempt to exercise one of them."

The mugwump — the independent — was the true patriot, and he should find satisfaction and strength in the knowledge that he came from an illustrious ancestry:

In the whole history of the race of men no single great and high and beneficent thing was ever done for the souls and bodies, the hearts and the brains, of the children of this world, but a Mugwump started it and Mugwumps carried it to victory. And their names are the stateliest in history; Washington, Garrison, Galileo, Luther, Christ. Loyalty to petrified opinions never yet broke a chain or freed a human soul in *this* world — and never will.

Twain never ceased upholding the doctrine of political independence and criticizing those who put party allegiance before principle. He accused the American voter of a dual moral standard. The same man who boasted of his independence in private life would "without a blush . . . vote for an unclean boss if that boss is his party's Moses." The same man who would stand "faithfully by the principles of honor and honesty" in everyday affairs, forgot these principles when he came forward "to exercise a public trust," and "can be confidently counted upon to betray that trust in nine cases out of ten, if 'party loyalty' shall require it." He expressed the absurdity of it all in an item in his unpublished notebook for 1900: "There are bigots who can accept nothing which their party-opposites approve. If you could work the multiplication table into a democratic platform the republicans w[oul]d vote it down at the election."

In 1884 Twain rejected the Republican Party primarily because of its questionable presidential candidate. With the passing years he renounced nearly all of that party's principles, particularly high protective tariffs. In *Tom Sawyer Abroad*, published in 1894, Tom described impost duties as "just hogging," and predicted that the blessings of the Lord would be taxed at the next session of Congress, because "there warn't nothing foreign that warn't taxed." In angrier vein, Twain wrote in his notebook a year later: "The man that invented protection belongs in hell."

Twain argued that the tariff discriminated against the Western areas, where the added shipping cost made the price of an imported article prohibitive. "The result is the same as if there were rows of custom-fences between the coast and the East." Furthermore, the continual shift in the rate between taxed and duty-free articles was a serious threat to importers. "A man invests years of work and a vast sum of money in a worthy enterprise, upon the faith of existing laws i.e. (tariffs); then the law is changed and the man is robbed by his own government." Most important was the fact that the tariff was the "life-source" of the trusts. "We swept [out] slavery & substituted Protection," Twain commented, predicting that high tariffs, by fostering monopoly, would impose a new slavery on the country. He charged the Republican Party with major responsibility: "By a system of extraordinary tariffs it has created a number of giant corporations in the interest of a few rich men & by most ingenious & persuasive reasoning it has convinced the multitudinous and grateful unrich that the tariffs were instituted in their interest."

Convinced that the Republican Party was acting solely in "the interest of a few rich men," Twain never went back to it. He refused to be persuaded that Theodore Roosevelt, as a "trust-buster," merited his support, contending that no man who championed high tariffs could be regarded as a real foe of monopoly. On the contrary, his policies had "hastened the day" when monopoly would dominate the entire economy.

Twain was not much impressed by another cardinal Republican principle of the 1890's — opposition to free silver. In reply to the hysterical Republican cry that victory for William Jennings Bryan on a free silver platform in 1896 would "paralyze all industries, strike prosperity dead, & bring upon the country a blight of poverty, disaster & desolation," Twain drew an analogy between slavery and free silver. He pointed out that the slaveholders had also warned that "to remove slavery would destroy prosperity, (and) it didn't do it." "Half our people are for silver — are all the fools on that side?" he queried in the midst of the presidential campaign. After William McKinley's election, Twain projected what might have happened if the Democratic candidate had won:

November came & Bryan was elected. By & by Free silver followed — this law to go into effect after [an] interval of three years. Europe was ashamed of America, & nearly half of the American people were ashamed of themselves. The world held its breath & waited for the catastrophe. . . . Meanwhile, all interested, both at home and abroad, did the natural thing. They invested such means as they could devise to soften the coming blow. Europe did not sell out its American securities at once, knowing that would make a panic & knock them down to nothing. They sold them to Americans.

The import and export trade declined and withered away to nothing; shipping ceased. "But we owed no foreigner a penny, & no foreigner owed us a penny. We had gradually scraped through & gotten out without serious injury, & our European friends had done the same. We were cut off from the world and must live by our own hands and brains." The three-year limit was approaching. "Yet the country was not excited. It was not holding its breath to see what was going to happen. It already knew that nothing was going to happen. It knew that the three-year interval had provided for all emergencies, & had long ago arranged that the prophet's bad dream should not come true." As the importing business fell off, money went into American factories; industry spread all over the country into regions never before industrialized, "supplying the home market in sufficient abundance with nearly all the things which we had formerly imported, & thus stopping an outgo of five or six hundred millions a year. . . . We had to pay wages never heard of before, but that was no matter, the country's colossal prosperity could stand it & not feel it." As soon as free silver was ushered in, the export trade leaped up, for the silver dollar, contrary to predictions, proved to be "as good as a gold one with us. Free silver proceeded on its comfortable way. People presently recognized that at last American currency was becoming stable, trustworthy, & emancipated from caprice & uncertainty. When a man got a coin, now, whether of gold or silver, it would keep its value."

Twain's observations on free silver, heretofore unpublished, reveal his views on a major issue in American politics. He was, however, not involved in the political struggles of the 1890's. From June 6, 1891 to October 15, 1900, except fleetingly in 1895, Twain was out of the country. He announced upon his return that he was still "a mugwump" and belonged to neither of the major parties. (A few months later, he referred to himself as "the only living representative" of the mugwumps.) Although, as we shall see, he became deeply involved in the national struggle over imperialism, his main political activity was in the battle in New York against Tammany Hall and its boss, Richard Croker.

In "The Revised Catechism" of 1871 and in *The Gilded Age* of 1874, Twain had condemned Tammany and its then boss, Tweed, for plundering New York City. He was not in the country in 1892 when Rev. Charles Henry Parkhurst exposed the alliance of organized politics with vice in New York, and when, two years later, the Lexow Investigation uncovered police extortion and blackmail and Tammany's control of the ballot-box. But Twain's full awareness of Tammany control of New York politics is illustrated in his description of an imaginary procession of floats, including one with "Mr. Croker with his arms in the city treasury up to the elbows," another, with a "Tammany agent collecting blackmail from gambling hells, and prostitutes" and the entire procession followed by a banner on which is inscribed "Tammany's famous sarcastic motto, 'What're you going to do about it?'"

In 1900 and 1901, reform groups in New York City were battling Tammany, and Bishop Henry Codman Potter called for and received Twain's support. On January 4, 1901, Twain shared the platform with Bishop Potter in a discussion, before the reform-minded City Club, of "The Causes of Our Present Municipal Degradation." The theme of Twain's speech was that the few corrupt politicians dominated the city because they were organized and the many decent voters were not. Illustrating this argument with a story of his childhood, in which part of a boy's organization was prevented from doughnut bribing by an Anti-Doughnut group, Twain proposed an Anti-Doughnut Party, with a purpose similar to that of his unpublished plan for a "Casting Vote Party" — to force the two major parties always to nominate their best men. He concluded by urging the City Club to emphasize organization, since forty-nine men out of fifty were honest and only needed to combine to disqualify the fiftieth. Excerpts from Twain's speech were widely published in the press, and the *New York Times* reported that "it was the opinion of those who heard him last night that the 'Anti-Doughnut Party' would be one of the slogans in the next municipal campaign."

Twain was active in the campaign to beat Tammany in 1901 and elect Seth Low, President of Columbia College, as mayor on a fusion ticket. He gained wide publicity for lecturing policemen in front of his house at Riverdale on the evils of Tammany rule and urging them to vote the fusion ticket. Newspapers published a letter to Twain from a policeman which informed him "that most all the men in the Police Department are for Seth. We sympathize with you in your efforts for the Hon. Seth Low."

Twain became a member of the Acorns, an anti-Tammany group, before whom he delivered a fierce arraignment of Tammany boss Croker and his hirelings. The speech was mainly a set of extracts from Edmund Burke's impeachment of Hastings, with the Great Council of Calcutta substituting for Tammany, and Croker for Hastings:

The Calcutta Tammany — like our own Tammany — had but one principle, but one policy, one moving spring of action — avarice, money-lust. So that it got money it cared not a rap about the means and the methods. It was always ready to lie, forge, betray, steal, swindle, cheat, rob, and no promise, no engagement, no contract, no treaty made by the Boss was worth the paper it was written on or the polluted breath that uttered it. Is the parallel still exact? It seems to me to be twins.

Copies of Twain's speech were printed and circulated in the thousands. When the fusion ticket won, Twain was given a large share of the credit. It was conceded that his energetic campaigning for clean government had immeasurably helped turn the election into a triumph over Tammany control. One paper wrote:

> Who killed Croker?
> I, said Mark Twain.
> I killed the Croker,
> I, the Jolly Joker.

The New York mayorality election marked the last time Twain participated in a political campaign. He could see nothing good in Republican promises or performances, and he felt that party was too firmly entrenched for the Democrats to be able to unseat it. Moreover, as in the past, he saw little difference between them, convinced that both parties functioned in the interest of wealth. While his formula for reforming corrupt politics still went no deeper than electing good men to office, he had lost faith in the ability to achieve even this through "sewer, party politics," managed by venal and corporation-serving politicians.

Thus Twain completed the circle so far as politics was concerned. He began with a feeling of loathing towards politics and politicians, and ended with the same feeling. In between, however, he made some notable contributions to the American political scene. He exposed corruption in politics and the forces mainly responsible for it; he advocated a series of reforms, including enfranchisement of women, to eradicate this evil, and he campaigned both as a Republican and as an independent voter to elect candidates pledged to end corruption. Despite his long absence from the country, despite the limitations of his insight and of his proposed reforms, he exercised more positive influence on the political thinking of the American people than most other writers of his day.

Democracy Versus Monarchy

It should not be assumed that Twain's disillusionment with the administration of government in the United States caused him to lose faith in its constitutional principles of democracy. There were times, as in 1875, when governmental maladministration left him "so unhappy and discontented" that he thought of "going to England to live." But these were transitory feelings; in the main, he believed the best government was a democracy after the American model. It was best because its constitution was based on the equality of all men:

The American dogma, rightly translated, makes this assertion: that every man is of right born free, that is, without master or owner; & also that every man is of right born his neighbor's political equal — that is, possessed of every legal right &

privilege which his neighbor enjoys & not debarred from aspiring to any dignity to which his neighbor may attain. When a man accepts this rendering of that gospel, it is the same as proclaiming that he believes that whoever is born & lives in a country where he is denied a privilege accorded his neighbor — even though his neighbor be a king — is not a freeman; that when he consents to wear the stigma described by the word "subject," he has merely consented to call himself a slave by a gentler epithet; & that where a king is there is but one person in that nation who is not a slave.

It was what he considered unjust and bigoted criticism of American democratic institutions by foreign critics that drew some of Twain's heaviest satirical fire, and particularly so when the criticism came from those who lived under a monarchy. Then Twain not merely defended the ideas and ideals of democracy, but voiced his growing hatred of the monarchial system.

In Twain's early writings, condemnation of monarchial rule is mixed with admiration for certain contemporary monarchs. Thus in *The Innocents Abroad* he condemns monarchies as agents of cruelty and oppression — the Sultan of Turkey is particularly damned as the "chief of a vast royalty ... a man who sees his people robbed and oppressed by soulless tax-gatherers, but speaks no word to save them." Yet, at the same time, he hails Napoleon III, the French monarch, as a "genius of Energy, Persistence, Enterprise."

Twain's admiration for royalty was always fleeting. It was usually a tribute to a monarch whom he assumed to be exceptional. What was permanent in his thinking and writing was his contempt for and hatred of monarchy as a conspiracy against the people and his defense of democratic government.

THE PRINCE AND THE PAUPER

The Prince and the Pauper, published in 1881, with its glorification of democracy and its indictment of the

British monarchy in the sixteenth century, is the first extended treatment of this subject. The plot by which beggar Tom Canty becomes king and Prince Edward, son of Henry VIII, a beggar, disposes of the flimsy assumption of royal divinity. The pauper boy and the young prince change places and the courtiers sense no difference.

At the outset, Twain dramatizes the evils of monarchial rule. The ruler of a great kingdom is a spoiled and pampered boy who learns no wisdom until he changes association with the "gilded vassals of the crown," for association with outlaws, beggars and commoners. From them he learns of England's cruel laws and of widespread injustice. He sees "small husbandmen turned shiftless and hungry upon the world because their farms were taken from them to be changed to sheep-ranges." He sees what his father's rape of the monasteries had meant to those turned out in the world "houseless and homeless." From a once-prosperous farmer he hears of the tragedy of a starved wife and children, hears his ironical toast to the "merciful English law that delivered [them] from the English hell!" He concludes that "the world is made wrong," that kings should go to school, see the operation of their laws, "and so learn mercy."

Undoubtedly a royal prince will rule better after an unroyal "education" in the tribulations of his people. The pauper "king" Tom Canty demonstrates this when he proves to be a noble sovereign. His first acts were "singularly merciful for those harsh times." Edward, after his new education, follows in the path of the pauper "king." His coronation day is distinguished by the unprecedented mercy of his judgements. When a great dignitary protests, he replies: "What dost *thou* know of suffering and oppression? I and my people know, but not thou."

Thus the "spectacle of England acquiring mercy at the hands of two children" ridicules the whole business of kingcraft. But *The Prince and the Pauper* was but a prelude to a more fully developed criticism of the feudal world. Here Twain did not pose the abolition of monarchy but its improvement, ending with Edward VI a better monarch for having worn the pauper's rags. Still its basic message is crystal clear. As Howells said in his review in the New York *Tribune* of October 25, 1881: "It is only touching the story at many points to speak of it as a satire on monarchy; in this sort it is a manual of republicanism which might fitly be introduced in the schools. It breathes throughout the spirit of humanity and the reason of democracy."

A CONNECTICUT YANKEE IN KING ARTHUR'S COURT

It is in *A Connecticut Yankee in King Arthur's Court* that we find most of the passages in which Twain expresses his full contempt for monarchy. Yet his original conception of the novel was remote from what finally emerged. The idea of the novel first came to him in 1884 after he had read Malory's *Morte d'Arthur*. "I began to make notes in my head for a b[oo]k," he wrote in his notebook. A sampling of the notes reveals the nature of Twain's original conception:

Dream of being a knight errant in armor, in the Middle Ages. Have the notions & habits of thought of the present day mixed with the necessities of that. No pockets in the armor. Can't scratch. Cold in the head — can't blow — can't get a handkerchief, can't use iron sleeve. Iron gets redhot in the sun — leaks in the rain, gets white with frost & freezes me solid in winter. Makes disagreeable clatter when I enter church. Can't dress or undress myself. Always getting struck by lightning. Fall down & can't get up.

In the five years between conception and publication, the novel evolved from a droll and gently satirical portrayal of ludicrous knight-errantry and chivalrous romances into a burning indictment of royalty and nobility and of the whole social order of the British Age of Chivalry together with a passionate affirmation of the principles of democracy. With some of the original, purely burlesque material, Twain kept the basic idea of "dumping the nineteenth century down into the sixth century and observing its consequences." But what had at first appealed to him as mainly comical gradually turned hateful, as he familiarized himself with the brutal realities of medieval life, its ignorance and superstition and inhumanity. These gradually submerged the Arthurian glamor and pageantry which had appealed to Twain.

This transition from sentimental romance to social criticism was hastened by his feeling that he had a "special mission" to vindicate American democracy from attacks by foreign critics, especially Matthew Arnold, who, during and following his tour of the United States in 1883-84, had characterized American civilization as mediocre and even barbarous. In several unpublished articles and in a public speech, Twain angrily retorted to Arnold, denouncing the evils of the British monarchial system and defending American democracy which, unlike the British system, was founded on the three principles basic to any "respect-compelling civilization — equality, liberty, and humanity." But it is clear from his notebook entries between April 1888 and December 1889, when the *Yankee* was published, that he intended his novel to be the definitive answer to Arnold.

Here are some examples:

It [monarchy] belongs to that state of culture that admires a ring in your nose, a head full of feathers, and your belly painted blue.

Show me a lord & I will show you a man who you couldn't tell from a journeyman shoemaker if he were stripped; and who, in all that is worth being, is the shoemaker's inferior. . . .

Arthur slept much. Kings & snakes are always best when asleep.

That worm-eaten & dilapidated social structure in England which Mr. Arnold regards as a "civilization."

Monarchy & nobility (hereditary) is a laughable departure from the law of survival of the fittest — a law obeyed in all other cases.

137

Better the Almighty Dollar than a tub of rancid guts, labeled king, noble & so on.

Monarchial govt is a system invented to secure the comfort, safety & prosperity of the few; (a) republican govt is a system invented to secure the liberty, comfort, safety & prosperity of the many.

The kingly office is entitled to no respect. It was originally procured by the highwayman's methods; it remains a perpetuated crime, can never be anything but the symbol of a crime. It is no more entitled to respect than is the flag of a pirate.

Loyalty is a word which has worked vast harm; for it has been made to trick men into being "loyal" to a thousand iniquities, whereas the true loyalty should have been to themselves — in which case there would have ensued a rebellion, and the throwing off of that deceptive yoke. *Note for the Yankee.* The first thing I want to teach is disloyalty, till they get used to discussing that word *loyalty* as representing a virtue. This will beget independence — which is loyalty to one's best self and principles, and this is often disloyalty to the general idols and fetishes.

In the summer of 1889, Twain turned to Howells for help in reading proofs of the *Yankee.* He had also wanted his friend's opinion of the work, and was delighted to receive his enthusiastic and unqualified approval: "It's a mighty great book, and it makes my heart burn with wrath. . . . The book is glorious — simply noble; what masses of virgin truth never touched in print before." Twain was particularly happy that Howells shared his sentiments concerning the liberating mission of the French Revolution:

I am glad you approve of what I say about the French Revolution. Few people will. It is odd that even to this day Americans still observe that immortal benefaction through English and other monarchial eyes, and have no shred of opinion about it that they didn't get at second-hand.

Next to the 4th of July and its results, it was the noblest and holiest thing and the most precious that ever happened in this earth. And its gracious work is not done yet — not anywhere in the remote neighborhoods of it.

Twain concluded the letter with an acknowledgment that he had not fully turned loose the torrent of his republican fervor in the novel: "Well, my book is written — let it go. But if it were only to write over again there wouldn't be so many things left out. They burn in me; and they keep multiplying and multiplying; but now they can't ever be said. And besides they would require a library — and a pen warmed up in hell."

Shortly after the letter was written and just before his novel was published, Twain saw his prediction regarding the continuing influence of the French Revolution vindicated. News arrived that the Brazilian monarchy had fallen. "Another throne has gone," Twain rejoiced in a letter to Sidney Baxter of the Boston *Herald*, "and I swim in oceans of satisfaction." He now predicted that by 1939 the thrones of Europe would sell at auction for old iron:

I believe I shall really see the end of what is surely the grotesquest of all the swindles ever invented by man — monarchy. It is enough to make a graven image laugh, to see apparently rational people ... still mouthing empty reverence for those moss-backed frauds and scoundrelisms, hereditary kingship and so-called "nobility." It is enough to make the monarchs and nobles themselves laugh — and in private they do.... Have you noticed the rumor that the Portuguese throne is unsteady, and that the Portuguese slaves are getting restive? Also, that the head slave-driver of Europe, Alexander III, has so reduced his usual monthly order for chains that the Russian foundries are running only half time now? ... In a few years from now we shall have nothing but played-out kings and dukes on the police.

Twain asked Baxter to note the striking similarity in the wording of the state papers in which the Brazilian republic was proclaimed and that used in his about-to-be published novel.

Meanwhile, Twain's London publishers, Chatto and Windus, after considering the manuscript, concluded that a novel in which a Connecticut Yankee announced the dissolution of King Arthur's monarchy and proclaimed a

British Republic, was too strong for English consumption. They sent an urgent appeal for an expurgated edition. Twain's indignant refusal was prompt and decisive. Asserting that the book had already undergone sufficient revision under the critical eyes of Mrs. Clemens, Howells, E. C. Stedman, and several Englishmen, Twain gave his British publishers the following ultimatum:

> Now, mind you, I have taken all these pains because I wanted to say a Yankee mechanic's say against monarchy and its several natural props, and yet make a book which you would be willing to print exactly as it comes to you, without altering a word....
>
> Now, as I say, I have taken laborious pains to so trim this book of offense that you might not lack the nerve to print it just as it stands. I am going to get the proofs to you just as early as I can. I want you to read it carefully. If you can publish it without altering a single word, go ahead. Otherwise, please hand it to J. R. Osgood in time for him to have it published at my expense....
>
> This is important, for the reasons that the book was not written for America; it was written for England. So many Englishmen have done their sincerest best to teach us something for our betterment that it seems to me high time that some of us should substantially recognize the good intent by trying to pry up the English nation to a little higher level of manhood in turn.

In spite of their trepidation, Chatto and Windus published the *Yankee* in unexpurgated form concurrently with the American edition.

What was it in *A Connecticut Yankee* that made London publishers hesitate to publish a book by one of the best-selling authors of all times? What was his message to the English people, designed to raise them "to a little higher level of manhood"?

Ever angry at injustice, Twain was never more irate than when he wrote *A Connecticut Yankee in King Arthur's Court.* "No nobility, no royalty or other fraud can face ridicule in a fair field and live," he had written in his notebook. He filled his novel with ridicule, but also with his hatred of the institutions which, after plaguing humanity in the Middle Ages, continued to operate in his contemporary world. (Twain's unpublished notebooks reveal his awareness of and concern over the increasing demands in the late 'eighties by wealthy Americans for the institution of a monarchy in the United States as a means of holding in check the "radical forces" represented by the organized workers and farmers.) He coupled this with a clarion call for democratic reform. The book satirized exploitation of labor, rule of one over many, social and political inequality and other injustices in the mythical kingdom of King Arthur's court, but its main fire is directed against three enemies of mankind:

1. The established church which inculcated feudal doctrines in the mass of the people; kept them in a state of poverty, ignorance and superstition in order to maintain its worldly power; suppressed freedom of thought and encouraged resignation to a sordid life by insisting that only life in the hereafter truly mattered.

2. The parasitical aristocracy which throve on the system the church sanctioned; paid lip service to Christian ideals as it plundered the peasants and other producing classes; perpetuated a rigid caste system in order to maintain dominance over the commoners and preserve its own privileges.

3. The monarchy which crowned and symbolized the decadent feudal order. Sanctioned by the church and subsidized by the aristocracy, and further propped up by the doctrine of divine right, it perpetuated itself by means of a vicious and degrading penal code.

In his animadversions on the church, which he regarded as the cornerstone of institutionalized evil, Twain was unsparing. We will, however, consider his attack on the established church in the chapter on "Religion." Here let us confine our discussion to two of the great enemies of progress: the monarchy and the aristocracy.

In *A Connecticut Yankee* Twain ripped up the basic premise of monarchy, the divine right of kings. Using a device already employed in *The Prince and the Pauper*, he has King Arthur wander incognito through his realm with the Yankee. Captured by slave-traders, Arthur is chained with other slaves in a convoy. The Yankee, musing on the king's inability to identify himself, concludes: "It only shows that there is nothing diviner about a king than there is about a tramp, after all. He is just a cheap and hollow artificiality when you don't know he is a king. But reveal his quality, and, dear me, it takes your very breath away to look at him."

For all the logic in the theory of divine rights, cats would make perfect kings. It was not absolutely necessary that there be a man on the throne before whom the abject subjects might crawl and worship. Cats might even be an improvement:

They would be as useful as any other royal family, they would know as much, they would have the same virtues and the same treacheries, the same disposition to get up shindies with other royal cats, they would be laughably vain and absurd and never know it, they would be wholly inexpensive: finally, they would have as sound a divine right as any other royal house, and "Tom VII., or Tom XI., or Tom XIV., by the Grace of God, King," would sound as well as it would when applied to the ordinary royal tom-cat with tights on. And as a rule ... the character of these cats would be considerably above the character of the average king, and this would be an immense moral advantage to the nation. . . . The worship of royalty being founded in unreason, these graceful and harmless cats would easily become as sacred as any other royalties, and indeed more so, because it would presently be noticed that they hanged nobody, beheaded nobody, imprisoned nobody, inflicted no cruelties or injustices of any sort, and so must be worthy of a deeper love and reverence than the customary human king, and would certainly get it.

The conception is worthy of Swift.

When he discussed the aristocracy, Twain grew hot with indignation. He could concede that some kind of religion is necessary to the average person, and that the church might have beneficial possibilities, but he could find absolutely nothing to justify an aristocratic order. The privileged existed only to enjoy their privileges. They exploited the producing classes in order to maintain themselves in luxury; they indulged the church as a propaganda agency, and supported a monarchy as the most efficient means of preserving the *status quo*. Added to all this was the aristocracy's hypocrisy. The Yankee observes: "I will say this much for the nobility: that, tyrannical, murderous, rapacious, and morally rotten as they were, they were deeply and enthusiastically religious. Nothing could divert them from the regular and faithful performance of the pieties enjoined by the Church. More than once I had seen a noble, who had gotten his enemy at a disadvantage, stop to pray before cutting his throat."

Centuries of inherited rule had exalted the nobility as a species above and apart from the general run of mankind and had instilled in all classes of society the belief that the lower classes were the mere property of the upper. This was the ideology of slavery in all places and at all times: "a privileged class, an aristocracy is but a band of slaveholders under another name. One needs but to hear an aristocrat speak of the classes that are below him to recognize — and in but indifferently modified measure — the very air and tone of the actual slaveholder, and behind these are the slaveholder's spirit, the slaveholder's blunted feeling."

Not only was the caste system of a "gilded minority" degrading to the lower classes, but it was in contradiction to the real interests of the nation. For the commoners were the real nation and the only part of it worthy of respect: "To subtract them would have been to subtract the Nation and leave behind some dregs, some refuse, in the shape of a king, nobility and gentry, idle, unproductive, acquainted mainly with the arts of wasting and destroying, and of no sort of use or value in any rationally controlled world."

The Yankee can have a title in King Arthur's realm if

he wants it. But up speaks the democrat, the Hartford, U.S.A. mechanic: "I could have got a title easy enough, and that would have raised me a large step in everybody's eyes: even in the king's, the giver of it. But I didn't ask for it; and I declined it when it was offered. I couldn't have enjoyed such a thing with my notions; and it wouldn't have been fair, anyway, because as far back as I could go, our tribe had always been short of the bar sinister. I couldn't have felt really and satisfactorily fine and proud and set-up over any title except one that should come from the nation itself — the only legitimate source."

He gets his title Freeman at last, winning and wearing it "with a high and clean pride." Does the title come from the king? Indeed not. "This title fell casually from the lips of a blacksmith, one day." The Hartford mechanic has attained his nobility from the only source he can respect.

Again and again in the *Yankee*, Twain points out that the material welfare and cultural achievements of civilization had derived entirely from the suppressed masses, and only in the masses of common men lay the seeds of a better social order. The supposition that the people were not as well fitted to govern themselves as some self-appointed rulers were to govern them was a manifest absurdity:

The master minds of all nations, in all ages, have sprung in affluent multitude from the mass of the nation ... only — not from its privileged classes; and so, no matter what the nation's intellectual grade was ... the bulk of its ability was in the long ranks of its nameless and its poor, and so it never saw the day that it had not the material in abundance whereby to govern itself. Which is to assert an always self-proven fact; that even the best-governed and most free and most enlightened monarchy is still behind the best condition attainable by its people; and that the same is true of kindred governments of lower grades.

In advancing this basis principle of democracy, Twain now praised universal suffrage which, we have seen, he once hoped would be abolished: "Men may write many fine and plausible arguments in support of monarchy, but the fact remains that where every man in a state has a vote, brutal laws are impossible."

Just as the citizens of any nation are capable of governing themselves, so they are also endowed with the manhood requisite for building any type of society they wanted, if they would but assert themselves. True, the Yankee is often disgusted that the mass of the people submit meekly to the tyranny imposed upon them:

It was pitiful for a person born in a wholesome free atmosphere to listen to their humble and hearty outpourings of loyalty toward their king and Church and nobility, as if they had any more occasion to love and honor [them] than a slave has to love and honor the lash. . . . Any kind of royalty, howsoever modified, any kind of aristocracy, howsoever pruned is rightly an insult; but if you are born and brought up under that sort of arrangement you probably never find it out yourself, and don't believe it when somebody else tells you. It is enough to make a body ashamed of his race to think of the sort of froth that has always occupied its throne without shadow of right or reason, and the seventh-rate people that have always figured as its aristocracies.

Yet the fundamental integrity and spirit of this "human muck" can never be destroyed — not even by centuries of oppression, nor by the notion imposed by all-powerful propaganda that God, in his wisdom, had chosen a few privileged individuals to dominate the mass of mankind for their profit and that it was the duty of the common people to submit meekly. The Yankee confidently affirms: "A man *is* a man, at bottom. Whole ages of abuse and oppression cannot crush the manhood clear out of him. . . . There is plenty good enough material for a republic in the most degraded people that ever existed — even in the Russians . . . even in the Germans — if one could but force it out of its timid and suspicious privacy, to overthrow and trample in the mud any throne that was ever set up and any nobility that ever supported it."

It is the Yankee's mission to help the people come to their senses. Disgusted though he was with the stupidity, perversity, and even cowardliness of the masses he wanted to help, the Yankee did not despair or sink into hopelessness. Although he finds himself in an England "where the right to say how the country should be governed was restricted to six persons in each thousand of its population," and where any signs of dissatisfaction "would have been so disloyal, so dishonorable, such putrid black treason," he assumed the role of a political messiah and decided that "what the nine hundred and ninety-four dupes needed was a new deal." So the Yankee set about to undermine men's loyalty and allegiance to institutions which degraded them, and to educate the masses up to their exalted position as "the nation, the actual Nation . . . about all that was useful or worth saving, or really respectworthy."

Specifically, the new deal aimed at an industrial revolution, popular education, making the Established Church an individual "go-as-you-please affair," replacing knight-errantry with something useful, and exchanging Merlin's hocus-pocus with nineteenth century science. All this would contribute much, the Yankee hoped, toward the reformation, but he concluded that only drastic measures would achieve a real democratic order. There was one great imperative: monarchy must be destroyed. To justify this radical change, Twain appropriated Carlyle's clothes metaphor:

> You see my kind of loyalty was loyalty to one's country, not to its institutions, or its office-holders. The country is the real thing, the substantial thing, the eternal thing; it is the thing to watch over, and care for, and be loyal to; institutions are extraneous, they are its mere clothing, and clothing can wear out, become ragged, cease to be comfortable, cease to protect the body from winter, disease, and death. To be loyal to rags, to shout for rags, to worship rags, to die for rags — that is a loyalty to unreason, it is pure animal; it belongs to monarchy, was invented by monarchy; let monarchy keep it.
>
> I was from Connecticut, whose Constitution declares "that all political power is inherent in the people, and all free governments

are founded on their authority and instituted for their benefits; and that they have at all times an undeniable and indefeasible right to alter their form of government in such a manner as they may think expedient."

Under that gospel, the citizen who thinks he sees that the commonwealth's political clothes are worn out, and yet holds his peace and does not agitate for a new suit, is disloyal; he is a traitor. That he may be the only one who thinks he sees this decay, does not excuse him; it is his duty to agitate anyway, and it is the duty of the others to vote him down if they do not see the matter as he does. . . .

In order to restore health to the nation, the feudal caste system must be transformed into a democracy. The only effective way to achieve such drastic change, the Yankee decides, is by violent revolution: "All gentle cant and philosophizing to the contrary notwithstanding, no people in the world ever did achieve their freedom by goody-goody talk and moral suasion; it being immutable law that all revolutions that will succeed must *begin* in blood, whatever may answer afterward. If history teaches anything, it teaches that. What this folk needed, then, was a Reign of Terror and a guillotine. . . ." The Terror of the Revolution would be as nothing compared to the Terror under which the people have been oppressed for centuries:

And here were these freemen assembled in the early morning to work on their lord and bishop's road three days each — gratis; every head of a family, and every son of a family, three days each, gratis, and a day or so added for their servants.

Why, it was like reading about France and the French, before the ever-memorable and blessed Revolution, which swept a thousand years of such villainy away in one swift tidal-wave of blood — one: a settlement of that hoary debt in the proportion of half a drop of blood for each hogshead of it that had been pressed by slow tortures out of that people in the weary stretch of 10 centuries of wrong and shame and misery the like of which was not to be mated but in hell.

There were two "Reigns of Terror," if we would but remember it and consider it; the one wrought murder in hot passion, the other in heartless cold blood; the one lasted mere months, the other had lasted a thousand years; the one inflicted death upon 10,000 persons, the other upon a hundred millions; but our shudders are all for the "horrors" of the minor Terror, the momentary Terror, so to speak; whereas, what is the horror of swift death by the axe, compared with life-long death from hunger, cold, insult, cruelty and heart-break?

What is swift death by lightning compared with death by slow fire at the stake? A city cemetery could contain the coffins filled by that brief Terror which we have all been so diligently taught to shiver at and mourn over; but all France could hardly contain the coffins filled by that older and real Terror — that unspeakably bitter and awful Terror which none of us has been taught to see in its vastness or pity as it deserves.

As it turned out, the revolution the Connecticut Yankee proposed was abortive. Thus the Yankee lost the final battle. With good reason, too! For he found that though he had truth and science on his side, and though he could fight with gunpowder and electricity, he lost when he was isolated from the people.

Though the effort to destroy sixth-century feudalism and knight-errantry by nineteenth-century Yankee ingenuity failed, the basic idea of the book remained: vigorous hatred of oppression, bigotry, tyranny and autocracy, sham pomp and pretension; assertion of the worth of the individual, and advocacy of the rights of man. Democracy's superiority to kingship and to despotism in general is the theme of *A Connecticut Yankee*. Written at white heat, it is a masterpiece of social criticism. And it presents Mark Twain's humor at its best. Indeed, it is quite rare to find a novel that is at once so angry and yet so witty. Howells put it well in the "Editor's Study" column of *Harper's*: "Here he is to the full the humorist, as we know him; but he is very much more, and his strong, indignant, often infuriate hate of injustice, and his love of equality, burn hot through the manifold adventures and experiences of the tale. . . . The delicious satire, the marvellous wit, the wild, free, fantastic humor are the colors of the tapestry, while the texture is a humanity that lives in every fibre. At every moment the scene amuses, but it all the time is an object-lesson in democracy. . . . We feel that in this book our arch-humorist imparts more of his personal quality than in anything else he has done."

None of the other American reviewers saw the book in the same light. Most of them contented themselves with cataloguing humorous incidents. Where they did mention Twain's social criticism, they dismissed it as unimportant, and predicted that "by the great majority of people . . . the book will be read for its humor, and of this there is an abundance." The *Literary World*, alone among American critics, condemned the *Yankee* from beginning to end. It called the book "the poorest of all his productions thus far," and found even its humor offensive. Twain deserved only the severest condemnation because "he prostitutes his humorous gift," and those who praised the book for its humor were to be pitied: "It is not calculated to make a reflecting person proud of a shallow and self-complacent generation which can enjoy such so-called humor."

The leading English journals, with one exception, ignored the book. The exception was the newly founded *Review of Reviews* which selected the *Yankee* for consideration as "Novel of the Month." W. T. Stead, its editor, conceded serious defects in the book, which he considered more a "political pamphlet" than a novel, but termed it "one of the most significant of our time" for its understanding of "what the mass of men who speak English are thinking." He complimented Twain for getting "directlier at the heart of the masses than any of the blue-china set of nimminy-pimminy criticasters."

Lesser British journals condemned the book as a coarse and vulgar travesty. Twain, in the opinion of *The Speaker*, was dull as well as offensive, and was especially dull when he wrote with a social purpose. *The Spectator* commented: "Mark Twain has surpassed himself as a low comedian in literature by the manner in which he has vaulted at a bound into the charmed circle of Arthurian romance."

"My interest in a book ceases with the printing of it," Twain had written to Twichell in 1874. This time, however, he was deeply concerned by the critical reception in England. He had expected to be maltreated, but to be snubbed by the major critics and called "dull" and "offensive" by the lesser ones, stung him. He asked the English critic, Andrew Lang, an old friend, to speak out in the book's defense. In his letter to Lang, Twain set forth what he considered his major function as an author. He protested that he was misunderstood by the English critics, who represented a literary standard to which he had made no pretensions; consequently he was the victim of cultural snobbishness:

The thin top crust of humanity — the cultivated — are worth pacifying, worth pleasing, worth coddling, worth nourishing and preserving with dainties and delicacies, it is true; but to be caterer to that little faction is no very dignified or valuable occupation, it seems to me; it is merely feeding the over-fed, and there must be small satisfaction in that. It is not that little minority who are already saved that are best worth trying to uplift, I should think, but the mighty mass of uncultivated who are underneath. . . .

Indeed, I have been misjudged from the very first. I have never tried in even one single instance, to help cultivate the cultivated classes. I was not equipped for it, either by native gifts or training. And I never had any ambition in that direction, but always hunted for bigger game — the masses.

Lang responded with a curious defense of the creator of *Huckleberry Finn*. In an article in the *London Illustrated News*, he announced that he had "abstained" from reading the *Yankee*, "because here Mark Twain is not, and cannot be, at the proper point of view. He has not the knowledge which would enable him to be a sound critic of the Middle Ages."

As late as 1907, Lang plumed himself on that abstention: "I have never read, and never will read *A Yankee at King Arthur's Court*." In that same year, another Englishman wrote to Twain: "I am persuaded that the future historian of America will find your work as indispensable to him as a French historian finds the political tracts of Voltaire." This man was George Bernard Shaw.

The critics who rejected the *Yankee* on the ground of bad taste were, of course, offended by Twain's use of the comic possibilities of feudal chivalry, through such incidents as having the medieval knights, dressed as sandwich men, carry advertisements for "Persimmons Soap — All the Prima Donne Use It"; the eleventh hour rescue of the King and the Yankee by Round Table knights on bicycles; and "Every year expeditions went out holy grailing, and the next year relief expeditions went out to hunt for *them*." But 250 years before Twain, Cervantes had also been criticized for his "tastelessness and want of tact" in satirizing medieval chivalry. In the case of both *Don Quixote* and *A Connecticut Yankee*, the critics evaded the real issues.

In dealing with the *Yankee*, the critics could not accept a serious treatment of vital social issues by a man whom they dismissed as a humorist, and a blood and fire indictment of traditions and institutions they regarded as holy. The book concentrates its fire on those who cynically proclaimed that the mass of the people were incapable of mastering their own fate but were destined by God, nature and their own innate incapacities to occupy an inferior status in society. Had Twain attacked the poverty-stricken instead of poverty; unjust monarchs rather than the institution of monarchy, and certain clerical practices instead of the idea of an established church, he would have fared far better at the hands of the critics. But Twain was not content merely with railing at symptoms — he attacked the specific root cause of the disease. The so-called "low comedian in literature" had baffled his critics by writing a "message novel" whose theme had universal application, and, despite the hostile attitude of the reviewers, was to be read by millions. Some of these readers might disagree or recoil from the burlesque-like comic quality, but none could help but feel greater respect for mankind and for democracy on reading *A Connecticut Yankee in King Arthur's Court.*

Two years after his tirades against monarchy in the *Yankee,* Twain voiced his pleasure at the warm reception extended him by Austrian royalty. He even wrote in his notebook: "There are princes which I cast in the *Echte* (genuine) princely mold, and they make me regret — again — that I am not a prince myself. It is not a new regret but a very old one. I have never been properly and humbly satisfied with my condition. I am a democrat only by principle, not by instinct — nobody is *that*."

Had Twain forgotten what he had written in the *Yankee?* For the moment, yes; but only for the moment. The restatement of his old opinions indicated that the mood was transitory.

JOAN OF ARC

Twain returned to the attack upon "monarchy and its several natural props" in *Joan of Arc,* published in 1896. The irresponsibility of a vacillating and treacherous ruling clique, a closed world of birth and breeding, has brought France to her knees, before the end of the Hundred Years' War. The country has been "betrayed and delivered over, hand and foot, to the enemy" when the Queen joined her daughter to the *butcher* of Agincourt. Royalty looked to its own, not to the people's immediate good. Indeed, the Dauphin had severed relations with his subjects, turned the army over to generals like La Hire, banished his most faithful councillor, Constable Richemont, and shut himself up "with his favorites and fools in inglorious idleness and poverty in a little patch of the kingdom," where he was surrounded by "schemers and traitors" like Georges de la Tremoille and that holy fox, the Archbishop of Rheims. Small wonder that the French army has done "nothing but run for near a century," that the nation "lay gasping out the remnants of an exhausted life." Because "the gilded children of privilege" had long been divorced from the "mighty underlying force" of the people, the spirit of France was dead indeed, and only odds and ends of the country yet remained "under that rare and almost forgotten rag, the banner of France."

Out of the ignored and inarticulate masses, the "marvelous child" of Domremy rose to check the degradation of France. Through her, the exhausted nation drew strength, and "dead France woke suddenly to life." Joan of Arc soon became "a mirror in which the lowly hosts of France were clearly reflected." Indeed, her phenomenal success is largely explained as the consolidation of the country's true fighting strength which had not been previously enlisted in the conflict — what Twain proudly hailed as "that vague, formless, inert mass, that mighty underlying force called the 'people.'"

With her to inspire them, there was no limit to their willingness to serve and sacrifice. These same humble folk, indeed, were her only supporters when she fell into the hands of France's great internal enemy, the Church. To their sorrow and humiliation, "this symbol of France made flesh" had been "sold to a French priest by a French prince, with the French nation standing thankless by and saying nothing."

Thus the legend of Joan of Arc becomes another fiery preachment against feudal injustice. Like *A Connecticut Yankee*, it is an object-lesson in democracy. The common man, Twain insists, is the strength of the nation, and the equal of those who set themselves up as his betters.

Right of Revolution

Twain continued to employ familiar themes to express his detestation of the crowned heads of nations and their claims of superiority. Using the clothes metaphor, he has the Russian Czar meditate as he surveys his nude form in the mirror: "Naked, what am I? A lank, skinny, spider-legged libel on the image of God! . . . Is it that a hundred and forty million Russians kiss the dust before me and worship? Manifestly not! . . . It is my clothes. Without my clothes I should be as destitute of authority as any other naked person. . . . One realizes that without his clothes a man would be nothing at all. . . . Titles — another artificiality — are a part of his clothing. . . . An Emperor . . . by the sheer might of these artificialities . . . can get himself worshipped as a deity by his people." It was behind such flimsy pretexts that the monarchs of the world operated. "Strip the human race, absolutely naked, and it would be a real democracy," Twain wrote. "But the introduction of even a rag of tiger skin, or a cowtail, could make a badge of distinction and be the beginnings of a monarchy."

Twain spent less of his energies now in exposing tyrants and more in blasting the downtrodden for submitting to them. The inertia of the populace, he kept repeating, was directly responsible for kings and their dissolute forms of government. He depicted the surprise among rulers like the Czar at being permitted to continue their tyrannies: "A curious invention . . . the human race! The swarming Russian millions have for centuries meekly allowed our Family to rob them, insult them, trample them under foot, while they lived and suffered and died with no purpose and no function but to make that Family comfortable! . . . Is the human race a joke? . . . Has it no respect for itself?" Leopold of Belgium, equally incredulous, sneered at the supposition that a monarch should want respect: "What king has valued the respect of the human race? He stands upon an eminence . . . and sees multitudes of meek human things . . . who are in no way better or finer than themselves. . . . If men were really *men*, how could a Czar be possible? and how could I be possible? But we *are* possible; we are quite safe. . . . The race will put up with us, in its docile immemorial way. It will . . . make large talk, but it will stay on its knees all the same. . . . It finds fault with me and my occupations, and forgets that neither of us [the Czar or Leopold] could exist an hour without its sanction."

The victim of tyranny was thus submitting to a condition of life of which he was the creator as well as the victim. "I thought caste created itself," one of Twain's characters in *The American Claimant* observes, "and perpetuated itself; but it seems quite true that it only creates itself, and is perpetuated by the people whom it despises, and who can dissolve it at any time." The solution, as Twain saw it, was simple: "the first ... second ... third ... and the only gospel in any monarchy should be Rebellion."

The glorification of revolution runs strongly through Twain's published and unpublished writings. He justified revolution as a means of overthrowing unjust or tyrannical governments. It was the last refuge of a tyrannized people, but its righteousness was implicit, for government must express the will of the people; and when government becomes tyranny, that will can be expressed only in revolution. "The natural right of the oppressed to rebel" is a phrase that occurs again and again in Twain's writings and speeches.

The Struggle Against Russian Czarism

Any sign of revolt against what seemed to him tyrannical authority afforded Twain pleasure, and he often helped revolutionaries with a speech or with money or an article. No cause, however, aroused his interest and enthusiasm more than did the struggle against Russian Czarism.

Horrified by reports of the suffering of masses of Russian political prisoners exiled to Siberia, Twain wrote a letter in 1890, at the request of the editor of *Free Russia*, urging the "liberation parties" to kill the Czar and organize a republic. To do otherwise, he argued, was to invite failure, for never in the history of the world had a despotism submitted to reform. The entire system had to be obliterated, not merely altered. America had paid for her freedom with blood; England had so bought her liberation from despots. "When we consider that not even the most responsible English monarch ever yielded back a stolen public right until it was wrenched from them [*sic*] by violence, is it rational to suppose that gentler methods can win privileges in Russia?" The proper way would be to demolish the throne by revolution; but since rebellion could not be organized in Russia, the Czar should be assassinated and the throne kept vacant until a republic could be established. Compromise with Czarism could only be disastrous.

The letter was never mailed because it seemed too openly revolutionary at that early period. In his notebooks, Twain continued to confide his belief that "assassination" of the Czar should be the first order of business in Russia. "The idiotic Crusades were gotten up to 'rescue' a valueless tomb from the Saracens," he wrote on September 9, 1891; "it seems to me that a crusade to make a bonfire of the Russian throne & fry the Czar in it w(oul)d have some sense."

Publicly, however, Twain said little until 1905. Then a massacre of Jews and the slaughter of nearly 1,500 men, women, and children in Moscow on "Bloody Sunday" (January 22, 1905), brought Twain's hatred of Czarism to a head, and he published "The Czar's Soliloquy," in the *North American Review* of March, 1905. He called for revolution, reiterated his demand that the Czar be assassinated, and condemned moralists who opposed the use of force to overthrow the barbaric Czarist despotism. He pictured the Czar as incredulous at the world's insistence that the moral axioms subscribed to in civilized countries should be applied to him and his system:

We [the Romanoffs] have done as we pleased for centuries. Our common trade has been crime, our common pastime murder, our common beverage blood.... Yet the pious moralist says it is a crime to assassinate us.... Ah! What could our Family do without the moralist? ... Today he is our *only* friend. Whenever there has been dark talk of assassination, he has come forward and saved us with his impressive maxim, "Forbear: nothing politically valuable was ever achieved by violence." There is no Romanoff of learning and experience but would reverse the maxim.

News of Russian defeats in the Russo-Japanese War delighted Twain. A smashing defeat for the Czarist forces would certainly be followed by a successful revolution and assassination of the Czar. When Twain learned in the Spring of 1905 that most of the Russian fleet had been captured or sunk by Admiral Teichachiro Togo's fleet, he wrote excitedly to Twichell: *"Togo forever!* I wish somebody would assassinate the Russian Family. So does every sane person in the world — but who has the grit to say so? Nobody. . . ."

It is not difficult, then, to imagine Twain's anger over the peace treaty ending the war which was negotiated at Portsmouth, New Hampshire, with the assistance of President Theodore Roosevelt. "That foolish brief truce which they call by the larger name of a 'peace,'" he wrote bitterly to his daughter. While others were hailing the Treaty of Portsmouth as a victory for civilization, he characterized it as "the greatest calamity that has ever befallen civilization. The Russians were within an inch of civil liberty, but it has been snatched from them. This seals the fate of billions of human souls who, on account of this peace, will have to live in bondage."

In response to a request from the Boston *Globe* asking him to join in "the expression of congratulations" at the announcement of peace, Twain forwarded a message which he insisted that the *Globe* "either publish all, without modifying a word, or suppress the whole of it & leave me unmentioned." The communication, published in the *Globe* of August 30, 1905, read:

Russia was on the high road to emancipation from an insane & intolerable slavery; I was hoping there would be no peace until Russian liberty was safe. I think that this was a holy war in the best & noblest sense of that abused term, & that no war was ever charged with a higher mission; I think there can be no doubt that

that mission is now defeated and Russia's chains re-riveted, this time to stay. I think the Czar will now withdraw the small humanities that have been forced from him, & resume his medieval barbarisms with a relieved spirit & an immeasurable joy. I think Russian liberty has had its last chance, & has lost it. I think nothing has been gained by the peace that is remotely comparable to what has been sacrificed by it. One more battle would have abolished the waiting chains of billions of billions of unborn Russians, and I wish it could have been fought. I hope I am mistaken, yet in all sincerity I believe that this peace is entitled to rank as the most conspicuous disaster in political history.

Twain's message was widely reprinted, and produced a number of editorials and many letters of approval. One correspondent wrote from Maine: "I wish to thank you for your brave utterance in reference to the Peace of Oyster Bay. The coming years will, I am sorry to believe, show you to have been absolutely right. The only significance this war ever had lay in the possibility of its bringing liberty to the Russian people."

Despite his public appeals for the overthrow of Czarism, Twain was invited to dine with the Russian officials who had negotiated the peace treaty. It is interesting to compare the original draft of the words in which he declined the invitation with the later and more formal version, and to note the underlying irony of the letter. The original read:

I am still a cripple, otherwise I should be more than glad of this opportunity to meet these illustrious magicians who with the pen have annulled, obliterated, & abolished every high achievement of the Japanese sword and turned the tragedy of a tremendous war into a gay & blithesome comedy. If I may, let me in all respect & honor salute them as my fellow-humorists, I taking third place, as becomes one who was not born to modesty, but by diligence & hard work, is acquiring it.

The telegram which he actually sent, and which the Russians asked permission to publish, and announced their intentions of showing to the Czar, was more reserved in its irony:

I should be more than glad ... to meet the illustrious magicians who came here equipped with nothing but a pen, & with it have divided the honors of the war with the sword. It is fair to presume that in thirty centuries history will not get done in admiring these men who attempted what the world regarded as the impossible & achieved it.

Congratulating Twain for having correctly labeled the "Peace of Portsmouth" a "disaster," Daniel De Leon, leader of the American Socialist Labor Party, nevertheless predicted "that causes unconsidered by the author of *A Connecticut Yankee in King Arthur's Court,* will thwart the purpose of the peace dictators." It was an accurate prediction. The Revolution of 1905 erupted in Russia just after the Treaty of Portsmouth was signed. A general strike broke out; the water supply and electricity was cut off in some cities; nearly all the railroads were halted; *soviets,* or councils of workers and peasants were established; and Czar Nicholas II and his Government became frightened. The Czar named Count Witte Premier and promised the people a constitution to be drawn up by the Duma, the first national legislature in Russia, elections which were to be held in March, 1906.

Emissaries representing the revolutionary forces left Russia on missions seeking financial and moral support. In the Spring of 1906, Nicolai Tchaikowsky, brother of the composer, and Maxim Gorky, the distinguished writer, came to the United States for this purpose. The American Socialists greeted them enthusiastically, and formed a committee to forward the cause. Mark Twain immediately signified his willingness to serve on it, and, on April 11, 1906, introduced Gorky at a meeting launching the organization:

If we can build a Russian republic to give to the persecuted people of the Tsar's domain the same measure of freedom that we enjoy, let us go ahead and do it. We need not discuss the methods by which that purpose is to be attained. Let us hope that fighting will be postponed or averted for a while, but if it must come —

I am most emphatically in sympathy with the movement, now on foot in Russia to make that country free.... Anybody whose ancestors were in this country when we were trying to free ourselves from oppression, must sympathize with those who now are trying to do the same thing in Russia.... If we keep our hearts in this matter Russia will be free.

The following day, Twain wrote a letter to be read by Tchaikowsky at a mass meeting in the Grand Central Palace. He could not attend because he was presiding that evening "at a meeting whose object is to find remunerative work for certain classes of our blind who would gladly support themselves if they had the oportunity," but he wrote to the gathering:

My sympathies are with the Russian revolution, of course. It goes without saying. I hope it will succeed, and now that I have talked with you I take heart to believe it will.

Government by falsified promises, by lies, by treacheries, and by the butcherknife for the aggrandizement of a single family of drones and its idle and vicious kin has been borne quite long enough in Russia, I should think, and it is to be hoped that the roused nation, now rising in its strength, will presently put an end to it and set up the republic in its place.

Some of us, even of the white-headed, may live to see the blessed day when Czars and Grand Dukes will be as scarce there as I trust they are in heaven.

On April 13, 1906, the New York *World* featured a cartoon depicting Mark Twain pushing the Czar off his throne with a pen. The caption read: "A Yankee in Czar Nicholas's Court."

Twain's activity for the Russian revolutionary cause ended on the very next day. He and Howells had both agreed to speak at a literary dinner honoring Gorky, when the newspapers disclosed that the actress who had accompanied the Russian author to the United States as his wife was not married to him. At once the press raised a howl, and the couple was evicted from a procession of hotels.

Twain's reaction was immediately recorded in his notebook: "Saturday (April 14, 1906). The morning papers revealed the Gorky secret. Of course it made a sensation . . . 'all is dead' was my thought. . . . I believe it is dead beyond resurrection. . . ." (The "it" referred to the purpose of Gorky's visit to the United States.) He was less positive in a public statement to reporters who interviewed him that same day:

Gorky came to this country to lend the influence of his great name — and it is great in the things he has written — to the work of raising funds to carry on the Revolution in Russia. By these disclosures he is disabled. It is unfortunate. I felt that he would be a prodigious power in helping the movement, but he is in a measure shorn of his strength. Such things as have been published relate to a condition that might be forgivable in Russia, but which offends against the customs in this country. I would not say that his usefulness has been destroyed, but his efficiency as a persuader is certainly impaired. Every country has its laws of conduct and of customs, and those who visit a country other than their own must expect to conform to the customs of that country.

Though Eugene V. Debs and other leading American Socialists came to Gorky's defense, the plans for the dinner honoring the Russian writer were dropped. Twain acquiesced in the decision. That he did so not out of moral scruples, is made clear in his note to Twichell commenting on "Gorky's bad mistake." "Poor fellow," he wrote, "he didn't understand our bigotry. Too bad!" He remarked to Dan Beard: "Gorky made an awful mistake, Dan. He might as well have come over here in his shirt-tail."

What Twain did not realize was that the status of his female companion really had little to do with the slander campaign against Gorky. The press would have overlooked the whole matter if Gorky had not committed what, in their eyes, was an even worse offense than traveling with a woman who was not his wife. On the very day that the press broke the news about Gorky's female companion, it also reported that the Russian author and revolutionary leader had sent a telegram to William ("Big Bill") Haywood and Charles Moyer, officers of the Western Federation of Miners, who were in the county jail at Caldwell, Idaho, falsely charged with having conspired to murder ex-Governor Steunenberg of Colorado. Gorky's telegram read: "Greetings to you, my brother Socialists. Courage! The day of justice and deliverance for the oppressed of all the world is at hand."

The message to the leaders of the nation's most militant labor union infuriated the corporation heads throughout the country. These men had been kidnapped by the police of Idaho without extradition papers, and were being held in jail without bail. Every effort was made to "railroad" them to death and thus remove a thorn in big business' side, and even President Theodore Roosevelt cooperated in the conspiracy by publicly condemning Haywood and Moyer as "undesirable citizens." When Gorky's message was made public, the press determined to counteract its influence by slandering the sender.

Eugene V. Debs understood this, and noted in the Socialist paper, *Appeal to Reason*, that Gorky's "real offense" was support for the imprisoned labor leaders and not his relations with his traveling companion. But Twain and Howells did not see through the propaganda surrounding the issue although it is likely that even had he understood the real basis of the attack on Gorky, Twain would have felt that public opinion had been so poisoned against the Russian writer that nothing could be achieved for a cause with which he was associated. He wrote in his notebook: "The efforts which have been made in Gorky's justification are entitled to all respect because of the magnanimity of the motive back of them, but I think the ink was wasted. Custom is custom; it is built of brass, boiler iron, granite; facts, reasoning, arguments have no more effect upon it than the idle winds have upon Gibraltar."

News of the slander campaign against one of its leading writers aroused great resentment in Russia, especially among the revolutionists, and Twain was criticized for failing to align himself with Debs in defending Gorky. But Gorky himself did not share this opinion. In a letter from the United States to friends in Russia, he urged them not to lump Twain, for whom he had the highest respect, with other critics of his conduct: "I am immune to all this poison. . . . The petty bourgeoisie cannot be without morals like an executioner cannot be without a noose. . . . Not only in America have I observed this horrible picture of moral poverty. I saw it in Russia too, and therefore one does not have to attack the esteemed Mark Twain. He is an excellent man. In this case . . . Twain is one of those people who is unclear as to the meaning of facts."

In his interview with the press on the day the Gorky incident broke, Twain refused to commit himself as to whether he would withdraw from the committee in aid of the Russian revolution. But he quickly added: "I am said to be a revolutionist in my sympathies, by birth, by breeding and by principle. I am always on the side of the revolutionists, because there never was a revolution unless there were some oppressive and intolerable conditions against which to revolute."

This principle Twain upheld to his dying day. He was always ready to lend his support to any revolutionary cause even if he could not play an active role. Typical of scores of letters he sent during the last years of his life to American friends of revolutionary causes in Europe, Asia and Africa was one he sent on March 20, 1907, to the Secretary of the Friends of Russian Freedom: "I am in full sympathy with the movement & am willing to have my name used, but as I am too full of duties I cannot furnish any active service." The name "Samuel L. Clemens" was to adorn the letterhead of many such organizations for freedom!

I think if a feller he'ps another feller when he's in trouble, and don't cuss, and don't do no mean things, nur nothin' he ain' no business to do, and don't spell the Saviour's name with a little g, he ain't runnin' no resks, — he's about as saift as if he b'longed to a church. [*A Tramp Abroad.*]

Early Religious Training

Recent research has altered considerably the traditional picture of Mark Twain's religious training as a boy in Hannibal, in which earlier critics emphasized the backward influence exercised by a Calvinistic household. We know today that Twain's father was no lover of Calvinism. On the contrary, John Clemens was a "free thinker," and the impression his father's heterodoxy made upon him was strong enough to cause Twain to recall in 1897: "My father was a refined and kindly gentleman, very grave, rather austere, of rigid probity, a sternly just and upright man, albeit he attended no church, and never spoke of religious matters, and had no part nor lot in the pious joys of his Presbyterian family, nor ever seemed to suffer from this deprivation."

Since Twain specifically states that his father never spoke of religious matters, it is easy to underrate John Clemens' influence upon his young son's beliefs. Minnie M. Brashear has conjectured that "Mark Twain's father, sojourning in Kentucky or coming down the Ohio in the 'thirties, may have acquired an interest in both Voltaire and Tom Paine, and ... his son may have caught from him hints of such an interest that aroused his curiosity and motivated his later reading." While it is extremely doubtful if John Clemens ever held discussions with his son on the liberal ideas he may have absorbed from these readings — in later life Twain recalled that he and his father did not enjoy an intimate relationship — he undoubtedly discussed them with his adult acquaintances, and we have ample evidence that young Mark was the proverbial "little pitcher with big ears." Certainly there were frequent religious discussions between John Clemens and Uncle John Quarles: Although Twain does not mention his uncle's religious views in any of his writings, there is no doubt that John Quarles' deviation from the orthodoxy of the day impressed him. "I have not come across a better man than he was," Twain wrote in his *Autobiography*. "I was his guest for two or three months every year, from the fourth year after we removed to Hannibal till I was eleven or twelve years old."

Unable to reconcile the question of human destiny with the Calvinist dogma, John Quarles became a Universalist — a believer in the doctrine that all mankind will be saved and not only the elect; that truth and righteousness are controlling powers in the universe, and that Good must therefore triumph over Evil. J. V. Bodine, Quarles' biographer, describes the current attitude towards men who espoused this doctrine: "It was even worse than being an 'Infidel,' and often converted a man into a social pariah, though John Quarles did not suffer this fate, his natural kindness and his usefulness as a man and citizen saving him from the common penalty."

Conflict between Calvinism and Universalism was intense in a small town like Hannibal. While it is unlikely that the boy understood the full significance of his uncle's unpopular views, their influence upon him is highly probable. Although Twain, as he later pointed out, was "brought up as Presbyterian," he at least must have been aware that many intelligent people held doctrines opposed to those he heard at church. Certainly a boy who was a cub printer at the age of twelve, could not have been totally unaffected by the currents of liberal thought which penetrated the predominately Calvinistic atmosphere — especially when he was himself finding that atmosphere oppressive. The critics who have dwelt on the repressive forces of the Calvinistic elements in Twain's training have neglected the influence exerted during these very years by the liberal views of his heretical father and uncle. Granted that there is a paucity of evidence about the exact nature of this influence, we do know that it was to find expression later in Twain's criticism of the intolerance and bigotry of organized religion.

The other male kinsman whose attitude toward religion may have influenced Twain was his older brother, Orion. Not much is known of Orion's religious opinions, but a study of his various newspapers reveals that he frequently printed anecdotes with an unorthodox flavor. One, printed in Orion's *Western Union,* is fairly typical: The "red man's answer to the bigot was a good 'un. 'Why do you not come to the House of God on the Sabbath and hear me preach?' said he once, to a 'perverted' Indian. 'Ugh!' replied the savage, 'me go in the woods, Sunday; God preach there!'" Such anecdotes, expressing Deistic thoughts, must have exerted an influence on young Mark Twain's thinking.

In the eyes of numerous critics, the heterodox views of Twain's male kinsmen were of slight importance in shaping his religious views. His mother, after all was a Presbyterian; and to Van Wyck Brooks, Harvey O'Higgins, Edward N. Reeds and other exponents of psychoanalytical literary criticism, this fact was the decisive influence. Indeed, the numbing role played in the formation of Mark Twain's character by the "grim Calvinism" of his mother has almost become part of American folklore. For Brooks, Jane Clemens was a tragic example of the Freudian possessive mother love, which injures that which it seeks most to nurture. She was "the embodiment of that old-fashioned, cast-iron Calvinism which had proved so favorable to the life of enterprising action but which perceived the scent of the devil in any least expression of what is known as the creative impulse." O'Higgins and Reeds are even more explicit: "She was an orthodox believer in a stern Calvinistic God . . . and she planted the fear of this avenging deity ineradicably in Mark Twain's young mind."

Actually there was little fire-and-brimstone in Jane Clemens' vocabulary; and very little in her make-up suggests that she spent her time warning her son of the torments of hell that awaited bad little boys. On the contrary, she was wholly unlike the type of person pictured by Twain's psychologically bent biographers. "She was of a sunshiny disposition," wrote her son, Mark Twain, "and her long life was mainly a holiday to her. She was a dancer, from childhood to the end, and as capable a one as the Presbyterian church could show among its communicants. . . . She was very bright, and was very fond of banter and playful duels of wit." A far cry from the type of person whose life was dominated by the darker teachings of Calvinism. Indeed, her descendants testify that "as far as religious convictions are concerned, Jane Clemens seems to have been unusually liberal for her day. . . . She was never one whose life centered in the church; she was not a very steady churchgoer. . . . She did not read the Bible a great deal." Her granddaughter, who lived with her for twenty-five years in St. Louis and Fredonia, and "heard her mention almost everything that was in her mind," does not recall that "she ever referred to the retribution of a stern Calvinistic God, or similar subjects." She does not remember that Jane Clemens went to church at all in St. Louis, and in Fredonia she went to church only now and then.

Such testimony casts doubt upon the accepted critical conclusions and even upon Albert Bigelow Paine's generalization that "she [Jane Clemens] joined the Presbyterian Church, and her religion was of that clear-cut, strenuous kind which regards as necessary institutions hell and Satan." The truth appears to be that, although she subscribed in general to the Presbyterian dogma, her creed was hardly "clear cut" in its orthodoxy.

The unorthodox thinking of Twain's father and uncle

and, to an extent, even of his mother, exerted influence on his religious convictions, but they certainly could not overcome all the effects of Hannibal's religious atmosphere with its emphasis on the constant battle between the elect of God and all the forces of the Prince of Darkness. "The Puritan Sabbath held Hannibal tightly in its grip," Dixon Wecter points out. All frivolous behavior was looked upon with suspicion, but, above all, Sunday was to be kept holy. Terrible things would happen to boys who violated the Sabbath by playing ball, fishing, etc. Hannibal families read aloud stories from the *Youth's Companion* which told of boys drowned swimming in violation of the Sabbath. In Sunday school students were supposed to memorize Bible texts. As an added incentive, successful recitations were rewarded with colored paper tickets. Twain once wrote that he had read the Bible through "before I was 15 years old."

"A boy's life is not all comedy," Twain mused in his old age; "much of the tragic enters into it." As a child he knew of murders, epidemics, drownings, and steamboat explosions. The impress of the darker teachings of Calvinism on a child's mind in an environment where death was so present is easy to evaluate. He was in terror lest the violence he witnessed prefigured punishment for his childish wrong-doing. The drunken tramp who was burned to death in the village jail, lay upon his conscience "a hundred nights afterward and filled them with hideous dreams." Pondering over these tragic events, he decided that they were direct warnings to him from God.

There is no doubt that Mark Twain never did free himself completely from the hold on his emotions which his early religious training had established. "When he invoked Hannibal," Bernard De Voto notes, "he found there not only the idyll of boyhood but anxiety, violence, supernatural horror, and an uncrystallized but enveloping dread." The truth of this observation does not mean that young Twain accepted the theological training without protest. Against the whole atmosphere of super-piety he was in early rebellion. "For we were little Christian children," he wrote in his *Autobiography*, "and had early been taught the value of forbidden fruit." Even as a boy he "detested Sunday-School" and played hooky. To escape the monotony of the Presbyterian training, he frequently attended the Methodist Sunday School. In fact, the teacher who made the most permanent impression upon his mind was a kindly stonemason named Richmond, who was a Methodist.

The influence of the Hannibal years upon Twain's religious beliefs was a mixed one. All scholars are agreed that primarily his environment was one of Calvinist-Puritan-Presbyterianism. This creed, with its emphasis on Holy Law and righteousness, an untiring pursuit of duty, especially the duty of work, and unbending opposition to what the Church regarded as evil, filled Twain with boredom, revulsion and fear, all of which "hovered like shadowy spectres in the background of his mind." Coupled with this influence, however, were the underlying currents of liberal and unorthodox doctrine which reached him from his father, his uncle, his brother, and even his mother. These currents implanted the seeds of his mature thought on the Church, the Bible, God, superstition and morality.

Deism and Freemasonry

While there is little agreement among students of Mark Twain as to what his religious convictions may have been during his boyhood, there is general agreement that they underwent a rapid transformation after he left Hannibal in 1853. "What a man wants with religion in these breadless times surpasses my comprehension," he wrote to his brother, Orion, in 1860 during the business panic caused by the secession crisis.

Some have attributed Twain's turning away from Hannibal Presbyterianism and his rejection of orthodox Christianity to the influence of the Scotsman named Macfarlane with whom he roomed in Cincinnati in 1856, and who impressed him with a pre-Darwinian, mechanistic, evolutionary theory. Others have emphasized Twain's exposure to Deism during his wanderings through the country, particularly during his life on the Mississippi. Although there is only a minor reference to Tom Paine in Twain's writings, there is no doubt that *The Age of Reason*, which he read as a cub pilot, helped direct his mind away from the Calvinism of his boyhood. Its exposition of Newtonian Deism, uncompromising rejection of the Church, ridicule of religious "superstition," and plea for a morality based upon natural religion, must have further unsettled Twain's wavering Presbyterianism.

Still another influence was his associations with the Freemasons. In 1861 Twain became a member of the Ancient, Free and Accepted Order of Masons, affiliating with the Polar Star Lodge Number 79 of St. Louis, the largest in the State. He rose rapidly in the ranks and soon became a Master Mason. As a Freemason, Twain was introduced to Deistic ideas which supplemented those gleaned from the writings of Tom Paine. The basic doctrine of the order was that all organized religions are mere sects, containing distorted versions of a universal Truth once held by all mankind. Christianity was merely one of these sects. This reduction of all religions to the same level was unquestionably significant in the formation of Twain's later attitudes. ("It is not the ability to reason that makes the Presbyterian, or the Baptist, or the Methodist, or the Catholic, or the Mohammedan, or the Buddhist, or the Mormon," he wrote years later, "it is the environment.") Likewise, the Freemason's concept of God is one which appears frequently in Twain's later works. ("The Being who is to me the real God," he wrote in 1898, "is the One who created this majestic universe and rules it. . . . His real character is written in plain words in his real Bible, which is Nature and her history.")

In 1869 Twain fell in love with Olivia Langdon. Although hardly a product of the orthodox Protestantism which he had rejected — the Langdons were pillars of the Park Church in Elmira, New York, whose minister, Thomas K. Beecher, was a leading exponent of liberal Protestantism — Olivia had been brought up in a distinctly religious climate. In his anxiety to win her parents' blessing for their marriage, Twain devised what Dixon Wecter calls a "lover's gambit." Livy was to assist him in finding his way back to the fold of religion, and he was to prove to her that his black sheep days were over by his efforts to acquire her religious feeling. Whether or not he was sincere, he was certainly not successful in equaling her faith. He wrote to her during the courtship:

I thank you for all you say, for everything you say, about religion, Livy, and I have as much confidence as yourself that I shall succeed at last, but oh, it is slow and often discouraging. I am happy in conducting myself rightly — but the emotion, the revealing religious emotion, Livy, will not come, it seems to me. I pray for it — it is all I can do. I know not how to *compel* an emotion. And I pray every day that you may not be impatient or lose confidence in my final conversion. I pray that you may keep your courage and be of good heart. And I pray that my poisonous and besetting *apathy* may pass from me. It is hard to be a Christian in *spirit*, Livy, though the mere letter of the law seems not very difficult as a general thing. I have hope.

It seemed for a while that both Livy's and Twain's efforts had succeeded: she in making a Christian out of him again and he in marrying her. Three days after their marriage, Twain informed his mother: "She [Livy] said she never could or would love me — but she set herself the task of making a Christian out of me. I said she would succeed but that in the meantime she would unwittingly dig a matrimonial pit & end by tumbling into it — & lo! the prophecy is fulfilled." A day later, writing to Will

Bowen, he admitted having succumbed to his bride's efforts to alter his religious thinking: "[Her] beautiful life is ordered by a religion that is all kindliness and unselfishness. Before the gentle majesty of her purity all evil things & evil deeds stand abashed, — then surrender."

For a time after their marriage, Twain attempted to observe the forms of Christian worship. He joined his wife in saying family prayers, repeating grace at table, and reading aloud daily from the Bible. But it is clear from his own description that it was all an effort:

Behold then Samuel L. Clemens — now become for everybody Mark Twain, the great American humorist — the rough days of his western life put behind him, settled down at number 472 Delaware Avenue, Buffalo, trying hard to be respectable. Here he lives the model life of a family man, joins in morning prayer and listens as best he can to the daily reading of the Scriptures. More than that, he even makes desperate efforts to give up smoking.

He has his wife at his side, his desk at his elbow, and the world at his feet. After all, what does tobacco matter? Let's have another chapter of Deuteronomy.

It obviously could not last. Twain's reasoning would not permit him to accept the Bible as a guide to spiritual salvation. He erupted into sudden and candid repudiation, saying to Olivia one day: "Livy you may keep this up if you want to, but I must ask you to excuse me from it. It is making me a hypocrite. I don't believe in this Bible. It contradicts my reason. I can't sit here and listen to it, letting you believe that I regard it, as you do, in the light of Gospel, the word of God." In the end it was not Twain's but Livy's beliefs that changed. That the transformation began early is shown by a letter she wrote to her husband in December, 1871: "It is so long since I have been to church. ... I did not tell her [Mrs. Warner] how almost perfectly cold I am toward God." Eight years later, she admitted to Susan Crane, her adopted sister, that she had ceased to believe in a personal God.

Twain's daughters did not attend Sunday School, and

Susy, at five, told a visitor once that she "had been in a church only once, and that was the day Bay [her sister Clara] was crucified [christened]." Though Twain rented a pew at the Asylum Hill Congregational Church in Hartford, he never joined the congregation as a formal member. While the family attended services, and Twain himself participated actively in the secular programs sponsored by the Church, he did so mainly because it was part of the social life of the community. Despite his close friendship with Reverend Joseph H. Twichell, pastor of the Church, and his respect for his "ethical convictions," nothing that he heard at the services retarded Twain's rapid return to the religious views he had held prior to his marriage. By 1873 he was referring to himself as "an entire & absolute unbeliever." In 1878 he said to Twichell: "Joe ... I'm going to make a confession. I don't believe in your religion at all. I've been living a lie right straight along whenever I pretended to. For a moment, sometimes, I have been almost a believer, but it immediately drifts away from me again."

In 1887, in an unpublished comment in his notebook, Twain indicated that his position was the same as he had outlined in his letter to Orion back in 1860: "I cannot see how man of any large degree of humorous perception can ever be religious — except he purposely shut the eyes of his mind & keep them shut by force." At about this time, he presented his creed in detail:

I believe in God the Almighty.

I do not believe He has ever sent a message to man by anybody, or delivered one to him by word of mouth, or made Himself visible to mortal eyes at any time in any place.

I believe that the Old and New Testaments were imagined and written by man, and that no line in them was authorized by God, much less inspired by Him.

I think the goodness, the justice, and the mercy of God are manifested in His works: I perceive that they are manifested toward me in this life; the logical conclusion is that they will be manifested toward me in the life to come, if there should be one.

I do not believe in special providences. I believe that the universe is governed by strict and immutable laws. If one man's family is swept away by a pestilence and another man's spared it is only the law working: God is not interfering in that small matter, either against the one man or in favor of the other.

I cannot see how eternal punishment hereafter could accomplish any good end, therefore I am not able to believe in it. To chasten a man in order to perfect him might be reasonable enough; to annihilate him when he shall have proved himself incapable of reaching perfection might be reasonable enough; but to roast him forever for the mere satisfaction of seeing him roast would not be reasonable — even the atrocious God imagined by the Jews would tire of the spectacle eventually.

There may be a hereafter and there may *not* be. I am wholly indifferent about it. If I am appointed to live again I feel sure it will be for some more sane and useful purpose than to flounder about for ages in a lake of fire and brimstone for having violated a confusion of ill-defined and contradictory rules said (but not evidenced) to be of divine institution. If annihilation is to follow death I shall not be aware of the annihilation, and therefore shall not care a straw about it.

I believe that the world's moral laws are the outcome of the world's experience. It needed no God to come down out of heaven to tell men that murder and theft and the other immoralities were bad, both for the individual who commits them and for society which suffers from them.

If I break all these moral laws I cannot see how I injure God by it, for He is beyond the reach of injury from me — I could as easily injure a planet by throwing mud at it. It seems to me that my misconduct could only injure me and other men. I cannot benefit God by obeying these moral laws — I could as easily benefit the planet by withholding my mud. (Let these sentences be read in the light of the fact that I believe I have received moral laws *only* from man — none whatever from God.) Consequently I do not see why I should be either punished or rewarded hereafter for the deeds I do here.

Clear though this exposition is, it is necessary to turn to the bulk of Twain's writings (including those which his wife dissuaded him from publishing) to understand his religious views fully.

The earliest of these is in a letter which Twain wrote to the Muscatine *Journal* in 1855, less than two years after he left Hannibal. Already we can see his contempt for clergymen who forgot immediate social reality and fixed their eyes instead on distant lands:

A widow woman with five children, destitute of money, half starved and almost naked, reached this city [St. Louis] yesterday from somewhere in Arkansas, and were on their way to join some relatives in Illinois. They had suffered dreadfully from cold and fatigue during their journey, and were truly objects of charity. The sight brought to mind the handsome sum our preacher collected in church last Sunday to obtain food and raiment for the poor, ignorant heathen in some part of the world; I thought, too, of the passage in the Bible instructing the disciples to carry their good works into all the world — *beginning first at Jerusalem.*

This critical view of church practices became increasingly more pronounced. It first took the form of lampoons against the traditional Sunday School book concept of behaviour, expressed in moralizing tales for children in which "the good little boy . . . always went to Heaven and the bad little boys . . . invariably got drowned on Sundays." Twain found them "pretty dreary books," and he resolved early to demolish the "model boy" of the Sunday School tale. He accomplished this in a series of sketches, written in 1863 and 1865, entitled "Stories for Good Little Boys and Girls," "The Story of the Good Little Boy Who Did Not Prosper," and "The Story of the Bad Little Boy Who Did Not Come to Grief." Jacob, the good little boy, "always obeyed his parents, no matter how absurd and unreasonable their demands were; and he always learned his book, and never was late at Sabbath-school." Unlike other boys in the community, Jacob did not play hooky, nor lie, nor play marbles on Sunday, nor rob birds' nests, nor give hot pennies to organ grinders' monkeys. The other boys, unable to understand the reason for Jacob's strange conduct, concluded that he was "afflicted."

The explanation for Jacob's conduct is his hopeless infatuation with Sunday School tracts. They were his "greatest delights," and his sole ambition was "to be put in a Sunday-School book. He wanted to be put in, with pictures representing him gloriously declining to lie to his mother, and her weeping for joy about it; and pictures representing him standing on the doorstep giving a penny to a poor beggar-woman with six children, and telling her to spend it freely, but not to be extravagant, because extravagance is a sin." Jacob knew that "it was not healthy to be good." All the Sunday School book heroes die in the last chapter, and he lives obsessed with thoughts of death. He decides to live right, hang on as long as he could, and he has his dying speech all ready. Meanwhile, he seeks to do good in order to perfect his soul, and, according to the Sunday School tracts, win the gratitude of his fellow men.

Jacob does do good, but all he reaps is misfortune. "When he found Jim Blake stealing apples, and went under the tree to read to him about the bad little boy who fell out of a neighbor's apple tree and broke his arm, Jim fell out of the tree, too, but he fell on *him* and broke *his* arm, and Jim wasn't hurt at all." He helps the blind man whom bad boys have pushed, and the blind man whacks *him* with his stick by mistake. He brings home a "hungry and persecuted" dog so that he can have "that dog's imperishable gratitude," and after he has fed him and was going to pet him, "the dog flew at him and tore all the clothes off him except those that were in front, and made a spectacle of him that was astonishing."

These mishaps astound Jacob. According to the tracts he should have been rewarded for his goodness; yet he only knows pain and ingratitude. The dog's conduct is especially puzzling. "It was of the same breed of dogs that was in the books, but it acted differently." Still his faith in the books is not diminished. He determines to go out into the world and earn an honest living. He examines his books and decides that the best course for a good boy was to ship out as cabin boy. As a recommendation, he shows the captain a Bible tract endorsed with the words, "To Jacob Blivens, from his affectionate teacher."

But the captain was a coarse, vulgar man, and he said, "Oh, that be blowed! *that* wasn't any proof that he knew how to wash dishes or handle a slush-bucket, and he guessed he didn't want him." This was altogether the most extraordinary thing that ever happened to Jacob all his life. A compliment from a teacher, on a tract, had never failed to move the honor and profit in their gift. . . .

Only the thought of a romantic death while performing an act of goodness now sustains Jacob. He does die in his next adventure, but it is hardly the anticipated romantic ending. He tries to keep bad boys from tying tin cans to some dogs. An alderman appears on the scene; the bad boys run off, but Jacob is swatted by the alderman who sets off a container of nitroglycerine, and sends the dogs, Jacob and himself to kingdom come.

In sharp contrast to what happened to sinful little boys in Sunday School books, Twain demonstrates that in real life they not only enjoy doing prohibited things but are rewarded for them. The bad boy of Twain's story climbs the tree to steal apples, and torments the dog. Yet he is the boy who gets the job with the sea captain, and ends up wealthy. Although he becomes "the infernalist wickedest scoundrel in his native village, [he] is universally respected, and belongs to the legislature."

Twain was by no means the first to poke fun at the drooling Sunday School tales, but went so far beyond the others in the effectiveness of his satire that Howells was deterred fom printing the sketches in the *Atlantic* for fear they would cost him the bulk of his subscribers. "The public wouldn't stand that sort of thing," Twain recalled later. The pieces were published in Western journals.

These early sketches contain, of course, the germ of

Tom Sawyer with its expanded tale about a bad little boy who ends up rich. Tom Sawyer pilfers, deceives Aunt Polly, plays hooky, and licks the model boy of the village. In the famous white-washing scene, Tom acquires his playmates' treasures, and tricks them into doing his chore besides, having discovered the "great law of human action ... that in order to make a man or boy covet a thing, it is only necessary to make the thing difficult to obtain." Worse still, the next morning at Sunday School the young sinner trades off his ill-gotten licorice, fish-hooks, and other profits, for blue and yellow tickets which certify his memorization of 2,000 Biblical verses, and qualify him for a Bible. Tom continues to sin, has a glorious time at it, and winds up with a half share in $12,000 of buried treasure.

Twain's scoffing at the dreary Sunday School tales is one expression of his dislike of the holier-than-thou Sabbath atmosphere. In a sketch reporting San Francisco's "new wildcat" religion of Spiritualism, he derides the boring Presbyterian church service:

> We get up of a Sunday morning and put on the best harness ... and enter the church; we stand up and duck our heads and bear down on a hymn book propped on the pew in front when the minister prays; we stand up again while our hired choir are singing, and look in the hymn book and check off the verses to see that they don't shirk any of the stanzas; we sit silent and grave while the minister is preaching, and count the waterfalls and bonnets furtively, and catch flies; we grab our hats and bonnets when the benediction is begun; when it is finished, we shove off, so to speak.

The life had departed out of the Presbyterian Sabbath, in which "good" church people go through the motions listessly, while they do lip service to a creed that promised "limitless fire and brimstone and thinned the predestined elect down to a company so small as to be hardly worth saving."

This dislike of the Sabbath atmosphere is sharply reflected in *The Innocents Abroad*, particularly in the original *Alta California* letters later revised for inclusion in the book, describing a group of fellow passengers embarked on a pilgrimage to the Holy Land. These Pilgrims refuse to set out to sea because of a storm and because they "could not properly begin a pleasure excursion on Sunday." The first day of the cruise is, therefore, spent in repetitions of church and prayer-meetings. Later, he excoriates the fanaticism of the Pilgrims who are ready to sacrifice everything in order to avoid breaking the Sabbath:

Properly, with the sorry relics we bestrode, it was a three days' journey to Damascus. It was necessary that we should do it in less than two. It was necessary because our three pilgrims would not travel on the Sabbath day, but there are times when to keep the *letter* of a sacred law whose spirit is righteous, becomes a sin, and this was a case in point. We pleaded for the tired, ill-treated horses, and tried to show that their faithful service deserved kindness in return, and their hard lot compassion. But when did ever self-righteousness know the sentiment of pity? What were a few long hours added to the hardships of some overtaxed brutes when weighted against the peril of those human souls? ... We said the Saviour, who pitied dumb beasts and taught that the ox must be rescued from the mire even on the Sabbath day, would not have counseled a forced march like this. We said the "long trip" was exhausting and therefore dangerous in the blistering heats of summer, even when the ordinary days' stages were traversed, and if we persisted in this hard march, some of us might be stricken down with the fevers of the country in consequence of it. Nothing could move the pilgrims. They *must* press on. Men might die, horses might die, but they must enter upon holy soil next week, with no Sabbath-breaking stain upon them. Thus they were willing to commit a sin against the spirit of religious law, in order that they might preserve the letter of it.

The Pious Hypocrites

In his *Autobiography* Twain refers to William Anderson Moffett who married his sister, Pamela, as "a fine man in every way." Moffett seldom went to church because he could not "bear to hear people talk piously on Sunday and cheat on pork on the middle of the week." Nothing disgusted Twain more than the conduct of so many of the wealthy pewholders at the Asylum Hill Congregational Church — the "Church of the Holy Speculators" he dubbed it — who spewed profit-seeking and Christian ideals in the same breath.

Twain had only scorn for John Wanamaker's work for the Bethany Sunday School (Presbyterian) which the Department Store tycoon founded in 1858: "Those two unspeakable shams, buttermouthed hypocrites, John Wanamaker & his Sunday School Times." Wanamaker saw no inconsistency in paying his female employees so poorly that many were forced into prostitution to supplement their meagre earnings, but to Twain the exposure of these conditions came as no surprise. He labeled the smug hypocrisies of the wealthy Sunday School patrons "as the John Wanamaker grade."

In this category Twain placed the Sunday School work of John D. Rockefeller, the multimillionaire Standard Oil monopolist who had crushed thousands of small businessmen and said God gave him the money he extracted from his competitors. "Satan twaddling sentimental silliness to a Sunday-School," Twain wrote in an unpublished portion of his *Autobiography*, "could be no burlesque upon John D. Rockefeller and his performances in his Cleveland Sunday-School. When John D. is employed in that way he strikes the utmost limit of grotesqueness. He can't be burlesqued — he is himself a burlesque."

In the unpublished story, "The International Lightning Trust," Twain cleverly satirized the type of Christianity represented by Wanamaker and Rockefeller in their Sunday School work. Two partners, Steve and Jasper, have built a gigantic trust in the lightning protection insurance field. Discussing the reasons for their success, Jasper attributes it all to "Providence" which has watched over them from the beginning. Steve, however, is not satisfied:

"Oh, I know it! I know all that; I know we deserve well; I know our sacrifices for the poor & the bereaved are observed by Providence; still my conscience is not at rest. I have no peace of mind these days."

"Why, Steve?"

"Because we do so much lying. Providence is noticing *that*, too, you may be sure & it will do us a damage!"

This thought went deep, & it made Jasper tremble. He had not thought of this. It sobered him. He remembered with pain that only the last Sabbath, in instructing his Bible class he had dwelt with feeling & impressiveness upon the sinfulness of lying, & now he was himself found guilty. He realized, with shame, that every new circular he issued contained fresh lies — lies essential to prosperity & expansion in the business, it was true, but lies all the same; he realized that the size of these lies was getting bigger & bigger with every new output & the thought of it made his cheek burn. He saw clearly that in contriving these unholy inventions he was imperilling his salvation, & he spoke up with decision, & said —

"I stop it right here. I will no longer soil my soul with it; we must hire a liar."

Steve responded with strong emotion —

"Oh, thank you for those blessed words, they heal my heart, & it was so sore, so wounded! Our sin removed, our purity restored, we are our own true selves again, dear Jasper, & I know there is rejoicing in heaven over this reform. I shall sleep again, now, as of yore, & be at peace, as knowing the approving angels are watching over me. Jasper, I am hungry to begin anew — have you thought of anyone for the place?"

Several names were mentioned & discussed, experts of known ability, all of them: interviewers, fishermen, big-game hunters, & such-like, but no decision was arrived at. In the end it was decided to call in twenty or thirty professionals & submit the prize to a competition. A man who had been trained by the inventor of the Keeley motor got the position.

In the remarkable "Letter from the Recording Angel," probably written in 1887, and originally planned for inclusion in *A Connecticut Yankee in King Arthur's Court,* Twain effectively ripped the mask off the pious hypocrisy of the "Holy Speculators." He shows the difference between selfish private prayers ("Secret Supplications of the

Heart") and unctuous, benevolent public prayers "uttered in Prayer Meeting, Sunday School Class Meeting, Family Worship, etc." The target is Andrew Langdon, the Buffalo coal dealer and uncle of Twain's wife. In a letter addressed to Langdon from the Office of the Recording Angel, Department of Petitions, the coal dealer is informed of the rulings on his private and public prayers for an entire week. The private prayers are dealt with first:

1. For weather to advance hard coal 15 cents per ton. Granted.
2. For influx of laborers to reduce wages 10 per cent. Granted.
3. For a break in rival soft coal prices. Granted.
4. For a visitation upon the man, or upon the family of the man, who has set up a competing retail coal-yard in Rochester. Granted, as follows: diphtheria, 2, 1 fatal; scarlet fever, 1, to result in deafness and imbecility.

Langdon's prayer for an increase in profits from $22,230 for December to $45,000 for January was also granted and the Recording Angel agreed to "perpetuate a proportionate monthly increase thereafter." Having granted these and other private prayers, the Angel rejects most of Langdon's public prayers on the grounds that they are in conflict with the Secret Supplications of the Heart. By "a rigid rule of this office, certain sorts of Public Prayers of Professional Christians are forbidden to take precedence of Secret Supplications of the Heart." Thus Langdon's public prayer "for weather mercifully tempered to the needs of the poor and naked" is denied because it is in conflict with private prayer, no. 1; his public prayer for better times and plentier food "for the hard-handed son of toil whose patient and exhausting labors make comfortable the homes and pleasant the ways, of the more fortunate" is denied as being in conflict with private prayer, no. 2. Of the 464 requests mentioned in Langdon's public prayers, only two are granted. One asked that "the clouds may continue to perform their office," and the other asked the same for the sun. "It was the divine purpose anyhow; it will gratify you to know that you have not disturbed it," the Angel explains.

The Angel adds a note of his own to the report:

When certain sorts of people do a sizeable good deed, we credit them up a thousand-fold more for it than we would in the case of a better man — on account of the strain. You stand far away above, your classification-record here shows because of certain self-sacrifices of yours which greatly exceed what could have been expected of you. Years ago, when you were worth only $100,000 and sent $2 to your impoverished cousin the widow when she appealed to you for help, there were many in heaven who were not able to believe it, and many more who believed that the money was counterfeit. Your character went up many degrees when it was shown that these suspicions were unfounded. A year or two later, when you sent the poor girl $4 in answer to another appeal, everybody believed it, and you were all the talk here for days together. Two years later you sent $6, upon supplication, when the widow's youngest child died, and that act made perfect your good fame. ... Your increasing donation, every two or three years, has kept your name on all lips, and warm in all hearts. All heaven watches you Sundays, as you drive to church in your handsome carriage; and when your hand retires from the contribution plate, the glad shout is heard even to the ruddy walls of remote Sheol, "Another nickel from Andrew!"

But the climax came a few days ago, when the widow wrote and said she could get a school in a far village to teach if she had $50 to get herself and her two surviving children over the long journey; and you counted up last month's clear profit from your three coal mines — $22,230 — and added to it the certain profit for the current month — $45,000 and a possible fifty — and then got down your pen and your check-book and mailed her fifteen whole dollars! Ah, Heaven bless and keep you forever and ever, generous heart! There was not a dry eye in the realms of bliss; and amidst the hand-shakings, and embracings, and praisings, the decree was thundered forth from the shining mount, that this deed should out-honor all the historic self-sacrifices of men and angels, and be recorded by itself upon a page of its own, for that the strain of it upon you had been heavier and bitterer than the strain it costs ten thousand martyrs to yield up their lives at the fiery stake.

Though the "Letter From the Recording Angel" remained in manuscript form throughout Twain's lifetime, its essential theme — that outward religious piety often hid greed — was made clear in his great story, "The Man That Corrupted Hadleyburg," published in 1899.

In a reputedly incorruptible town, which proudly advertises its "fine old reputation" for piety, honesty, and integrity, and prays that its "example would now spread far and wide over the American world, and be epoch-making in the matter of moral regeneration," nineteen leading citizens readily succumb when tempted. Each of the representative families perjures itself, in the very sanctity of the church, and at the very moment when the town's boasted incorruptibility was on display.

In his tale, Twain draws a real distinction between organized religion and Christianity, presenting a marvelous satire on Christian hypocrisy and social cant. "The weakest of all weak things," he notes, "is a virtue which has not been tested in fire." Through one of the villagers he develops this thesis:

It's been one everlasting training and training and training in honesty — honesty shielded from the very cradle, against every possible temptation, and so it's *artificial* honesty, and weak as water when temptation comes.... It is my belief that this town's honesty is as rotten as mine is.... It is a mean town, a hard, stingy town, and hasn't a virtue in the world but this honesty it is so celebrated for and so conceited about; and so help me, I do believe that if ever the day comes that its honesty falls under great temptation, its grand reputation will go to ruin like a house of cards.

The *artificial honesty* is illustrated in the successful efforts of the villagers to salve their consciences. One very religious couple who permitted an innocent man, whom they might have saved, to be indicted, are relieved of any sense of shame or feeling of guilt when they learn that he does not suspect their betrayal. The wife exclaims: "Oh ... I am glad of that! As long as he doesn't know that you could have saved him, he — he — well, that makes it a great deal better."

Throughout the tale Twain mocks an artificial, untried piety, and advocates omitting the negative in the line of the Lord's Prayer: "Lead us not into temptation." He urges the pious, smug moralists, with their shallow, hypocritical rectitude, "to request that they be led into temptation, rather than away from it, in order that they might make their moral fibre strong enough through use instead of rotten through inactivity." He was thus reaffirming the creed of John Milton, who had written almost three hundred years before: "I cannot praise a fugitive and cloistered virtue unexercised and unbreathed, that never sallies out and seeks her adversary but slinks out of the race, where the immortal garland is to be run for, not without dust and heat."

In an unpublished comment in his notebook, set down about the time he was writing "The Man That Corrupted Hadleyburg," Twain indicated the chief lesson of the story: "The Land of Cant. That is always a land where the great bulk of the people are sincerely religious." Sincerity in religion was not enough; it nurtured hypocrites, not truly religious people. What was needed was a religion which would create people willing to act in public life on the religious principles they professed in private life. "There are Christian Private Morals," Twain noted, "but there are no Christian Public Morals." He called upon all citizens "to throw away their public morals and use none but their private ones henceforth in all their activities."

The Venal Clergy

The representatives of the clergy who drew Twain's sharpest satire were those who showed more interest in cash than in converts. As early as 1865, Twain pointedly attacked the venal clergy through an imaginary exchange of letters in two issues of the *Californian* with three ministers from New York, Philadelphia and Chicago regarding a call to the post at Grace Church in San Francisco. Twain depicted himself as willing to be "helpful" in the matter even though he was not a member of the congregation. His action is motivated solely by conscience: "What I have done in the matter I did of my own free will and accord, without any solicitation from anybody, and my actions were dictated solely by a spirit of enlarged charity and good feeling toward the congregation of Grace Cathedral. I seek no reward for my services; I desire none but the approval of my own conscience and the satisfaction of knowing I have done that which I conceived to be my duty, to the best of my ability." His first letter is to the Reverend Bishop Hawks of New York who has just rejected an offer to come to Grace Cathedral for $7,000 a year. He advises the Bishop to

say nothing to anybody — keep dark — but just pack up your traps and come along out here — I will see that it is all right. That $7000 dodge was only a *bid* — nothing more. They never expected you to clinch a bargain like that. I will go to work and get up a little competition among the cloth, and the result of it will be that you will make more money in six months here than you would in New York in a year. I can do it. I have a great deal of influence with the clergy here ... I can get them to strike for higher wages any time.

Twain must have known that his suggestion of a clerical strike for higher wages would horrify Bishop Hawks. It was a time when "Protestantism presented a massive, almost unbroken front in its defense of the social *status quo*." Protestant clergymen not only did not strike; they condemned all strikes as illegal, and a violation of economic law. The *Congregationalist*, a Boston weekly, expressed prevailing Protestant opinion when it recommended lowering wages to "the lowest attainable point," and condemned a strike as "akin to violence in its very seminal idea."

Continuing the letter, Twain describes for Bishop

Hawks how easy the work would be at Grace Cathedral. The West is a haven of sin, and "the flattest old sermon a man can grind out is bound to corral half a dozen [sinners]. ... Bring along a barrel of your old obsolete sermons; the people here will never know the difference." And as for the money, Bishop Hawks need have no concern:

... don't you fret about the salary. I'll make *that* all right, you know. ... You can depend upon me. I'll see you through this business as straight as a shingle; I haven't been drifting around all my life for nothing. ... And although I am not of the elect, so to speak, I take a strong interest in these things, nevertheless, and I am not going to stand by and see them come to any seven-thousand-dollar arrangement over you. I have sent them word in your name that you won't take less than $18,000 and that you can get $25,000 in greenbacks at home.

Thus Twain reduces the spiritual pretensions of the man of God to the cash denominator. And Bishop Hawks, in his letter of reply, though rejecting the offer, talks the same language. In an unctuous, yet down-to-earth tone, he writes: "I see that you understand how it is with us poor laborers in the vine-yard, and feel for us in our struggles to gain a livelihood. ... My refusal of the position at $7,000 a year was not precisely meant to be final, but was intended for what the ungodly term a 'flyer' — the object being, of course, to bring about an increase of the amount." Although he is not able to accept the position, the offer has been useful: "The timely arrival of the 'call' from San Francisco insured success to me. The people appreciated my merits at once." His New York congregation hurried to raise the bid to $10,000, and promised to purchase for him "The Church of St. George the Martyr, up town."

I closed with them on these terms, My dear Mark, for I feel that so long as not even the little sparrows are suffered to fall to the ground unnoted, I shall be mercifully cared for! and besides, I know that come what may I can always eke out an existence so

187

long as the cotton trade holds as good as it is now. I am in cotton to some extent, you understand, and that is one reason why I cannot leave here just at present. . . . You see I have some small investments in that line which are as yet in an undecided state, and must be looked after.

Twain commends Dr. Hawks for having followed the example of a shrewd Wall Street stock speculator. The Bishop, he notes approvingly, "is not going to take his chances altogether with St. George — the — Martyr-er — he has a judicious eye on cotton. And he is right, too. Nobody deserves to be helped who don't try to help himself, and 'faith without works' is a risky doctrine." Twain concludes the first half of the sketch with the promise to publish his correspondence with the other two clergymen the following week. But by then they had refused to have their letters published. Both Reverend Phillip Brooks and Cummings telegraph Twain declining the post in San Francisco because they were making money in their pastorates, and because their respective investments required their constant attention. Reverend Brooks, Twain explains, is "in petroleum to some extent, also," and the other is "speculating a little in grain."

As a result of the published offer, a flood of applicants descends upon Twain. He prints one letter from this "swarm of low-priced back-country preachers," some of whom offer to come at "any price": "I feel that I am 'called,' and it is not for me, an humble instrument to disobey. : : : It stirs the deepest emotion in my breast to think that I shall soon leave my beloved flock: . . . for I have reared this dear flock, and tendered it for years, and I fed it with spiritual food, and sheared it — ah, me, and sheared it — I cannot go on — the subject is too harrowing."

In his "Important Correspondence" concerning the post at the Grace Cathedral, Twain records his belief that the clergy do not live up to the Christian standards they profess. Money motivates their conduct just as it does other men of influence and power. Godliness was in alliance with wealth, and too many clergymen made business values the criterion of religious conduct. Although the "Correspondence" was imaginary, the press of the period carried sufficient reports of the adoption of "business ethics" by clergymen to give it reality.

Twain had no tolerance for snobbery of any kind, but nothing infuriated him more than religious snobbery. He wrote a caustic piece publicly denouncing a Reverend Mr. Sabine, who declined to hold church burial services for an old actor, as a "crawling, slimy, sanctimonious, self-righteous reptile." In a biting satire, "About Smells," he took Reverend T. De Witt Talmage of Brooklyn to task for closing his church to working people because of their bad smell. "I have a good Christian friend," Talmage wrote in defense of his action in *The Independent*, a religious weekly, "who, if he sat in the front pew in church, and a working man should enter the door at the other end, would smell him instantly. My friend is not to blame for the sensitiveness of his nose, any more than you would flog a pointer for being keener on the scent than a stupid watchdog. The fact is, if you had all the churches free, by reason of the mixing up of the common people with the uncommon, you would keep one-half of Christendom sick at their stomach. If you are going to kill the church thus with bad smells, I will have nothing to do with this work of evangelization."

To do justice to Twain's comment we must reprint it in full:

We have reason to believe that there will be laboring men in heaven; and also a number of negroes, and Esquimaux, and Terra del Fuegans, and Arabs, and a few Indians, and possibly even some Spaniards and Portuguese. All things are possible with God. We shall have all these sorts of people in heaven; but alas! in getting them we shall lose the society of Dr. Talmage. Which is to say, we shall lose the company of one who could give more real "tone" to celestial society than any other contribution Brooklyn could furnish. And what would eternal happiness be without the Doctor?

Blissful, unquestionably — we know that well enough — but would it be *distingué*, would it be *recherché* without him? St. Matthew without stockings or sandals; St. Jerome bareheaded, and with a coarse brown blanket robe dragging the ground; St. Sebastian with scarcely any raiment at all — these we should see, and should enjoy seeing them; but would we not miss a spike-tailed coat and kids, and turn away regretfully, and say to parties from the Orient: "These are well enough, but you ought to see Talmage of Brooklyn." I fear me that in the better world we shall not even have Dr. Talmage's "good Christian friend." For if he were sitting under the glory of the Throne, and the keeper of the keys admitted a Benjamin Franklin or other laboring man, that "friend," with his fine natural powers infinitely augmented by emancipation from hampering flesh, would detect him with a single sniff, and immediately take his hat and ask to be excused.

To all outward seeming, the Rev. T. De Witt Talmage is of the same material as that used in the construction of his early predecessors in the ministry; and yet one feels that there must be a difference somewhere between him and the Saviour's first disciples. It may be because here, in the nineteenth century, Dr. T. has had advantages which Paul and Peter and the others could not and did not have. There was a lack of polish about them, and a looseness of etiquette, and a want of exclusiveness, which one cannot help noticing. They healed the very beggars, and held intercourse with people of a villainous odor every day. If the subject of these remarks had been among the original Twelve Apostles, he would not have associated with the rest, because he could not have stood the fishy smell of some of his comrades who came from around the Sea of Galilee. He would have resigned his commission with some such remark as he makes in the extract quoted above: "Master, if thou art going to kill the church thus with bad smells, I will have nothing to do with this work of evangelization." He is a disciple, and makes that remark to the Master; the only difference is, that he makes it in the nineteenth instead of the first century.

Is there a choir in Mr. T.'s church? And does it ever occur that they have no better manners than to sing that hymn which is so suggestive of laborers and mechanics:

> "Son of the Carpenter! receive
> This humble work of mine?"

Now, can it be possible that in a handful of centuries the Christian character has fallen away from an imposing heroism that scorned even the stake, the cross, and the axe, to a poor little effeminacy that withers and wilts under an unsavory smell? We are not prepared to believe so, the reverend Doctor and his friend to the contrary notwithstanding.

Tributes to Clergymen

As the concluding sentence implies, Twain did not engage in a blanket condemnation of all men of the cloth. Among clergymen who retained the "heroism" of the early "Christian character," he placed Reverend Thomas K. Beecher of Elmira, New York, who had been expelled from the Ministerial Union for having held services in a theatre. "Happy, happy world," Twain wrote in the Elmira *Advertiser*, "that knows at last that a little congress of congregationless clergymen, of whom it never heard before have crushed a famous Beecher and reduced his audiences from fifteen hundred down to fourteen hundred and seventy-five in one fell blow."

Twain endorsed Rev. Beecher's project for a model church providing rooms for a public library, social gatherings, family reunions, games and dances, and to which people of all creeds or no creed could come. "You will notice," Twain wrote approvingly, "in every feature of this new church one predominant idea and purpose discernable — the banding together of the congregation as a *family*, and the making of the church a home ... It is the great central, ruling idea."

Such efforts of representatives of the cloth to employ religion to help mankind to a freer, happier life always earned Twain's praise. The belief that the missionaries were working towards that end led him, at one time, to praise their activity in the Sandwich Islands as "pious, hard-working; hard-praying; self-sacrificing ... devoted to the well-being of this people." Later, he was to become one of the sharpest critics of the missionary movement, but in the period following his visit to the Sandwich Islands, his attitude, was, in the main, favorable. "The missionaries," he wrote in *Roughing It*, "have clothed them (the inhabitants of the islands), educated them, broken up the tyrannous authority of their chiefs, and given them freedom and the right to enjoy whatever their hands and brains produce, with equal laws for all, and punishment for all alike who transgress them." Twain had special praise for the role of the Catholic clergy in the Sandwich Islands. "The Catholic clergy," he wrote, "are honest, straightforward, frank and open; they are industrious and devoted to their religion and their work; they never meddle; whatever they do can be relied on as being prompted by a good and worthy motive."

It is quite clear that Twain did not lump all clergymen with Hawks, Brooks, Sabine, and Talmage. Clergymen were among his closest friends, and he went out of his way to make their acquaintance. For clergymen who preached and practiced a constructive, progressive religious doctrine, he had great praise, ranking them second only to the medical profession in the service of mankind.

The Catholic Church

Twain's praise of the Catholic clergy in the Sandwich Islands may come as a surprise to some, since Catholic critics have characterized him as an implacable enemy. One Catholic writer charges Twain with "habitual irreverence [toward the Catholic Church] ... blasphemous rhetoric and witty desecrations." Twain himself conceded, in *The Innocents Abroad*, that his relationship to the Roman Catholic Church was not "an entirely friendly one." "I have been educated to enmity toward everything that is Catholic, and sometimes, in consequence of this, I find it much easier to discover Catholic faults than Catholic merits."

In Twain's boyhood anti-Catholic sentiment was widespread and violent. Hannibal, not far from the Catholic stronghold of St. Louis, seethed with propaganda to the effect that the Pope was conspiring, through the American

Catholics, to destroy Protestantism and republican government in the United States.

Orion Clemens did not subscribe to this vicious propaganda. In his *Journal*, he even supported a building-fund appeal for a Catholic Church in Hannibal. But Orion did condemn the Catholic Church for its role in halting social progress. In an editorial entitled "Catholic rule," he wrote in 1853: "Wherever there is Catholic rule there is blight. ... Roman Catholic rule was beneficial in the Dark Ages, but politically it has served its time... during the last three centuries, her efforts have been aimed to stunt the growth of the human mind. Every advance in the freedom, knowledge and national wealth has been resisted by her where it was possible for resistance to be effectual. ... We do not attack the *Religion* of the Church of Rome, but her *politics*."

Twain was to voice much the same viewpoint in his writings, but with an important difference. While Orion regarded the Catholic Church as *the* stumbling block to social progress, Twain regarded *every* Church as such. During a visit to London he jotted in his notebook that "the church here rests under the usual charge — an obstructor and fighter of progress; until progress arrives, then she takes the credit." The Church — and by the "Church" Twain meant any form of institutionalized religion — had always lagged, had always condemned progress as heresy, had always retarded the advance of civilization; indeed, history proved that "whatever it opposes prospers — like anti-slavery and evolution."

When Twain left home in 1853, he took with him a hostility to "priestcraft,"which was to deepen when he reached Europe in the *Quaker City* excursion and found himself "in the heart and home of priestcraft — of a happy, cheerful, contented ignorance, superstition, degradation, poverty, indolence, and everlasting unaspiring worthlessness." When he gazed upon the shovel-hatted, long-robed, well-fed priests" all "fat and serene," he could think only of the miserable poverty of the Italian masses. In "priest-ridden Italy" he saw a land which "for fifteen hundred years, has turned all her energies, all her finances, and all her industry to the building up of a vast array of wonderful church edifices, and so starving half her citizens to accomplish it. She is today one vast museum of magnificence and misery. . . . It is the wretchedest, princeliest land on earth."

For the terrible poverty which surrounded its magnificent cathedrals, Twain condemned the Catholic Church, which was the largest property owner in the country. "All this country belongs to the Papal States," he wrote indignantly. When confiscation of church property began, he urged the citizens to speed up the process: "On, sons of classic Italy, *is* the spirit of enterprise, of self-reliance, of noble endeavor, utterly dead within ye? Curse your indolent worthlessness, why don't you rob your church?"

"I feel," Twain wrote in *The Innocents Abroad*, "that after talking so freely about the priests and the churches, justice demands that if I know anything good about either I ought to say it." And say it he did. Thus he noted that "there is one thing I feel no disposition to forget; and that is, the honest gratitude I and all pilgrims owe the Convent Fathers in Palestine." Their door was always open, and there was always a welcome for anyone who came "whether he comes in rags or clad in purple. . . . Our party, pilgrims and all, will always be willing to touch glasses and drink health, prosperity, and long life to the Convent Fathers of Palestine."

He was even more enthusiastic in his praise for the Dominican Friars in Italy:

. . . men who wear a coarse, heavy brown robe and a cowl, in this hot climate and go barefoot. They live on alms altogether, I believe. They must unquestionably love their religion, to suffer so much for it. When the cholera was raging in Naples; when the people were dying by hundreds and hundreds every day; when every concern for the public welfare was swallowed up in selfish private interest, and every citizen made the taking care of himself his sole object, these men banded themselves together and went about nurs-

194

ing the sick and burying the dead. Their noble efforts cost many of them their lives. They laid them down cheerfully and well they might. Creeds mathematically precise, and hair-splitting niceties of doctrine, are absolutely necessary for the salvation of some kinds of souls, but surely the charity, the purity, the unselfishness that are in the hearts of men like these would save their souls though they were bankrupt in the true religion.

This was, to Twain, the true essence of religion. It provides a key to his religious philosophy. The "charity, the purity, the unselfishness," that existed in the heart of good men and women would save their souls though they be "bankrupt" in traditional, orthodox religion. On such a basis any man or woman of good will could work out his or her own salvation, and to Twain it was unimportant whether the person was Presbyterian, Catholic, Jewish, or Moslem.

That Twain's respect for the humanitarian acts of individual Catholics and Catholic groups was lasting is shown by his immediate response in 1873 (a depression year), to Father Hawley's appeal for funds to aid people in Hartford who were starving. He offered to deliver a lecture free, and "to bear an equal proportion of whatever expenses were incurred by the committee of eight who agreed to join in forwarding the project." In 1910, the year of his death, he responded promptly to Mrs. Lathrop, who had asked him to contribute something to her periodical, *Christ's Poor*. He considered it a compliment to be invited to write for the periodical: "If there is one unassailably good cause in the world, it is the one undertaken by the Dominican Sisters of housing and nourishing the most pathetically unfortunate of all the afflicted among us — men and women sentenced to a painful and lingering death by incurable disease."

Critical though he was of certain Catholic practices, Twain never approved the stand taken by bigots who made the term Catholic synonymous with *evil*. In *A Tramp Abroad*, he describes "a rabid Protestant" who finds fault with everything Catholic. Twain tries to argue with him, but finally decides to let the matter drop, for "it was a waste of breath to argue with a bigot." While he himself could not accept Catholic dogma, he respected the right of others to believe in it, and extended this even to members of his own family. In a touching letter to his wife in the early 1890's, he wrote of his daughter that he was "very, very glad that Jean is in a convent. And away deep down in my heart I feel that if they make a good strong unshakable Catholic out of her I shan't be in the least bit sorry."

Twain had indeed traveled far from the early days in Hannibal when he had been "educated to enmity toward everything that is Catholic." But he never surrendered his contempt for the priests who lived off the poverty of the people. Two entries in his unpublished notebooks for 1897 reveal his unchanging attitude: "Salzburg. Sept. 24 '97. From the din of unpleasant church bells it woud seem that this village of 27,600 people is made up mainly of churches. Money represents labor, sweat, weariness. And that is what these useless churches have cost these people & are still costing them to support the useless priests & monks." Five months later, he wrote: "The priesthood and church impoverishes a people by propagating ignorance, superstition & slavery among them, & then godifies itself for its fine & noble work in furnishing crumbs of relief, procured by begging — not from its own coffers but from the pockets of the paupers it has created."

The Established Church

Twain's criticism of the Catholic Church as an institution was closely interrelated with a theme which had been maturing in his mind for some years — the evils of an established church. Its beginnings are abundantly evident in *The Innocents Abroad*, and the theme recurs in his other writings, mainly in brief comments such as the following note on the founding of Kamehameha's empire in Honolulu: "He destroyed His Established Church, and his kingdom is a republic today, in consequences of that act." It is in *A Connecticut Yankee in King Arthur's Court* that he developed his ideas on the subject in greatest detail.

Although he uses the Roman Catholic Church as his example in the book, Twain's quarrel was, in reality, with any church that might say: "The Church giveth law to all; and what she wills to do, that she may do, hurt whom it may." It was his firm conviction that any Established Church is an established crime, an established slave-pen." He made it clear that his attack was leveled upon all such churches, not merely the Roman Catholic:

One of the men had ten children; and he said that last year when a priest came and of his ten pigs took the fattest one for tithes, the wife burst out upon him, and offered him a child and said:

"Thou beast without bowels of mercy, why leave my child, yet rob me of the wherewithal to feed it?"

How curious. The same thing had happened in the Wales of my day, under the same old Established Church, which was supposed to have changed its nature when it changed its disguise.

Again, in another passage, the Yankee, speaking for Twain, points out: "Why, in my own former days — in remote centuries not yet stirring in the womb of time — there were old Englishmen who imagined that they had been born in a free country: a 'free' country with the Corporation Act and the Test still in force in it — timbers propped against men's liberties and dishonored conscience to shore up an Established Anachronism with."

The Yankee admits that religion is necessary, but he proposes to limit its threat to the State by encouraging a wide variety of sects: "Concentration of power in a political machine is bad; and an Established Church is only a political machine; it was invented for that; it is nursed, cradled, preserved for that; it is an enemy to human liberty, and does no good which it could not better do in a split-up and scattered condition." A highly unified religion would mean only a repetition of life under the Established

197

Church. Hence, although the Yankee hoped "to overthrow the Catholic Church and set up the Protestant faith on its ruins," this new faith was specifically to be organized "not as an Established Church, but as a go-as-you-please one." Education would be completely divorced from religion: "But I confined public religious teaching to the churches and the Sunday-Schools, permitting nothing of it in my other educational buildings."

The Yankee considers decreeing that everyone must be a Presbyterian — his own sect — but he decides against it. For one thing, he knows that "a man is only at his best, morally, when he is equipped with the religious garment whose color and shape and size most nicely accommodate themselves to the spiritual complexion, angularities, and stature of the individual who wears it." More important: "I was afraid of a United Church; it makes a mighty Power, the mightiest conceivable, and then when it by and by gets into selfish hands, as it is always bound to do, it means death to human liberty and paralysis to human thought." The "poor ostensible freemen" of King Arthur's realm inform the Yankee that "it hadn't even occurred to them that a nation could be so situated so that every man *could* have a say in the government." The Yankee's reply to this voices one of the main themes in the book: "I said I had seen one — and that it would last until it had an Established Church."

The country the Yankee was referring to was, of course, the United States. In *The Innocents Abroad,* Twain had recommended that the Italians visit the United States to see "a country which has no overshadowing Mother Church, and yet the people survive." In later years, he was not so sure; indeed, he began to fear that there was a real danger that a powerful, rich minority would set up an established church in the United States to protect its favored position. This danger did not arise from the Catholic Church whose power had been "dying ... for many centuries." It was Christian Science, Twain felt, that would eventually become an established church.

Twain regarded Mrs. Mary Baker Eddy, founder of Christian Science as "the queen of frauds and hypocrites," viewing her as a shrewd businesswoman who had converted mental healing into a religion by tacking on the name Christian to long-established practices. But he had no objection to Christian Science as a form of therapy, and, indeed, he allowed its healers to practice on members of his family. He even liked "several features" of the Christian Science philosophy, and was convinced that by "driving one's mind away from its own concerns and riveting it upon something else ... it brings healing to the spirit."

When Twain denounced Christian Science so violently in 1901, he did so because he feared that it would eventually become an established church. He felt that the sect, representing an alliance of power and wealth, would grow so rapidly that by 1940 it would be "the governing power in the Republic — to remain that permanently." He felt, too, that "the [Christian Science] Trust ... will then be the most insolent and unscrupulous and tyrannical politico-religious master that has dominated a people since the palmy days of the Inquisition." Perhaps, as Stephen Leacock points out, Twain was "attacking a grass-bird with a cannon" in his diatribe against Christian Science. But his fear of powerful religious institutions was so great that he refused to remain silent when he discerned a danger on the horizon. The American people had to be made to understand that if they continued to permit the centering of power and wealth in a religious sect, they risked loss of their freedom and independence.

Was Twain an "Infidel"?

On more than one occasion during his lifetime, Mark Twain was denounced as "that great infidel" who was America's leading emissary from the Prince of Darkness. "This son of the Devil, Mark Twain," was a title bestowed upon him rather freely.

It is true that, rather early in life, Twain began to doubt the truth of his religious teachings, and, as his faith in Christian dogma vanished, he rejected orthodox religion. Nevertheless, Twain was deeply interested in the relationship of institutionalized religion to man and society, particularly in reconciling Christian ethics and the social structure of his own day. Hence, while he incited the influence of religion and the church when it served to fetter man and society, he also called for a religion and a church which would help man and society. A sincere, courageous, vital, realistic, dynamic religion for him meant one which would inspire people to create a better world. He urged all churches, as a major step toward this goal, to tear from Christianity all the camouflage of self-deception, hollow sham and hypocrisy, to strip it of the ornamentation of the ages and to return to the original, sound principles of Jesus Christ — the ethics of humanity. Preoccupation with traditional theology had blinded the righteous to their true task — to deal realistically with the world as it was. Realism should become the foundation on which to build a real religion, "having for its base God and Man as they are, and not as the elaborately masked and disguised artificialities they are represented to be in most philosophies and in all religions." Therein is the key to Twain's religious philosophy. He was never the atheist some thought him. He sought to arouse the people to discard conventional faith and establish one that would help civilization.

As we shall see, Twain's disgust with conventional faiths increased by the turn of the century as he witnessed the pulpit abetting the triumph of imperialism. Observing how clergymen exalted the imperialists and squared their conscience with Heaven, he wrote in his notebook: "If Christ were here now, there is one thing he would *not* be — a Christian."

Chapter Five
CAPITAL AND LABOR

"Who are the oppressors? The few: the king, the capitalist, and a handful of other overseers and superintendents. Who are the oppressed? The many: The nations of the earth; the valuable personages; the workers; they that *make* the bread that the soft-handed and idle eat." [From speech, "Knights of Labor — The New Dynasty," March 22, 1886.]

"The frontier made Mark Twain, the Gilded Age ruined him," one scholar has written. The idea, as elaborated by numerous critics, is that Twain became a victim of the Gilded Age and its money-worshipping, corrupt environment; that his financial ventures, his desire to become a successful businessman, his dream of becoming a multi-millionaire, his associations with ultra-respectable, wealthy neighbors in Hartford and with millionaires like Andrew Carnegie and particularly Henry Rogers, vice-president of the Standard Oil Company, forced him to identify himself with the business interests and to refrain from attacking the hard materialism and tyrannical capitalism he saw about him. In short, these critics say, as Browning said of Wordsworth, that "Just for a handful of silver he left us, Just for a riband to stick in his coat."

Actually, Mark Twain's attitude toward the rampaging development of American capitalism following the Civil War is a complex one. More than on any other subject, his thinking on this issue displays a dichotomy, an ambivalence which must be analyzed with care.

The Cash Nexus

It is, of course, true that Twain chose many of the external standards of the wealthy as his own. He liked big houses, good clothes, fine whisky, travel, the trappings of economic success. Each book had to give him a very good living, and he often appeared to regard literature as primarily a way of making a lot of money. "The lack of money is the root of all evil," he once wrote in his notebooks. He was constantly trying to prove that he could be a successful businessman, and he was proud that he could state, at the age of fifty, "that whatever I touch turns to gold." He liked to spend hours with the financial and industrial tycoons of his day, as if the fact of his being with "big money" was proof that he too was a "smart" businessman.

All this is easy to discover. One has but to read Twain's autobiography, his letters, and his notebooks. For he himself freely acknowledged how strongly he possessed the "universal human desire for success." But the reader who pursues this problem further will quickly discern that there is another side to the story. Mark Twain never believed that success justified itself *per se*, and while he did not automatically condemn wealth, he hated and despised the ruthlessness, corruption and hypocrisy of the businessmen of his era who sacrificed human values to their interest in profits, and operated on the single principle: "Get money. Get it quickly. Get it in abundance. Get it dishonestly if you can, honestly if you must."

Twain expressed his disdain for this doctrine early in his writings. In a short sketch called "An Inquiry About Insurance," which appeared in his first book, he exposed the widespread corruption in insurance companies which fleeced both the living and the dead, and condemned the promoters behind these companies for growing wealthy on human misfortune. In another early sketch, "Daniel in the Lion's Den — and Out Again All Right," published in the *Californian* in November, 1864, he blistered the fleecing of innocent investors by stockbrokers. The entire operation of the stock exchange, he notes satirically, is based on "respectable stealing": "The place where stocks are daily bought and sold is called by interested parties the Hall of the San Francisco Board of Brokers, but by the impartial and disinterested, the Den of Forty Thieves;

the latter name is regarded as the most poetic, but the former is considered the most polite."

After spending several days "visiting the Board of Brokers ... and swapping lies with them," Twain comes away convinced that their work has deprived them of whatever good they were born with. He is satisfied that "brokers come into the world with souls," but they "wear them out in the course of a long career of stock-jobbing." Still, being thieves of standing in the community, "offenders of importance," it is not likely that they will be arrested by the police or condemned by the Church. Moreover, there is even a good chance that they will get to heaven: "Mind," he writes with tongue in cheek, "I do not say that a broker will be saved, or even that it is uncommon likely that such a thing will happen — I only say that Lazarus was raised from the dead, the five thousand were fed with twelve loaves of bread, the water was turned into wine, the Israelites crossed the Red Sea dry-shod, and a broker *can* be saved. True, the angel that accomplishes the task may require all eternity to rest himself in, but has that got anything to do with the establishment of the proposition?"

The Robber Barons

In *The Innocents Abroad,* discussing the pretensions of riches, Twain remarks that in the United States, wealth, no matter how acquired, had become the sole criterion for honor and distinction — "because ... if a man be rich, he is greatly honored, and can become a legislator, a governor, a general, a senator, no matter how ignorant an ass he is." No doubt many readers took this as a typical Twain joke. Actually, he was dead serious. Nothing infuriated and disgusted him so much as did the eulogies bestowed upon the industrial and financial buccaneers of the post-Civil War era. In sermons of clergymen, principally Protestant, in newspaper and magazine articles, even in novels, these men were hailed as superior people who had reached the top because God had rewarded them for their self-reliance, their will and perseverance, their sobriety and frugality. To be sure, went the refrain these men worked primarily for their own gain, but "an over-ruling and wise Providence" had so directed their activities that whatever they did "inure[d] to the benefit of the people." As one panegyrist put it: "Men of colossal fortunes are in effect, if not in fact, trustees of the public."

When Mark Twain saw America plundered by these "pre-eminent persons," saw the exploitation of men, women and children and the crippling of so many lives by the rich and powerful few, he could not accept the hero-worshipping accounts. These men, he was convinced, merited the obloquy and not the gratitude of the nation, and their panegyrists the contempt of all decent citizens.

Many intellectuals in the Gilded-Age America, sickened by the glorification of the business buccaneers, took to the sidelines as embittered observers and otherwise retreated into themselves. Twain refused to do either. In March, 1869, there appeared in *Packard's Monthly* a piece by him which stood in sharp contrast to the estimate of the self-made men devised by their encomiasts. It was a satirical denunciation of one of the most unscrupulous and ruthless "Robber Barons" of the era — Commodore Cornelius Vanderbilt. Through the art of stock-watering, Vanderbilt had built a fortune of $105,000,000. In carrying through various steamship and railway schemes by which this vast sum was accumulated, Vanderbilt had bribed legislators, judges, newspapers, even ministers. So contemptuous of the government and the people was the "Commodore" that he shouted on one occasion: "Law! What do I care about the Law? Hain't I got the power?"

Vanderbilt had indeed "got the power" — and the fortune that came with it. Both brought him a whole flock of eulogists in newspaper offices, university chairs, and pulpits who hailed Vanderbilt as a self-made man whom God had providentially rewarded for a useful life. At the unveiling of a statue to Vanderbilt in 1869, the Right Rev.

Bishop Janes delivered the invocation, and predicted that by his work in piling up riches, Vanderbilt was making certain to "lay up treasures in heaven." Mayor Oakley Hall of New York City compared Vanderbilt to Franklin, Jackson, and Lincoln — "a remarkable prototype of the rough-hewn American character... which can carve the way of every humbly born boy to national eminence."

In his "Open Letter to Com. Vanderbilt," Twain turned on these trucklers the fullness of his wrath, and, at the same time, exposed Vanderbilt for what he really was — a rascal who had pillaged the nation and had been elevated to respectability by a society which placed a premium on money-chasing and created a success cult which corrupted and distorted the best traditions of American democracy.

Twain poses as a man who seeks to help the Commodore by forcing him to grasp the truth about himself. He warns him that he was not getting his money's worth from his paid hirelings, "for these infatuated worshippers of dollars not their own seem to make no distinctions, but swing their hats and shout hallelujah every time you do *anything* no matter what it is." Indeed, the Commodore's "subjects" were injuring his reputation while lauding him to the skies:

One day one of your subjects comes out with a column or two detailing your rise from penury to affluance, and praising you as if you were the last and noblest work of God, but unconsciously telling how exquisitely mean a man has to be in order to achieve what you have achieved. Then another subject tells how you drive in the Park, with your scornful head down, never deigning to look to the right or the left, and make glad the thousands who covet a glance of your eye, but driving straight ahead, heedlessly and recklessly, taking the road by force, with a bearing which plainly says, "Let these people get out of the way if they can; but if they can't, and I run over them, and kill them, no matter, I'll pay for them." And then how the retailer of the pleasant anecdote does grovel in the dust and glorify you, Vanderbilt! Next, a subject of yours prints a long article to show how, in some shrewd, underhanded way, you have "come it" over the public with some Erie dodge or other, and added another million or so to your greasy greenbacks; and behold *he* praises you, and never hints the immoral practices, in so prominent a place as you occupy, are a damning example to the rising commercial generation — more, a damning thing to the whole nation, while there are insects like your subjects to make virtues of them in print.... And next, a subject tells how when you owned the California line of steamers you used to have your pursers make out false lists of passengers, and thus carry some hundreds more than the law allowed — in this way breaking the laws of your country and jeopardizing the lives of your passengers by overcrowding them during a long, sweltering voyage over tropical seas, and through a disease-poisoned atmosphere. And this shrewdness was duly glorified too....

There are other anecdotes told of you by your glorifying subjects, but let us pass them by, they only damage you. They only show how unfortunate and how narrowing a thing it is for a man to have wealth who makes a god of it instead of a servant. They only show how soulless it can make him — like that petty anecdote that tells how a young lawyer charged you $500 for a service, and how you deemed the charge too high, and so went shrewdly to work and won his confidence, and persuaded him to borrow money and put it in Erie, when you knew the stock was going down, and so held him in the trap until he was a ruined man, and then you were revenged; and you gloated over it; and, as usual, your admiring friends told the story in print, and lauded you to the skies. No let us drop the anecdotes. I don't remember ever reading anything about which you oughtn't be ashamed of.

Twain has but one request to make of Vanderbilt. He urges the Commodore

to crush out your native instincts and go and do something *worthy* of praise — go and do something you need not blush to see in print — do something that may arouse one solitary good impulse in the breasts of your horde of worshippers; prove one solitary good example to the thousands of young men who emulate your energy and your industry; shine as one solitary grain of pure gold upon the heaped rubbish of your life. Do this, I beseech you, else through your example we shall shortly have in our midst five hundred Vanderbilts, which God forbid. Go, now please go, and do one worthy act. Go, boldly, grandly, nobly, and give four dollars to some great public charity. It will break your heart, no doubt; but no matter, you have but a little while to live, and it is better to die suddenly and nobly than live a century longer the same Vanderbilt you are now. . . .

Go and surprise the whole country by doing something right. Cease to do and say unworthy things, and excessively *little* things, for those reptile friends of yours to magnify in the papers. Snub them thus, or else throttle them.

In the midst of the "Open Letter," Twain presents a serious analysis of the tyranny of wealth and the deterioration of those who fall slave to the lust for money. Vanderbilt's paid hirelings, he remarks, have pictured him as a happy man, who, having acquired millions by dint of hard work, had reached a stage of contentment. Twain knows better. As he sees it, Vanderbilt is to be pitied, and pity him he does:

Poor Vanderbilt! How I do pity you; and this is honest. You are an old man, and ought to have some rest, and yet you have to struggle and struggle, and deny yourself, and rob yourself of restful sleep and peace of mind, because you need money so badly. I always feel for a man who is so poverty ridden as you. Don't misunderstand me, Vanderbilt. I know you own seventy millions; but then you know and I know that it isn't what a man has that constitutes wealth. No — it is to be *satisfied* with what one has; that is wealth. As long as one sorely *needs* a certain additional amount, that man isn't rich. Seventy times seventy millions can't make him rich as long as his poor heart is breaking for more. I am just about rich enough to buy the least valuable horse in your stable, perhaps, but I cannot sincerely and honestly take an oath that I need any more now. And so I am rich. But you! You have got seventy millions, and you need five hundred millions, and are really suffering for it. Your poverty is something appalling. I tell you truly that I do not believe I could live twenty-four hours with the awful weight of four hundred and thirty millions of abject want crushing down upon me. I should die under it. My soul is so wrought upon by your hapless poverty, that if you came by me now I would freely put ten cents in your tin cup, if you carry one, and say, "God pity you, poor unfortunate."

Although the irony here does not quite come off, the paragraph reveals that Twain was well aware of the dangers involved in the quest for wealth. He knew that money has a certain infinity. Of all else, he pointed out, the end is surfeit: of greed for food or drink, even of lust. But of the love of money there is no limit, and once stricken by the malady, a man had to be on constant guard lest it destroy his body and soul.

Money Lust

The doctrine of wealth set forth in the "Open Letter to Com. Vanderbilt" was to appear again and again in Twain's writing. It was expressed, as we have already seen, in "The Revised Catechism," in "The Letter From the Recording Angel," *The Gilded Age*, and "The Man That Corrupted Hadleyburg." We also find it in a fragment about a man who went mad through "money-lust," imagined that there was thirty centuries' interest due him, "and he kept calculating & compounding it & laying before lawyers to help him collect it or tell him where to apply. He is *always* calculating it & worrying over it." We find it, too, in a little story about an Esquimau maiden whose life was ruined when her father became rich. Tracing the deterioration of the girl's father, Twain depicts how wealth hardens a man's heart and coarsens his character. He shows how the opinions of the rich man were enhanced by his money in the eyes of society, although they were the same stupid ideas formerly ignored by the same society. "He has lowered the tone of all our tribe," the daughter tells the narrator. "Once they were a frank and manly race, now they are measly hypocrites, and sodden with servility. In my heart of hearts I hate all the ways of millionaires."

Twain's celebrated short story, "The Million Pound Bank Note," recently made into a delightful film by the British moviemaker Ronald Neame, presents his acid comments on a society that treats people according to how much money they have. The tale revolves about a bet between two immensely rich old Londoners over whether the simple possession of a million pound note would be enough to insure the future of the man who held it, even if he never cashed it. To resolve the argument they turn the bill over to an impoverished American passer-by, with the instructions to return it in a month's time and claim his reward. At once a despised tramp is changed into the object of respect and veneration. And the irony of it all is that it is the appearance of money and not the money itself that really counts. As long as the American has his scrap of paper, his credit is unlimited. The finest restaurants, tailors, and hotels — even the finest homes — are open to him. An occasional flash of the note is sufficient to establish his credit. He can make stocks rise at the mere mention of his interest in them. And, of course, he promptly becomes England's most eligible bachelor.

Twain's farcical story brilliantly satirizes a system based not so much on money as the appearance of money. Again Twain makes the point that it is not character but possession of wealth that determines a man's standing in his contemporary society. The possession of great wealth did not give the American in the story real happiness. Yet, Twain points out, people threw away their whole lives for it, only to discover that its pleasures were feverish and transient. As he put it in the closing paragraph of the story "$30,000 Bequest," in which this theme is developed: "Vast wealth, acquired by sudden and unwholesome means, is a snare."

Turning Point in American History

Although he repeatedly and effectively ridiculed the business code of his day — "Get rich; dishonestly if we can; honestly if we must" — Twain never published an explicit theory that would explain the forces responsible for the doctrine. In a number of unpublished manuscripts, however, he did advance such a theory. In his "Notes for a Social History of the United States from 1850 to 1900," which he planned to write, Twain asserts that the big difference between America before and after 1850 was the influence exerted on American life by the "lust for money" and the "hardness and cynicism" which accompanied it. Prior to 1850, there were wealthy people, but, in the main, they acquired their wealth honestly. More important, there was little "worship of money or of its possessor." The youth of America in those days were not dominated by the sole thought of how "to get rich." Their heroes were not financial and industrial buccaneers who set wealth as the only worthy goal in life, but statesmen and literary giants — men "moved by lofty impulses."

The real change in American life and which, in Twain's opinion, ultimately corroded the very soul of the nation, was introduced by the California gold rush. The "Californian sudden-riches disease" spread rapidly during the Civil War, and the chief carriers of infection were the Wall Street bankers who financed the war and, together with the railroad promoters, looted the nation's resources during and after the conflict. They established domination over the nation, state, and city governments. They openly declared that the ethical values of pre-war 1850 America held no significance for the new industrialized and commercialized America. They emphasized that principles and scruples of conscience were cumbersome obstacles on the road to opulence. Opportunity lay open and people were expected to seize it.

Thus was foisted upon the nation, Twain noted, a new set of values which hastened the "moral rot" introduced by the California gold rush and accelerated by the Civil War. To be sure, the exponents of these new values pointed with pride to the financial, industrial and mechanical miracles achieved by the new industrial America, and hailed as heroes the financiers and industrialists who "triumphed over nature and harnessed it for the country's good." Twain conceded that many mechanical advances had been achieved since 1850, but contended that the blessings of inventions and mechanical developments had been distorted by a business civilization which emphasized that only material riches count: "It is a civilization which has destroyed the simplicity and repose of life; replaced its contentment, its poetry, its soft romantic-dreams and visions with the money-fever, sordid ideals, vulgar ambitions, and the sleep which does not refresh; it has invented a thousand useless luxuries, and turned them into necessities, and satisfied none of them; it has dethroned God and set up a shekel in His place."

In many of his manuscripts Twain blistered the men he held largely responsible for the change in American life after 1850, specifically mentioning J. P. Morgan, John D. Rockefeller, John Wanamaker, Cornelius Vanderbilt and other millionaire financiers and industrialists. But the chief villain in Twain's incompleted social history of the United States, was Jay Gould. He singled out the unscrupulous railroad promoter, industrialist and newspaper owner as "the mightiest disaster which has ever befallen this country," because he had left behind the gospel that "Money is God." "The people had *desired* money before his day, but *he* taught them to fall down and worship it. They had respected men of means before his day, but along with this respect was joined the respect due to the character and industry which had accumulated it. But Jay Gould taught the entire nation to make a god of money and the man, no matter how the money might have been acquired."

Twain's interpretation of American history is symptomatic of a widespread tendency among intellectuals of the Gilded Age who, shocked by the social corrosions of expanding capitalism, longed to regain the serenity they credited to pre-industrial, pre-gold rush, pre-Civil War America. Apart from the fact that these days were gone by and unrecapturable, this concept of American society before 1850 could not stand the strain put upon it by history. Fourteen years before the gold rush, de Tocqueville noted that a characteristic of American society was the pernicious influence exerted by "a large number of men whose fortune is on the increase, but whose desires grow much faster than their fortunes, and who gloat upon the gifts of wealth in anticipation." He pointed specifically to the increasing gulf between the ideals of the American Revolution and this lust for wealth.

The next few decades witnessed the deepening of the gulf as the slave system expanded, and church, state and press hastened to protect and increase the profits of the slaveholders. In 1846, Emerson observed that cotton thread united Southern slaveholders and Northern capitalists in a fraternity of profit seekers. The press, he noted, hailed it as an alliance of "the solid portion of the community," but in reality it was an alliance of "sharpers" to whom profit was the sole value. It was inevitable that a conflict should arise between the democratic element and this alliance of profit seekers from whom "no act of honor or benevolence or justice is to be expected." "When I speak of the democratic element, I do not mean that ill thing, vain and loud, which writes lying newspapers, spouts at caucuses, and sells its lies for gold; but that spirit of love for the general good whose name this assumes. There is nothing of the true democratic element in what is called Democracy; it must fall, being wholly commercial." Thus Emerson, writing before the gold rush and the post-bellum "Robber Barons," already saw how the profit motive was corroding national life.

Actually, Twain was aware that it was an oversimplification to surround pre-Civil War America with an idealistic halo. He conceded that even in the early days of the Republic, tremendous influence was exerted upon American life by the "worship[p]ers of the Almighty Dollar" who had inherited the "instinct" from "our English fathers, the worship[p]ers of the Almighty Farthing." In describing a rich "scoundrel," named Asa Hoover, in a pre-Civil War village on the Mississippi, he noted: "Just how rich he was nobody knew; it was only known that there seemed to be no bottom to his purse. Everybody looked up to him, bowed down to him, flattered him, & everybody stood in mortal fear of him, & would go [to] any length to keep from getting his ill will." Evidently Twain forgot about Asa Hoover when he wrote: "In my youth there was nothing resembling a worship of money or of its possessor."

Although Twain went much too far in investing pre-Civil War America with an idealistic haze, he was correct in emphasizing the tremendous decline in business morality during and after the Civil War. There is not space within the limits of this work to spell out the evidence for Twain's observation. Whole books have been written on the cynical corruption that flourished in business and government during the period 1861-1875, of the emergence of a new group of capitalists who interpreted every event in terms of profit and loss, and of the concurrent emergence of the slogan, "Get rich!" Becoming rich legitimized the means, whether fair or foul. "This country is fast becoming filled with gigantic corporations, wielding and controlling immense aggregations of money and thereby commanding great influence and power," a Congressional committee warned the nation in 1873. "It is notorious in many state legislatures that these influences are often controlling, so that in effect they become the ruling power of the State. ... The belief is far too general that all men can be ruled with money, and that the use of such means to carry public measures is legitimate and proper."

Reasons for Poverty

While the "hogs run wild," as Walt Whitman dubbed the titans of industry, cynically flaunted their riches in conspicuous consumption, corrupted legislatures, judges and governors, hundreds of thousands of Americans lived in abject poverty. But the millionaires and their panegyrists either treated poverty as a "blessing in disguise" or blamed it on its victims as "the obvious consequences of sloth and sinfulness." Just as wealth was interpreted as proof of the possessor's superior qualities, so poverty was considered the result of laziness, drunkenness or other faults. As John

Hay said: "That you have property is proof of industry and foresight on your part or your father's; that you have nothing is a judgment on your laziness and vices, or on your improvidence. The world is a moral world, which it would not be if virtue and vice received the same reward."

Early in his career, Twain rejected this smug defense of the *status quo*. During his stay in New York City in 1867, Twain several times visited its worst slums and saw "the squalid want, criminal woe, wretchedness and suffering" of men, women, and children. In dispatches to the *Alta California*, he described vividly the "cholera-breeding" slums where half of the city's million people were "packed away in holes and dens and cellars of tenement houses." Lashing out at the slum landlords who doomed their tenants to death from cholera by their refusal to spend a penny on sanitary improvement, he noted ironically that respectable people did not die of cholera, but "only the poor, the criminally, sinfully, and wickedly poor and destitute starvelings in the purlieus of the great cities." He attacked the concept spread by the wealthy and their allies that honest poverty was a "blessing in disguise." He never knew a wealthy proponent of this doctrine to exchange his ill-gotten riches for honest poverty. As for himself: "Honest poverty is a gem that even a king might feel proud to call his own but I wish to sell out. I have sported that kind of jewelry long enough. I want some variety. I wish to become rich, so that I can instruct the people and glorify honest poverty a little, like those good, kind-hearted, fat, benevolent people do."

Aiming his shaft at the pious hypocrites who wept over the poor while they compelled them to work and live under conditions that bred poverty, Twain announced a plant that would relieve them of their concern. Modeling himself after Swift's "Modest Proposal," he raised the cry: "Desicate the poor workingman; stuff him into sausage." "I regard the poor man, in his present condition, as so much wasted raw material. Cut up and properly canned, he might be made useful to fatten the natives of the Cannibal Islands and to improve our export trade with that region." What could be a more perfect solution? The wealthy could increase their profits at the same time that they salved their conscience!

It was bad enough, Twain pointed out, that "hunger, persecution and death are the wages of poverty in the mighty cities of the land." What was worse was that to this was added the "humiliation" of being told that poverty was the poorer classes' own fault. The poor were thus robbed not only of their comforts, their health, their living standards, but worse yet, of their human dignity.

Twain was especially outraged by the oft-repeated charge that the poor were in want solely because they squandered their wages at a tavern. He knew the horrors of alcoholism among the poor, but insisted that the true causes of habitual drunkenness were poverty, misery, and dirt. He argued that when men worked long hours in dangerous and unsanitary surroundings for earnings so small they and their families were half-starved, it was to be expected that they would seek some outlet for their misery in alcohol. He saw red at the pious hypocrisy of the temperance reformers who, instead of blaming poverty for drunkenness, blamed drunkenness for poverty. He wrote to his sister in 1875: "Nothing can persuade me to read a temperance tract or be a party to the dissemination of such injurious publications."

Nothing, moreover, could make Twain believe that industry would be ruined unless labor was enslaved to low wages, long hours of work, and dangerous and unsanitary working conditions. He scornfully rejected the factory owners' lament that they would be forced out of business by a living wage and an eight-hour day. Commenting in his notebook on the "capitalist-employer" demand that the "eight-hour scheme . . . be left to voluntary action, that is, no legislation," he wrote: "The English laws don't allow a man to shoot himself, but you see these people don't want to make a law to prevent a man's committing half-suicide & being other-half murdered by overwork – & his family left destitute. No legislation to strengthen the hands of the despised struggles. Why doesn't the Church (which is a part of the aristocracy) leave tithes & other robberies to 'voluntary action?'"

Trade Unionism

Workers, Twain insisted, had a right to leisure and enjoyment in their lives. But they would never achieve either if they depended on the "voluntary action" of the employers. Nothing but force would bring results, and the working class by weight of its numbers was the only group capable of applying it effectively — provided they organized thoroughly. Only by associating could they stand up against the immense preponderance of power arrayed against them.

Twain illustrated this theme in *Life on the Mississippi* with the story of how the river pilots organized a closed-shop union in 1861 and gained higher wages and improved working conditions.

With employers bringing in a flock of new and inexperienced pilots to undermine wages, the monthly wages fell rapidly from $250 to $100. At this point the pilots organized an association with provisions for unemployment and death benefits, and demanded $250 a month. The employers retaliated by refusing to hire any association members. Soon "all the members were outcast and tabooed and no one would employ them." The employers laughed derisively at the association; still, to keep pilots from joining, wages were raised to $125 and $150 a month. The pilots stuck to their guns, and as non-union workers realized that the increased wages were due to the existence of the union, many joined its ranks. Meanwhile, business was booming; pilots were in great demand, and were scarce. The employers' anti-union policies were boomeranging:

Captain - - - - was the first man who found it necessary to take the dose, and he had been the loudest derider of the organization. He hunted up one of the best association pilots and said:

"Well, you boys have rather got the best of us for a little while, so I'll give in with as good a grace as I can. I've come to hire you; get your trunk aboard right away. I want to leave at twelve o'clock."

"I don't know about that. Who is your other pilot?"

"I've got I. S. Why?"

"I can't go along with him. He don't belong to the association."

"What!"

"It's so."

"Do you mean to tell me that you won't turn a wheel with one of the very best and oldest pilots on the river because he don't belong to your association?"

"Yes, I do."

"Well, if this isn't putting on airs! I supposed I was doing you a benevolence; but I begin to think that I am the party that wants a favor done. Are you acting under a law of the concern?"

"Yes."

"Show it to me."

So they stepped into the association rooms, and the secretary soon satisfied the captain, who said:

"Well, what am I to do? I have hired Mr. S. for the entire season."

"I will provide for you," said the secretary, "I will detail a pilot to go with you, and he shall be on board at twelve o'clock."

"But if I discharge S., he will come on me for the whole season's wages."

"Of course that is a matter between you and Mr. S., Captain. We cannot meddle in your private affairs."

The captain stormed, but to no purpose. In the end he had to discharge S., pay him about a thousand dollars, and take an association pilot in his place. The laugh was beginning to turn the other way, now. Every day thenceforward, a new victim fell; every day some outraged captain discharged a non-association pet, with tears and profanity, and installed a hated association man in his berth. In a very little while idle non-associationists began to be pretty plenty, brisk as business was, and much as their services were desired. The laugh was shifting to the other side of their mouths most palpably.

The employers vowed to discharge every Association pilot once the business "spurt" was over. But the union had a trick up its sleeve. It ruled that its members should never give information about the channel to any "outsider." The non-union pilots suddenly found themselves compelled to run 500 miles of river on information that was a week or ten days old.

Now came another perfectly logical result. The outsiders began to ground steamboats, sink them, and get into all sorts of trouble, whereas accidents seemed to keep entirely away from the association. Wherefore even the owners and captains of boats furnished exclusively with outsiders, and previously considered to be wholly independent of the association and free to comfort themselves with brag and laughter, began to feel pretty uncomfortable.

Still, they made a show of keeping up the brag, until one black day when every captain of the lot was formally ordered to immediately discharge his outsiders and take association pilots in their stead. And who was it that had the dashing presumption to do that? Alas, it came from a power behind the throne that was greater than the throne itself. It was the underwriters!

It was no time to "swap knives." Every outsider had to take his trunk ashore at once. Of course it was supposed that there was collusion between the association and the underwriters, but this was not so. The latter had come to comprehend the excellence of the "report" system of the association and the safety it secured, and so they had made their decision among themselves and upon plain business principles.

There was weeping and wailing and gnashing of teeth in the camp of the outsiders now. But no matter, there was but one course for them to pursue, and they pursued it. They came forward in couples and groups, and . . . asked for membership.

Wages rose rapidly to $500 and even $700 a month. "The Association had a good bank account and was very strong. There was no longer an outsider." The union thrived until after the Civil War when the railroads diverted travel from the steamers. Soon "the Association and the noble science of piloting were things of the dead and pathetic past."

But Twain's account of the pilots' union was very much of the present. Published in 1883, when the Knights of Labor was beginning its meteoric rise, the story of the union gained considerable notice. With the press sounding warnings about the dangers of "labor monopoly," and charging that trade unionism was a foreign importation by European Communists, Socialists, and Anarchists, Twain's account of a closed-shop union which was born and thrived before and during the Civil War was a valuable antidote to the hysterical cries. The story was reprinted in a number of labor journals, and *John Swinton's Paper*, the leading labor organ of the period, praised Twain for having made "a powerful contribution to labor's struggle for justice."

Twain followed the career of the Knights of Labor with great interest. He was impressed by its slogan — "An Injury to One is the Concern of All" — and by the fact that it brought together into one organization all workers, skilled and unskilled, men and women, North and South, Negro and white, native American and foreign-born, and of all religious and political beliefs. When the Knights won a great victory over Jay Gould in 1885, and organized the tycoon's southwestern railroad system, Twain hailed it as a triumph for all who believed in democracy. The fact that the man whom he regarded as the greatest menace to the nation had been forced to yield to the power of the Knights of Labor was proof to Twain that the future American democracy, even world democracy, rested with organized labor. Fired by the success of the Knights, he advanced the idea that the organization was the nucleus of a broader body which would "include, in one grand league, labor of whatever form, and, in the end, all mankind in a final millennium."

But businessmen and their allies viewed the Knights as a menace that "must be crushed," and launched a vicious campaign picturing the organization as headed by self-seekers and leeches and the men they led as lawless and violent. Calling for the outlawing of the Knights of Labor, the Salem (Mass.) *Gazette* declared editorially early in 1886:

The American "birthright" is quite fully set forth in the preamble of our constitution and the bill of rights. It is not the "birthright" of any class of men who have availed themselves of the care and protection of our constitution and laws to band themselves into a secret organization, like the Knights of Labor, which seeks to honeycomb American society with foreign agitators, which seeks to subvert our constitutional government and to set up an oligarchy of Communists and Anarchists in its place. There is no room in the United States for an organization which is bent upon overthrowing our republican institutions and the government which is organized to support such institutions.

On March 22, 1886, at the very height of the campaign of slander against the organization, Mark Twain delivered a speech before the Monday Evening Club in Hartford which was entitled, "Knights of Labor — The New Dynasty." Previously mentioned only through a brief reference in Paine's biography of Twain, the full text of the speech was only recently discovered among the Mark Twain Papers at the University of California. It reveals as does nothing else how staunch a friend of organized labor was Mark Twain.

Twain begins by pointing out to the Hartford business and professional men who made up the membership of the Monday Evening Club that through the centuries power has been used for oppression and exploitation. He then proceeds to ask and answer a series of significant questions:

"Who are the oppressors? The few: the king, the capitalist, and a handful of other overseers and superintendents. Who are the oppressed? The many: The nations of the earth; the valuable personages; the workers; they that *make* the bread that the soft-handed and idle eat. Why is it right that there is not a fairer division of the spoil all around? *Because laws and constitutions have ordered otherwise.* Then it follows that if the laws and constitutions should change around and say there *shall* be a more nearly equal division, *that* would have to be recognized as right. That is to confess, then, that in *political societies, it is the prerogative of Might to determine what is Right;* that it is the prerogative of

Might to create Right — and uncreate it, at will. It is to confess that if the banded voters among a laboring kinship of 45,000,000 persons shall speak out to the other 12,000,000 or 15,000,000 of a nation and command that an existing system has in that moment, in an absolutely clear and clean and legal way, become an obsolete and vanished thing, then it has utterly ceased to exist, and no creature in all the 15,000,000 is in the least degree privileged to find fault with the act."

For centuries, the king and "the scattering few" have held in their hands the power to determine what was right and what was not. "Now was that power real or was it a fiction," Twain asks, and he answers:

"Until to-day it was real; but *from* to-day in *this country*, I take heart of grace to believe, it is forever mere dust and ashes. For a greater [power] than any king has arisen upon this the only soil in this world that is truly sacred to liberty; and you that have eyes to see and ears to hear may catch the sheen of his banners and the tramp of his marching hosts; and men may cavil, and sneer, and make wordy argument — but please God he will mount his throne; and he will stretch out his sceptre, and there will be bread for the hungry, clothing for the naked, and hope in the eyes unused to hoping; and the sham nobilities will pass away, and the rightful lord will come to his own."

Twain again resorts to historical evidence to drive home his point. Throughout history, he notes, the ruling classes have sneered at the idea that their power to oppress and exploit might some day be snatched from them by the very objects of their oppression. They had good reason to sneer. For "the huge inert mass of mankind" had wept over its lot throughout all ages, and once in a generation in all lands, "a little block of this inert mass has stirred, and risen with noise; and said it could no longer endure its oppressions, its degradation, its misery — and then after a few days it has sunk back, vanquished, mute again, and laughed at." Likewise, in the era of the capitalist ruling class, single mechanical trades banded together in trade unions, rose "hopefully and demanded a chance in this world's fight." But it was always an isolated struggle — the other trades were either unorganized or, if organized, "went uninterested about their own affairs — it was not their quarrel; — and that also was a time to sneer — and men did sneer."

"But when *all* the bricklayers, and all the machinists, and all the miners, and blacksmiths, and printers, and hod-carriers, and stevedores, and house-painters, and brakemen, and engineers, and conductors, and factory hands, and horse-car drivers, and all the shop-girls, and all the sewing-women, and all the telegraph operators; in a word, all the myriads of toilers in whom is slumbering the reality of that thing which you call *Power*, not its age-worn sham and substanceless spectre, — when these rise, call the vast spectacle by any deluding name that will please your ear, but the fact remains a *Nation* has risen."

This new power was not something for the future. It was already here. Twain then proceeded to describe how tremendously he had been moved by an incident at a Senate Committee hearing on copyright legislation which had been held in January, 1886. While he was waiting to testify, a spokesman for labor appeared before the Senate Committee to support this legislation. He was James Walsh, President of Philadelphia Typographical Union, No. 2, affiliated with the Knights of Labor. Unpretentious in appearance compared with the prominent authors of the day and the Senators, the labor spokesman made by far the greatest impression. For he said: "I am not here as a printer; I am not here as a brick-layer, or a mason, or a carpenter, or as any other peculiar or particular handicrafts man; but I stand here to represent *all* the trades, *all* the industries, all brethren of *any* calling that labor with their daily bread and the bread of their wives and their little children, from Maine to the Gulf, and from the Atlantic to the Pacific; and when I speak, out of my mouth issues the voice of five millions of men." The Senators stopped looking bored and listened with respect — for here was the master speaking, the representative of the new and only real power, and "his command will be heeded."

"This was the first time in this world, perhaps, that ever a nation did actually and in its own person, not by proxy, speak. And by grace of fortune I was there to hear and see. It seemed to me that all the gauds and shows and spectacles of history somehow lost their splendor in this presence; their tinsel and lacquer and feathers seemed confessed and poor, contrasted with this real blood and flesh of majesty and greatness. And I thought then, and still think, that our country, so wastefully rich in things for her people to be proud of, had here added a thing which transcended all that went before. Here was the nation in person speaking; and its servants, *real* — not masters *called* servants by canting trick of speech — listening. The like could not be seen in any other country, or in any other age.

"They whom the printer represented are in truth the nation; and they are still speaking."

Turning next to the Manifesto of Wrongs and Demands of the Knights of Labor, a document adopted in 1878, Twain urged his audience to read it carefully. At first glance, it might appear that such statements in the Manifesto as the desire of the Knights "to secure to the toilers a proper share of the wealth that they create," such assertions as the "alarming development and aggressiveness of great capitalists and corporations [which] unless checked will lead to the pauperization and hopeless degradation of the toiling masses," and such demands as prohibition of the employment of children under fourteen years of age; equal pay for equal work for both sexes; the adoption of laws providing for the safety of those engaged in mining, manufacturing industries; ownership by the government "of all telegraphs, telephones and railroads," and "the reduction of the hours of labor to eight per day, so that the laborers may have more time for social enjoyment and intellectual improvement, and be enabled to reap the advantages conferred by the labor-saving machinery which their brains have created" — were all new, dangerous, and, indeed, revolutionary. Actually, Twain insisted, the fundamental objective of the Manifesto was not all new. "It is the oldest thing in this world — being as old as the human voice. In one form or another it has wearied the ears of the fortunate and the powerful in all the years of all the ages." But heretofore it had been laughed at; regarded as the hopeless dream of people "who were crying for the moon, crying for the impossible." Now these words had acquired real meaning because they were supported by mass organization of the working class. No longer could they be sneered at. Now all were compelled to pay attention.

It is with this historical background in mind, Twain continued; that the Manifesto should be read. The reader must then ask in surprise:

" 'Is it possible that so plain and manifest a piece of justice as this, is actually lacking to these men, and must be asked for? — has been lacking to them for ages, and the world's fortunate ones did not know it; or knowing it could be indifferent to it, could endure the shame of it, the inhumanity of it?' And the thought follows in your mind, 'Why is this as strange as that a famishing child should want its common right, the breast, and the mother-heart not divine it; or, divining it, turn away indifferent.'

"Read their Manifesto; read it in a judicial spirit, and ponder it. It impeaches certain of us of high treason against the rightful sovereignty of this world, the indictment is found by a competent jury, and in no long time we must stand before the bar of the Republic and answer it. And you will assuredly find counts in it which not any logic of ours can controvert."

Twain rejoiced that the working class had finally found the means by which to redress their justifiable grievances. "Many a time," he declared, "when I have seen a man abusing a horse, I have wished I knew that horse's language, so that I could whisper in his ear, 'Fool, you are master here, if you but knew it. Launch out with your heels!'" For countless centuries labor had been in the same position:

"The working millions, in all the ages, have been horses — were horses; all they needed was a capable leader to organize their strength and tell them how to use it, and they would in that moment be master. They have *found* that *leader* somewhere, to-day and they *are* master — the only time in this world that ever the true king wore the purple; the only time in this world that 'By the grace of God, King' was ever uttered when it was not a lie."

The forces of wealth had spread lies about this new king, charging that he represented a threat to society. Twain denied this, insisting that only *he* stood for the preservation of what was best in society, and was, actually, a bulwark against movements which aimed to destroy the entire social order. To be sure, this new king would use his power to oppress at first, "for he is not better than the masters that went before; nor pretends to be." But there was a significant difference now that had never existed before:

"The only difference is he will oppress the few, they oppressed the many; he will oppress the thousands, they oppressed the millions; but he will imprison nobody, he will massacre, burn, flay, torture, exile nobody, nor work any subject eighteen hours a day, nor starve his family. He will see to it that there is fair play, fair working hours, fair wages: and further than that, when his might has become securely massed and his authority recognized, he will not go, let us hope, and determine also [what] to believe. He will be strenuous, firm, sometimes hard — he *must* be — for a while, till all his craftsmen be gathered into his citadel and his throne established. Until then let us be patient."

Twain concluded on a stirring and confident note:

"It is not long to wait; his day is close at hand: his clans are gathering, they are on their way; his bugles are sounding the call, they are answering; every week that comes and goes, sees ten thousand new crusaders swing into line and add their pulsing footfalls to the thunder-thread of his mighty battalions.

"He is the most stupendous product of the highest civilization the world has ever seen — and the worthiest and the best; and in no age but this, no land but this, and no lower civilization than this, could he ever have been brought forth. The average of his genuine, practical, valuable knowledge — and knowledge is the truest right divine to power — is an education contrasted to which the education possessed by the kings and nobles who ruled him for a hundred centuries is the untaught twaddle of a nursery, and beneath contempt. . . .

"His was a weary journey and long: the constellations have drifted far from the anchorages which they knew in the skies when it began; but at last he is here. He is here — and he will remain. He is the birth of the greatest age the nations of the world have known. You cannot sneer at him — that time has gone by. He has before him the most righteous work that was ever given in the hand of man to do; and he will do it. Yes, he is here; and the question is not — as it has been heretofore during a thousand ages — What shall we do with him? For the first time in history we are relieved of the necessity of managing his affairs for him. He is not a broken dam this time — he is the Flood!"

It is not difficult to pick minor flaws in Twain's magnificent speech. Twain's estimate of the Knights of Labor membership, based on the testimony of James Walsh, was a considerable exaggeration over the Knights' actual membership of about 750,000. His conception that the appearance of a powerful, unified labor movement was a purely American phenomenon and could not occur in any other country is ridiculous when one considers the fact that trade unionism in England at this time was even more advanced than it was in the United States. His enthusiastic portrayal of the labor movement as the new power in the United States which had practically replaced rule by the capitalist class was overoptimistic to say the least.

With all these weaknesses, Twain's "The New Destiny" is unquestionably the most eloquent defense of organized labor during the 1880's, and one of the most eloquent in all of American history. The bulk of American intellectuals in the 'eighties not only did not support labor's objectives and methods; they regarded them as dangerous in general, and the Knights of Labor, in particular, as equivalent to insurrection. A few intellectuals — Henry Demarest Lloyd and William Dean Howells being outstanding examples — championed labor's cause, but not even these writers so vigorously defended not only the right of labor to organize to redress its grievances but the complete justice of its being the ruling force in society. No one so effectively argued that the working class and the nation were interchangeable since the workers were the nation.

Even Howells, to whom Twain sent a copy of his speech in the form of an essay, conceded that no one had so effectively presented the case for organized labor. He wrote Twain that he had read the "Knights of Labor — The new dynasty" "with thrills amounting to yells of satisfaction," and declared it to be "the best thing yet said on the subject. . . ." Apparently Howells had tried to get the essay published and had failed, for he wrote to Twain: "You can't get a single newspaper to face the facts of the situation. . . . If ever a public was betrayed by its press, it's ours. . . ."

Twain's speech remained buried for over seventy years, but the ideas embodied in it could not be buried. The Knights of Labor declined and disappeared, but the labor movement continued, and, despite frequent setbacks, grew in strength and influence. No truer words were ever spoken or written by Mark Twain than those he used in describing the organized worker: "He is here — and he will remain. . . . He is not a broken dam this time — he is the Flood!"

Having demonstrated so effectively the relationship between the labor movement of the 1880's and every past struggle of the working masses throughout history, it is not surprising that Twain utilized his defense of the Knights of Labor as the basis of his discussion of trade unionism and trade-unions haters in Chapter XXXIII of *A Connecticut Yankee in King Arthur's Court*, entitled "Sixth Century Economy." Hank Morgan, the Yankee, explains to a group of onlookers in 6th Century England that due to the combined strength of labor "wages will keep on rising, little by little, as steadily as a tree grows," and that as a consequence, workers in 19th Century America will earn more in one day than they made in a month. The onlookers exclaim in amazement, "It is the income of an earl!" Morgan, however, reminds them that they must never forget a basic economic principle, namely, that "it isn't what sum you get, it's how much you can buy with it . . . that tells whether your wages are high in fact or only high in name." The solution of this and other problems facing the workers, the Yankee predicts, will come when the few who do not work ("nobles, rich men, the prosperous generally") will no longer determine what pay the vast majority who do the work shall have. That time was coming:

"These few, who do no work, determine what pay the vast hives shall have who *do* work. You see? You see? They're a 'combine' — a trade-union, to coin a new phrase — who band themselves together to force their lowly brother to take what they choose to give. Thirteen hundred years hence — so says the unwritten law — the 'combine' will be the other way, and then how these fine people's posterity will fume and fret and grit their teeth over the insolent tyranny of trade-unions! Yes, indeed! the magistrate will tranquilly arrange the wages from now clear way down into the nineteenth century; and then all of a sudden the wage-earner will consider that a couple of thousand years or so is enough of this one-sided sort of thing; and he will rise up and take a hand in fixing his wages himself. Ah, he will have a long and bitter account of wrong and humiliation to settle."

"Do ye believe —"

"That he actually will help to fix his own wages? Yes, indeed. And he will be strong and able then."

Twain's vigorous defense of organized labor in his own day did not go unnoticed by readers of the *Yankee*. A number of critics rated Twain's analysis well-nigh worthless, setting it down as a mass of half-truths. Others simply refused to regard the novel as having any significance for the problems of the nineteenth century. On the other hand, Howells, who reviewed the *Yankee* in *Harper's Monthly* shortly after it appeared, stressed its meaning for his own day. He praised Twain's defense of trade unionism, and pointed out that what the Yankee said about sixth-century "freemen" applied almost as well to company-town mill workers and coal miners in America of the 1880's.

... the noble of Arthur's day who fattened on the blood and sweat of his bondmen, is one in essence with the capitalist of Mr. [Benjamin] Harrison's day who grows rich on the labor of his underpaid wagemen. .... With shocks of consciousness, one recognizes ... that the laws are still made for the few against the many, and the preservation of things, not men, is still the ideal of legislation. There are incidents in this wonder-book which wring the heart for what has been of cruelty and wrong in the past, and leave it burning with shame and hate for the conditions which are of like effect in the present. It is one of its magical properties that the fantastic fable of Arthur's far-off time is also too often the sad truth of ours.

That the *Yankee* said something for the working class and to the working class of the 1880's and 1890's is seen by the choice of it wherever workers assembled. Excerpts from the novel, especially Chapter XXXIII, were read aloud at trade union meetings and labor picnics, and were reprinted in many labor papers in America and England. In February, 1890, barely two months after its publication, W. T. Stead ranked the *Yankee* along with Henry George's *Progress and Poverty* and Edward Bellamy's *Looking Backward* as the three literary contributions "which have given the greatest impetus to the social-democratic movement in recent years."

Socialism and Howells' Influence

The listing of the *Connecticut Yankee* as a book that advanced the Socialist cause must have surprised readers of Twain's earlier works. In these he had rejected government ownership and operation of industry as slow and inefficient, and had characterized the idea of dividing and sharing wealth equally as idiotic. Yet by the time the

Yankee was published, Twain had already started to re-evaluate his thinking on the issue, and was slowly coming to the conclusion that the only way to protect the public from private greed was to have the government take the country's industries out of private hands and operate them for the good of the people. He did not abandon his fear that public agencies under government ownership and operation would be corrupted by powerful influences, but he now felt that this danger would have to be risked if the injustices of modern society were to be amended.

Twain's change in attitude was influenced by his close association with William Dean Howells. Howells' conviction that most of the social problems of modern life were the consequences of inherent evils in the capitalist system was arrived at only through long painstaking deliberation. His thinking reached a crucial point in the fall of 1887 when the sentence of the "Chicago Anarchists" was upheld by the Supreme Court. Howells, convinced that the condemned men were innocent of the bombing incident at Haymarket Square on May 4, 1886 — a conviction shared by many trade unionists, Socialists and liberals here and abroad — sent a letter conveying this belief to the New York *Tribune*. He urged all "who believe that it would either be injustice or impolicy" to execute the condemned men to join him in petitioning the Governor of Illinois to mitigate their punishment.

Governor Oglesby commuted two of the sentences to life imprisonment, but one man committed suicide (or was murdered in his cell), and four were hanged. Howells wrote indignantly to his father: "All is over now, except the judgment that begins at once for every unjust and evil deed, and goes on forever. The historical perspective is that this free Republic has killed five men for their opinions."

Howells himself recognized that his defense of the Haymarket martyrs had contributed to his own development. He admitted to Hamlin Garland that his "horizons have been indefinitely widened by the process," and that he was "reading and thinking about questions that carry me beyond myself and my miserable literary idolatries of the past."

The reading that converted Howells to socialism consisted of the works of Tolstoy, and three contemporary books published in America: Laurence Gronlund's *The Coöperative Commonwealth*, Edward Bellamy's *Looking Backward*, and Henry George's *Progress and Poverty*.

The influence of Tolstoy on Howells is avowed by him many times and in many ways. With his discovery of Tolstoy in the late 'eighties, his thinking took a definite socialist turn; indeed, it is generally acknowledged that Tolstoy was one of the most important sources of Howells' socialism.

Although he was strongly attached to Henry George's single-tax program, Howells believed that it did not go far enough in solving the social and economic problems of his day, and George's influence on his writings is slight. More influential were the theories of Gronlund and Bellamy, both of whom emphasized that the solution for the evils of capitalism was simple: substitute a society based on co-operation for a society based on competition. This new society would be reached by a gradual extension of state ownership and operation of the means of production. Both writers proclaimed that the transition to socialism would come peacefully — indeed, with the consent and co-operation of the capitalists themselves.

Such a gentle, peaceful solution to the evils of capitalism appealed to Howells, and he advanced this concept in his novels, especially *A Hazard of New Fortunes, A Traveller from Altruria,* and *Through the Eye of the Needle.* Perhaps the best concise statement of Howells' belief is set forth in the following paragraph:

The system of competitive capitalism, with its accompanying ideal of individual success, is no longer satisfactory. It produces only a heartless struggle for survival, governed largely by chance, in which no life is secure; in which even invention, fruit of man's ingenuity, only adds to the misery of the unemployed. It produces, contrary to the equalitarian ideals of America, insuperable distinctions between the rich and the poor. Competitive capitalism should therefore be replaced by socialism; the machinery of government should be employed to control production in the interest of all rather than in the interest of the exploiting few. This socialism should not be the effect or agent of class conflict, but should represent the will of the majority, peaceably expressed by suffrage.

Essentially then, Howells, as a socialist, was opposed to confiscation, stood for gradual collectivization of industry, beginning with telegraphs and railroads, and believed that the change would come without class conflict. Like Gronlund and Bellamy, Howells believed that the intelligent classes should lead the way to socialism, with the workers playing an important but secondary role, and that the capitalists could be convinced that their best interests, in the long run, would be advanced if they too joined the crusade. That this was a Utopian brand of socialism is obvious, but it is also clear that it was based on the deep belief that the only hope for mankind was not reform but the exchange of a barbarous, competitive economic system for a rational, co-operative one.

Howells imparted his socialist creed to Mark Twain. During the long, animated talks which Howells describes so glowingly in *My Mark Twain*, there was a general exchange of ideas on the subject. Howells recommended specific books to Twain, including Tolstoy's works and Bellamy's *Looking Backward*. Twain did not fully appreciate Tolstoy — "I haven't got him in focus yet," he wrote Howells — but he was impressed by Bellamy. "Began 'Looking Backward' Nov. 5, 1889 on the train. A fascinating book," he recorded in his notebook.

Shortly afterwards, Twain arranged to meet Bellamy and discussed his ideas with him. Still later, in *The American Claimant*, describing a meeting of the Mechanics' Club, made up "mainly of the working class," he shows how deeply the workers were inspired by *Looking Backward*. But much as he admired Bellamy's brilliant analysis of the principle faults of the "dog-eat-dog" system of competitive capitalism; his exposé of the church, the schools and the press as agencies of "Big Business," and his detailed elaboration of how, in his imaginary co-operative commonwealth, poverty and want are abolished through the production of goods and services to meet the needs of the people, Twain did not share his confidence in the ability to achieve the new society without class conflict and through the co-operation of employers and workers.

Nevertheless, Howells was delighted to find Twain in such close accord with his own ideas of socialism. Speaking of Twain, he wrote to his father on February 2, 1890: "He and his wife and Elinor and I are all of accord in our way of thinking: that is, we are theoretical socialists, and practical aristocrats. But it is a comfort to be right theoretically and to be ashamed of one's self practically."

How fundamental Twain's "socialism" was at this time remains a question. Howells himself later modified the view he had expressed to his father. "He [Twain]," he wrote in *My Mark Twain*, "never went so far in socialism as I have gone, if he went that way at all." Certainly Twain never went so far in a Utopian direction as did Howells. He did not believe that socialism could be achieved without a class struggle and even with the co-operation of the more enlightened capitalists. He acknowledged that there were industrialists earnestly desirous of improving the conditions in mines and factories. But even these were so caught in the complex web of the economic system that there was little they could do as individuals; and the great body of the capitalists were so immersed in reaping profits from exploitation of labor that nothing but fear or force would make them yield a fraction of an inch. Just as it had been naive to have expected the slave-owners to respond to appeals to their intelligence and shame and join the movement to abolish slavery; just as it would be naive to expect the Czar and all other absolute monarchs to concede the virtues of the appeals for repre-

233

sentative government; so, too, it was naive to expect to achieve socialism by appealing to the intelligence and good will of the capitalists.

Twain also rejected the concept that the intelligent classes should lead the movement for socialism and that the workers should occupy a secondary role. He firmly believed that the only power in modern society capable of eradicating the evils of capitalism was organized labor. As Howells himself points out: "he had a luminous vision of organized labor as the only present help for workingmen."

While Twain shared Howells' hatred of the crimes of capitalism, he did not go as far as his friend in the advocacy of socialism to remedy these evils, but neither did he believe in the Utopian program advanced by men like Bellamy and endorsed by Howells. He placed his faith in organized labor.

Organized Labor: Civilization's Hope

Twain was not uncritical of organized labor. He condemned the practice of craft unions in barring membership to unskilled workers, especially the barriers placed in the path of foreign-born workers who sought to join these unions. He felt, too, that the opposition of unions to the introduction of new machinery was mistaken, convinced that "for every man deprived of work by the M[achine], 10 will get work, through it." But he never ceased to believe that, its faults notwithstanding, trade unionism was labor's only way of taking an effective "stand against injustice and oppression," and he was confident that labor would be triumphant in the end. For the workers' struggle, through the unions, for a decent livelihood and human dignity, was part of mankind's unending battle for ever-greater freedom. As a worker at the Mechanics' Club debate in *The American Claimant* points out, it was part of the long struggle against the "petted and privileged few" who have gained wealth and comfort "at the cost of the blood and sweat and poverty of the unconsidered masses who achieved them, but might not enter in and partake of them." Endorsing a strike of mine workers, Twain characterized it as "a strike for liberty. . . . It was Barons and John, over again, it was Hampden and Ship-Money; it was Concord and Lexington."

A worker in the Mechanics' Club debate, speaking for Twain, declares that the nation's most important resource was happy men and women, and that the test of a nation's progress was the security it afforded its working people. The achievement of this goal rested with labor through its organization.

This outlook remained with Twain to the end. Paine tells of one of the last evenings Howells spent with Twain. "The talk drifted to sociology and to the labor-unions, which Clemens defended as being the only means by which the workman could obtain recognition of his rights." His own description of himself in this connection is revealed in his characterization of a woman friend with whose deeply religious views he sharply disagreed, but "she is [for] laborers' rights and approves trades unions and strikes, and that is me."

Twain took particular pride in the admiration tendered him by the working class. He was delighted that his description of the Pilots' Union in *Life on the Mississippi* and his Chapter XXXIII from the *Connecticut Yankee* were reprinted in the labor press. He described the rousing welcome he received when he arrived in England in 1907 in these terms: "Who began it? The very people of all people in the world whom I would have chosen: a hundred men of my own class — grimy sons of labor, the real builders of empires and civilizations, the stevedores! They stood in a body on the deck and charged their masculine lungs, and gave me a welcome which went to the marrow of me." One may overlook the reference to "my own class" – he was probably thinking in terms of his early days as printer and pilot — but the deep sincerity of Twain's feelings is unmistakable.

Following the Equator has a passage in which Twain describes the sovereignty of the worker in South Australia: "his vote is the desire of the politician — indeed, it is the very breath of the politician's being; the parliament exists to deliver the will of the workingman, and the Government exists to execute it. The workingman is a great power everywhere in Australia, but South Australia is his paradise. He has had a hard time in this world, and has earned a paradise. I am glad he has found it." In his notebook, Twain inserted the observation: "Australia is the modern heaven — it is bossed absolutely by the workingmen."

Such statements refute the charge made frequently in Mark Twain's day, and in ours, that he took refuge in the 6th century because he lacked the courage to speak out concerning his own. Though he was reluctant to leave the writer's desk and become involved in the actual contest between capital and labor, he made it unmistakably clear again and again that in this struggle he sided with the workers. "His mind and soul," Howells pointed out, "were with those who do the hard work of the world, in fear of those who give them a chance for their livelihood and underpay them all they can."

Twain summed up his attitude toward the working class in a single sentence: "They are the creators of wealth; they build civilization; and without them no civilization can be built." Going further, he declared that the working class alone could save democratic institutions from being destroyed by "moneyed corporations." In his vision of a democratic America, free of the "moral rot" caused by the "money-fever," he counted upon the workers to be its architects. It would, he predicted, be the workers' own making, by their own efforts, through organization and the use of the ballot.

"One of my theories is, that the hearts of men are about alike, all over the world, no matter what their skin-complexions may be." [From letter to Ray J. Friedman, New York, March 19, 1901, Mark Twain Papers, University of California.]

"I am quite sure," Mark Twain wrote, "that (bar one) I have no race prejudices, and I think I have no color prejudices nor caste prejudices nor creed prejudices. . . . All that I care to know is that a man is a human being — that is enough for me; he can't be worse." The concluding portion of the statement reflects Mark Twain's deep pessimism about the entire human race expressed in his later years. But with the exception of his one bias (against the French), this summarizes Twain's mature approach to peoples of all colors, creeds, and nationalities. Its essence is contained in the following principle of action: "There is but one first thing to do when a man is wounded and suffering: *relieve* him. If we have a curiosity to know his nationality, that is a matter of no consequence, and can wait."

We have spoken of Twain's "mature approach" advisedly, for it was something he grew into only gradually, and only to the extent that he overcame some of the most destructive prejudices of his time.

Early Prejudices

Twain's boyhood was spent in a community in which feeling against "foreigners" was strengthened by anti-Catholicism and nativist politics. When he left Hannibal in 1853 to seek his fortune, he took with him a contempt for and intolerance of the foreign-born (particularly the Irish-Catholics) which was to color much of his early writings. His prejudice against the Catholic Church was to soften into toleration only with the passage of a half century. Even apart from anti-Catholicism, Twain's earliest comments on the foreign-born differed little from those appearing in the intolerant native-American journals of the period.

At the age of eighteen, he was expressing indignation over the number of foreigners in the Eastern cities. In August, 1853, he wrote home that he was appalled by the "mass of human vermin" he encountered in the immigrant districts of New York. In Philadelphia, three months later, he was similarly appalled by the number of foreigners there. When the Philadelphia printers failed to raise enough money to build a statue of Franklin, Twain wrote indignantly to his brother Orion: "There are so many abominable foreigners here ... who hate everything American, that I am very certain as much money for such a purpose could be raised in St. Louis, as in Philadelphia. I was in Franklin's old office this morning ... and there was at least one foreigner for every American at work there."

Twain recalled many years later that the above letters were written at a time when "the Know-Nothing disturbances were brisk." Although there is nothing to indicate that he participated in this movement, there is no doubt that he sympathized, at this stage in his development, with its objectives of checking immigration and making it more difficult for the foreign-born to become citizens. In a letter to Frank E. Burrough in 1876, he admitted his "intolerance" at the age of nineteen and twenty. Yet the truth is that this intolerance persisted for several more years. It appears even so late as in *Roughing It* (published in 1872) in expressions of prejudice against the foreign-born, particularly the Irish.

Yet this same man was later to become a foremost champion of the foreign-born, and was to condemn all anti-foreign sentiment. In 1899 he wrote in his notebook: "Patriotism is being carried to insane excess. I know men who do not love God because He is a foreigner."

It did not take long for Mark Twain to understand that his like or dislike for a minority group had nothing to do with the fact that they were entitled to the rights promised them under the Declaration of Independence and the Constitution. "I am not fond of Chinamen," he wrote in a public letter in 1868, "but I am still less fond of seeing them wronged and abused." Unless all minorities did enjoy the same rights as the majority, the boast that America was the land of the free was a mockery. As Twain put it in *Roughing It*, commenting on the exclusion of Chinese from the protection of the law: "Ours is the 'land of the free' — nobody denies that — nobody challenges it. (Maybe it is because we won't let other people testify.)"

Twain's championship of the rights of the Chinese in America emerged gradually. His description of the Chinese quarters of New York City and Virginia City, Nevada, reflects the stereotype so prominent in the anti-Chinese literature of the day. But in California he made the discovery that this stereotype was not based on actual experience with, or accurate observation of Chinese immigrants, that the conduct of the hard-working Chinese was generally the very opposite of that caricatured in the current slanders and jokes.

During a visit to San Francisco, late in 1863, Twain first took note of the persecution of the Chinese. In a sketch published in the New York *Sunday Mercury*, he commented: "God pity any Chinaman who chances to come in the way of the boys hereabout, for the eye of the law regardeth him not." In his newspaper work in San Francisco, he witnessed many incidents of brutality against the Chinese, and sought to voice his indignation in print. Among other pieces, he attacked certain Brannan Street butchers "who set their dogs on a Chinaman who was quietly passing with a basket of clothes on his head; and while the dogs mutilated his flesh, a butcher increased the hilarity of the occasion by knocking some of the Chinaman's teeth down his throat with half a brick." But the indignant piece was not published; the city-editor tossed it out "because it might offend some of the peculiar element that subscribed for the paper."

The Burlingame Treaty

After he left the Coast, Twain published a number of articles indicting the systematic persecution of the Chinese. On August 4, 1868, the New York *Tribune* featured his four-column article under the heading: "The Treaty With China. Its Provisions Explained." The treaty, signed by Secretary of State William H. Seward and Anson Burlingame, and ratified by the U.S. Senate, contained additions to an earlier treaty (1858), amplifying its powers.

Twain hailed the provisions giving the Chinese government the right to appoint Consuls with the same rights, privileges and powers as the Consuls of Great Britain and Russia. He was confident that even though the Consuls would be Americans, they would "be men who are capable of feeling pity for persecuted Chinamen and will call to a strict account all who wrong them." It gave him "infinite satisfaction" to think of the anguish on the face of the "cobblestone artists of California" when they read the consular clauses providing that:

They can never beat and bang and set the dogs on the Chinamen any more. These pastimes are lost to them forever. In San Francisco, a large part of the most interesting local news in the daily papers consists of gorgeous compliments to the 'able and efficient' Officer This and That for arresting Ah Foo, or Ching Wang, or Song Hi for stealing a chicken; but when some white brute breaks an unoffending Chinaman's head with a brick, the paper does not compliment any officer for arresting the assaulter, for the simple reason that the officer does not make the arrest; the shedding of Chinese blood only makes him laugh; he considers it fun of the most entertaining description. I have seen dogs almost tear helpless Chinamen to pieces in broad daylight in San Francisco, and I have seen hod-carriers who help to make Presidents stand around and enjoy the sport. I have seen troops of boys assault a Chinaman with stones when he was walking quietly along about his business, and send him bruised and bleeding home. I have seen Chinamen abused and maltreated in all the mean, cowardly ways possible to the invention of a degraded nature, but I never saw a Chinaman righted in a court of justice for wrongs thus done him. The California laws do not allow Chinamen to testify against white men. California is one of the most liberal and progressive States in the Union, and the best and worthiest of her citizens will be glad to know that the days of persecuting Chinamen are over, in California.

Still more intense, Twain predicted, would be their outraged feelings when they read Article 6 of the treaty. This gave the Chinese in the United States the privileges and immunities pertaining to "residence" by the "citizens or subjects of the most favored nation." To be sure, the same clause specified that it did not confer the right of naturalization on the subjects of China in the United States. But Twain dismissed this as insignificant, pointing out: "One of the chief privileges pertaining to 'residence' among us is that of taking the oath and becoming full citizens after that residence has been extended to the legal and customary period. . . . It would hardly be worth while for a treaty to *confer* naturalization in the last clause of an article wherein it had already provided for the acquirement of naturalization by the proper and usual course."

Unable to contain his enthusiasm, Twain characterized Article 6 as working "a miracle" which put Aladdin's achievements in the shade. It "lifts a degraded, snubbed, vilified, and hated race of men out of the mud and invests them with the purple of American sovereignty. It makes men out of the beasts of burden." It would wipe out the iniquitous and burdensome mining tax imposed upon Chinese in California — a tax imposed upon no other miners, native or foreign. It would allow the Chinese to acquire real estate, to testify against a white man in court, to sit on juries. "The time is near at hand when they will vote . . . when they will be eligible for office and may run for Congress, if such be the will of God." Especially important to Twain was the fact that, under Article 6, "the children of Chinese citizens will have the entry of the public schools on the same footing as white children." Therefore, he anticipated as the inevitable nativist reaction on the Pacific Coast a "weeping and wailing, and gnashing of teeth. . . . For, at one sweep, all the crippling, intolerant, and unconstitutional laws framed by California against Chinamen pass away, and 'discover' (in stage parlance) 20,000 prospective Hong Kong and Suchow voters and office-holders!"

Twain conceded that "the idea of seeing a Chinaman a citizen of the United States would have been almost appalling to me a few years ago, but I suppose I can live through it now." The Chinese were a hard-working, thrifty, quiet, orderly, and peaceable people, who "possess the rare and probably peculiarly barbarous faculty of minding their own business." They were "remarkably quick and intelligent, and they can all read, write, and cipher." Why, then, not confer the rights of citizenship on them? "Do not they compare favorably with the mass of other immigrants? Will they not make good citizens? Are they not able to confer a sound and solid prosperity upon a State?"

Events soon demonstrated, however, that the Burlingame treaty had not ushered in the millennium for the Chinese in the United States. On the contrary, by promoting the importation of Chinese laborers to the Pacific Coast, particularly for construction work on the Union Pacific Railroad which had been experiencing labor difficulties, the treaty intensified antagonism toward the Chinese. When completion of the transcontinental line in 1869 threw many laborers out of work, labor organizations in California blamed the Chinese. A few clearsighted leaders in the labor movement emphasized that the proper solution was to organize the Chinese; but their voices were drowned out in the loud cry that "The Chinese Must Go!"

Twain was aware that much of the opposition to the Chinese in California came from workers who believed that their living standards were being undermined by "coolie competition." The fact that the Chinese workers were imported to labor for incredibly low wages, gave these beliefs plausibility. At first, Twain saw nothing wrong in the importation of "coolie" labor, and urged the Californians to use "coolie" labor instead of agitating to bar the Chinese from the country. In his letters from Honolulu to the Sacramento *Union*, in 1866, Twain wrote: "You will not always go on paying $80 and $100 a month for labor which you can hire for $5. The sooner California adopts coolie labor the better it will be for her. It cheapens no labor of man's hands save the hardest and most exhausting drudgery ... which all white men abhor and are glad to escape from." But Twain began to regret his fulsome support of "coolie" labor. In his article on the Burlingame treaty, he called for "the breaking up of the infamous Coolie trade." Once this was achieved, there would be little fear of the Chinese undermining the standard of living of white workers. Indeed, Twain believed that, even in California which received the bulk of Chinese immigrants, the competition from Chinese labor was never as menacing as the agitators claimed. Much of this agitation, he believed, was deliberately stirred up by men of wealth who stood to benefit by deluding white workers that all their grievances would be solved once the Chinese were driven out. By channeling labor discontent into anti-Chinese activities, the wealthier classes diverted it from themselves.

Twain did not greatly concern himself with the economic effects of the problem, but recent research tends to substantiate the correctness of what he did write on the subject. He mainly devoted himself to exposing "the brutally outrageous treatment" of the Chinese in the land of the free, a subject which engaged the attention of few American writers of the period.

One of Twain's most effective pieces on this subject is the brilliant but little-known satire, "Disgraceful Persecution of a Boy," published in the *Galaxy* magazine in 1870. "In San Francisco, the other day," the sketch begins, "a well-dressed boy, on his way to Sunday-school, was arrested and thrown into the city prison for stoning Chinamen. What a commentary is this upon human justice! What sad prominence it gives to our human disposition to tyrannize over the weak. San Francisco has little right to take credit to herself for her treatment of this poor boy. What had the child's education been? How should he suppose it was wrong to stone a Chinaman? Before we side against him, along with outraged San Francisco, let us give him a chance — let us hear the testimony for the defense." Twain then points out that since the boy was "well-dressed ... and a Sunday-school scholar," it is to be assumed that his parents were "intelligent, well-to-do people, with just enough natural villainy in their composition to make them yearn after the daily papers, and enjoy them; and so this boy had opportunities to learn all through the week how to do right, as well as on Sunday." In this manner, the boy learned that "the great Commonwealth of California" imposed "an unlawful mining-tax" upon the Chinese, and that "a respectable number of the taxgatherers" collected this tax twice instead of once, and that since they did this "solely to discourage Chinese immigration into the mines, it is a thing that is much applauded, and likewise regarded as being singularly facetious." He also learned that when a white man, no matter of what nationality, robbed a sluice-box, he was forced to leave the camp; "and when a Chinaman does that thing, they hang him"; and that, "in many districts of the vast Pacific coast so strong is the wild, free love of justice in the hearts of the people, that whenever any secret and mysterious crime is committed, they say, 'Let justice be done, though the heavens fall', and go straightway and swing a Chinaman." In this way, too, he learned "that the legislature, being aware that the Constitution has made America an asylum for the poor and the oppressed of all nations, and that, therefore, the poor and oppressed who fly to our shelter must not be charged a disabling admission fee, made a law that every Chinaman, upon landing, must be *vaccinated* upon the wharf; and pay to the State's appointed officer *ten dollars* for the service, when there are plenty of doctors in San Francisco who would be glad enough to do it for him for fifty cents." Twain then sums up the case for the defense:

It was in this way that the boy found out that a Chinaman had no rights that any man was bound to respect; that he had no sorrows that any man was bound to pity; that neither his life nor his liberty was worth the purchase of a penny when a white man needed a scape-goat; that nobody loved Chinamen, nobody befriended them, nobody spared them suffering when it was convenient to inflict it; everybody, individuals, communities, the majesty of the State itself, joined in hating, abusing, and persecuting these humble strangers.

And, therefore, what *could* have been more natural than for this sunny-hearted boy, tripping along to Sunday-school, with his mind teeming with freshly-learned incentives to high and virtuous action, to say to himself: "Ah, there goes a Chinaman! God will not love me if I do not stone him." And for this he was arrested and put in the city jail.

Twain concludes his sketch on a note of savage irony: "Everything conspired to teach him that it was a high and holy thing to stone a Chinaman, and yet he no sooner attempts to do his duty that he is punished *for* it."

"Goldsmith's Friend Abroad Again"

Twain probed still more deeply into the wide range of discrimination against and persecution of the Chinese in a satire published serially in the *Galaxy* magazine, in 1870 and 1871, under the title, "Goldsmith's Friend Abroad Again." The series purports to be letters from Ah Song Hi, a Chinese emigrant to the United States, to his friend in China, Ching Foo. In his introductory note, Twain makes it clear that while the letters were imaginary, their contents were based on reality: "No experience is set down in the following letters which had to be invented. Fancy is not needed to give variety to the history of a Chinaman's sojourn in America. Plain fact is amply sufficient."

The first letter is written from Shanghai as the excited Ah Song Hi is about to set sail for the promised land:

It is all settled, and I am to leave my oppressed and over-burdened native land and cross the sea to that noble realm where all are free and equal, and none reviled or abused — America! America, whose precious privilege it is to call herself the Land of the Free and the Home of the Brave. We and all that are about us here look over the waves longingly, contrasting the privations of this our birthplace with the opulent comfort of that happy refuge. We know how America has welcomed the Germans and the Frenchmen and the stricken and sorrowing Irish, and we know how she has given them bread and work and liberty, and how grateful they are. And we know that America stands ready to welcome all other oppressed peoples and offer her abundance to all that come, without asking what their nationality is or their creed or color.

Once on board the ship, Ah Song Hi discovers that, in order to pay for his passage he must turn over to the partner of the employer in the United States, who has advanced the money (sixty dollars), "my wife, my boy, and my two daughters ... for security for the payment of the ship's fare." He also discovers that out of the twelve dollars a month he was to receive as wages, he must pay two dollars to the American Consul for the certificate that he was shipped in the steamer. Under the laws, the Consul is supposed to collect two dollars per steamer, but he collects two dollars per passenger. Since there were 1,300 Chinese on board, he pocketed $2,600 for certificates. "My employer tells me," Ah Song Hi informs his friend, Ching Foo, "that the Government at Washington knows of this fraud, and are so bitterly opposed to the existence of such a wrong that they tried to have the extor — the fee, I mean, legalised by the last Congress, but as the bill did not pass, the Consul will have to take the fee dishonestly until next Congress makes it legitimate. It is a great and good and noble country, and hates all forms of vice and chicanery."

Chinese always travel in steerage, Ah Song Hi points out. "It is kept for us, my employer says, because it is not subject to changes of temperature and dangerous drafts of air. It is only another instance of the loving unselfishness of the Americans for all unfortunate foreigners. The steerage is a little crowded, and rather warm and close, but no doubt it is best for us that it should be so." The discomforts of the voyage are made bearable by the promise that in ten days, Ah Song Hi would "step upon the shore of America, and be received by her great-hearted people; and I shall straighten myself and feel that I am a free man among freemen."

The voyage lasted much longer, but finally Ah Song Hi arrived in San Francisco. He stopped ashore jubilantly, wanting "to dance, shout, sing, worship the generous Land of the Free and Home of the Brave." Alas! As he walked off the gangplank, policemen beat him up with their clubs, and confiscated his baggage. He was forced to be vaccinated by the official doctor whose fee was ten dollars. This took his last penny — "my ten dollars which were the hard savings of nearly a year and a half of labour and privation."

Ah Song Hi assures his friend that these incidents had not dampened his enthusiasm. For one thing, he was convinced, that "if the law-makers had only known there were plenty of doctors in the city glad of a chance to vaccinate people for a dollar or two, they would never have put the price up so high against a poor friendless Irish, or Italian, or Chinese pauper fleeing to the good land to escape hunger and hard times."

After a month in San Francisco, Ah Song Hi is a free man. His employer's business had failed, and he agreed to release Ah Song Hi from his contract on the condition that he be repaid for the passage money from the first wages Ah Song Hi earned. Penniless, without a friend, a stranger in a strange land, Ah Song Hi feels like a pauper. But then he remembers that he is in America, "the heaven-provided refuge of the oppressed and the forsaken!"

The comforting thought does not last long. He is attacked by several young men who set their dog upon him, and soon he is "just rags and blood from head to foot." Luckily a passer-by calls the police. Ah Song Hi is rescued in a peculiar way. He is arrested, beaten up, thrown into a stone-paved dungeon, and charged with "being disorderly and disturbing the peace." His pleas of innocence are met with the warning that the court will stand for none of his "d — d insolence." Being unable to pay the fine or furnish bail, he is beaten to a pulp and thrown back into the dungeon. The last words he remembers as he is kicked into the cell are: "Rot there, ye furrin spawn, till ye lairn that there's no room in America for the likes of ye or your nation."

Ah Song Hi informs his friend that he is rapidly becoming disillusioned. The very idea of prisons in America had seemed inconceivable to him, for prisons, he had believed, "are a contrivance of despots for keeping restless patriots out of mischief," and "Americans, being free, had no need of prisons." Equally disillusioning is the knowledge that there are some people in America who are not punished for their crimes. A boy of fourteen is in the jail with him, sentenced because he had enticed young girls from the public schools to the lodgings of prominent gentlemen down town. Imagine Ah Song Hi's consternation when he learns that "there was a strong disposition to punish the gentlemen who had employed the boy to entice the girls, but as that could not be done without making public the names of those gentlemen and thus injuring them socially, the idea was finally given up."

But the complete disillusionment comes during the trial. Ah Song Hi discovers that Irishmen can often evade punishment because of the friendly disposition of the judges; that "Negroes were promptly punished, when there was the slightest preponderance of testimony against them," and that "Chinamen were punished *always*." When he proposes to call several Chinese witnesses to testify that he was attacked without any provocation on his part, he is informed coldly by the interpreter: "That won't work. In this country white men can testify against Chinamen all they want to, but *Chinamen ain't allowed to testify against white men*." This is beyond his comprehension:

What a chill went through me! And then I felt the indignant blood rise to my cheek at this libel upon the Home of the Oppressed, where all men are free and equal — perfectly equal — perfectly free and perfectly equal. I despised this Chinese-speaking Spaniard for his mean slander of the land that was sheltering and feeding him. I sorely wanted to sear his eyes with that sentence from the great and good American Declaration of Independence which we have copied in letters of gold in China and keep hung up over our family altars and in our temples — I mean the one about all men being created free and equal.

But woe is me, Ching Foo, the man was right. He was right, after all. There were my witnesses, but I could not use them. . . .

Ah Song Hi is fined five dollars or ten days. Along with him, twelve to fifteen other Chinese are fined and imprisoned — solely on the testimony of a white person; and all were barred from calling Chinese witnesses in their defense.

The correspondence closes with the trial. The last (and seventh) letter to Ching Foo ends: "By noon all the business of the court was finished, and then several of us who had not fared well were remanded to prison; the judge went home; the lawyers and officers, and spectators departed their several ways, and left the uncomely courtroom to silence, solitude, and Stiggers, the newspaper reporter, which latter would now write up his items (said an ancient Chinaman to me), in which he would praise all the policemen indiscriminately and abuse the Chinamen and dead people."

"Goldsmith's Friend Abroad Again" has been listed by bibliographers under the heading of "Whimsical Sketches." But there is nothing "whimsical" about this exposure of the brutal treatment accorded the Chinese immigrants in the land they had imagined to be the haven of the oppressed. It is true that the Irish characters in the sketch are stereotypes; but this is its only flaw. No one has given us a more devastating portrayal of the contrast between the myth and reality of American democracy so far as the Chinese in this country were concerned.

Negro Slavery in Hannibal

In his article in the New York *Tribune* of August 4, 1868, "The Treaty with China," Mark Twain explained that his endorsement of citizenship for Chinese-Americans was part of a general process of change in his thinking on the whole subject of citizenship for minority groups. The key to this change, he pointed out, was his attitude toward citizenship for the Negro: "The idea of making negroes citizens of the United States was startling and disagreeable to me, but I have become reconciled to it, and the ice being broken and the principle established, I am ready now for all comers." The man who wrote these words was soon to explain to a close friend that he "held himself responsible for the wrong which the white race had done the black race in slavery," and that in paying the way of a Negro student through Yale, "he was doing it as part of the reparation due from every white to every black man."

Mark Twain had reason to feel personally responsible for that "wrong." He grew up in a slaveholding community, and his father and uncle both owned slaves. But he was, during most of his early life, wholly unconscious of the contradiction presented by the presence of slavery in a land settled by seekers for freedom. Looking backward over his childhood, he later admitted that in his schooldays he had no aversion to slavery, and went on to explain apologetically: "I was not aware that there was anything wrong about it. No one arraigned it in my hearing; the local papers said nothing against it; the local pulpit taught us that God approved it, that it was a holy thing, and that the doubter need only look to the Bible to settle his mind ... and then the texts were read aloud to us to make the matter sure; if the slaves themselves had any aversion to slavery, they were wise and said nothing. In Hannibal we seldom saw a slave misused, on the farm, never."

Twain offers the same explanation for the fact that his kind-hearted mother (whom he describes as "the natural ally and friend to the friendless," and who "would not have allowed a rat to be restrained of its liberty") condoned human slavery: "I think she was not conscious that slavery was a bold, grotesque and unwarrantable usurpation. She had never heard it assailed in any pulpit, but she had heard it defended and sanctified in a thousand, her ears were familiar with the Bible text that approved it, but if there were any that assailed it they had not been quoted by her pastor; as far as her experience went, the wise and the good and the holy were unanimous in the conviction that slavery was right, righteous, the peculiar pet of the deity, and a condition which the slave himself ought to be duly and nightly thankful for. Manifestly, training and association can accomplish strange miracles. As a rule our slaves were convinced and content."

It is quite true that slavery bore less harshly on the Negro slave in Missouri than on the large plantations of the deep South. It is also true that the intermingling of Negro and white, young and old, was quite common in Hannibal, and gave Twain the opportunity to develop early friendships with Negroes. He recalled, years later, that he preferred the society of his Negro playmates "to that of the elect." Referring to summers spent on the farm of his uncle who owned thirty slaves, he wrote in his *Autobiography:* "All the negroes were friends of ours and with those of our own age we were in effect comrades. I say in effect, using the phrase as a modification. We were comrades; color and condition interposed a subtle line which both parties were conscious of and which rendered complete fusion impossible. . . . It was on the farm that I got my strong liking for the race and my appreciation of certain of its fine qualities. This feeling and this estimate have stood the test of sixty years and more, and have suffered no impairment. The black face is as welcome to me now as it was then."

All this, however, could not mitigate the fact that slavery was still slavery whether on the small farms of Missouri or the large plantations of the lower Mississippi. Twain's statement that slaves were seldom misused in Hannibal is open to question. One of his most poignant memories was of the sad faces — "the saddest faces I have ever seen" — of a dozen Negro men and women, chained together on the Hannibal wharf, awaiting shipment to southern slave markets. There were other hideous memories too: of a Negro being killed when his master flung a lump of iron-ore at his head; of the house girl, Jennie, her wrists bound with a bridle rein, being flogged with a cowhide by Mark Twain's father because she dared to snatch the whip with which his mother had threatened to punish her; of Negro slaves being burned to death by Missouri lynch mobs; and of recaptured runaway slaves being tied up with ropes and left lying on the ground, wounded and groaning. The number of advertisements in Hannibal newspapers describing fugitive slaves and offering rewards for their capture, casts doubt on Twain's statement that the slaves of the area were usually "content." Orion Clemens' paper carried such advertisements, so Mark certainly knew that there were slaves in Hannibal ready to risk life and limb to escape "contentment" in Missouri.

Twain's statement that no one "arraigned" slavery within his "hearing" may be true; but he certainly knew that even in Hannibal there had been people who denounced the system and demanded its abolition. President David Nelson of Marion College, located in West Ely near Hannibal, was a militant abolitionist in pro-slavery Marion county, fifteen hundred of whose ten thousand inhabitants were slaves in 1840. An anti-abolition lynch-crusade by the local slaveholders forced President Nelson out of the state. In addition, "several persons living about or near the College, suspected of entertaining abolition sentiments, had to leave the county with the utmost precipitation." While Mark Twain was only one year old when these events took place, he must have known of them, for they were long talked of in Hannibal. He himself used them as the basis for the sketch, "A Scrap of Curious History." He certainly was aware that his own father, a local magistrate, sentenced abolitionists to jail.

That young Twain knew of and had no sympathy for the struggle against slavery being waged in the North by the abolitionists is made clear in his early letters. He told his mother, in 1853, that when he saw the Court House in Syracuse, on his way to New York City, "it called to my mind the time when it was surrounded with chains and companies of soldiers, to prevent the rescue of McReynold's nigger, by the infernal abolitionists." Other of these letters express annoyance over the fact that Negroes in the North enjoyed liberties which were entirely unknown in Hannibal. He resented having to force his way, in New York, through crowds of Negroes, mulattoes, quadroons, and other "trash." He wrote home that "to wade through this mass of human vermin, would raise the ire of the most patient person that ever lived." Several such experiences caused him to write indignantly to his mother: "I reckon I had better black my face, for in these Eastern States niggers are considerably better than white people." He longed for the pro-slavery society of Hannibal where a Negro knew his place. In a letter to his brother Orion, he exclaimed: "I would like amazingly to see a good old-fashioned negro."

Of Orion, Twain once said that although "born and reared among slaves and slaveholders, he was yet an abolitionist from boyhood to his death." One can, of course, ask why it was possible for Orion Clemens to regard slavery as morally wrong though reared among slaveholders, and for Mark and his mother to see nothing wrong in slavery *because* they were reared in the same environment. Apart from this, one must note that Twain's characterization of his brother as an abolitionist was quite exaggerated — almost as much as his statement that his father, though owning slaves, held that "slavery was a great wrong." Actually, Orion Clemens maintained that he was "entirely conservative" on the slavery question, expressed "contempt for the abolitionists of the North," and attacked the Free Soil movement. He did, however, regard slavery as an evil, defended the civil rights of free Negroes in Hannibal, and became a Lincoln Republican on the eve of the Civil War.

Twain's Role in the Civil War

Believing that slavery was an evil, Orion was a staunch supporter of the Union cause during the Civil War. Mark Twain, a pilot on the Mississippi, could not make up his mind which side to support. Indeed, he showed little interest in the issues and events which were leading the country to Civil War. By February, 1861, Louisiana had joined the other seceding states, yet Twain's letter to Orion from New Orleans, dated February 6, 1861, did not mention secession talk, or any special excitement in the city, or the approaching inauguration of President-elect Lincoln.

In the "Private History of a Campaign that Failed," published in 1865, Twain recalled the state of mind of the pilots before and after the cannonading of Fort Sumter with which the war began: "During the first months of the great trouble ... it was hard for us to get our bearings. ... My pilot mate was a New-Yorker. He was strong for the Union; so was I. But he would not listen to me with any patience; my loyalty was smirched, to his eye, because my father had owned slaves. ... A month later the secession atmosphere had considerably thickened on the Lower Mississippi, and I became a rebel, so did he. ... In the following summer he was piloting a Federal gunboat and shouting for the Union again, and I was in the Confederate army."

For several months then, Twain swung, without conviction between the Union and Confederate cause. He finally decided to go home and reflect on the matter. The result of his reflection was that he became a Confederate volunteer. After three weeks service, he deserted. This constituted his total war record.

There is little to indicate that Twain deserted because he became conscience-stricken over fighting to uphold human slavery. To be sure, some of his biographers have ventured that opinion, but he himself nowhere supports it. Another explanation may be that he came to oppose war in general. He explained that, at the age of eleven, during the Mexican War, he had wanted to be a soldier, but was of course, not accepted. And "before I had a chance in another war the desire to kill people to whom I had not been introduced had passed away." Certainly a boil, a sprained ankle, and heavy rains combined to destroy whatever remained of the desire, and hastened his desertion. It was to take a long time, however, before Twain lived down his three weeks' participation in the Confederate military service. More than once after the war he was called "a damned Secessionist."

As soon as he recovered sufficiently from the injury to his ankle to travel, Twain went to Orion's home in Keokuk, Iowa. Orion had an offer of a good job as secretary to the Governor of the Territory of Nevada. He urged his brother to go with him, partly for financial aid (Twain had his earnings from his work on the river), and partly "to wean Sam away from his rebel cause." Thrown out of a well-paid profession by the outbreak of war, Twain decided to join Orion in the move West.

Edgar Lee Masters charges that Twain went West in 1861 to escape the military draft, and that his sudden departure should be labeled abject cowardice. It is true that he wanted no part of the fighting and saw no reason "to get up into a glass perch and be shot at by either side."

But it is extremely improbable that Twain foresaw the draft in May or June, 1861, when he first entertained the idea of going West with Orion. It is much more probable that the reports in the St. Louis papers of gold and silver discoveries in Nevada, coupled with the prospect of adventure, induced him to leave for the Territory. Doubtless he believed that the war would be quickly settled and that he could return to his old place on the river after a vacation in the West. Later, when Twain wrote of his trip to Nevada in *Roughing It*, he implied that he had not planned to remain long: "In two or three weeks I had grown wonderfully fascinated with the curious new country, and concluded to put off my return to 'the States' awhile."

Though it need not have been cowardice that prompted his decision to leave for Nevada, it certainly can be said that he displayed little interest in the greatest crisis the country had ever faced, and that he remained indifferent to the vital issues of the war. This is illustrated in a letter to his mother from Carson City in January, 1862, which included some verse he had written:

> *How sleep the brave who sink to rest*
> *Far, from the battle-field's dreadful array,*
> *With cheerful ease and succulent repast*
> *Now ask the sun to lend his steaming ray.*

"Bully, isn't it," comments Twain. "I mean the poetry, madam, of course. Doesn't it make you feel 'stuck up' to think that your son is a — Bard?" A latter-day critic had a more appropriate comment to make when he asked: "Does not his poem betray a levity about a deeply serious national crisis that is not altogether commendable even in a humorist?" The same observation can be made of the following sentence in one of Twain's letters home in late 1861: "If the war will let us alone we can make Mr. Moffett rich."

But the war did not leave Nevada or Twain alone. By

the time he joined the staff of the *Territorial Enterprise* at Washoe, the Territory was divided over the issues of the conflict, with fist fights among the Nevadan miners an almost daily occurrence. Twain's reporting for the ardently pro-Union *Enterprise* did not lead to his active involvement in the struggle. He did help in the campaign of the Union Sanitary Fund, but he was comparatively uninterested in the reasons for it. In a semi-humorous slur on the women of Virginia City who had raised money at a Sanitary Fund Fancy Dress Ball, he charged that the money "had been diverted from its legitimate course, and was to be sent to aid a Miscegenation Society somewhere in the East." Although Twain apologized to the ladies, his use of the expression "a Miscegenation Society" reveals that he was not unsympathetic to one of the most vicious arguments used to besmirch the Union cause.

Probably the closest thing to an affirmation of Twain's support of the Union cause, during the war, is a piece he published in the Virginia City *Evening Bulletin* of July 31, 1863. Here he described the inspiring effect of the emergence of the flag of the United States on Mount Davidson out of the gloom of an electric storm. This aroused great excitement because of a "superstition . . . that this was a mystic courier come with great news from the war." It turned out that the telegraph operator, who was sworn to secrecy, knew that great things had happened that day in the East — "Vicksburg fallen, and the Union armies victorious at Gettysburg!" Twain reports that had "the glorious flag on Mount Davidson" been able to speak and tell of its joyous news, it would have been "saluted and resaluted . . . as long as there was a charge of powder to thunder with; the city would have been illuminated; and every man that had any respect for himself would have got drunk."

This is all we have from Mark Twain's pen to indicate that he was ever moved by the issues of the bloody conflict. In none of his sketches, written during or shortly after the war, are the issues of the struggle touched on. Apart from the piece about the flag, Twain remained silent from the beginning till the end of the war. Throughout the conflict he seems to have been reluctant to commit himself.

Twain's Analysis of Negro Slavery

Twain's writings on the question of slavery before and during the Civil War reveal either indifference or opposition to the anti-slavery forces. Nothing in these writings could lead one to expect that he would come to view slavery as a tremendous injustice and a basic contradiction to the precepts put forth by the founding fathers; or to suggest that he would devote a major portion of his creative writing to exposing the evils of slavery. His hatred of the institution he had accepted and even defended as a boy and a young man, flashed in his later novels, sketches, speeches and notebooks. The notebooks, the bulk of which are still unpublished, reveal how strongly Twain felt that he had to "atone" for his previous indifference to and support of human bondage. The whole structure of chattel slavery comes under his scrutiny in these notes which assembled the ammunition for the attacks he was to make in his novels and stories. No one who had read the complete notebooks can disagree with William Dean Howells' remark about the Mark Twain he knew in the post-Civil War era: "No man more perfectly sensed and more entirely abhorred slavery."

An analysis of Twain's post-Civil War writings reveals that he understood clearly that the foundation of slavery had been the profit motive. One of Twain's characters, speaking for the author, asks what "crime" did the first Negro commit that the fate of slavery "was decreed for him"? And the answer is that there was no "crime." It was the white man's greed for profits that made "this awful difference between white and black." Fundamentally there was no difference between the two. A black skin did not render a woman incapable of knowing mother love. "Ain't you my chile?" a Negro mother in one of Twain's novels asks her son who is unable to understand her willingness to be sold back into slavery for his sake. "In de inside, mothers is all de same. De good Lord he made 'em so."

Because the slaveholders robbed the Negro people of their natural right — their freedom — Twain justified all measures they took against their oppressors. In his novel, *Pudd'nhead Wilson*, Twain boldly asserts that the Negro slaves were fully justified in stealing from their masters: "They had an unfair show in the battle of life, and they held it no sin to take military advantage of the enemy in a small way. . . . They would smouch provisions . . . small articles of clothing, or any other property of light value . . . perfectly sure that in taking this trifle from the man who daily robbed them of an inestimable treasure — their liberty — they were not committing any sin that God would remember . . . in the Last Great Day."

Thus Twain rejected the concepts of literary figures in post-Civil War America — headed by Thomas Nelson Page — who glorified the plantation tradition, provided their readers with nostalgic pictures of "happy and faithful slaves," "kind and considerate masters," and "wretched and disillusioned freedmen" who longed to return to the "care-free happiness" of slavery. Twain dismissed the oft-repeated description of slaveowners as men whose interests compelled them to care for their slaves' welfare, with the terse comment: "He would be a fool & *called* a fool, who should claim that when the master makes the laws that are to govern both himself & his slave, he will take as much care of the slave's interest as of his own."

In his notebook, Twain recorded the following conversation of Negroes he had met on the Mississippi, and indicated that it was to be used as ammunition against "the Wretched Freedman who longed for Slavery" school of literature:

At one place one of them said: "That's a mighty beautiful plantation."

The other replied, "Lordy, lordy, many a poor nigger has been killed there, just for nuffin, & flung into that river thar' & that's the last of — 'em."

After a pause the first said, "If we could only have the old times back again, just for a minute, just to see how it would seem."

"Oh Lordy *I* don't want 'em back again for a minute. It was mighty rough time on the niggers."

"That's so. I come mighty near being sold down here once; & if I had been I wouldn't been here now; been the last of me."

The other said, "I was sold once down as far as Miss[issippi]. I was afraid I'd go furder down. If I had I'd never been here."

Twain minced no words in evaluating the inhumanity of slavery and the suffering it entailed on the Negro people. At its worst, slavery meant "working a Negro to death," and at its best, it meant "a life of misery." As the mother in Langston Hughes' poem, "Mother to Son," puts it:

> *Well, son, I'll tell you:*
> *Life for me ain't ben no crystal stain.*
> *Its had tacks in it,*
> *And splinters,*
> *And boards torn up,*
> *And places with no carpet on the floor —*
> *Bare.*

"Lincoln's proclamation . . . not only set the black slaves free, but set the white man free also," Twain once said. Slavery for the Negro smothered the white conscience, robbed the white man's sense of self-respect, and turned the white man into an unchristian, undemocratic, and inhuman tyrant. Slavery particularly brutalized the slaveholder and removed his finer sensibilities if he had any. Twain reminded himself in his notebook to make sure to "tell how I once saw a planter gamble a negro away. Make it realistic." He likewise noted that "women slaves (were) stripped and whipped," that "families (were) sold on (the) auction block," and that no protests came from "the best families." Men and women had become so hardened by long familiarity with oppression that when a slave-woman was lashed into unconsciousness, they commented only "on the expert way in which the whip is handled." Twain observes succinctly: "This is what slavery could do, in the way of ossifying what one may call the superior lobe of human feeling."

While staying at a Bombay hotel during his lecture tour in India, Twain saw the German manager strike a native on the jaw for failing to execute a command properly. The train of thought which this incident started carried him back to the Missouri of his childhood. "I had not seen the like of this for fifty years," he reflected. "It flashed upon me the forgotten fact that this was the *usual* way of explaining one's desires to a slave." Recalling how, as a child of ten, he had seen a Negro killed for doing something awkwardly, he wrote bitterly in an unpublished passage in his *Autobiography:* "Everybody seemed indifferent about it — as regarded the slave — though considerable sympathy was felt for the slave's owner, who had been bereft of valuable property by a worthless person who was not able to pay for it."

This was the kind of callousness which slavery strengthened in men. "To admit that slavery exists in any country," Twain summed it up, "is to admit that you may describe any form of brutal treatment which you can imagine and go there and find it . . . applied."

Slavery, Twain pointed out, had bred a society in the South in which many white people considered it beneath their dignity to work with their hands. Such a society was dear to the literary figures who were reconstructing the ante-bellum South as a glorified American Eden. But Twain had only contempt for it.

"Sir Walter Disease"

Next to slavery, Twain attributed the evils of Southern society to the "Sir Walter disease." From Scott's Waverley novels came the Southern obsession with genealogy, knighthood, and chivalry. It was Scott, Twain charged, who had resurrected in the South the medieval "chivalry silliness" which undid the work of a greater writer, Cervantes, who "swept the world's admiration for the medieval chivalry silliness out of existence." The advance of civilization had been checked in the South by the debilitating influence of Scott's romances.

Warming to his subject, Twain even charged that Scott had caused the Civil War. "It was Sir Walter that made every gentleman in the South, a major or a colonel, or a general or a judge, before the war; and it was he, also, that made these gentlemen value these bogus decorations. ... Sir Walter had so large a hand in making Southern character, as it existed before the war, that he is in a great measure responsible for the war."

Admittedly this personal devil interpretation of American history was superficial. (Twain himself agreed that it was a "wild proposition.") Yet he did put his finger on one cause of Southern backwardness, and did expose the highly glamorized "aristocracy" of the ante-bellum South, revealing what actually lay behind the moonlight and magnolias. Compared to the bogus Southern aristocrats, with their "silliness and emptiness, sham grandeurs, sham gauds, and sham chivalries of a brainless and worthless long-vanished society," the Negro characters in Twain's novels and stories stand out as true heroes and heroines of the South.

"A True Story"

Reviewing *Sketches Old and New* by Mark Twain, William Dean Howells wrote in the *Atlantic Monthly* of December, 1875: "by far the most perfect piece of work in the book is 'A True Story'. ... The rugged truth of the sketch leaves all other stories of slave life infinitely far behind, and reveals a gift in the author for the simple, dramatic report of reality which we have seen equalled in no other American writer."

262

Every reader of "A True Story" will agree with Howells' evaluation. It is truly a masterpiece. The story, which Twain states is "repeated word for word as I heard it," begins with a description of the Negro servant, Aunt Rachel, "a cheerful, hearty soul" who, at the end of the day's work, would "let off peal after peal of laughter." One summer evening, Twain asks her: "Aunt Rachel, how is that you've lived sixty years and never had any trouble?" After assuring herself that he is really serious, Aunt Rachel, "full of earnestness," replies:

"Has I had any trouble? Misto C - - - -, I's gwyne to tell you, den I leave it to you. I was bawn down 'mongst de slaves; I knows all 'bout slavery, 'case I ben one of 'em my own se'f. Well, sah, my ole man — dat's my husban' — he was lovin' an' kind to me, jist as kind as you is to yo' own wife. An' we had chil'en — seven chil'en — an' we loved dem chil'en just de same as you loves yo' chil'en. Dey was black, but de Lord can't make no chil'en so black but what dey mother loves 'em an' wouldn't give 'em up, no, not for anything dat's in dis whole world. . . .

"Well bymeby my ole mistis says she's broke, an' she got to sell all de niggers on de place. An' when I heah dat dey gwyne to sell us all off at oction in Richmon', oh, de good gracious! I know what dat mean!"

Aunt Rachel had gradually risen, while she warmed to her subject, and now she towered above us, black against the stars.

"Dey put chains on us an' put us on a stan' as high as dis pooch — twenty foot high — an' all de people stood aroun', crowds an' crowds. An' dey'd come up dah an' look us all roun', and squeeze our arm, an' make us git up an' walk, an' den say, 'Dis one too ole,' or 'Dis one lame,' or 'Dis one don't 'mount to much.' An' dey sole my ole man, an' took him away, an' dey begin to sell my chil'en an' take *dem* away, an' I begin to cry; an' de man say, 'Shet up yo' dam blubberin',' an' hit me on de mouf wid his han'. An' when de las' one was gone but my little Henry, I grab' *him* clost up to my breas' so, an' I ris up an' says, 'You shan't take him away,' I says; 'I'll kill de man dat tetches him!' I says. But my little Henry whisper an' say, 'I gwyne to run away, an' den I work an' buy yo' freedom.' Oh, bless de chile, he always so good! But dey got him — dey got him, de men did; but I took and tear de cloe's mos' off of 'em an' beat 'em over de head wid my chain; an' *dey* give it to *me,* too, but I didn't mine dat.

"Well, dah was my ole man gone, an' all my chil'en, all my seven chil'en — an' six of 'em I hain't set eyes on ag'n to dis day, an' dat's twenty-two year ago las' Easter."

Aunt Rachel then relates how she was taken to Newbern by her new master. When the Civil War broke out, her master became a Confederate colonel, and she was the family's cook. The white people ran away when the Union army came, leaving Aunt Rachel and the other Negro slaves "in dat mons'us big house." Aunt Rachel was asked by the Union officers who moved in if she would cook for them. "'Lord bless you,' says I, 'dat's what I's *for.*'" Aunt Rachel tells the Union officers the story of her life and especially "bout my Henry. Dey a-listening to my troubles, jist de same as if I was white folks; an' I says, 'What I come for is beca'se if he got away and got up Norf whar you gemmen comes from, you might 'a' seen him, maybe, an' could tell me so as I could fine him ag'in; he was very little, an' he had a sk-yar on his lef' wris' an' at de top of his forehead.' Den dey look mournful, an' de Gen'l says, 'How long sence you los' him?' an' I say, 'Thirteen year.' Den de Gen'l say, 'He wouldn't be little no mo' now — he's a man!'"

Eventually, Aunt Rachel learns that Henry had escaped to the North and had become a barber. When the war came, he decided to give up his trade and look for his mother. "So he sole out an' went to whar dey was recruitin', an' hired hissel'f out to de colonel for his servant; an' den he went all froo de battles everywhah, huntin' for his ole mamy; yes, indeed, he'd hire to fust one officer an' den another, tell he'd ransacked de whole Souf; but you see *I* didn' know nuffin 'bout *dis.* How was I gwyne to know it?"

One night there was a soldier's ball at Newbern, and a whole platoon from a Negro regiment came into the house. One of the Negro soldiers decided to stay behind in the house after the dance, for there was something on his mind, and he knew that he would not be able to sleep that night:

"Dis was 'bout one o'clock in de mawnin'. Well, 'bout seven, I was up an' on han', gettin' de officers' breakfast. I was a-stoppin' down by de stove — jist so, same as if yo' foot was de stove — an' I'd opened de stove do' wid my right han' — so, pushin' back, jist as I pushes yo' foot — an' I'd jist got de pan o' hot biscuits in my han' an' was 'bout to raise up, when I see a black face come aroun' under mine, an' de eyes a-lookin' up into mine, jist as I's a-lookin' up clost under yo' face now; an' I jist stopped *right dah*, an' never budged! Jist gazed an' gazed so; an' de pan begin to tremble, an' all of a sudden I *knowed*! De pan drop' on do flo' an' I grab his lef' han' an' shove back his sleeve — jist so, as I's doin' to you — an' den I goes for his forehead an' push de hair back so, an' 'Boy!' I says, 'if you ain't my Henry, what is you doin' wid dis welt on yo' wris' an' dat sk-yar on yo' forehead? De Lord God ob heaven be praise', I got my own ag'in!"

"Oh, no Misto C - - - -, I hain't had no trouble. An' no joy!"

In these few pages, Twain tells us more about the Negro people, the true nature of slavery, the Civil War, the role of the Negro people in that conflict, than is achieved in many volumes. He makes clearly evident: 1. The dignity of the Negro woman; 2. That to characterize the Negro people as fun-loving children who have no real concerns or problems of importance is a canard; 3. The love of the Negro family — of the Negro slave husband and wife for each other, the Negro slave mother for her children; 4. The hideous nature of slavery, that tears families apart; 5. The desertion of their plantations by the slaveowners, leaving the slaves to shift for themselves; 6. The liberating role of the Union army; 7. The devotion of the Negro slaves to the Union army; and their eagerness to aid the Union soldiers; 8. The role of the Negro people in fighting for their own liberation by participation in the Union army by military and other service; 9. The sympathy of the Union officers for the slave woman, revealing the significance of the entrance of the Union army into the South; 10. The search of the son for his mother as typifying what took place during and after the Civil War as thousands of former slaves moved about the South looking to reunite their families, separated during slavery.

THE ADVENTURES OF HUCKLEBERRY FINN

The idea for *Huckleberry Finn* was forming in Mark Twain's mind at the time he wrote "A True Story"; hence it is not surprising that his greatest work should contain numerous passages which are almost a continuation and development of the brief story. And if, in the earlier work, Twain created one of the finest woman characters in American literature, so in *The Adventures of Huckleberry Finn*, published in 1884, he gave us one of the greatest male characters — Huck Finn's companion and friend, the Negro runaway slave, Jim. "Jim," Sterling Brown has pointed out, "is the best example in 19th century fiction of the average Negro slave (not the tragic mulatto or the noble savage), illiterate, superstitious, yet clinging to his hope for freedom, to his love for his own. And he is completely believable."

Jim is the real hero of the novel. He is a warm human being, lovable and admirable. His nobility shines through the entire book. Whether it was risking his life and freedom to save Tom Sawyer or shielding little Huck from the knowledge that the corpse aboard the raft is Huck's father, Jim represents all that is good in man. Even the doctor, steeped in the Southern white supremacy ideology, pays tribute to Jim's courage in aiding Tom when he was wounded. He tells the slave hunters who have captured Jim after his escape from slavery, that he never saw a Negro who "was a better nuss or faithfuller and yet he was risking his freedom to do it." Twain does not portray Jim's devotion to Tom in the servile stereotyped manner typical of the plantation tradition novels. Rather he shows Jim as naturally kind, staunch and brave.

266

Huck's development is a constant struggle. He has the task of throwing off the load of slave society conventions. The true greatness of the book lies in its exposition of how this is accomplished.

Huck begins by regarding Jim very much as the white Southerner regarded a slave. Gradually, he discovers that Jim, despite the efforts of society to brutalize him, is a noble human being who deserves his protection, friendship and love. This change takes place slowly in Huck, always accompanied by an inner struggle between the ideology and mores of a slave society and the humanity of the boy. In one instance, Huck, having hurt Jim's feelings by a particularly mean trick, says: "It was fifteen minutes before I could work myself up to go and humble myself to a nigger; but I done it, and I warn't ever sorry for it afterward, neither. I didn't do him no mean tricks, and I wouldn't done that one if I'd 'a' knowed it would make him feel that way." On another occasion, Huck awakens on the raft and hears Jim moaning to himself. Huck is puzzled but he finally concludes: "I knowed what it was about. He was thinking about his wife and children, up yonder, and he was low and homesick... I do believe he cared just as much for his people as white folks does for their'n. It don't seem natural, but I reckon it's so."

But it is in the famous "conscience" scene, growing out of Jim's escape to freedom, that Huck makes his final break with the conventions of Southern slave society. One day Jim learns to his horrified amazement that he was about to be sold "down the river." As Jim explains to Huck:

"Well you see it 'uz disway. Ole missus — dat's Miss Watson — she pecks on me all de time en treats me pooty rough, but she awlus said she wouldn't sell me down to Orleans. But I noticed dey wuz a nigger trader roun' de place considerable lately, en I begin to get uneasy, well one night I creeps to de do' pooty late, en de do' warn't quite shet, en I hear ole missus tel de widder she gwyne to sell me to Orleans, but she didn't want to, but she could git eight hund'd dollars for me, 'en it 'uz such a big stack of money she couldn' resis'. De widder she try to git her to say she wouldn't do it, but I never waited to hear de res'. I mighty quick lit out I tell you."

In Jim's plight, Twain dramatizes the cruelty of slavery. He is to be sold down the river for the sufficient reason that he will bring $800 in New Orleans. Moreover, everyone in the village is entirely reconciled to such inhumanity; none felt it to be inconsistent with their praise of the Declaration of Independence on the fourth of July. Even generous-hearted Huck, a person of no family — his father having "no more quality than a sudcat" — shares the village's attitude toward slavery. He cannot understand Tom Sawyer's proposal to help Jim escape from bondage: "Well, one thing was dead sure, and that was that Tom Sawyer was in earnest, and was actually going to help steal that nigger out of slavery. That was the thing that was too many for me. Here was a boy that was respectable and well brung up; and had a character to lose; and folks at home that had character; and he was bright and not leather-headed; and knowing and not ignorant; and not mean, but kind; and yet here he was, without any more pride, or rightness, or feeling, than to stoop to this business, and make himself a shame, before everybody." When he is asked to assist in the escape, Huck contemplates with horror the thought of being called a "nigger-stealer" or "low-down" abolitionist. In an unpublished comment in his notebook, set down in 1895, Twain explains Huck's feelings:

In those old slave-holding days the whole community was agreed as to one thing — the awful sacredness of slave property. To help steal a horse or a cow was a low crime, but to help a hunted slave, or feed him or shelter him, or hide him, or comfort him, in his trouble, his terrors, his despair, or hesitate to promptly betray him to the slave-catcher when opportunity offered was a much baser crime, & carried with it a stain, a moral smirch which nothing could wipe away. That this sentiment should exist among slave-owners is comprehensible — there were good commercial reasons for it — but that it should exist & did exist among the paupers, the loafers, the tag-rag & bobtail of the community, & in a passionate & uncompromising form, is not in our remote day realizable. It seemed natural enough that Huck & his father the worthless loafer should feel it & approve it, though it seems now absurd. It shows that that strange thing, the conscience — the unerring monitor — can be trained to approve any wild thing you *want* it to approve if you begin its education early & stick to it.

Huck decides to help Jim make good his escape, but he is constantly wrestling with his "ill-trained conscience," as Twain put it in his notebook. In one of his many moments of vacillation, his soul tormented by the "crime" he is committing, he takes pity on "poor Miss Watson" who is being deprived of her "property": "Conscience says to me, 'What had poor Miss Watson done to you that you could see her nigger go off right under your eyes and never say one single word? What did that poor old woman do to you that you could treat her so mean?'" When Huck hears Jim describe his plan, once he had gained his freedom, to buy his wife and children out of slavery, all his Southern rearing comes to the fore:

It most froze me to hear such talk. He wouldn' ever dared to talk such talk in his life beforen. Just see what a difference it made in him the minute he judged he was about free. It was according to the old saying, "Give a nigger an inch and he'll take an ell."

Here was this nigger which I had as good as helped to run away, coming right out flat footed and saying he would steal his children — children that belonged to a man I didn't even know; a man that hadn't done me no harm. . . .

Huck weighs the question of betraying Jim. He tries to persuade himself that Jim would be better off at home, after all, with his family. He considers the advantage to himself, realizing that he would become a hero in the eyes of his home town. But he cannot do it. His conscience pulls at him in all directions:

My conscience got to stirring me up hotter than ever, until at last I say to it, "Let up on me — it *ain't* too late yet — I'll paddle ashore at the first light and tell. . . ."

By and by one showed, Jim sings out, "We's safe, Huck, we's safe! you know." And as I shoved off he says: "Pooty soon I'll be a shout'n for you, en I'll say its all on account o' Huck I's a free man. . . . Jim wont ever fergit you, Huck; you's de bes' fren' Jim's ever had; en you's de only fren' ole Jim's got now."

I was paddling off all in a sweat to tell on him but when he says this, it seemed to kind of take the tuck all out of me . . . when I was fifty yards off, Jim says: "Dah you goes, de ole true Huck; de on'y white genlman dat ever kep' his promise to ole Jim."

Well, I just fell sick. But I says I got to do it. . . . I can't get out of it.

Huck decides to try to find an answer through prayer. He tells himself that if he had gone to Sunday School he would not be in this predicament, that he would have learned that helping a slave gain his freedom meant going to "everlasting fire. . . . So I kneeled down. But the words wouldn't come . . . I was trying to make my mouth say I would do the right thing and the clean thing, and go and write to that nigger's owner, and tell where he was; but deep down in me I knowed it was a lie and He knowed it. You can't pray a lie — I found that out." At last Huck had an idea, astonishing in its simplicity. Why, he'd write the letter first and then try to pray. So he wrote a letter to Miss Watson informing her of Jim's whereabouts:

I felt good and washed clean of sin for the first time I had ever felt so in my life, and I knowed I could pray now. But I didn't do it straight off but laid the paper down and set there thinking — thinking how good it was all this happened so and how near I came to being lost and going to hell. And went on thinking. And got to thinking over our trip down that river; and I see Jim before me all the time; in the day and in the night time, sometimes moonlight, sometimes storms, and we a-floating along, talking and singing and laughing. But somehow I couldn't seem to strike no places to harden me against him, but only the other kind. I'd see him standing my watch on top of his'n 'stead of calling me, so I could go on sleeping; and seen him how glad he was when I came back out of the fog; and when I come to him again in the swamp, up there where the feud was; and such like times; and would always call me honey and pet me, and do everything he could think of for me, and how good he always was; and at last I struck the time I'd saved him by telling the men we had smallpox aboard, and he was so grateful and said I was the best friend old Jim ever had in the world, and the *only* one he got now, and then I happened to look around an see that paper.

It was a close place. I took it up, and held it in my hand. I was a-trembling, because I'd got to decide, forever, betwixt two things and I knowed it. I studied a minute, sort of holding my breath, and says to myself, "*All right,* then, I'll go to hell," and tore it up.

"A sound heart & a deformed conscience came into collision & conscience suffers defeat," Twain summed it up, years later, in his notebook. The conscience scene on the river is one of the most moving in American literature. Nowhere else is so effectively pictured the contradiction between the holy institutions which upheld slavery and the humane feelings of a decent human being.

Huck's tearing up the letter is the crux of the novel, but the book is filled with devastating thrusts at the whole idea of white supremacy. When a free Negro from Ohio comes to town with a white shirt, a gold watch and chain and a silver-headed cane, who is it that flies into a rage and sounds off about shiftless Negroes? Why, it is Huck's drunken old father, who never did a stroke of work in his life if he could help it. Who is it who insists that the Negroes deserve to be enslaved because they are not mentally equipped to be free? Why, it is the same whites who show how stupid they are by falling prey to two old frauds who swindle them by posing as the Duke of Bilgewater and the Dauphin of France. Who is it who claims that the Negroes are savages? Why, none other than the whites who spend their time feuding with each other for nothing.

The Adventures of Huckleberry Finn is climaxed by the remarkable piece of irony towards the end of the novel in which Huck explains that the delay in the boat's arrival was caused by the blowing of a cylinderhead. "Goodness gracious! anybody hurt?" Aunt Sally, a pious Christian woman asks. "No'm. Killed a nigger," Huck answers. "Well, it's lucky; because sometimes people do get hurt," Aunt Sally says thankfully.

It is in such eloquent passages, especially the "Conscience" scene, notes De Voto, that "literature does what it can to repay the bondman's 250 years of unrequited toil." Twain, like his fellow novelist and lecture companion, George W. Cable, helped to counterbalance the derogatory stereotypes of the Negro characteristic of most American fiction in the post-Reconstruction era. With "Mark Twain's Jim," notes the London *Times Literary Supplement* in 1954, evaluating the development of American literature, "there begins an attempt to portray the Negro as an individual rather than as a stock character." There begins, too, the attempt to demolish in literature the myth that the Negro slave was acquiescent and subservient to the slavocracy. The historical truth, as set forth in *Huckleberry Finn* and before it, in "A True Story," is that the Negro slave challenged, through struggle, the whole system of oppression in the South.

Small wonder, then, that *Huckleberry Finn* was barred from certain libraries and schools. While the reasons advanced by the authorities was "the book's endemic lying, the petty thefts, the denigration of respectability and religion, the bad language, and the bad grammar," it was clear to anyone who read the attacks on the book thoughtfully, that the authorities regarded the exposure of the evils of slavery and the heroic portrayals of the Negro characters as "hideously subversive." And, as Twain pointed out bitingly, the fathers of these same authorities had "shouted the same blasphemies a generation earlier when they were closing their doors against the hunted slave, beating his handful of humane defenders with Bible text, and billies, and pocketing the insults and licking the shoes of his Southern masters."

PUDD'NHEAD WILSON

Twain's next novel concerning the South in general and slavery in particular, *Pudd'nhead Wilson,* published in 1893, was no *Huckleberry Finn.* Yet it is permeated with acute and detailed observations on the nature and effects of white-supremacy oppression. The very fact that Twain dealt with this theme in fiction in the early 1890's is significant. George W. Cable's *John March, Southerner,* published in 1894, caricatured its Negroes, in sharp contrast to his heroic "Bras-Coupe" of the *Grandissimes,* published ten years before. William Dean Howells' *An Imperative Duty,* published in 1893, concerned itself with the tragic problem of an octoroon girl whom a white man seeks in marriage. Neither Cable's nor Howells' novels dealt with Negro history or oppression. In those same years, moreover, a flood of anti-Negro fiction came pouring from the presses, "stressing the Negro's divergence from an Anglo-Saxon norm to the flattery of the latter." Against this racist literary production, Mark Twain's *Pudd'nhead Wilson,* despite certain faults, stands in refreshing and sharp contrast. While this much neglected novel does not rise to the greatness of *Huckleberry Finn,* it is also a masterpiece. In several ways, it more sharply conveys Twain's intense contempt for the slavocracy's ideology than any of his other books.

It opens with a masterfully ironical portrayal of the ruling class of Dawson's Landing, the Missouri town where the novel is set. We are immediately shown how a slaveholding culture breeds an aristocratic, feudal tradition in a democratic society. "To be a gentleman — a gentleman without stain or blemish — was his only religion, and to it he was always faithful," is the way Twain sums up the philosophy of the leading slaveholder in the community. For the gentleman, he notes further, "honor stood first," and the laws of honor "required certain things of him which his religion might forbid him: then his religion must yield — the laws could not be relaxed to accommodate religion or anything else." With such an aristocratic code of conduct to guide them, it is not surprising, Twain points out, that these "gentlemen" thought nothing of separating slave families by selling mothers, fathers and children down the river. When Percy Driscoll, "a gentleman," withdraws his threat to sell his slaves down the river, he is so amazed at his own magnanimity that "that night he set the incident down in his diary, so that his son might read it in after years and be thereby moved to deeds of gentleness and humanity himself." It never occurs to him, Twain makes clear in this ironic portrayal, that by enslaving human beings he has deprived himself of the right to consider himself in terms of "humanity."

Just as Jim, the Negro slave, is the hero of *Huckleberry Finn*, so Roxy, the slave girl, is the heroine of *Pudd'nhead Wilson*. Indeed, according to Henry Seidel Canby, she is "the only completely real woman in his [Twain's] books."

She was of majestic form and stature [Twain says in introducing her], her attitudes were imposing and statuesque, and her gestures and movements distinguished by a noble and stately grace. Her complexion was very fair, with the rosy glow of vigorous health in the cheeks, her face was full of character and expression, her eyes were brown and liquid, and she had a heavy suit of fine soft hair which was also brown, but the fact was not apparent because her head was bound about with a checkered handkerchief and the hair was concealed under it. Her face was shapely, intelligent, and comely — even beautiful. She had an easy, independent carriage — when she was among her own caste — and a high and 'sassy' way, withal; but of course she was meek and humble enough where white people were.

This meekness and humility, Twain makes clear as the story develops, was no more than a façade. Roxy is ready to defy the whole system of oppression to save her infant son from the degradation of slavery. Through Jim, Twain showed the basic humanity and heroism of the Negro male; and through Roxy, he portrays, as in "A True Story," the unbreakable strength of the Negro woman.

The central theme of the novel revolves about the interchange of two babies, one Negro, the other white, in their cradles. Through his masterly handling of this theme, Twain demonstrates the fraud and myth of racial superiority. Roxana (Roxy) and her master's wife give birth to two baby boys on the same day, February 1, 1830. "Roxana was twenty years old. She was up and around the same day, with her hands full, for she was tending both babies." So Twain depicts the callous lack of regard for the slave mother, not permitted a single day alone with her new-born child; she must work so that the white mother can rest. When the white mother dies within the week, both babies continue to be cared for by Roxy.

Twain scoffs at the manifest absurdity of the slavocracy's doctrine that justified enslavement of any person with the slightest infusion of Negro blood in his or her veins. "Only one-sixteenth of her was black, and that sixteenth did not show. . . . To all intents and purposes Roxy was as white as anybody, but the one-sixteenth of her which was black outvoted the other fifteen parts and made her a negro. She was a slave and salable as such. Her child was thirty-one parts white, and he, too, was a slave, and by a fiction of law and custom, a negro." So much alike did Roxy's child and that of her master's look that one could tell them apart only by their clothing, "for the white babe wore ruffled soft muslin and a coral necklace, while the other wore merely a coarse tow-linen shirt which barely reached to its knees, and no jewelry."

Roxy discovers to her amazement that her baby could some day be sold down the river. As she watches the white baby sleeping, Roxy cries out:

'What has my po' baby done, dat he couldn't have yo' luck? He hadn't done nothin'. God was good to you; why warn't he good to him? Dey can't sell *you* down de river. I hates yo' pappy; he hain't got no heart — for niggers he hain't anyways. I hates him, en I could kill him! . . . .

'Oh, I got to kill *my* chile, dey ain't no yether way — killin' *him* wouldn't save de chile fum goin' down de river. Oh, I got to do it, yo' po' mammy's got to kill you to save you, honey.... Mammy's got to kill you — how *kin* I do it! But yo' mammy ain't gwine to desert you — no, no; *dah*, don't cry — she gwine *wid* you, she gwine to kill herself, too. Come along, honey, come along wid mammy; we gwine to jump in de river, den de troubles o' dis worl' is all over — dey don't sell po' niggers down the river over yonder.'

In the process of clothing the baby so the angels would "'mire" him and not feel he was dressed "too indelicate," Roxy put the master's baby's ribboned and ruffled gown on her own child. She was amazed at his loveliness, but more so at the perfect resemblance between the two babies. Suddenly her problem was solved. Roxy switches everything from her baby to the little master, and rejoices that her child is saved: "dey ain't no man kin ever sell mammy's po' little honey down de river now!" As she looks at the little master, now sleeping in her own child's "unpainted pine cradle," she says movingly: "I's sorry for you, honey; I's sorry, God knows I is, — but what *kin* I do, what *could* I do? Yo' pappy would sell him to somebody, some time, en den he'd go down de river, sho', en I couldn't, *couldn't* stan' it." As she thinks further on the problem, she concludes that she would be committing no sin, for the real sin was committed in the first place by the white folks who enslaved the Negro people.

To make sure that the switching of the children was perfect, Roxy took them to the one person whom she felt might be keen enough to note the difference. It was the person whom everyone but Roxy considered a fool — Pudd'nhead Wilson. The test was passed. Pudd'nhead took their fingerprints — he took all fingerprints in the area — labeled them in a routine fashion, paid Roxy the usual compliments, and went on with his work. Roxy's child thus becomes the master's son and the master's own son become his slave! The father himself cannot tell his own child from the other. With what irony, Twain depicts how the master's cruel, but confidently righteous, severity imposes the abjectness of slave mentality upon his own child, who becomes the servant of the slave's child.

To be sure, as the story unfolds, Twain appears to be swallowing the spurious "blood will tell" doctrine in his explanation of the evil conduct of Roxy's child once he is installed as the master's son. But this does not detract from his effective demolition of the structure upon which the justification of slavery rested. In the end, Pudd'nhead Wilson discovers the secret and reveals how Roxy switched the children after birth. Even here Twain scores a number of additional points against slavery. He shows how difficult it is for the master's son, reared in slavery, to think and act as a free man now that he has been restored to his place at the head of the plantation. Slavery has conditioned him to regard himself as an inferior being, a crime it had committed against countless Negroes.

The conclusion of the story is a crowning irony. After Roxy's child confesses to a murder committed while he occupied the status of the master's son, he was sentenced to life imprisonment. However, since he has been transformed into a slave and has become a valuable piece of property, the creditors to the estate complain against the sentence. The entire white population saw their point: "Everybody granted that if Tom were white and free it would be right to punish him — it would be no loss to anybody; but to shut up a valuable slave for life — that was quite another matter. As soon as the Governor understood the case, he pardoned Tom at once, and the creditors sold him down the river." Once again Twain makes the point that the profit motive is at the root of the slave system. Legal and ideological theories raised to justify slavery are mere devices to buttress the extraction of wealth from the uncompensated labor of the Negro people.

Did Twain Degrade the Negro People?

From time to time, Twain's novels and stories have been criticized as being "racially offensive" to the Negro people. This is based both on the use of dialect and derogatory references such as the word "nigger." The issue received considerable publicity recently when the press reported on September 12, 1957, that the New York City Board of Education had quietly dropped *The Adventures of Huckleberry Finn* from the approved textbook lists for the elementary and junior high schools. The reason for the action was reported to be that the book "has been criticized by some Negroes as 'racially offensive.'" The press quoted a spokesman for the National Association for the Advancement of Colored People as stating that while his organization had not protested to the Board of Education about the book, it "strongly objected to the 'racial slurs' and 'belittling racial designations' in Mark Twain's works."

The news produced a series of editorials and letters, the vast majority of which expressed indignation at the removal of *Huck Finn* from the approved textbook lists, and pointed out that to do so on the ground that it was "racially offensive" to the Negro people was to overlook the fact that the book's central theme was that slavery and racial inequality are evil. The *New York Times* editorialized: "The truth is that Huckleberry Finn is one of the deadliest satires that was ever written on some of the nonsense that goes with the inequality of races. . . . It should . . . be available for use in New York schools. One is not so certain about the Central High School of Little Rock, Ark(ansas)."

The New York *Herald Tribune* took the same editorial position. But it went still further, sponsoring an essay contest among elementary and high school students on "What 'Huck Finn' Means to Me." The essays submitted vigorously opposed banning the book, revealing clearly that the reading of Twain's novel had opened the eyes of the young people to the evils of slavery, had deepened their respect for the heroism of the Negro slaves, and their understanding of the broad significance of Huck's final decision to help Jim escape.

The defenders of this masterpiece of American and indeed of world literature are clearly in the right in deploring its banning. Yet it is necessary to point out that there is a real problem here which must be solved. Men and women, deeply concerned that this might assist the cause of the white supremacists, have argued that in exactly reproducing dialect and in degrading references to Negroes, Twain's books help to perpetuate the myth of Negro inferiority.

The solution to this problem is not to ban the books and deprive young people of acquaintance with great literature and great documents in the progress of human relations and understanding, but to require teachers to explain the background of the language used by Mark Twain, and why words accepted passively in the 1880's are today labeled terms of opprobrium.

Twain himself explained that he had made a most careful study of the Missouri vernacular before writing *Huckleberry Finn*: "In this book a number of dialects are used, to wit: the Missouri Negro dialect, the extremest form of the backwoods Southwestern dialect, the ordinary 'Pike County' dialect, and four modified varieties of this last. The shadings have not been done in a haphazard fashion or by guesswork, but painstakingly and with the trustworthy guidance and support of personal familiarity with these several forms of speech." James Nathan Tidewell, a distinguished linguistic scholar, has established that Twain completely succeeded in his attempt to reproduce with painstaking accuracy the multiple dialect of the Negroes in the Missouri of his time. He "revealed the salient, low colloquial Southern and Negro features of Jim's speech, not by a thoroughly 'consistent' spelling of every word, but by what is better, an accurate one."

While appreciating the motives for protesting the use

of dialect, its authentic reproduction does not, by itself, slander the Negro people. No less a figure than Frederick Douglass, the greatest Negro of the nineteenth century, acknowledged the "slave accent" and reproduced dialect in his writings. It could not, he pointed out, be ignored as a cultural manifestation in Negro speech.

In explaining the derogatory references to Negroes in Twain's works, it must be pointed out that apart from the fact that these were used in most of the literature of the period, it was inevitable that a book written about Missouri when it was slave territory would contain references from which decent Americans would recoil today. It would have been a violation of reality to put twentieth century anti-racist expressions and concepts in the mouths either of the Missouri slaveowners or its backwoods people.

Criticizing the New York City Board of Education for dropping *Huckleberry Finn* from approved public school textbook lists, Elmer A. Carter, a Negro member of the New York State Commission Against Discrimination, declared: "No harm can be done to Negroes by Mark Twain." This is true, for Twain never deliberately vilified the Negro people. To be sure, there are stereotyped portraits of Negroes in his novels and stories. But, unlike most of his contemporaries, Twain does not present these familiar stereotypes to support the Plantation Tradition of the ante-bellum South. In almost every case, such material is balanced by the portrayal of the Negro as the hero or the heroine of the story. It is quite understandable why many Southerners read Twain's books with "revulsion of feeling." One critic, reviewing *Pudd'nhead Wilson* in the *Southern Magazine* in 1894, said that the book should have been properly entitled "The Decline and Fall of Mark Twain." The novelist was accused of "substituting circus-posters for accurate photographs of life and people in the South." Yet he could not be said to have "sinned ignorantly against half his countrymen," for he himself was a Southerner. "How come you to be so sinfully reconstructed" a Southern correspondent asked Twain, after reading *Huckleberry Finn* and *Pudd'nhead Wilson.*

Yes, Mark Twain was a Southerner, and it is to be expected that his novels should be filled with traditional images of steamboats on the river, cotton plantations, the great house, and the slave quarters. Novels in his day provided readers with the same set of stock scenes and characters. But Mark Twain added something different — wonderful scenes in which the evils of slavery are laid bare; quiet, tender scenes in which Negroes voice their longings for freedom; and dramatic scenes picturing Negro heroism. Twain's novels proclaimed to the world that the Negro had never accepted slavery, had fought for his freedom, and was entitled to enjoy the full fruits of democracy.

Were the Negro People Really Free?

In 1869 Mark Twain urged "Petroleum V. Nasby" (David Ross Locke) to join him in a lecture tour of the West, on which Nasby would give his famous denunciation of slavery, "Cussed Be Canaan." Nasby refused, objecting that the slavery lecture had lost its meaning: "You know that lemon, our African brother, juicy as he was in his day, has been squeezed dry. Why howl about his wrongs after said wrongs have been redressed? ... You see, friend Twain, the Fifteenth Amendment busted 'Cussed Be Canaan.' I howled feelingly on the subject while it was a living issue ... but now that we have won our fight, why dance frantically on the dead corpse of our enemy."

Although Twain's awakening to the slavery issue came much later than Nasby's, he, at least, understood that the fight for the freedom of the Negro people was by no means "won" with the adoption of the 13th, 14th, and 15th amendments. Indeed, in *The Innocents Abroad*, published the same year (1869) in which he proposed the lecture tour to Nasby, Twain shows his understanding of the fact that the Negro in the United States was still far from being fully free. In this book, Twain introduces a Negro who

281

acted as a guide during his tour of Venice. He reports that his guide "was born in South Carolina of slave parents. They came to Venice while he was an infant. He had grown up here. He is well educated. He reads, writes and speaks, English, Italian, Spanish and French, is a worshiper of art and thoroughly conversant with it; knows the history of Venice by heart and never tires of talking of her illustrious career." Twain left his guide with this interesting observation: "Negroes are deemed as good as white people, in Venice, and so this man feels no desire to go back to his native land. His judgment is correct." This tribute to the Negro guide as a cultured person, and his recognition that in most parts of the United States, he would be regarded as inferior to the least-cultured white man, shows that Twain understood that the Emancipation Proclamation had not really freed the Negro.

Twain and Frederick Douglass

In that same year, 1869, Twain made the acquaintance of a Negro who had risen from slavery to the position where he was recognized as the militant spokesman for his people. He wrote to his wife on December 14: "Had a talk with Fred Douglass, to-day, who seemed exceedingly glad to see me — & I certainly was glad to see *him* for I do so admire his spunk." What Twain admired in Douglass was the Negro leader's insistence that emancipation of the Negro slaves was not enough; that to make it meaningful, political, economic and civil rights had to be added; and his constant emphasis that only through militant struggle would the Negro people win full freedom. So great was Twain's respect for and admiration of Douglass, that in 1881, he wrote to President-elect James A. Garfield, urging him to retain the Negro spokesman as Marshal of the District of Columbia. This was his sole request of Garfield, for whose election he had campaigned vigorously. He wrote to the President-elect on January 12, 1881:

I offer this petition with peculiar pleasure and strong desire, because I so honor this man's high and blemishless character and so admire his brave, long crusade for the liberties and elevation of his race.

He is a personal friend of mine, but that is nothing to the point, his history would move me to say these things without that, and I feel them too.

Twain was proud to claim Frederick Douglass as a "personal friend." Negroes were welcomed to his home as equals. When he was living in Lucerne, Switzerland, he received and entertained six Jubilee Singers at his home. He wrote the following day: "Three of the six were born in slavery, the others were children of slaves. How charming they were — in spirit, manner, language ... carriage, clothes — in every detail that goes to make up the real lady and gentleman, and welcome guest." Twain would lecture any time in a Negro church even if he was too busy to speak for a white congregation. He paid the way of one Negro student through a Southern institution, and that of another through the Yale Law School.

Lynching of Negroes

Once Twain was asked whether he, as a Southerner, thought that lynching of Negroes was necessary as a protection for the whites. He retorted angrily that even the asking of the question was an insult; that when a hundred men killed one trembling, terrified Negro, they were guilty of both murder and fantastic cowardice. And their crime was compounded by the fact that, in more than half the cases, the lynchers put to death an innocent man.

This last point was based on more than conjecture. Twain had read many accounts of lynchings which concluded that "the night riders lynched the wrong man." In August, 1869, he published an editorial in the Buffalo *Express* entitled, "Only a Nigger." The editorial opens by reporting that it has been discovered that a Negro who had been lynched in Tennessee for "having ravished a young lady" was innocent. Twain then comments:

Ah, well! Too bad, to be sure! A little blunder in the administration of justice by Southern mob-law; but nothing to speak of. Only "a nigger" killed by mistake — that is all. Of course, every high-toned gentleman whose chivalric impulses were so unfortunately misled in this affair ... is as sorry about it as a high-toned gentleman can be expected to be sorry about the unlucky fate of "a nigger." But mistakes will happen, even in the conduct of the best regulated and most high-toned mobs, and surely there is no good reason why Southern gentlemen should worry themselves with useless regrets, so long as only an innocent "nigger" is hanged, or roasted or knouted to death, now and then. What if the blunder of lynching the wrong man does happen once in four or five cases? Is that any fair argument against the cultivation and indulgence of those fine chivalric passions and that noble Southern spirit which will not brook the slow and cold formalities of regular law, when outraged white womanhood appeals for vengeance? Perish the thought so unworthy of a Southern soul! Leave it to the sentimentalism and humanitarianism of a cold-blooded Yankee civilization! What are the lives of a few "niggers" in comparison of the impetuous instincts of a proud and fiery race? Keep ready the halter, therefore, oh chivalry of Memphis! Keep the lash knotted; keep the brand and the faggots in waiting, for prompt work with the next "nigger" who may be suspected of any damnable crime! Wreak a swift vengeance upon him, for the satisfaction of the noble impulses that animate knightly hearts, and then leave time and accident to discover, if they will, whether he was guilty or no.

A few weeks later, Twain inserted the following note in his column, "People and Things," in the Buffalo *Express*: "Another trifling mistake by Judge Lynch: The negro found hanging near Dresden, Tennessee, a few years ago, and who was supposed to have been hung for committing a rape on a small girl, has proved not to be the right person."

Twain's hatred of and contempt for lynchers was brilliantly expressed in the powerful scene in *Huckleberry Finn* where Colonel Shelburne's scorn withers the bravados of the mob. The Colonel, shotgun in hand, sneers at the gang formed to lynch him: "I know you clear through. ... Your newspapers call you a brave people so much that you think *you are*. ... You didn't want to come. The average man don't like trouble and anger. ... But if only *half* a man shouts ... 'Lynch him!' You're afraid to back down — afraid you'll be found out to be what you are — *cowards*. The pitifulest thing out is a mob."

In 1901, a particularly barbarous lynching occurred in Missouri, Mark Twain's native state. A young white woman on her way to church was murdered. Three Negroes were lynched — two of them very old — five Negro households were burned out, and thirty Negro families were driven into the woods. Twain was so deeply revolted by the terrible crime that he wrote "an acid article" on the whole subject which he called "The United States of Lyncherdom." The lynching, in Missouri, he said, has stained the entire nation, for the lynchers "have given us a character and labeled us with a name, and to the dwellers in the four quarters of the earth we are 'lynchers' now, and ever shall be."

Twain gives figures on the increase in the number of lynchings, and then asks what accounts for the wave of lynching which was sweeping the country. He answers that whenever a Negro was burned at the stake, the act brings in its wake a host of imitators. Hence "a much-talked-of lynching will infallibly produce other lynchings here and there and yonder, and that in time these will breed a mania, a fashion; a fashion that will spread wide and wider, year by year, covering state after state, as with an advancing disease." Thus far the "disease" had mainly infected the South, especially the four Southern states of Alabama, Georgia, Louisiana, and Mississippi; but it had also begun to make headway in Colorado, California, Missouri; unless it was stamped out, the time might come when one would see "a negro burned in Union Square, New York, with fifty thousand people present, and not a sheriff visible, not a governor, not a constable, not a colonel, not a clergyman, not a law-and-order representative of any sort." A lynching mob, Twain points out, consists largely of a momentarily insane group. What brought the sane members into it? Fear of unpleasantly standing out from the crowd. Usually one domineering man in the mob was able to browbeat the other members into acts of violence. Logically, therefore, a possible method of preventing lynchings was to find a man with the moral courage to face the lynching mob without flinching. If such a man could be located and stationed in every community — one morally brave man — lynchings would end. The sheriff should be that man, but he was usually in league with the lynchers.

Twain, therefore, suggested that the missionaries in China be recalled from their futile attempt to Christianize "the heathen," and that they be distributed throughout the lynching area. It seemed to him that this would provide the forces necessary to stop "this epidemic of bloody insanities." "O kind missionary," he pleaded, "O compassionate missionary, leave China! come home and convert these [lynching] Christians."

The article reveals that Twain had thought deeply about the problem. That some of his observations and conclusions are superficial is true. He failed to link the increase in lynchings at the turn of the century with the rising militancy of the Negro people. His argument that the source of lynching was moral cowardice had elements of truth, but it ignored the role of the Southern ruling class in stirring up lynch mobs to keep the Negro people subservient. Nevertheless, his contention that the way to combat the lynchers was through moral courage touched upon the key to the question. He developed this to its logical and correct conclusion in a separate proposal, writing: "The government should ... police the South so thoroughly that wherever a negro steps he bumps into an officer of the peace, and these same officers must control the lynchers in their criminal defiance of the law."

Twain planned to have "The United States of Lyncherdom" published in the *North American Review,* and specifically had the November, 1901, issue in mind. But the article was not printed until 1923 when Albert Bigelow Paine included it in the volume of Twain's writings entitled, *Europe and Elsewhere.* Evidently Twain decided not to publish the article by itself but to include it as an introduction to a book he was preparing to write on the history of lynching. On August 26, 1901, one day after he had completed "The United States of Lyncherdom," he wrote to a friend:

The thing I am full of, now, is a large subscription book to be called "History of Lynching in America" — or "Rise and Progress of Lynching" — or some such title.

I want you to hire for me a competent *pair of scissors.* That is all. He needn't have any brains, or any literary talent, he needs to have only the great talent of industry, and with it the quality which interests its possessor in patiently tracking out and hunting down any case which he has heard of, cost what it may of time and correspondence. For I want the details of *all* the lynchings — from the earliest days down to the present.

There may be 3,000 of them.

If I make only one volume I will use some of the accounts just as they stand, re-write others, and *mention* the rest.

If I make several volumes, I shall give myself more space and more liberty.

But I want pretty full accounts and these can probably be better obtained from the local press than from the curtailed telegrams sent to the papers of the whole country. . . .

Nothing but such a book can rouse up the sheriffs to put down the mobs and end the lynchings — which are growing in number and spreading northwards.

Unfortunately, the book was never finished and the article that was to serve "as an introduction to the book" was not published during Twain's lifetime. Yet "The United States of Lyncherdom" had lost none of its significance when it was finally published. Indeed, as one reads Twain's essay on lynching, today, fifty years after Twain penned it, one realizes that his words remain meaningful.

It was one of Mark Twain's chief objectives after the Civil War to atone for slavery and his own part in supporting it. One can state quite flatly that he did much towards achieving his goal. He fought with his pen against the whole myth built up for decades to justify the Negroes' enslavement before the Civil War, and their continued bondage after their freedom was supposed to have been achieved. By assisting to demolish the myth of the Negroes' "helpless passivity" under slavery; by casting many of his Negro characters in a heroic mould and depicting their struggle to end their bondage; by showing them to be human beings with the same feelings and thoughts as white people, Twain delivered sharp and effective blows agains the ideological foundation of exploitation that came up out of slavery. The fact that the struggle against discrimination in all its forms is still continuing and even increasing in intensity, makes Twain's writings on this whole subject as timely as the day that they were written.

Overcoming Anti-Semitic Prejudice

"Accept no courtesies of the Twilight Club; it thinks itself better than Jews," Mark Twain wrote in his notebook in 1888.

It was at school in Hannibal that Twain met the Levin boys — "the first Jews I had ever seen." In his notebook, Twain reported that they made "an awful impression among us." A "shudder" went through every boy in town, and discussions took place over the question: "Shall we crucify them?" Twain also recorded that the Levin boys were chased and stoned by the other children in town, and noted: "It was believed that the drowning of (the) writer Levering was a judgment on him & his parents because his great-grandmother had given the 11 [Levin] boys protection when they were being chased & stoned." Twain notes, too, that "the ground was all prepared" for the treatment the Levin boys encountered. Anti-Semitic feeling was drummed into the youth of Hannibal at Sunday School, and the town's newspapers published frequent accounts of supposed trickery by Jewish merchants at the expense of non-Jews. According to his biographers, Twain himself did not fall prey to this anti-Semitic propaganda. Dixon Wecter states flatly: "Despite frequent gibes at Jews, their alleged commercial tricks and rapacity, which appear so often in Hannibal newspapers in the latter 1840's, Sam Clemens seems never to have been indoctrinated with this prejudice."

The evidence does not sustain this conclusion. It demonstrates, on the contrary, that just as he had to abandon early acquired prejudices against other minorities, Mark Twain had to overcome an anti-Semitic prejudice. In a letter from Philadelphia, November, 1853, Twain remarks that the presence of Jewish occupants "desecrated" two historic houses in the City of Brotherly Love. Again, at the age of twenty, as a reporter in Cincinnati, he wrote a piece for the Keokuk (Iowa) *Daily Post* of April 10, 1857, in which he repeated the typical aspersions cast on the Jews which had appeared "so often in the Hannibal newspapers of the latter 1840's." In a humorous vein he described the cold winter of 1857 in Cincinnati, and reported how the price of coal soared until: "Gold dust warn't worth no more'n coal dust, and in course the blasted Jews got to adulterating the fuel. They mixed it up half and half — a ton of coal dust to a ton of ground pepper, and sold it for the genuine article. But they ketched them at last, and they do say that some of the indignant inhabitants took a hoss whip and castigated one of 'em till he warn't fit to associate with Jeemes Gordon Bennett hisself."

It certainly is impossible to conclude that the young man who wrote the above piece was "never ... indoctrinated" with anti-Semitic prejudice. Yet it must be said that the stereotype of the Jew is entirely absent from Mark Twain's subsequent writings. In this connection, Susy Clemens' report of her father's conversations is particularly significant:

Papa said that a Mr. Wood an equaintance [*sic*] of his, knew a rich Jew who read papa's books a great deal. One day this Jew said that papa was the only great humorist who had ever written without poking some fun against a Jew, and that as the Jews were such a good subject for fun and funny ridicule, he had often wondered why in all his stories not one said or had anything in it against the Jews. And he asked Mr. Wood the next time he saw papa to ask him how this happened.

Mr. Wood soon did see papa and spoke to him upon this subject. Papa at first did not know himself why it was that he had never spoken unkindly of the Jews in any of his books, but after thinking awhile he decided that the Jews had always seemed to him a race much to be respected; also they had suffered much, and had been greatly persecuted, so to ridicule or make fun of them seemed to be like attacking a man that was already down. And of course that fact took away whatever there was funny in the ridicule of a Jew.

It was an "ancient" river pilot, George Newhouse, according to Twain, who helped him to change his whole approach toward the Jews. On a trip to New Orleans in 1860, Twain was standing with Newhouse in the pilot house when a passenger entered, "began to be sociable, and presently made a scurrilous general remark about the Jews." Mr. Newhouse turned him out, and when Twain, somewhat surprised, asked him why he had done this, the pilot replied that it had been fifteen years "since he would allow a Jew to be abused where he was. This . . . was for the sake of one Jew, in memory of one Jew." He proceeded to tell a story that moved the young man deeply.

"Newhouse's Jew Story," as Twain listed the tale in his manuscripts, is an account of a game of poker on a river steamer around the year 1845. The professional gambler in this particular game, a man named Jackson, was notorious for coming down hard on any loser who dared to protest. The moment he was accused of cheating, he would maneuver his accuser into challenging him to a duel so as to be able to name the weapons himself. He always named bowie knives, and so expert was he with the weapon that few dared to face him. An abject apology would come from the accuser, and it was furnished before all onlookers. Occasionally, a man was foolish enough to accept Jackson's terms, but he never lived to play another game of cards. One day Jackson was in a game of poker with a rich Louisiana planter, and was openly robbing him. The planter had already lost all of his cash, two slaves, and was gambling his daughter's slave maid away. The latter had been the daughter's playmate and companion as well as servant from birth.

Newhouse and a young Jew, having heard that the planter was at the mercy of the notorious Jackson, went into the social hall to see the outcome. By that time the planter had lost the maid to Jackson, and to every plea that he be allowed to buy her back, the gambler turned a deaf ear. Not even the appeals of the planter's daughter, offering twice her value in money, could move him. "The wench is mine and money can't buy her," he told the daughter. Publicly called a coward by the girl, Jackson turned to her father and said, "I can't punish a child for that, but I'll slap your face for it." He was about to do it,

when the young Jew jumped for him and hit him on the mouth with the back of his hand, and the crowd gave him cheer. Jackson's voice shook with anger when he said —

"Do you know the price of that? What did you do it for?"

"Because I know your game. You wanted to make him challenge you, and then apologize before everybody when you named the weapons, or go ashore and get himself butchered. What are you going to do about it?"

"I know what *you* are going to do about it. You are going to fight *me*."

"Good. It is pistols this time. Will somebody ask the captain to land the boat?"

The boat is landed; the duelists each chose a second, went ashore, and disappeared in the woods. Pistol shots were heard. "Then," Newhouse told Twain, "three of the men came aboard again, and we backed out and went on down the river." After a while, Twain asked impatiently, "Which one did you leave ashore?" Newhouse gave him a satisfied grin, and said: "Well, it wasn't the Jew."

Twain also reports how a similar event influenced a banker he knew to alter his opinion of Jews. He quotes Mr. Randall, president of the Farmer's Bank, as telling his friends: "You have all known me a great many years ... but none of you have ever heard me say an ill word about the Jews when I could think of a good one in place of it — and I always could. I have said the good word and suppressed the ill one for forty-four years, now; and I've done it for the sake of a Jew that I knew once, and for the sake of a thing which he did.... Before it happened I wasn't able to see any good thing in the Jews and didn't believe there was any good thing in them to see."

Twain then relates the story told him by Mr. Randall which is essentially the same story Captain Newhouse told. Here, too, a young Jew rescues a slave girl from a gambler by outwitting him in a duel, and returns her to her master. At the end, the banker describes the Jew as "an all-around man; a man cast in a large mould; and for his sake, and in memory of that thing which he did, I have weighed his people ever since in scales which are not loaded."

One can certainly point out that in both cases, the Jews could have performed a real deed of humanity by giving the slave girls their freedom instead of returning them to a life of slavery. Though Twain misses this point, it is clear that these stories helped considerably to eradicate the stereotype of the Jew which had heretofore influenced his thinking. Indeed, these stories may have influenced him to accept a pro-Jewish stereotype which could easily be twisted to their own purposes by anti-Semites. In 1879 he wrote in his notebook: "Sampson was a Jew — therefore not a fool. The Jews have the best average brain of any people in the world. The Jews are the only race who work wholly with their brains and never with their hands. There are no Jewish beggars, no Jew tramps, no Jew ditchers, hod-carriers, day laborers or followers of toilsome, mechanical trades. They are peculiarily and conspicuously the world's intellectual aristocracy."

These observations were unpublished. Otherwise Jewish commentators could have shown Twain that, with a twist and a turn, such praise could be used to support the false charges of anti-Semitic propagandists that the Jews shrewdly lived off others' labors. Or they might have nullified any value Twain's statement might have had by proving that it had no basis in fact. They could have pointed to the presence of Jewish beggars in the United States at that very time, and of sweated Jewish workers in the cigar-making trade, the capmaking, and men's and ladies' garment industries. Hundreds of Jewish workers had participated in the New York capmakers' general strike of 1874, and in the great cigarmakers' strike in the same city from October 15, 1877 to February 3, 1878. In short, Twain, despite his good intentions, accepted, though from a favorable viewpoint, certain features of the anti-Semitic stereotype. But these observations of the 1870's remained unpublished, which was, for the time being, fortunate.

"Concerning the Jews"

Then in September, 1899 appeared Twain's "Concerning the Jews," and the controversy was on! The essay emerged from a previous article dealing with the political situation in Austria. In 1897, while Twain was living in Vienna, there occurred one of the periodic riots in the *Reichsrath* (Parliament) over the *Ausgleich* between Austria and Hungary. The inciting cause this time was that the Czech tongue was made the official language in Bohemia in place of the German. The posting of government troops in Parliament to stop the riots only provoked more serious outbreaks in various parts of the country, especially in Bohemia. As was customary, the ruling class sought to deal with them by diverting the discontent of the people against

293

the government, towards the Jews, who became the victims of widespread attacks.

Mark Twain's account of the episode under the title, "Stirring Times in Austria," was published in *Harper's Magazine* for March, 1898. At the very close of the lengthy article, he mentioned, without comment, the attacks on the Jews, pointing out that, although they were innocent parties in the political dispute, they had been "harried and plundered," and that "in all cases the Jew had to roast, no matter which side he was on."

Various Jewish readers wrote to Twain asking him to explain more clearly why their people had been attacked, "harried and plundered" in Austria, even though they were innocent. One letter especially impressed Twain. The correspondent, a Jewish lawyer, asked:

"Now will you tell me why, in your judgment, the Jews have thus ever been, and are even now, in these days of supposed intelligence, the butt of baseless, vicious animosities? I dare say that for centuries there has been no more quiet, undisturbing, and well-behaved citizens, as a class, than that same Jew. It seems to me that ignorance and fanaticism cannot alone account for these horrible and unjust persecutions.

"Tell me, therefore, from your vantage-point of cold view, what in your mind is the cause. Can American Jews do anything to correct it either in America or abroad? Will it ever come to an end? Will a Jew be permitted to live honestly, decently, and peaceably like the rest of mankind? What has become of the golden rule?"

Twain determined to answer this writer and other correspondents by examining the whole Jewish problem. He wrote "Concerning the Jews" in the summer of 1898 and it was published in *Harper's Monthly* the following year.

After making it clear that he was using "the word Jew as if it stood for both religion and race" — an approach which is not accepted today by most scientific anthropologists and many social scientists — Twain begins his inquiry into the causes of anti-Semitism. This is divided into several points. Under the first, the civic qualities of the Jew,

Twain emphasizes his industry, his family life, his self-sufficiency, as proof of his "good citizenship." While the Jew may possess "certain discreditable ways" and a reputation for petty cheating, usury, sharp business practices and "an unpatriotic disinclination to stand by the flag as a soldier," he has no monopoly of "discreditable features." When one balances creditable and discreditable features, one must conclude that "the Christian can claim no superiority over the Jew in the matter of good citizenship." "Yet," Twain concludes the first subdivision of his essay, "in all countries, from the dawn of history, the Jew has been persistently and implacably hated, and with frequency persecuted."

The second subdivision undertakes to answer the question: can religious fanaticism alone account for the world's harsh treatment of the Jew? Twain rejects this. Insisting that the Jews are the most intelligent people in the world, he attributes the persecution to the inferiority and consequent envy of other people. The persecution of the Jews flowed basically from economic pressure: "In Russia, Austria, and Germany nine-tenths of the hostility to the Jew comes from the average Christian's inability to compete successfully with the average Jew in business — in either straight business or the questionable sort." Twain quotes, as evidence, the speech of a German lawyer who wanted the Jews driven from Berlin because "*eighty-five percent* of the successful lawyers of Berlin were Jews, and ... about the same percentage of the great and lucrative businesses of all sorts in Germany were in the hands of the Jewish race." The Christians were being pushed to the wall by the Jews, their livelihood was in peril, and "to human beings this is a much more hate-inspiring thing than is any detail connected with religion."

The essay goes on to advise the Jews to organize politically. Twain argues that the Jew has not participated in an organized movement to end persecution. The Jew, he contends, received his freedom in France and England without his having participated in the campaign to remove discriminatory legislation. In the United States "he was created free in the beginning — he did not need to help, of course." He maintains also that, in the great battle in France led by Emile Zola for the exoneration of Captain Alfred Dreyfus, "the most infamously misused Jew of modern times" — a battle which he believed and hoped would be won — no "great or rich or illustrious Jew" participated.

With all his capacities and achievements, Twain argues, the Jew was not politically active in any country. Numerical weakness was no excuse, since the Irish had managed to grab more than their share of political power while immensely inferior to the Jew in intellect and numbers. As a remedy for this situation, he proposes the following "plan": "In England and America put every Jew in the census book *as* a Jew. . . . Get up volunteer regiments composed of Jews solely . . . so as to remove the reproach that . . . you feed on a country but don't like to fight for it. Next, in politics, organize your strength . . . and deliver the casting vote where you can. . . . And then from America and England you can encourage your race in Austria, France and Germany."

Twain finally addresses himself to the question: will the persecution of the Jews ever come to an end? He states flatly that the Golden Rule has no place in the discussion of this question. "It is strictly religious furniture like an acolyte, or a contribution-plate, or any of these things. It has never been intruded into business; and Jewish persecution is not a religious passion. It is a business passion." He concludes that dislike of the Jew will probably continue, for "by his make and ways he is substantially a foreigner wherever he may be, and even the angels dislike a foreigner." Nevertheless, persecution, he thinks, will end, in fact is already ending. "That is, here and there in spots around the world, where a barbarous ignorance and a sort of animal civilization prevail (persecution will continue); but I do not think that elsewhere the Jew need now stand in any fear of being robbed and raided."

296

After this prophecy — all too soon to be tragically disproved — Twain closes his essay with a moving tribute to the Jewish people:

If the statistics are right, the Jews constitute but *one percent* of the human race. It suggests a nebulous dim puff of star dust lost in the blaze of the Milky Way. Properly the Jew ought hardly to be heard of; but he is heard of, has always been heard of. He is as prominent on the planet as any of her people, and his commercial importance is extravagantly out of proportion to the smallness of his bulk. His contributions to the world's list of great names in literature, science, art, music, finance, medicine, and abtruse learning are also away out of proportion to the weakness of his numbers. He has made a marvelous fight in this world, in all the ages; and has done it with his hands tied behind him. He could be vain of himself, and be excused for it. The Egyptian, the Babylonian, and the Persian rose, filled the planet with sound and splendor, then faded to dream-stuff and passed away; the Greek and Roman followed, and made a vast noise, and they are gone; other peoples have sprung up and held their torch high for a time, but it burned out, and they sit in twilight now, or have vanished. The Jew saw them all, beat them all, and is now what he always was, exhibiting no decadence, no infirmities of age, no weakening of his parts, no slowing of his energies, no dulling of his alert and aggressive mind. All things are mortal but the Jew; all other forces pass, but he remains. What is the secret of his immortality?

This concluding paragraph, like other portions of the essay, exhibits Mark Twain's sincere admiration for the Jewish people. Probably this led Albert Bigelow Paine to characterize "Concerning the Jews" as the best presentation of the Jewish character of its day. But the plain fact is that, despite his respect for and admiration of the Jews, Mark Twain had, unwittingly, written a piece replete with untruths and half-truths — and some of the most typical anti-Semitic slanders.

Criticism of "Concerning the Jews"

Twain himself took great pride in his essay, writing to Henry Rogers: "The Jew article is my 'gem of the ocean'.

.·. Neither Jew nor Christian will approve of it, but people who are neither Jews *nor* Christian will, for they are in a condition to know the truth when they see it." Just what this meant or proved is not quite clear, and certainly it was a peculiar measuring-rod to set for the significance of the essay. In any case, while there is little evidence to indicate that Christians did not approve of the essay, there is ample to prove that Jews definitely did not.

Discussions of "Concerning the Jews" followed in the Jewish-American, Yiddish, and German-Jewish press all over the world shortly after it appeared in *Harper's Monthly*. Most of the commentators acknowledged Twain's respect for the Jews and his desire to contribute to the ending of persecution and discrimination. But they insisted that he had distorted social, economic and political history and contemporary facts in picturing the Jew as a non-participant in the struggle to achieve freedom, as the dominant and dominating force in business and the professions, and as a citizen who contributed little or nothing to his country's military achievements. Some critics were especially incensed by Twain's statement that the Jews had not participated in the movement to acquit and free Captain Dreyfus. They cited evidence to contradict this remark, and they pointed out that, other than this comment in the essay, Twain himself had played no role in the Dreyfus affair.

There was truth in all of these criticisms. As far as the Dreyfus case was concerned, however, Twain did write unpublished comments on the affair which showed unmistakably where he stood. In 1898, in an unpublished essay, he described the French as "the fastidious people who have sent an innocent man [Dreyfus] to a living hell, taken to their embraces the slimy guilty one, and submitted to a thousand indignities Emile Zola — the manliest man in France." In September, 1899, in a letter to Simon Wolf, the Jewish lawyer, publicist, communal worker and historian, Twain rejoiced in the fact that "D[reyfus] has now won for a second time the highest honor in the gift of

France. I hope he knows how to value that, but he must not accept a pardon anyway. An innocent man should spare himself that smirch, and Dreyfus would. I think he is a manly man."

Of course, if Twain's Jewish critics had known that, in the same letter, he had written that "the Jews did wisely in keeping quiet during the Dreyfus agitation," they would have been further incensed. For precisely at the time Twain's essay was published, the American press was reporting that President McKinley was besieged daily with letters, petitions, and resolutions from Jewish organizations and individual Jews all over the country urging his mediation in behalf of Dreyfus; that the Jews were clamoring for the withdrawal of the United States from the French Exposition of 1900, and that mass meetings were held in Jewish neighborhoods, voicing resentment over the Dreyfus affair.

A lengthy editorial on Twain's essay appeared on October .13, 1899, in *Die Welt*, German-Jewish weekly published in Vienna. Its publication in the very city which saw the events that led Twain to deal at length with the problem of anti-Semitism, is especially significant. The editorial opened with a tribute to Twain as a serious thinker and social critic: "It is a generally accepted but mistaken idea that Mark Twain can utter nothing but jokes. If one mentions his name, seriousness goes out of the windows, and to do him honor, the most stodgy people allow themselves a brief smile. . . . The truth is this; he can be very serious indeed. This is proven by an article from his pen appearing in 'Harper's Magazine,' in which he treats with a bitterly serious matter: the Jewish question."

The editorial praised Twain's "sharp eye" for discerning the poisonous misstatements in the propaganda of the professional anti-Semites; but it expressed regret that even "this freest mind of a free country is tainted with several prejudices and that he repeated in his essay more than one false and long since disproven assertion." Statistical errors — such as the statement that the number of Jews in Austria amounted to five million and in the United States to 250,000 — could be forgiven. "Those are errors from which no conclusions can be drawn and which therefore cannot harm us. Less harmless are certain accusations against the Jewish character which can be explained only through the fact that smears repeated a thousand times, will finally find their way into the mind of even the least prejudiced observer." Specifically, the editorial cited the reflection on the so-called commercial rapacity of the Jews and their "unpatriotic dislike against bearing arms," and it noted sharply: "It seems this could have been written just as well by some European anti-Semites, and it is certain that Mark Twain, if challenged to produce the sources of his statements, would have had to admit to his own astonishment that they are drawn from reading rather than experience. One cannot live in Vienna for several years without being influenced by certain newspapers which Twain may have read eagerly."

Unlike *Die Welt*, some Jewish critics did not even concede that Twain was unprejudiced. Most caustic in his attack on Twain was the article by Rabbi M. S. Levy, "A Rabbi's Reply to Mark Twain," published in the *Overland Monthly* of October, 1899. Throughout Twain's essay, Rabbi Levy contended, there was evidence of prejudice against the Jews which "the author denies at the outset. From the many statements Mark Twain makes regarding the various traits of the Jews, it is plain that they are not only tinged with malice and prejudice, but are incorrect and false."

Rabbi Levy accused Twain of ignorance of American history in writing that in the United States the Jew "was created free in the beginning — he did not need to help, of course." Examples of Jewish participation in the Revolutionary cause as fighters, supporters, and financiers are cited to prove that the American Jew "fought and bled for his country." In the light of this evidence, Rabbi Levy condemned Twain's statement as "a libel on his [the Jew's] manhood and an outrage historically." Nor was this a minor issue in the battle against anti-Semitism. "This accusation is one that touches us to the core, implying as it does, that the Jew has done little for the privileges he enjoys." The record of the Jew's patriotism, Rabbi Levy continues, was not confined to the Revolutionary War. It was repeated in the War of 1812, the Civil War, and in every other war since then. Nor was this only an American story. The same story of Jewish patriotism "can be abundantly proven from the records of all countries. . . . Let these all testify, and then no more will an honest man declare that the Jew shows an unpatriotic disinclination to stand by the flag of his country as a soldier." Rabbi Levy then turns to Twain's statement that "the Jew is a money-getter," observing sardonically that this came from an author who was well supplied with "fat wealth." He answers angrily and effectively:

Money-getters? The Vanderbilts, Goulds, Astors, Havemeyers, Rockefellers, Mackays, Huntingtons, Armours, Carnegies, Sloanes, Whitneys, are not Jews, and yet they control and possess more than twenty-five per cent of all the circulated wealth of the United States. . . .

The tobacco, beer, sugar, oil, and beef trusts, and all the other trusts in which the commodities of life largely figure, are in the hands of men who are not Jews. . . .

It is not necessary to deny the existence of rapacious Jewish business men to agree with Rabbi Levy's criticism. Certainly the author of *The Gilded Age* was well aware that the vast majority of America's ruling class was non-Jewish. His failure to make this clear in his essay contributed to the anti-Jewish stereotype and thus helped the work of anti-Semites.

The whole point of Twain's essay — that the envy of inferior but more powerful peoples has been the real cause of the persecution of the Jews — was an oversimplified, distorted version of the origin and rise of anti-Semitism. While anti-Semitism *was* used as a weapon by non-Jewish businessmen to gain advantages over their Jewish rivals, it was more frequently employed by non-Jewish, monopoly capitalists and feudal landowners to divert emerging social unrest. This all-important aspect of anti-Semitism is ignored in Twain's essay. Ignored, too, is the existence of the Jewish working class whose interests were identified with the interests of all other workers. Nor is there any understanding of the relationship between the respective classes in Jewish life. Nowhere does Twain show any grasp of the fact that Jewish employers were joining hands with their non-Jewish associates to combat working-class organizations of Jews and non-Jews alike.

The plain truth is that Mark Twain had no gifts for a deep analysis of so complex a subject as anti-Semitism. The kind of documentation that served him well for the broad effect of fiction and even for his satirical exposés of social evils was too imprecise for detailed historical and economic analysis, and betrayed him into many errors of fact. Moreover, in his zeal to offset the stereotypes found in much of the writing of his day, he used a different type of distortion. The hook-nosed, pawnshop owner was replaced by the intellectual genius who far outshone everyone else in the world of commerce and the professions, and who thereby aroused the envy of the lesser breeds of humanity. It is hardly surprising that this picture of the Jew — presented in all sincerity as a token of admiration and respect — was used to place the blame for anti-Semitism on the Jews themselves. Four years after "Concerning the Jews" appeared, Reverend John Walsh, in an article in the *Catholic Mirror*, used Twain's explanation for the existence of anti-Semitism, as retaliation for Jewish scorn for inferior people. "Scorn will be met with scorn," Reverend Walsh concluded.

Twain's Reaction

Mark Twain was not unduly disturbed by the criticism of his essay in the Jewish press, for he seems to have expected it. But that he was willing to concede that he was in error when facts were presented to him is made clear in his correspondence with Simon Wolf. The Jewish-American historian, author of *The American Jew as Patriot, Soldier and Citizen,* published in 1895, was upset by Twain's statement "reflecting on the loyalty of the Jews during the Civil War." He wrote to Twain, sending along a copy of his book. Twain conceded that, on the basis of the evidence presented, he had written his statement about the role of the Jews in the Civil War "very awkwardly and stupidly." He assured Wolf that he was considering adding a postscript to the essay "showing the value of your publications."

In this postscript, published in 1904 under the title, "The American Jew as a Soldier," and widely publicized, Twain reported that he had spent time examining the official U.S. Government statistics and had discovered that Jews had served in great numbers as soldiers and high officers during the Civil War, the War of 1812, and the Mexican War — great numbers, that is, in terms of their percentage of the population. For the statistics of Jewish participation in the Civil War, demonstrated that Jews who fought in the Army and Navy on the side of the North and South constituted ten per cent of their numerical strength. Though this was the same percentage as Christian Americans, it signified more: "It clearly proves that the patriotism of the Jews exceeds that of the Christian. For if a Christian volunteer arrived at the camp he was greeted with applause and joy, while a Jew was usually humiliated and insulted. His company was unwanted and he was made to feel that. But since he controlled his wounded pride and offered his blood for his flag, his patriotism is lifted above the norm. He had shown in the battle that he is capable, faithful and brave, like any other soldier. This is true of both Jewish officers and Jewish soldiers."

In conclusion, Twain quoted Major General O. O. Howard's comment in his Civil War dispatches to Washington in which he emphasized that his Jewish soldiers and staff officers were "the bravest and best," and that "there are no soldiers who show more patriotism than those of Hebrew origin, whether they served in the higher ranks or as ordinary soldiers." Twain's postscript did much to assuage the indignation of many of his Jewish critics, even though they pointed out, in a friendly way, that it was hardly necessary to prove the Jew's patriotism by making him appear to be more patriotic than his fellow Americans of different persuasions.

Anti-Semitic Use of "Concerning the Jews"

Although there is no evidence that Twain's essay was used by the Nazis in Germany in their vile anti-Semitic propaganda, it was made use of by agents of the Nazis in the United States. In 1935, a writer, reviewing anti-Semitic propaganda in the United States, commented: "A glance at an article by Mark Twain, written thirty-five years ago, under the title 'Concerning the Jews,' will show that almost the same charges (against the Jews) with which we are now familiar were then being urged." He went on to note that these charges were being repeated in the vicious anti-Semitic leaflets and pamphlets issued by American agents of Hitler.

In 1939, an anti-Semitic leaflet, entitled "Jewish Persecution A Business Passion — Mark Twain," was circulated by Robert Edward Edmondson, an American professional Jew-baiter. Although based on excerpts from Twain's essay, it was, as Bernard De Voto pointed out, "a vile and dishonest misrepresentation ... (and) as vicious a bit of propaganda as I have ever seen." The scurrilous leaflet asserted that in his essay, Twain had "compiled a devastating analysis of Jewish activities," and accused his daughter, Clara Clemens Gabrilowitsch, of having deliberately deleted "Concerning the Jews" from an edition of Twain's writings, published in 1928. The leaflet then quoted excerpts which it claimed were from Twain's essay, but did it in a way that distorted much of their original meaning. Thus Twain wrote: "If he [the Jew] set up as a doctor, he was the best one, and he took the business." In the anti-Semitic leaflet, the sentence appeared: "If he set up as a doctor, he took the business."

The leaflet was effectively exposed by Bernard De Voto in the *Jewish Frontier* of May, 1939. In addition to revealing the distortions, De Voto, the literary executor of the Mark Twain Estate, proved that the statement that Twain's daughter had deliberately withheld publication of "Concerning the Jews" was false. The work was included, he pointed out, in the volume *In Defense of Harriet Shelley and Other Essays*, where it properly belonged. Not only was this book, including the essay, still in print in 1939, but "Concerning the Jews" had been published separately as a pamphlet in 1934 and was still on sale five years later.

Of the essay itself De Voto writes: "It is not, in my opinion, a very profound or very searching analysis (of anti-Semitism), but certainly it is extremely favorable to the Jews." One can agree with the first part of De Voto's statement. As for the second part, we need only to recall that when it was first published it appeared to most Jews as anything but favorable to the Jewish people — a fact which, incidentally, De Voto does not mention. All in all, one may conclude that the absence of the essay from Mark Twain's collected works would be no great loss.

Twain and the Jewish People

In New York's teeming East Side, the Jewish immigrants regarded Mark Twain in the most affectionate terms, and nothing that critics of his essay said seems to have influenced their affection for him. Many a time in the early years of the century, Twain visited the East Side and found numerous admirers and followers there. On several occasions, he was the honored guest at performances of "The Prince and the Pauper," presented by Jewish boys and girls of the East Side, at the University Settlement or the Educational Alliance. "The East Side turned out in force to greet Mark Twain," read a report of one such performance in the New York *Tribune*.

In 1909, Clara Clemens married the Russian-Jewish pianist, Ossip Gabrilowitsch. She revealed later that when she informed her father that she and Ossip were engaged, he exclaimed that "any girl could be proud to marry him. He is a man — a real man." In long discussions together preceding the engagement, Gabrilowitsch and Twain examined the whole problem of race prejudice in general and anti-Semitism in particular. Twain agreed with Gabrilowitsch's observation that "a race is just what other races make it," and the pianist long remembered his future father-in-law's comment that, because we may not like a Negro's feature or color, "we forget to notice that his heart is often a damned sight better than ours."

It was the "heart" rather than the "head," Twain repeatedly emphasized, that enabled a person to overcome the poisonous influence of race prejudice instilled in his mind from early childhood. He makes this point vividly in a beautiful passage in the last book he published, in October, 1909, six months before his death, called *Extract from Captain Stormfield's Visit to Heaven*. The first traveler Captain Stormfield meets on his visit to heaven is Solomon Goldstein, a Jew. "It was a great improvement, having company," the Captain reports. "I was born sociable, and never could stand solitude. I was trained to a prejudice against Jews — Christians always are, you know — but such of it as I had was in my head, there wasn't any in my heart."

After Solomon Goldstein learns that he and the Captain are going to hell, he begins to sigh and cry which annoys Stormfield no end. He rages to himself: "Just like a Jew! he has promised some hayseed or other a coat for four dollars, and now he has made up his mind that if he was back he could work off a worse one on him for five. They haven't any heart — that race — nor any principles." Finally, in anger, he tells his Jewish companion to forget about the "damn" coat, and discovers that Goldstein does not have slightest idea of what he is talking about. Stormfield rudely blurts out that he was referring to his crying about a coat. Goldstein then tells him that he is crying because he will never again see his little daughter who had just died, since she would be in heaven. "It breaks my heart!" Goldstein cries. "By God," writes Captain Stormfield, "it went through me like a knife! I wouldn't feel so mean again, and so grieved, not for a fleet of ships. And I spoke out and said what I felt; and went on damning myself for a hound till he was so distressed that I had to stop; but I wasn't half through. He begged me not to talk so, and said I oughtn't to make so much of what I had done; he said it was only a mistake, and a mistake wasn't a crime. There now — wasn't it magnanimous? I ask you — wasn't it? I think so."

When Mark Twain died in 1910, the unfortunate controversy over "Concerning the Jews" had long been forgotten. Editorials in the Jewish press the world over pointed to translations of his classic works into Yiddish and Hebrew, paid tribute to his humane social philosophy, his championship of the oppressed, and acclaimed him as a great friend and defender of the Jewish people. Widely reprinted was the following remark of President Meyer of the Hebrew Technical School for Girls who had said, in introducing Twain at a meeting of the School held in the Temple Emmanuel, January 20, 1901: "In one of Mr. Clemens' works he expressed his opinion of men, saying he had no choice between Hebrew and Gentile, black men or white; to him all men were alike."

The Indians

In 1882, Mark Twain recorded the following observation in his notebook:

U.S. Government:
We have killed 200 Indians.
What did it cost?

$ 2,000,000.

You could have given them a college education for that.

As the slaughter of Indians to drive them off land coveted by speculators and settlers continued, Twain found it impossible to confine his protest to his notebook. In 1885, he urged President Cleveland to protect the Indians in the West from barbaric treatment by government officials and private citizens. "You not only have the power to destroy scoundrelism of many kinds in this country," he appealed, "but you have amply proved that you have also the unwavering disposition and purpose to do it." As evidence that this "power" was needed immediately, he enclosed the following official notice from the *Southwest Sentinel* of Silver City, New Mexico:

$ 250 REWARD

The above reward will be paid by the Board of County Commissioners of Grant County to any citizens of said county for each and every hostile renegade Apache killed by such citizen, on presentation to said board of the scalp of such Indian.

By Order of the Board, E. Stine, Clerk.

Twain's protest to President Cleveland is significant in light of the charge that he was prejudiced against the Indians and indifferent to the shameful treatment they were subjected to. The charge is based to a large extent on Twain's campaign to demolish "the Noble Savage" stereotype in Romantic literature, particularly that of James Fenimore Cooper. Along with Francis Parkman, Bret Harte, and other critics, Twain regarded Cooper's Indians as products of sheer fantasy, or as Twain put it, "viewing him [the Indian] through the mellow moonshine of romance."

It is true that Twain's discussion of the Indian was, in large part, a burlesque in which he tended to emphasize the coarser elements of Indian life. His writings too often present the Indians in their worst light, and he dwells too strongly on their uncouthness. But he also shows the misery of these people, and points out that basically it stemmed not so much from any defect of the Indian character as from the fact that the white settlers in America had stolen the land from the Indians and reduced them to a state of peonage. "My first American ancestor, gentlemen, was an Indian, an early Indian," he told an audience at the annual dinner of the New England Society in 1881. "Your ancestors skinned him alive, and I am an orphan."

Mark Twain's emergence as a champion of the oppressed of all races, colors and religions was, as we have seen, a slow process. His early letters and sketches contained disparaging references to those of alien origin. In time, he outgrew most of this, and became a spokesman for the rights of the Negro people, a foe of anti-Semitism, and a vigorous critic of the persecution of the Chinese-Americans. In the last book he published, *Extract from Captain Stormfield's Visit to Heaven,* he peopled heaven with men and women of all races, creeds, and colors — American Indians, Negroes, Chinese, Jews, Mohammedans, and white Christians untiring in a universal brotherhood of man.

Chapter Seven
IMPERIALISM

"Against our traditions we are entering upon an unjust and trivial war, a war against a helpless people and for a base object — robbery." ["Glances at History," 1906-07.]

"I am an anti-imperialist. I am opposed to having the eagle put its talons on any other land." So Mark Twain told the press on the day of his return to the United States in the autumn of 1900 after a nine year absence. He added that he had not always taken this position; indeed, at one time he had even been a "red-hot imperialist." But he had soon learned better and changed his mind.

Early Stand on Annexation of Territory

Twain's "red-hot imperialist" period was very brief. In his letters to the Sacramento *Union* from the Sandwich (Hawaiian) Islands in the late summer of 1866, he rhapsodized over the sugar acres awaiting exploitation by American capital. To make certain that the islands would be dominated by American rather than European businessmen, he recommended a line of fast steamers between California and the islands: "They would soon populate these islands with Americans, and loosen that French and English grip which is gradually closing around them.... If California can send capitalists down in seven or eight days time and take them back in nine or ten, she can fill these islands full of Americans and regain her lost foothold." Twain described in detail the great profit to capitalists to be derived from American control, emphasizing the availability of cheap labor — Kanaka men and women and Chinese coolies — working under strict contract-labor laws. Control of the islands, he predicted, would lead inevitably to control of the entire Pacific — the realization of America's destiny. "American enterprise will penetrate to the heart and center of its hoarded treasures, its imperial affluence."

In his first public lecture after his return, "The Sandwich Islands," delivered October 2, 1866, Twain urged that the United States annex the Sandwich Islands, and let the "go-ahead Americans" step in and take possession of their rich sugar, cotton, and rice fields. Using language that was to characterize the apologists for American imperialism at the turn of the century, he argued: "The property has got to fall to some heir, and why not the United States?"

Twain was to repeat the Sandwich Islands lecture for several years; but he soon omitted the annexation passages. Within a year following his return from the Islands, he was publicly ranked with the anti-expansionists. In 1867, his satire helped defeat Secretary of State William H. Seward's schemes to annex the Danish island of St. Thomas. In a hilarious sketch, he described the woes of his uncle who sought "to settle down and be quiet and unostentatious" on the island of St. Thomas, only to be subjected successively to a destructive hurricane, a tidal wave, and a series of earthquake shocks. His uncle tried Alaska, but the bears chased him out. When he again tried St. Thomas, he contracted seven kinds of fever, had one of his farms washed away in a storm and two others destroyed by an earthquake and a volcano. On a later return to the island "in a couple of ships of war," a tidal wave hoisted both of the ships out into one of the interior countries. Hearing that the Government "is thinking about buying Porto Rico . . . he wishes to try Porto Rico. If it is a quiet place."

Twain's satire attracted wide attention, especially since the very arguments advanced by the groups favoring annexation of St. Thomas had been used by Twain himself a year before, in advocating acquisition of the Sandwich Islands. His explanation for his *volte face* was the same he advanced thirty-four years later; he had learned better. The anti-expansionists were satisfied with the explanation, especially since his satire had a devastating effect on the move to annex St. Thomas.

Any doubt of the sincerity of Twain's abandonment of his earlier pro-annexation views was set to rest by the stand he took in 1873 on the question of annexing the Sandwich Islands. At the death, late in 1872, of Kahehameha V, king of the Sandwich Islands, the expansionist elements in the United States called loudly for immediate annexation. The New York *Tribune*, which came out unequivocally against annexation, invited Mark Twain to express his views. Twain contributed two long letters to the paper in January, 1873.

His first communication gave a vivid description of the islands, its climate, the white and Hawaiian population, the influence of the missionaries, and the nature of the sugar industry. Especially effective was his analysis of the terrible effects of imperialism on the native population: "The natives of the islands number only about 50,000, and the whites about 3,000, chiefly Americans. According to Capt. Cook, the natives numbered 400,000 less than a hundred years ago. But the traders brought labor and fancy disease — in other words, long, deliberate, infallible destruction, and the missionaries brought the means of grace and got them ready. So the two forces are working along harmoniously, and anybody who knows about figures can tell you exactly when the last Kanaka will be in Abraham's bosom and the islands in the hands of the whites." It was such ironic observations that caused the *Tribune* to comment, editorially: "Mr. Clemens, as those who know him will testify, is not only a wit, but a shrewd and accurate observer, and so our readers will find, in the pithy communication published today, not merely food for laughter, but subjects for reflection."

In this first communication, Twain touched only slightly on the annexation issue, noting, in passing, that the sugar planters were the islands' chief advocates of annexation, through which they hoped to remove the duty in the United States against Hawaiian sugar. Annexation would mean that "some of those heavy planters who can hardly keep their heads above water now, would clear $75,000 a year and upward." So much, then, for the moral arguments advanced in favor of annexation! In the second letter, Twain came to grips with the annexation question. He upheld the claim of Prince William Lunalilo (whom he called "Prince Bill") to the vacant throne of the islands, and excoriated the white men who had drifted to the islands and, by unscrupulous means, had gained positions of wealth and power which they hoped to retain by annexation. Finally, satirizing the whole annexation scheme, he ironically urged that the islands be taken over by the United States:

We must annex these people. We can afflict them with our wise and beneficent government. We can introduce the novelty of thieves, all the way up from street-car pickpockets to municipal robbers and Government defaulters and show them how amusing it is to arrest them and try them and then turn them loose — some for cash, and some for "political influence." We can make them ashamed of their simple and primitive justice. . . . We can give them juries composed of the most simple and charming leather-heads. We can give them railway corporations who will buy their Legislatures like old clothes, and run over their best citizens. . . . We can give them Tweed. . . . We can furnish them some Jay Goulds who will do away with their old-time notion that stealing is not respectable. . . . We can give them lecturers! I will go myself. . . .

Some later critics have interpreted Twain's letters as support of annexation; but this is clearly based on a misreading of the contents. For contemporary readers Twain effectively used his marvelous gift of irony to demolish the case in favor of annexation. Indeed, when the movement for annexation was defeated, and Prince Lunalilo was

formally proclaimed King of the Sandwich Islands, the New York *Tribune* credited Twain with having played an important role in the outcome. "The fact that his letters have unquestionably put Prince Bill on the throne, establishes his claim to the title of Pacific Warwick."

Face-to-Face with Imperialism: FOLLOWING THE EQUATOR

Mark Twain's first-hand acquaintance with the evil effects of imperialism on colonial populations was confined, until the mid-1890's, to his brief stay in the Sandwich Islands. In July, 1895, bankrupted by the failure of his publishing enterprises, he set out on a world-wide lecture tour as a means of repaying his debts. The tour took in the British colonial possessions of the South Pacific, Asia and Africa. An appalling picture of colonial enslavement unfolded before the world traveler; and both in his notebooks kept during the journey, and in *Following the Equator*, published in 1897, Twain bitterly indicted imperialist colonial policy. The book dealt mainly with the British Empire, but the author left no doubt in his readers' minds that the indictment was also aimed at France's, Germany's, Russia's and Belgium's colonial empires, and, indeed, at all colonial empires.

Twain scornfully swept aside the word "civilization," used to camouflage the crimes of the imperialists. Touching on the colonialization of Australia, he wrote:

We are obliged to believe that a nation that could look on, unmoved, and see starving or freezing women hanged for stealing twenty-six cents' worth of bacon or rags, and boys snatched from their mothers, and men from their families, and sent to the other side of the world for long terms of years for similar trifling offenses, was a nation to whom the term "civilized" could not in any large way be applied. And we must also believe that a nation that knew, during more than forty years, what was happening to these exiles and was still content with it, was not advancing in any slow way toward a higher grade of civilization.

For the term "civilized" as applied to a policy which had harshly subjugated and virtually exterminated the peoples of Australia, New Guinea, New Zealand, Tasmania and other countries of the Pacific and Africa, Twain substituted the word "robbery." England had systematically robbed India for a hundred and fifty years. Nor was she the only guilty party. Russia, Germany and other governments had stolen whole empires. "Africa has been as cooly divided up and partitioned out among the gang as if they had bought it and paid for it." Each of the so-called civilized nations continued to steal from each other territory which they had, in the first place, stolen from the colonial peoples:

Dear me, robbery by European nations of each other's territories has never been a sin, is not a sin to-day. To the several cabinets the several political establishments of the world are clotheslines; and a large part of the official duty of these cabinets is to keep an eye on each other's wash and grab what they can of it as opportunity offers. All the territorial possessions of all the political establishments in the earth — including America, of course, consist of pilferings from other people's wash. . . . In Europe and Asia and Africa every acre of ground has been stolen several millions of times. A crime persevered in a thousand centuries ceases to become a crime, and becomes a virtue. This is the law of custom, and custom supersedes all other forms of law. Christian governments are as frank to-day, as open and above-board, in discussing projects for raiding each other's clothes-lines as ever they were before the Golden Rule came smiling into this inhospitable world and couldn't get a night's lodging anywhere. . . . In fact, in our day, land-robbery, claim-jumping, is become a European governmental frenzy.

Getting down to specifics, Twain cited the example of "Mr. Rhodes and his gang" in South Africa whose activities were characterized by the apologists of imperialism as "bringing civilization to the natives," but which Twain labeled "slavery." He exposed the brutality of slave-catchers of the Queensland planters who recruited the Kanakas from Hawaii to their immense holdings in Australia. Such agents of "civilization" existed among all nations: "To learn what France is doing to spread the blessings of civilization in her distant dependencies we may turn with advantage to New Caledonia. With a view to attracting free settlers . . . the Governor forcibly expropriated the Kanaka cultivators from the best of their plantations, with a derisory compensation. . . . Such immigrants as could be induced across the seas thus found themselves in possession of thousands of coffee, cocoa, banana, and bread-fruit trees, the raising of which had cost the wretched natives years of toil; whilst the latter had a few five-franc pieces to spend in the liquor stores."

The process, Twain concluded, was a combination of "robbery, humiliation, and slow, slow murder, through poverty and the white man's whiskey." In a masterful indictment of imperialism in general, he exclaimed:

In many countries we have chained the savage and starved him to death . . . in many countries we have burned the savage at the stake. . . . In more than one country we have hunted the savage and his little children and their mother with dogs and guns through the woods and swamps for an afternoon's sport, and filled the region with happy laughter over their sprawling and stumbling flight, and their wild supplications for mercy. . . . In many countries we have taken the savage's land from him, and made him our slave, and lashed him every day, and broken his pride and made death his only friend, and overworked him till he dropped in his tracks.

Twain disposed of the "the white man's burden" doctrine, used to justify imperialism — the doctrine that it was the white man's duty to elevate the less civilized colonial people — in one sentence: "There are many humorous things in the world; among them the white man's notion that he is less savage than other savages."

The struggles of the colonial people against their enslavers are admiringly reported in *Following the Equator*. Twain dwelt on the resistance of the Tasmanians, "Spartans of Australia," who had held out until the last man and woman had died. Speaking of their extermination, he commented caustically: "These were indeed wonderful people, the natives. They ought not to have been wasted. They should have been crossed with the Whites. It would have improved the Whites and done the Natives no harm."

Twain also hailed the Maori people who, though virtually unarmed, had won some of their battles against the English conquerors of New Zealand. He stressed the nobility and self-sacrifice of the Maori patriots who "fought for their homes ... fought for their country ... bravely fought and bravely fell." But he had only contempt for the few Maoris who fought with the British *against their own people.* He was scornful of the monument the British erected to these traitors. Writing in his notebook on December 8, 1895, he commented: "'Sacred to the memory of the brave men who fell on the 4th May '64, etc.' On one side are the names of about 20 Maoris — so it is a monument to a lot of traitors to their country. They were fighting countrymen of theirs who were risking their lives in defence of their fatherland against alien oppressors. Change the monument. Pull it down. It is a disgrace to both parties — the traitors & those who praise them." This comment remained unpublished, but in *Following the Equator,* Twain wrote of the same monument: "It is not a fancy of mine; the monument exists. I saw it. It is an object-lesson to the rising generation. It invites to treachery, disloyalty, unpatriotism. Its lesson, in frank terms is, 'Desert your flag, slay your people, burn their homes, shame your nationality — we honor such.'" The reader draws the logical conclusion that the colonial people are waging a desperate, sometimes hopeless, but always righteous struggle against the imperialist exploiters. The conclusion is that, no matter how strong the oppressors, they must be fought.

The critical reception to *Following the Equator* was about what could be expected of a book that dared to rip through the sham pretenses of imperialism and to expose the reality. Liberal commentators praised it highly. James Whitcomb Riley, the "Hoosier poet," wrote to Twain: "For a solid week ... I have been glorying in your last book — and if you've ever done anything better, stronger, or of more wholesome uplift I can't recall it." *The Dial* said of it: "the dominant note in this book is not jest but earnestness, moral and humane, — an earnest desire for sincerity and genuineness, but tearing sham to pieces and flinging it to the winds." Commenting in the *North American Review*, William Dean Howells observed: "It is by such handling of such questions ... that Mark Twain has won his claim to be heard on any public matter, and achieved the odd sort of primacy which he now enjoys." But these were minority reports. The majority of the critics were furious because the great humorist had dared to expose the so-called upholders of civilization. *The Critic* found the book's subject matter "depressing," since it dealt with "tyranny, leprosy, slavery, savagery, mutiny, war, disease, cruelty, and so forth — a gruesome procession." The *Chap Book* lamented that Twain was no longer the humorist, but had become "ethical-minded and solemn." It was clear that the greatness of the man was over, and "there is no hope for him."

In England, the critics echoed these judgments. The book contained "arid wastes of descriptive and statistical matter," something hardly to be expected from a writer whose purpose was to entertain his readers. Unfortunately, the Twain of *Following the Equator* was "less funny" than he should be, and "the quality for which nine out of every ten persons buy his books — his fun — is not what it was." Most important of all, British imperialism was a subject that should not concern an American author who wished to sell large quantities of his books to English readers. Said the British journal, *Academy*, sternly: "The majority of English readers do not greatly care for the political and serious opinions of an American author to whom they once confidently resorted for laughter. When they wish to be instructed concerning Great Britain, they prefer that it should be done by an Englishman."

Mark Twain's eyes had been opened to the barbarities practiced by the imperialists. He perceived that, masked behind high-sounding motives like the desire "to spread the blessings of their civilization in distant dependencies" was sheer lust for profits. He saw that the imperialists would stop at nothing, and that, unless the voices of the truly civilized people were heard in opposition, "all sav-age & semi-civilized countries are going to be grabbed." He was ready to lend his own voice to this protest, regard-less of the opinion of critics or the effect it would have on the sale of his books.

United States Turns Imperialist

Mark Twain sailed with his family for Europe in June, 1891. Except for intermittent visits, he remained in Europe until May, 1895. Then in July, 1895, he departed on a global tour. He did not return to the United States until mid-October, 1901. During Twain's nine years of almost continuous absence, the United States turned imperialist, joining the European powers in carving up the Orient and Africa.

While earlier, American capitalists had expanded mainly within the nation's own border, all during the 1880's and 1890's voices were raised urging American cap-italism to enter quickly into the struggle for colonies and naval outposts, before they were all snatched up by Eng-land, France, Belgium, Germany, Russia and other Euro-pean powers. Economic trends in the country reinforced these arguments. American capitalism entered the stage of monopoly capitalism in the 1880's, and this development continued at an accelerated pace through the 1890's. The New York *World* reported on March 26, 1899: "More in-dustrial trusts and monopolistic 'combines' were formed in 1898 than in the entire quarter of a century since the Stand-ard Oil Company, parent and pattern of American mo-nopoly, first began to destroy competition in illuminating oil." During this year, gigantic mergers took place in cop-per, lead, sugar, paper, salt, powder, cans, whiskey, coal, steel and other lines.

At the same time, the banking system had come under the domination of a few large banks controlled by the House of Morgan, the Rockefellers, Kuhn-Loeb, the Mel-lon group, and others. By the turn of the century, the big industrialists and bankers had fused into an oligarchy of finance capital. Finance capital (the merger of industrial capital with bank capital) had become dominant in the United States by the closing years of the nineteenth century. "The conquest of the United States economy by finance capital," notes one student, "led to the accumulation of a superabundance of capital in a few hands. . . . The monopolies had to find new fields for investment of their surplus capital. Failing this, their profits would decline in the resulting economic crisis."

The depression which began in 1893 and continued for five years, sharply pointed up the monopolies' need for new outlets for surplus goods and capital outside the United States. Increased productivity of the workers had widened the gap between what they produced and what they could purchase with their wages. The surplus goods piled up, bursting the warehouses for lack of foreign markets. On March 16, 1898, the Senate Committee on Foreign Relations reported: "The unoccupied territory has been taken up, and while much remains to be done, the creative energy of the American people can no longer be confined within the borders of the Union. Production has so outrun consumption in both agricultural and manufactured products that foreign markets must be secured or stagnation will ensue."

Actually, the American people could have consumed all and more that the factories and farms produced; but the monopoly capitalists were interested in super-profits and not in meeting the people's needs. Thus, when Carroll D. Wright, United States Commissioner of Labor, proposed "a higher standard of living" among the working classes as the solution, the New York *Journal of Commerce and Commercial Bulletin* remarked coldly in February, 1898: "We have the highest respect for Mr. Wright's humanitarian sympathies; but the sphere of benevolence lies outside the sphere of economic philosophy." The solution to the problem, it went on, lay in an expansion overseas that would yield new markets and new fields for investments.

The stage was set. All that was needed was an "incident" which American imperialism could use as the jump-off into the struggle to redivide the world and come up with huge booty. This was furnished by the revolution for Cuban independence from Spain. "Free Cuba," declared Henry Cabot Lodge, a blatant advocate of imperialism, in 1896, "would mean an excellent opportunity for American capital invited there by signal exemptions. But we have a broader political interest in Cuba." That "broader interest" was Spain's colonial possessions — Puerto Rico, Guam, the Virgin Islands, and the Philippine Islands.

The problem for American imperialists was to convert the sympathy of the American people for the local Cuban independence movement into support of a war against Spain. In this conspiracy the imperialists had the support of the jingo press, headed by William R. Hearst's New York *Journal* and Joseph Pulitzer's New York *World*. These unscrupulously played upon the American people's sympathy for the Cuban cause to raise circulation figures, and did all they could to drive the United States into war.

On February 15, 1898, the *Maine* blew up in the harbor of Havana, and the death of 250 American enlisted men and officers fanned the flames of war. A naval court of inquiry investigated the explosion. Its report was scrupulously careful not to imply that Spain was responsible for the disaster. But the jingo press and the imperialist spokesmen in Congress and in the McKinley administration ignored it, denounced Spain and called for war. Indeed, while the naval court of inquiry was conducting its investigation, President McKinley was already working upon a war bill, and his assistant secretary of the navy, Theodore Roosevelt, with Senator Lodge's assistance, was writing a telegram to Commodore George Dewey, ordering him to hold his squadron ready for "offensive operations in the Philippine Islands." On March 19, 1898, the *Wall Street Journal* reported that "a great many people in Wall

Street" were demanding action against Spain at once. Congress, meanwhile, was being deluged with petitions from powerful business groups urging it to support a policy of expansion. On April 9, 1898, Spain completely capitulated to every demand raised by the United States government to achieve a peaceful settlement of the Cuban question. But the political agents of imperialism were not interested in a peaceful solution. On April 11, two days after he had received Spain's capitulation, President McKinley sent his war message to Congress. He devoted nine closely printed pages to arguments based on the assumption that Spain had not capitulated, and two short paragraphs to the fact that it had. In short, the President deliberately concealed from the American people the news that Spain had already conceded every one of the United States demands.

Imperialist Peace Treaty

War was declared on April 25, 1898. As Charles and Mary Beard put it: "The hour had come for the planners of world politics to steer the country out on the course of imperialism." Events soon exposed the aims of the imperialists. On August 12, the war ended with Spain's signing the peace protocol. The terms glaringly revealed the imperialist nature of the conflict and raised the curtain on the Grand Deception. Spain was to relinquish Cuba; Puerto Rico and all its other islands in the West Indies were to be ceded to the United States, and one of the Ladrones (islands in the China sea) was to be chosen as war indemnity. One clause was ambiguous — the stipulation that "the United States is entitled to occupy, and will hold, the city, bay, and harbor of Manila pending the conclusion of a treaty of peace which shall determine the control, disposition, and government of the Philippines." This ambiguous clause was soon clarified. President McKinley's appetite increased. From just occupying Manila, he instructed the United States peace commissioners that by December, 1898, "by the single consideration of duty and humanity the cessation must be of the whole archipelago" — meaning the entire Philippine Islands. Later, McKinley told a Methodist delegation at the White House that, in answer to his prayers for guidance on the question of holding the Philippines, the revelation had one night come to him that "there was nothing left for us to do but to take them all, and to educate the Filipinos, and uplift and civilize and Christianize them, and by God's grace do the very best we could by them as our fellow-men for whom Christ also died." But in his instructions to the peace commissioners, Mc Kinley dropped the mask: "Incidental to our tenure in the Philippines is the commercial opportunity to which American statesmanship cannot be indifferent. It is just to use every legitimate means for the enlargement of American trade."

On December 10, 1898, the Treaty of Paris was executed. Cuba, it was understood, was to be held by the United States, with the immediate prospect of autonomy. Puerto Rico and the Philippine Islands were ceded to the United States. Eleven days later, President McKinley proclaimed to the Philippines a policy of "benevolent assimilation," and, at the same time, urged General Harrison Grey Otis, the military commander of the islands, to gain control of important towns and cities as quickly as possible.

To "gain control" meant to wrest the islands by military force from the Filipino people who had fought thirty-six rebellions against Spain, who had captured Manila for the U.S. forces, and who were fighting for independence!

A new revolutionary uprising in the Philippines against Spanish colonial government had begun in 1896, two years before the Spanish-American War. Emilio Aguinaldo, president of the Katipunan, a revolutionary body, led the uprising, which ended late in 1897 with arbitration and the pact of Biac-na-Bato. The insurgents were promised basic reforms, while Aguinaldo and other revolutionary leaders went into exile in Hong Kong. With war imminent between the United States and Spain early in 1898, hope for independence revived in the Philippines, particularly when Commodore Dewey invited Aguinaldo to cooperate with him and arranged that he be taken to the islands on an American naval vessel. The Filipinos were elated in June, 1898, when Dewey expressed the belief that they were more capable of self-government than the Cubans who had been promised their independence by the United States.

In July, three American expeditionary forces arrived in the Philippines and the Filipinos prepared to assist them in taking Manila. On August 6, Aguinaldo published a declaration of independence; and by the end of September, a revolutionary Congress had convened at Malos, ratified Philippine independence, and elected Aguinaldo president. But while the Filipinos, led by Aguinaldo, were digging trenches outside Manila, mopping up Spanish garrisons in other parts of Luzon, and taking thousands of Spanish prisoners, the plot to snatch the country from the Filipino people was being hatched in Washington. When the American army was ready to attack Manila, Dewey (now an Admiral) and the commanders of the land forces notified Aguinaldo that insurgent troops were not to enter the city, warning that force would be used, if necessary, to keep them out. The Filipino leader could only assent to the order and, on August 13, Manila fell almost without resistance. Tension between the Americans and the Filipinos increased when the news of the terms of the Treaty of Paris reached the islands. The Filipinos, however, looked to the American people, hopeful that the rising anti-imperialist movement in the United States would prevent ratification.

Anti-Imperialist League

Vast masses of the American people, Negro and white, opposed the imperialist policy of their government. Their opposition took organized form even before the close of the Spanish-American War, as it became clear that the war was now openly one for conquest. The organization through which this opposition was expressed was the Anti-Imperialist League.

The American Anti-Imperialist League was born on June 15, 1898 at a mass meeting in Boston's Faneuil Hall, site of numerous historical meetings in the American Revolution and the anti-slavery struggle. The assembled audience adopted protest resolutions against the war of conquest, declaring that it would be time enough to think of governing others "when we have shown that we can protect the rights of men within our own borders like the colored race of the South and the Indians of the West, and that we can govern great cities like New York, Philadelphia, and Chicago." The meeting selected an anti-imperialist committee of correspondence to contact "persons and organizations throughout the country." Special attention was to be given to winning labor's support; the committee of correspondence made an appropriation "for the distribution of an anti-imperialist speech recently made by President Samuel Gompers of the American Federation of Labor," and appointed a sub-committee to "prepare and circulate an appeal to the workingmen of the country to oppose imperialism by resolutions and others." The Anti-Imperialist League, and its local affiliates, spearheaded the drive to influence the U.S. Senate to reject the Spanish peace treaty. Petitions flooded the Senate protesting "against any extension of the sovereignty of the United States over the Philippine Islands." As the Senators prepared to cast their votes, thousands of petitions poured into Washington urging them to amend the peace treaty to exclude the annexation of the Philippines and Puerto Rico. Small wonder Henry Cabot Lodge, leader of the imperialists in the Senate, wrote to his jingo colleague, Theodore Roosevelt: "We are going to have trouble over the treaty."

The treaty was passed by only one vote. Thirty-three Senators stood firm in opposition. Lodge, breathing a sigh of relief, described the struggle for ratification as "the closest, hardest fight I have ever known."

On February 4, 1899, two days before the Senate ratification, U.S. troops fired on a group of Philippine soldiers, and the war for the conquest of the Philippines was on. This "war of conquest," as Walter Millis wrote, "was to flicker on for several years, which was to cost us as much in life and effort as the whole of the War with Spain, and which was to repeat in a kind of grotesque analogy almost everything which we had charged against the Spaniards since the 1895 outbreak in Cuba." The reference was to the brutality of American military forces in the Philippines. Reports from the islands, including letters from American soldiers, told of the Filipinos being rounded up and placed in concentration camps, of whole villages being wiped out, of prisoners of war being subjected to the "water cure" or shot down in cold blood, and of other tactics which made the charges of the United States against Spain's policy in Cuba seem mild indeed. And all this was supposedly for the purpose "of extending Christian civilization to the Filipinos." The nature of this "civilizing" was reflected in an American army ballad which went:

Damn, damn the Filipinos
Cross-eyed Kakiack ladrones
Underneath our starry flag, civilize 'em with a Krag,
And return us to our beloved homes.

The war of conquest lasted several years longer, but the backbone of Filipino resistance to American imperialism was broken on March 23, 1901 when Aguinaldo was captured. Of the outcome, W. Cameron Forbes writes: "In ... unequal warfare between the Americans, well commanded, well armed and equipped and amply supplied ... and the Filipinos, comparatively without leadership, resources and equipment, the inevitable had occurred, the Philippine organization had been defeated."

The years 1898-1900 witnessed in South Africa and China the same type of struggle against imperialism that was going on in the Philippines. In South Africa, the Boers, led by President "Oom Paul" Kruger, fought British imperialism, symbolized by Cecil Rhodes' South African Company. Like the American imperialists in the Philippines, the British rounded up the Boers in a series of "drives" which put 40,000 Boers, including thousands of women and children, into concentration camps. Still, it took three years and 450,000 trained British troops to overwhelm 66,000 Boers, and annex the Boer republics of Transvaal and the Orange Free State to the British Empire.

In China, meanwhile, the people, led by the "Boxers," rose up against the territorial encroachments upon their country by foreign imperialists, and the division of the thirteen richest, most populous, and most desirable of the eighteen Chinese provinces into "spheres of influence." War was the imperialists' answer to the attempt of the Chinese people to keep their country for themselves. In June, 1900, an international fleet bombarded and captured the Taku forts, which commanded the approach to Peking; and the American Admiral Kempff cooperated in the attack. Although the slaying of 242 foreigners, chiefly missionaries, was the pretext for the war against China, the slaying actually did not begin until the opening days of July, three weeks after hostilities had started. Some 18,000 international troops of eight powers, including 2,000 American soldiers, attacked China, plundered the country, executed leaders of the anti-imperialist movement, and imposed a humiliating treaty of peace. China was compelled to execute certain officials who had opposed division of the country into "spheres of influence," import no arms or ammunition for two years, suspend official examinations for five years in towns where foreigners had been mistreated, amend her treaties of commerce and navigation, and pay a then enormous indemnity of about

$353,000,000. The dismemberment of China continued. France took Annam and Tonkin, later to be called French Indochina; Britain took Burma; Russia took Port Arthur; Japan took Korea, and Germany reserved Shantung province as its "sphere of influence," and took twelve miles of territory. Although the United States, advocate of the "Open Door," took no territory, American imperialism gained control of important sections of China's economic resources through numerous consortiums, or loans under usurious conditions, forced upon China by international bankers, among whom those from the United States were most prominent.

Thus the turn of the century was marked by imperialist wars of aggression in South Africa, China, and the Philippines. No friend of freedom, no man who had a burning hatred of oppression could ignore the attacks on colonial peoples by the powerful nations of the day — least of all Mark Twain.

Twain and the Spanish-American War

Throughout the spring and summer of 1898, Mark Twain was living in Vienna. On August 30, 1898, he wrote to Howells from Kaltenleutgeben, near the Austrian capital: "This morning I read to Mrs. Clemens your visit to the Spanish prisoners, & have just finished reading it again — & lord, how fine it is & beautiful, & how gracious & moving. You have the gifts — of mind & heart." The reference was to Howells' "Our Spanish Prisoners at Portsmouth," published in *Harper's Weekly*, August 20, 1898. The article, an account of what Howells observed on two visits to the prisoners captured during the Spanish-American War, opened dramatically: "I have not much stomach for any war, and little or none at all for a war which began for humanity, and then by the ruling of an inscrutable Providence, or perhaps an ironic destiny, became a war of territory, or at least for coaling stations." After a poignant description of the river, the meadows and orchards surrounding the prison island, Howells raised the question of whether the United States had been justified in declaring war against Spain. He answered emphatically that there was no such justification!

There was certainly nothing surprising in Howells' bitter references to the Spanish-American War. Early in April, 1898, he wrote to his sister:

Of course, we are deafened by war-talk here. I hope you will not be surprised to hear that I think we are wickedly wrong. We have no right to interfere in Cuba, and we have no cause of quarrel with Spain. At the very best we propose to do evil that good may come. If we have war, it will be at the cost of a thousand times more suffering than Spain has inflicted or could inflict on Cuba. After war will come the piling up of big fortunes again; the craze for wealth will fill all brains, and every good cause will be set back. We shall have an era of blood-bought prosperity, and the chains of capitalism will be welded on the nation more firmly than ever.

If then there was nothing in Howells' article on the Spanish prisoners that was not in keeping with his views on the war, the same cannot be said of Mark Twain's approval of its contents. Unlike Howells, Henry James, William James, Charles Eliot Norton, Ambrose Bierce, Finley Peter Dunne (Mr. Dooley) and other American men of letters who could see no good in fighting Spain, Mark Twain looked upon the war as a "just and righteous one," to liberate Cuba from a tyrannical Spain and deliver it into the arms of independence and liberty. Consumed by his passion for liberty, Twain at the outset wholeheartedly supported the war.

Twain's support of "Cuba Libre" in 1898 represents a shift in his position. At the time of the first outbreak of the Cuban revolution against Spain in October, 1868, he had called for a hands-off policy by the United States. Recognizing that the expansionist forces were using American sympathy for the insurgents to achieve intervention in the island and its annexation to the Union, Twain then joined the foes of expansion in protesting against any action that would pave the way for such annexation. In a letter to the Buffalo *Express* of December 25, 1869, he blamed the absence of "thoroughly impartial news accounts of the doings in Cuba" for the fact that so many Americans fell prey to the expansionist plot to use sympathy for the Cuban patriots to achieve annexation of the island. As for himself, he wrote: "I do not love the Cuban patriot or the Cuban oppressor either, and never want to see our government 'recognize' anything of theirs but their respective corpses. If the Buffalo *Express* thinks differently let it say it in its editorials, but not over the signature of yours, with emotion, Mark Twain."

In 1869, the opponents of expansion were victorious. But the issue of "Cuba Libre" and the use of it for expansionist purposes did not disappear. When it arose again, even more sharply in the 1890's and became the pretext for war against Spain, Mark Twain failed to see through to the essential facts behind the demagogic propaganda. Carried away by his enthusiasm for what appeared to him, as it did to many Americans, "a war for the liberation of Cuba from Spanish dominion — an altruistic, moral war," he forgot the stand he had taken on the issue thirty years previously. Writing on May 17, 1898, a month after the war began, he stated in almost Hearstian terms: "I think we ought to have taken hold of the Cuban matter & d[r]iven Spain out fifty years ago. But better late than never — both for Spain's sake & the world's."

Living in Vienna, Mark Twain understood little of the sinister forces that were using the cause of Cuban freedom to lead the United States down the road to war and imperialism. But he was troubled by comments from his Austrian friends accusing the United States of championing the Cuban cause for imperialist rather than humanitarian motives. When his brother-in-law, Charles Langdon, arrived in Vienna, Twain asked for his views. Langdon assured Twain that the aims of the United States were completely disinterested, and in no ways tainted by imperialism. He cited the Teller Amendment to the Cuban resolution, adopted by Congress at the time war was declared against Spain, which specifically renounced annexationist designs in Cuba. He did not, however, tell his brother-in-law that Senator Henry M. Teller of Colorado had made it clear that his amendment applied only to Cuba, and that the United States was not restricted by its provisions with respect to acquisition of Spain's other colonies — especially the Philippines and Puerto Rico.

Twain was happy. He could defend his country's policies against the Austrian arguments with a clear conscience. Moreover, he could defend the war without abandoning his hatred of war, for this was a different type of war, a righteous war. "This is a good war with a dignified cause to fight for," he wrote to Major J. B. Pond, his lecture manager, on June 17, 1898, "a thing not to be said of the average war." The following day, he wrote to Joseph Twichell whose son had enlisted in the war: "I have never enjoyed a war — even in written history — as I am enjoying this one. For this is the worthiest one that was ever fought, so far as my knowledge goes. It is a worthy thing to fight for one's freedom; it is another sight finer to fight for another man's. And I think this is the first time it has been done." The phrase in this letter, "so far as my knowledge goes," provides the key to Twain's uncritical support of the war. Far removed from the sources of information, he could not see through the fog of propaganda. He was convinced that the purpose of American intervention as stated, was to free Cuba; and he was satisfied that a war to aid an oppressed people in their revolt for freedom was a just one. Furthermore, the fact that the Austrians and other Europeans and even Americans living abroad, whom he met in Vienna, condemned the United States for its role in the Cuban crisis increased his determination to justify his own country's actions.

While Twain did not alter his position that the Cuban war was just, until years later, he began to draw a distinction between the war in Cuba and the war in the Philippines. Less than two years after the outbreak of the Spanish-American War, he wrote: "When the United States sent word that the Cuban atrocities must end, she occupied the highest moral position ever taken by a nation since the Almighty made the Earth. But when she snatched the Philippines and butchered a poverty-stricken, priest-ridden nation of children, she stained the flag. That's what we have today — a stained flag." Just when did Twain conclude that the flag was "stained?" He gave the answer to this question upon his return to the United States in the fall of 1900. He had had, he told reporters, access to little unbiased news of the events surrounding the Spanish-American War. A careful reading of the Treaty of Paris had convinced him that the war for humanity had become a war for conquest.

Reading the terms of the Treaty of Paris, Twain felt betrayed, and he wrote bitterly to Twichell: "Apparently we are not proposing to set the Filipinos free and give their islands to them; and apparently we are not proposing to hang the priests and confiscate their property. If these things are so, the war out there has no interest for me." Twichell expected more from Twain than the mere avowal of a lack of interest in the war of conquest against the Filipinos. "Why don't you say something about it?" he wrote to Twain from Hartford. But, distracted by the illness of his daughter and deeply immersed in work to pay off his creditors, Twain wrote almost nothing in 1899 about American imperialism in the Philippines. He did, however, write a great deal about British imperialism in South Africa, but published little on the subject.

Twain and the Boer War

Mark Twain arrived in South Africa in 1896 during his tour around the world. It was a stirring time. The attempts of the British imperialists to seize the Boer republics in the raid led by the adventurer, Jameson, had ended in scandalous failure. Jameson had been utterly defeated. In his notebooks and in *Following the Equator*, Twain recorded these events and his reaction to them. He condemned both the Boers and the British for enslaving the native population in their own land. "The natives hate the Boers — and well they may," he commented in his notebook. Nevertheless, he ardently supported Boer independence. Twain understood that behind the British adventurers and military were the real fomenters of war in South Africa — the English capitalists who coveted the land and mines of the Boer republics. He put his finger on the chief warmonger, Cecil Rhodes, devoting several pages to him. While he conceded that no one could ignore Rhodes' capacity, he made it clear that the tycoon's rise to power was based on inhuman exploitation. "I admire him, I frankly confess it; and when his time comes I shall buy a piece of the rope for keepsake," he wrote sardonically in *Following the Equator*. In his notebook, he expanded on this theme: "They [the people of South Africa] think Rhodes ought to have been hanged 30 years ago. I think that is exaggerated feeling, spite, malignity, not justice, & I would not be unjust to any one, even Mr. Rhodes, though I am far from approving of him. That he sh[oul]d have been hanged 30 yrs. ago is in my opinion an over-severe judgment; but if you make it twenty-nine & a half, I am with you."

On the day that arch-imperialist, Colonial Secretary Joseph Chamberlain, announced officially that the Boer War had begun, Twain recorded angrily in his notebook: "London, 3:07 P.M., *Wednesday, October 11, 1899*. The time is up! Without a doubt the first shot in the war is being fired to-day in South Africa at *this moment. Some* man had to be the first to fall; he has fallen. Whose heart is broken by this murder? For, be he Boer or be he Briton, it is murder & England committed it by the hand of Chamberlain & the Cabinet, the lackeys of Cecil Rhodes & his Forty Thieves, the South Africa Company." Two months later, in a published article dealing with the ways in which people may and do lie, Twain described the lie of silent assertion and illustrated it by saying that "the lie ... was over England lately, a good half of the population silently letting on that they were not aware that Mr. Chamberlain was trying to manufacture a war in South Africa and was willing to pay fancy prices for the materials."

Twain was pleased to learn from Howells that his condemnation of Rhodes and the South Africa Company in *Following the Equator* was being used in the United States to aid the Boer cause. As for himself, he informed Howells, he was finding it increasingly difficult to speak out. "Privately speaking this is a criminal war, and in every way shameful and excuseless. Every day I write (in my head) bitter magazine articles about it, but I have to stop it. For England must not fail; it would mean an inundation of Russian and German political degradations which would envelop the globe and steep it in a sort of Middle-Age night and slavery which would last till Christ comes again." Hence, though he knew that England was wrong, he could not bring himself to attack her publicly. He summed up his attitude in the sentence: "My head is with the Briton, but my heart and such rags of morals as I have are with the Boer."

At one point Twain's heart almost got the better of his head, and he wrote a pro-Boer article for anonymous publication in the London *Times*. At the last moment, however, he reconsidered and withheld publication. In *Das Europabild Mark Twains*, Dr. Günther Moehle argues that Twain sided with England against the Boers because he could not wholly escape the "racial" ties uniting the Anglo-Saxon people. Actually, of course, Twain sided with the Boers; but there is no doubt that one reason for his silence was his desire not to disturb "this close relationship between England and America." Yet the picture would not be complete unless one adds that Mark Twain was convinced that England's political tradition made her an ally of democratic forces against the anti-democratic threat of Imperial Germany and Czarist Russia.

Both Twain's heart and head were definitely, from the very beginning, with China in its "war against the world." As far back as 1868, in his article, "The Treaty With China," he had condemned the foreign "concession" wrested from China, and had called for abolition of these communities in which white foreigners conducted themselves on Chinese soil as if they owned the areas:

The foreigners residing upon these tracts create courts of justice, organize police forces, and govern themselves by laws of their own framing. They levy and collect taxes, they pave their streets, they light them with gas. . . . Again, these foreign communities took it upon themselves to levy taxes upon Chinamen residing upon their so-called "concessions," and enforce their collection. Perhaps those Chinamen were just as well governed as they would have been anywhere in China, and perhaps it was entirely just that they should pay for good government — but the *principle* was wrong. . . . The municipal council which taxed these Chinamen was composed altogether of foreigners, so there was taxation without representation — a policy which we fought seven long years to overthrow.

Twain was particularly incensed by the contemptuous attitude towards the Chinese of the white foreigners who lived in these "concessions." They looked upon the Chinese "as degraded barbarians, and not entitled to charity — as helpless, and therefore to be trodden underfoot." The white foreigners were "a tyrannical class who say openly that the Chinese should be *forced* to do thus and so; that foreigners know what is best for them, better than they do themselves, and therefore it would be but Christian kindness to take them by the throat and compel them to see their real interests, as the enlightened foreigners see them."

As early as 1868, Twain had warned that, unless this vicious system of "concessions" was ended and unless the white foreigners began to treat the Chinese with some semblance of respect and dignity, the people of China would someday rise up in bloody combat to oust all foreigners. It came as no surprise to Twain, therefore, when the Chinese people did rise up in the "Boxer Rebellion." Although he knew the Chinese could not successfully resist the rape of their country by the troops of eight powers, the United States among them, he was heart and soul with their cause. On August 12, 1900, a day before the international troops entered Peking, he wrote to Twichell: "It is all China now, and my sympathies are with the Chinese. They have been villainously dealt with by the sceptred thieves of Europe, and I hope they will drive all foreigners out and keep them out for good. I only wish it; of course I don't really expect it." But even if China were defeated, it would only be a temporary setback. In the end, he predicted, "China [will] go free & save herself."

Twain Joins Anti-Imperialist Movement

"Like yourself, we are partisans of the Chinese," Twichell wrote to Twain, informing him that his friends in the United States share his views on China. He added that they had asked him to urge Twain to return home and lend his voice to the anti-imperialist cause. Some of the anti-imperialists were becoming discouraged, thinking that "the country is going to the dogs and has no men able to save her." He himself was not of this opinion — "not by a good deal," and many shared his views. But everywhere he went, men and women engaged in the anti-imperialist movement kept asking him "when the Clemenses are coming home."

It may appear that there was little that Twain could have added to the anti-imperialist forces in the United States. He had not as yet arrived at a clear position on the question of American imperialism in relation to the Spanish-American War; he had, he explained, read "only . . . scraps and snatches of news" in the papers about developments in the United States. But one thing his friends who were awaiting his return did know: Mark Twain was fundamentally an anti-imperialist, and once he understood clearly the character of the war being waged in the Philippines, he would lend his powerful support to the whole anti-imperialist movement.

Twain left Europe troubled in mind about the role his country was playing in the world-wide imperialist scramble for markets, and with a deepening distrust of American purposes in the Philippines. As he told a London correspondent for the New York *World* on October 6, 1900, immediately before embarking for America, he was still groping for the truth about the role the United States was playing in the Philippines, but he already knew enough to cause him great concern. Asked specifically where he stood on the question of imperialism, he replied:

You ask me about what is called imperialism. Well, I have formed views about that question. I am at a disadvantage of not knowing whether our people are for or against spreading themselves over the face of the globe. I should be sorry if they are, for I don't think that it is wise or a necessary development.... We have no more business in China than in any other country that is not ours. There is the case of the Philippines. I have tried hard, and yet I cannot for the life of me comprehend how we got into that mess. Perhaps we could have avoided it — perhaps it was inevitable that we should come to be fighting the natives of those islands — but I cannot understand it, and have never been able to get at the bottom of the origin of our antagonism to the natives. I thought we should act as their protector — not try to get them under our heel. We were to relieve them from Spanish tyranny to enable them to set up a government of their own, and we were to stand by and see that it got a fair trial. It was not to be a government according to our ideas, but a government that represented the feeling of the majority of the Filipinos, a government according to Filipino ideas. That would have been a worthy mission for the United States. But now — why, we have got into a mess, a quagmire from which each fresh step renders the difficulty of extrication immensely greater. I'm sure I wish I could see what we were getting out of it, and all it means to us as a nation.

Twain's confusions and uncertainties vanished shortly after he came home. From the day he stepped off the boat in New York harbor on October 15, 1900, until the middle of 1903, scarcely a month passed in which he did not give an interview, make a speech, sign a petition, or write a letter or pamphlet excoriating imperialism and the imperialists. These reached millions, for people all over the country were eager to hear and read what America's greatest writer had to say on any subject.

Twain Attacks Imperialism

"No sooner had he landed than he pricked with his wit the bubble of Imperialism," *The Nation* announced joyfully in welcoming Twain home. On the evening of his arrival in New York, where he received the warmest welcome he had ever experienced, Twain gave his first interview. For the first time he publicly lauded the Boers, and praised President Kruger who had been forced by the British to leave South Africa for Europe. He was certain "the heroic old man" and the cause he represented would ultimately triumph. Nor did Twain mince words in condemning United States policy in the Philippines. He was quoted in the New York *Herald* as saying:

I have read carefully the treaty of Paris, and I have seen that we do not intend to free but to subjugate the people of the Philippines. We have gone there to conquer, not to redeem.

We have also pledged the power of this country to maintain and protect the abominable system established in the Philippines by the Friars.

It should, it seems to me, be our pleasure and duty to make those people free, and let them deal with their own domestic questions in their own way. And so I am an anti-imperialist. I am opposed to having the eagle put its talons on any other land.

"You've been quoted here as an anti-imperialist," the reporter for the Chicago *Tribune* asked during the interview. "Well, I am," Mark Twain replied.

Thousands of Americans were giving the same answer to this question. By the time Twain landed in New York harbor, anti-imperialist leagues had sprung up all over the country. In October, 1899, at a mammoth convention in Chicago, these local leagues had combined into a central association, the American Anti-Imperialist League. The national body, with headquarters in Chicago, grew into an organization of one-half million members. The national and local leagues held conferences and public meetings, published thousands of manifestoes, pamphlets, poems, speeches and magazine articles. The national organization, alone, circulated 1,164,188 items of printed matter, and sent out 169,700 chain cards — urging "all lovers of freedom" to cooperate to achieve a suspension of hostilities in the Philippines, and the guarantee by Congress that the United States "will recognize the independence of the Philippines and its equality among nations, and gradually withdraw all military and naval forces." The anti-imperialist movement won the support of America's outstanding writers. Although not all were officially connected with the leagues, men like William Dean Howells, Henry and William James, Edwin Arlington Robinson, Edgar Lee Masters, Dr. W. E. B. Du Bois, Peter Finley Dunne, Joaquin Miller, William Vaughn Moody, Moncure Daniel Conway, Edwin Lawrence Godkin, Henry Demarest Lloyd, Charles Eliot Norton, Frederick Douglass, Jr., and Hamlin Garland contributed articles, essays, poems and short stories to the literature of anti-imperialism. Now Mark Twain was to take his stand alongside "virtually all the good writers of the Republic" in firm patriotic opposition to wars for plunder.

Twain arrived in the United States during the height of the Presidential campaign of 1900. Earlier that year, anti-imperialists had sought to organize a third party, feeling that the two major parties had played a Tweedledee-Tweedledum role on the issue of imperialism — the treaty of peace having been adopted in the Senate with Democratic as well as Republican votes. When this movement fell through, the anti-imperialists were left with a choice between the two major party candidates, neither of whom was to their liking. The Republicans had renominated McKinley on an openly imperialist platform, while the Democrats had nominated Bryan on a platform which denounced imperialism but advocated a protectorate for the Philippines. To the anti-imperialists this was literally an endorsement of imperialism. Moreover, Bryan's support of the imperialist Treaty of Paris annexing the Philippines had made his name anathema to them. Reluctantly and with much misgiving, the Indianapolis Convention of the American Anti-Imperialist League on August 16, 1900, chose the "lesser evil," and voted to support Bryan. But many rejected this decision, and the rest were half-hearted. The result was confusion and apathy which kept large numbers away from the polls. The total vote cast in 1900 was 13,964,567, only 64,710 more than in 1896. Denied a real choice, the voters re-elected McKinley by a vote of 7, 218,491. Bryan recorded an impressive 6,402,926, indicating that, had his record been such as to convince the people that he was really anti-imperialist, he would have been elected.

Like many other Americans, Mark Twain was disgusted by the choice of candidates. Several weeks after the election, he wrote in restrospect: "Oh, the Philippine mess! I wish I had been here two months before the Presidential election. I would have gone on the stump against both candidates." Instead, he had simply stayed away from the polls. Speaking before the New York City Club early in 1901, he explained his action: "Not long ago we had two men running for the President. There was Mr. McKinley on one hand and Mr. Bryan on the other. If we'd have had an 'Anti-Doughnut Party' neither would have been elected. I don't know much about finance, but some friends told me that Bryan was all wrong on the money question, so I didn't vote for him. I knew enough about the Philippines to have a strong aversion to sending our bright boys out there to fight with a disgraced musket under a polluted flag, so I didn't vote for the other fellow."

Twain went on to remind his audience that he still had

his vote and was ready to use it whenever a party was organized that would whole-heartedly oppose the imperialist policies of the McKinley administration. It is clear that he refused to accept the re-election of McKinley as a people's mandate endorsing imperialism, and did not share with the general discouragement. He did not agree that "the opposition to it [the administration's policy] might as well fold up its protests and become witnesses to what is done." On the contrary, the election was no sooner over than Twain was thinking of ways to reverse the administration's policies in the Philippines. "Won't you please see Mr. [Grover] Cleveland," he wrote to Laurence Hutton on December 3, 1900, "& ask him this question for me: Would it be possible to get the Spanish Treaty of Paris before the Supreme Court for examination & decision as to its constitutionality & legality? And if so: What steps must be taken in order to bring the matter before the court?"

Twain's most effective attacks upon imperialism in general and American imperialism in particular, came after the Presidential election of 1900. His stand, as one auditor at Twain's City Club speech put it, was a "sursum corda" (an uplifting of the spirits) to the anti-imperialist movement.

Four days after the election, on November 10, Twain spoke at a dinner in his honor tendered by the Lotos Club in New York. He criticized American policy in the Philippines and spoke out in defense of China. Two weeks later, in an address before the Public Education Association, he publicly announced, "I am a Boxer":

Why shouldn't all the foreign powers withdraw from China and leave her free to attend to her own business?

It is the foreigners who are making all the trouble in China, and if they would only get out how pleasant everything would be!

As far as America is concerned we don't allow the Chinese to come here, and we would be doing the graceful thing to allow China to decide whether she will allow us to go there. China never wanted any foreigners, and when it comes to a settlement of this immigrant question I am with the Boxer every time.

The Boxer is a patriot; he is the only patriot China has, and I wish him success.

During the address, Twain commented on a news dispatch headed, "Russia proposes to retrench." He at first assumed that this referred to the 30,000 Russian soldiers in Manchuria, whom the Czarist government was "going to take . . . out of there and send . . . back to their farms to live in peace. . . . Full of this dream of peace, I went on reading the cable dispatch. Alas! it went on to say that the Chinese war was so expensive that Russia had decided to retrench by withdrawing the appropriation for public schools. To spend money on war they retrench on schools." Twain heightened the point of his story with an anecdote about a Mississippi town of his youth. A proposal to close the school was successfully opposed by an old farmer who observed that every time they closed a school, they would have to build a jail. "It was like feeding a dog on his own tail; you'll never fatten the dog," he concluded.

At the news that Twain had publicly proclaimed himself a "Boxer," the infuriated imperialist press charged him with allying himself with murderers and assassins." The Louisville *Courier-Journal*, however, hailed the announcement as logical. "That he should champion the cause of the Chinese when he has championed the cause of the aborigines of every land is not surprising," it editorialized.

On December 13, 1900, Twain introduced Winston Churchill, then a war correspondent, to a distinguished audience gathered at a banquet in the Waldorf-Astoria Hotel. Churchill had fought in South Africa, had been captured and released by the Boers, and had come to the United States to lecture on his experiences. There were those who felt that Twain should not have participated in the banquet, but he made use of the occasion to deliver some sharp thrusts at the so-called upholders of civilization and bringers of light to "backward" people.

Behold America [Twain said in the course of his introduction], the refuge of the oppressed from everywhere (who can pay $10 admission) — everyone except a Chinaman — standing up for human rights everywhere, even helping to make China let people in free when she wants to collect $50 from them. And how piously America has wrought for that open door in all cases where it was not her own.

How generous England and America have been in not compelling China to pay exorbitantly for extinguished missionaries. They are willing to take produce for them — fire-crackers and such; while the Germans must have monuments and any other boodle that is lying around. They've made Christianity so expensive that China can't afford German missionaries any more.

And he concluded with a direct attack upon British and American imperialism to which he cleverly tied the guest of honor, Winston Churchill himself:

Yes, as a missionary I've sung my songs of praise; and yet I think that England sinned when she got herself into a war in South Africa which she could have avoided, just as we have sinned in getting into a similar war in the Philippines. Mr. Churchill by his father is an Englishman; by his mother he is an American; no doubt a blend that makes the perfect man. England and America: yes, we are kin. And now that we are also kin in sin, there is nothing more to be desired. The harmony is complete, the blend is perfect — like Mr. Churchill himself, whom I now have the honor to present to you.

Later in the evening Churchill and Twain argued about the Boer War. "After some interchanges," Churchill wrote later, "I found myself beaten back to the citadel 'My country right or wrong.' 'Ah,' said the old gentleman 'when the poor country is fighting for its life, I agree. But this was not your case.'"

Twain's introductory speech makes clear that he saw the basic similarity between British imperialism in South Africa and American imperialism in the Philippines, and was not afraid to point this out publicly despite his desire for a "closer relationship between England and America."

Yet his remarks were polite compared to what he wrote privately at the same time. In a letter penned on the last day of the year 1900, he wrote: "McKinley's war is as discreditable as Chamberlain's. I wish to God the public would lynch both these frauds."

Twain's final public utterance in 1900 was one of the most effective and widely distributed pieces in the entire literature of anti-imperialism. It was the remarkable "A Salutation-speech from the Nineteenth Century to the Twentieth taken down in short-hand by Mark Twain." The piece, in the form of a toast, was originally written for the Red Cross Society and was to be read at a series of watch meetings throughout the country on New Year's Eve, together with "greetings" composed by other famous people. But when Twain learned that only his name was listed in the announcement, he wrote the management of the Red Cross: "The list thus far issued by you contains only vague generalizations, and one definite name, mine — 'Some kings and queens and Mark Twain.' Now I am not enjoying this sparkling solitude and distinction, which has not been authorized by me, and which makes me feel like a circus-poster in a graveyard or like any other advertisement improperly placed." The Red Cross Manager, finding it impossible to publish a list of names as Twain had requested, returned the "Greeting." Twain then sent it to the New York *Herald* which published it on December 30, 1900. It read:

A salutation-speech from the Nineteenth Century to the Twentieth, taken down in short-hand by Mark Twain:
"I bring you the stately matron named Christendom, returning bedraggled, besmirched, and dishonored from pirate-raids in Kiao-Chou, Manchuria, South Africa & the Philippines, with her soul full of meanness, her pocket full of boodle and her mouth full of pious hypocrisies. Give her soap and a towel, but hide the looking-glass."

The "Greeting" was widely reprinted, especially in the anti-imperialist press. In addition, it was printed on small cards and distributed throughout the nation by the branches of the American Anti-Imperialist League. The cards contained two additional lines probably written by Twain. Following the final sentence, "Give her soap and a towel, but hide the looking-glass," there was the couplet:

> *Give her the glass; it may from error free her,*
> *When she shall see herself as others see her.*

Anti-Imperialists Slandered

"It is by the goodness of God," Twain wrote in *Following the Equator*, "that in our country we have those three precious things: freedom of speech, freedom of conscience — and the prudence never to practice any of them." It did not take him long after his return from Europe to see that the anti-imperialist movement did not attract prudent people. Anti-imperialist writers were denounced as "traitors" in the jingo press; they were threatened with physical violence; and their writings were barred from the mails. Even a conservative scholar like Charles Eliot Norton of Harvard, translator of Dante and a leading art historian, was subjected to a campaign of vilification for daring to call for peace. In his lecture on "True Patriotism," Norton had upheld the duty of opposing an unjust war, like that being waged in the Philippines. He wrote his friend Leslie Stephens in England: "My mail [after the lecture] was loaded down with letters and post cards full of abuse, mostly anonymous, some of them going so far as to bid me to look for a stray bullet."

Of the hideous events, of that sort, that had transpired before his return from Europe, Twain knew from conversations with Howells and other anti-imperialist men of letters. He was not at all frightened. He had made his position clear as far back as 1884 when his friends had asked him where he would stand if the United States went to war for an unjust cause with the approval of the great majority of the people. He replied:

If I thought it an unrighteous war I would say so. If I were invited to shoulder a musket in that cause and march under that flag, I should decline.... If the country *obliged* me to shoulder the musket, I could not help myself, but I would never volunteer. To volunteer would be the act of a traitor to myself, and consequently traitor to my country. If I refused to volunteer, I should be *called* a traitor, I am well aware of that — but that would not make me a traitor. The unanimous vote of the sixty millions could not make me a traitor. I should still be a patriot, and in my opinion, the only one in the country.

In 1901 Twain still adhered to this position. He refused, therefore, to heed the counsel of friends who advised caution. When Twichell warned him to avoid the subject of imperialism lest he damage the sale of his books and injure himself and his publisher, Twain was stirred to anger: "I can't understand it! You are a public guide and teacher, Joe, and you are under a heavy responsibility to men, young and old; if you teach your people — as you teach me — to hide their opinions when they believe the flag is being abused and dishonored, lest the utterance do them and a publisher a damage, how do you answer for it to your conscience? You are sorry for me; in the fair way of give and take, I am willing to be a little sorry for you."

There were those among the anti-imperialists who felt that Twain was late in joining their ranks, and that he gave voice publicly to opposition to the war in the Philippines when it could no longer accomplish much good. But most anti-imperialists felt that Twain's emergence as a vehement critic of American foreign policy was an invaluable asset to the cause. *The Nation*, praising Twain for his courage in risking popularity and income by making himself obnoxious "to the people [who] hold the purse strings," and this at a time when he had finished paying off his creditors, discussed this question in an editorial entitled, "Mark Twain: American Citizen."

He is a man to be reckoned with in this business. The ordinary epithets cannot be flung at him. Mark Twain is no bilious, white-livered, wall-eyed hermit of a timid and foreign-aping Little American. He is entirely American ... the strong native product of our Great West. ... Growth of our soil and travelled observer of other nations, Mark Twain comes home to tell our flaunting imperialists that he sees through their hypocrisies. Tell us what you think of him, champions of Imperialism ... give us your honest opinion of this typical and whole-hearted American, who stepped from the pilot-house of a Mississippi steamboat into first a national and then a European fame, and now fearlessly sides with the Filipinos against their American oppressors.

Mark Twain, American Citizen, remains what he was, a homely and vigorous republican, let who will, trick themselves out in the gauds and paste jewels of Imperialism.

In a letter to the *New York Times,* headed "Mark Twain, Literature and War," Moncure Daniel Conway (himself a staunch anti-imperialist who viewed the war in the Philippines "as an effort to lynch the humble Washingtons and Hancocks of that region") welcomed Twain to the ranks of the anti-imperialist writers. The noted biographer of Thomas Paine pointed out that Twain was following in the path of American writers who, a half-century earlier, had opposed the war of aggression against Mexico and had spoken out for peace.

The cause of peace has certainly declined in the past fifty years. The authors who gave America its literary fame in the middle of the last century, Emerson, Longfellow, Sparks, Hawthorne, Bryant, Holmes, Lowell, Whittier, Motley — to name only some — were celebrants of peace. ...

I have these many years recognized that Mark Twain's humor is apt to feather a very serious arrow, and I venture to predict that the indignant "patriots" who are demanding his explanations will not have long to wait. The nation has already heard the protests of some of its finest intellects, among them Howells and Charles Norton, and it may be now hoped that the bugle call of Samuel Clemens will be the signal for an uprising of intellectual forces in America similar to that which in France [in the Dreyfus Case] has just laid low the militant dragon and plucked the spoil out of its teeth.

347

The "bugle call" was already being prepared when Conway's letter was published in the *Times* on January 11, 1901. A week before, Twain had told a reporter for the New York *Herald* that he was writing "an article" on the subject of imperialism. It was "To the Person Sitting in Darkness," Mark Twain's most important anti-imperialist writing.

"To the Person Sitting in Darkness"

"I've written another article; you better hurry down and help Livy squelch it." So Twain wrote to Twichell on January 29, 1901, revealing that he had finished "To the Person Sitting in Darkness." Evidently Twichell's argument that publication of the article would hurt Twain's book sales did not influence Mrs. Clemens. Twain's daughter, Clara, reports that before publishing the article, "Father secured the approbation of both my mother and Mr. Howells, whose opinions alone could enable him to stand like the Statue of Liberty, unweakened by the waters of condemnation that washed up to his feet."

That Twain anticipated a flood of the "waters of condemnation" is clear. Meeting Dan Beard on the street, he remarked: "By the way, I have just written something you'll like. It is called 'To the Person Sitting in Darkness.' I read it to Howells, and Howells said I ought to have that published.... Howells also said I must go hang myself first, and when I asked him what I should do that for, he said to save the public the trouble, because when that story appeared in print they would surely hang me." Twain was, then, fully aware of the harm, personal and financial, publication of the article might do him. But he ignored all warnings. "He had given out his innermost convictions, and nothing could make him regret it," his daughter writes.

"To the Person Sitting in Darkness" appeared in the *North American Review* in February, 1901. The title, derived from the Bible (Matt:4:16, Verses 13-17), is a satirical use of the imperialist concept of the colonial peoples — the Chinese, the Boer, the African, the Filipino — to whom the imperialists claimed to be bringing the gospels of Christ and the benefits of civilization. The article is addressed to the "person" ostensibly to reconcile him to the receipt of the blessings bestowed upon him by imperialism. The essay opens with two quotations which had appeared in the New York *Sun*. One described the terrible conditions in New York's East Side districts *"where naked women dance by night in the streets ... where the education of the infants begins with the knowledge of prostitution ... where the children that have adult diseases are the chief patrons of the hospitals and dispensaries."* The other, a letter from China, reported that the Rev. Mr. William Ament of the American Board of Foreign Missions, had returned from a trip into the interior of China to collect indemnities for damages done by the Boxer uprising. The hundred Chinese Christians under the guardianship of the American Board had been killed, and Rev. Ament had collected 300 taels for each, had compelled full compensation for all property that had been destroyed, and had also assessed fines amounting to thirteen times the amount of the indemnity. This money, Rev. Ament announced, would be used for the propagation of the Gospel.

Justifying the sum extracted from the Chinese, Rev. Ament pointed out that the exactions of the American Board were moderate compared with the amounts collected by the Catholics who demanded, in addition to money, head for head. They extorted 500 taels for each convert killed; and, in addition, when 680 of their converts were massacred in the Wenchiu district, they demanded 680 heads. While denying that the missionaries generally were extortionists, Rev. Ament criticized the Americans for treating the Chinese with a soft hand unlike the Germans who knew how to use the mailed fist. "If you deal with the Chinese with a soft hand they will take advantage of it," Rev. Ament concluded.

It is good, says Mark Twain, that this glad tidings arrives on Christmas Eve, just in time to enable us to celebrate the day with proper gaiety and enthusiasm. The Rev. Ament is the right man in the right place. He represents the American spirit, and that of the oldest Americans, the Pawnees, whose idea is that it is only fair and right that the innocent should be made to suffer for the guilty, and that it is better that ninety and nine innocent should suffer than that one guilty person should escape.

Ament's "magnanimity," Twain points out, deserved a monument, the designs for which must include a representation of the thirteen-fold indemnity, and must "exhibit 680 Heads, so disposed as to give a pleasing and pretty effect, for the Catholics have done nicely, and are entitled to notice in the monument." Twain then lashes out at Ament's robbery of the Chinese. What matter if Chinese women and children had to starve in order to raise the blood money squeezed out of pauper peasants? Would it not be *used for the propagation of the Gospel*," Twain notes, underlining Ament's words. All told, "the act and the words, taken together, concrete a blasphemy so hideous and so colossal that without doubt its mate is not findable in this or any other age."

Twain had a deeper purpose than to hold Ament's conduct up to ridicule. He charged that the entire missionary movement was an agency of imperialism. Nor did he offer merely his own opinion as evidence; he quoted the New York *Tribune*'s Tokyo correspondent who advocated the suppression of missionary organizations in the Orient because they act as "filibustering expeditions" for the Western Powers, and "constitute a constant menace to peaceful international relations." The American people, Twain insists, must face up to this big question:

That is, shall we go on conferring our Civilization upon the peoples that sit in darkness, or shall we give those poor things a rest? Shall we bang right ahead in our old-time, loud, pious way, and commit the new century to the game; or shall we sober up and sit down and think it over first? Would it not be prudent to get our

Civilization tools together and see how much stock is left on hand in the way of Glass Beads and Theology, and Maxim Guns and Hymn Books, and Trade Gin and Torches of Progress and Enlightenment (patent adjustable ones, good to fire villages with, upon occasion), and balance the books and arrive at the profit and loss, so that we may intelligently decide whether to continue the business or sell out the property and start a new Civilization scheme on the proceeds?

In the past, Twain continues, extending the Blessings of Civilization had paid extremely well, "and there is money in it yet, if carefully worked." But it must be administered carefully; the People who Sit in Darkness were becoming scarce and shy. "We have been injudicious." "The Blessings-of-Civilization Trust, wisely and cautiously administered, is a Daisy. There is more money in it, more territory, more sovereignty and other kinds of emolument, than there is in any other game that is played."

But Christendom has been playing it badly. She has been too greedy, and the People who Sit in Darkness have become suspicious, and have begun to examine the blessings of civilization. The business was being ruined by the ineptitude of McKinley, Chamberlain, the Kaiser, the Czar, and the French. The previous managers of the "Blessings-of-Civilization Trust" had at least tried to conceal its ruthless colonial policy under slogans of "Love, Justice, Gentleness, Christianity, Protection to the Weak, Temperance, Law and Order, Liberty, Equality, Honorable Dealing, Mercy, Education" — a brand of goods, which, Twain notes, is "strictly for export" and confined to the cover. "Inside . . . is the Actual Thing that the Customer Sitting in Darkness buys with his blood and tears and land and liberty." The ineptitude of the contemporary imperialists, Twain points out, is illustrated by the fact that they have been exporting Civilization *"with the outside cover left off."* No longer does the customer sitting in darkness believe he is buying merchandise like Love, Liberty, Christianity, Justice. He now sees the real thing immediately.

Twain then censures the imperialist governments of

England, Germany, Russia and the United States in turn, showing how each has ruined the business by its ruthless policies. England, for example, under Chamberlain, "manufactures a war out of materials so inadequate and so fanciful that they make the boxes grieve and the gallery laugh, and he tries to persuade himself that it isn't purely a private raid for cash." This "exposes the Actual Thing to Them that Sit in Darkness." These people cannot help knowing something of British "harryings and burnings and desert-makings in the Transvaal," and of British privates' letters which boast of giving Boer soldiers the "long spoon" — the bayonet — even when they had dropped their guns and were begging for mercy.

The German imperialists, Twain notes, dealt a severe blow to the "Blessings-of-Civilization Trust." The Kaiser entered the game without first mastering it. He took $200,000 from China as well as twelve miles of territory worth $20,000,000, a monument and a Christian Church, all this as compensation for two missionaries killed in a Shantung riot. This was overcharging and, therefore, bad business. A missionary, like a doctor or a sheriff, or an editor, is worth much, but he is not worth the earth. The person sitting in darkness has not been deceived; he knows the Chinese have been overcharged, and he wonders if he can afford the "Blessings of Civilization." He also reasons that Germany would never dare to send troops through the United States with orders to slay, giving no quarter. But in China, which is helpless, he sees German troops loot and slay as they please. No wonder he begins to ask: "Can we afford Civilization?"

Russia also plays the game badly. With "its banner of the Prince of Peace in one hand, and its loot-basket and its butcher-knife in the other," it seizes Manchuria, raids its villages, and chokes its great river with swollen corpses of countless massacred peasants. And the person sitting in darkness, noting every move Russia makes, says to himself: "It is yet *another* civilized Power. . . . Is this then the Civilization we are supposed to buy?"

If Twain showed his contempt for European imperialism up to this point in his essay, his bitterest attacks are now delivered against the imperialism of his own country. Fully half the article is devoted to the Spanish-American War and the war in the Philippines.

Twain still clings to the idealistic interpretation of the origin of the Spanish-American War, and draws a picture of McKinley, acting in the best American tradition, leading the nation into a just war for Cuba's freedom. He was playing the American game in the Cuban campaign, and he could not lose. McKinley, our "Master of the Game," held the strength of seventy million sympathizers and the resources of the United States to back Cuba's struggle for freedom. "Nothing but Europe combined could call that hand and Europe cannot combine on anything." Moved by a high inspiration, the Master had even proclaimed forcible annexation to be "criminal aggression." "The memory of that fine saying will be outlived by the remembrance of no act of his but one — that he forgot it within the twelvemonth, and its honorable gospel along with it."

In the Philippines, McKinley began to play the European game, the Chamberlain game. As a consequence, those who sit in darkness are becoming convinced that just as there are two brands of Civilization, one for home consumption and one for export, there must be two Americas: "One that sets the captive free, and one that takes a once-captive's new freedom away from him, and picks a quarrel with him with nothing to found it on, then kills him to get his land." This, Twain asserts, is going to be bad for the Business. Indeed, "for the sake of the Business," the Person in the Darkness must be persuaded "to look at the Philippine matter in another and healthier way." Having stated the problem, Twain makes his "modest proposal." It is simply, following Mr. Chamberlain and even going beyond him, to "present the whole of the facts, shirking none, then explain them according to Mr. Chamberlain's formula." This runs: "Twice 2 are 14, and 2 from 9 leaves 35."

The "facts" follow in the form of a summarized history of American imperialism in the Philippines. Twain traces the military role played by the Filipinos in capturing Manila, their invaluable aid as allies, their patriotism and love of freedom; to this he contrasts the deceitful course followed by Dewey and others in the American command, the pretext used to prevent Aguinaldo and the Filipino soldiers from entering Manila, and the buying of territory from Spain which she no longer owned. He sums it all up as follows: "What we wanted ... was the Archipelago, unencumbered by patriots struggling for independence; and War was what we needed. We clinched our opportunity. It was Mr. Chamberlain's case over again ... and we played the game as adroitly as he played it himself."

Twain compares America's loss of 268 killed and 750 wounded to the Filipino loss of 3,227 killed and 694 wounded — facts proudly set forth in Major General Arthur MacArthur's reports. Then follows the scorching indictment contained in a letter from an American soldier in the Philippines to his mother, describing the victorious finish to the battle: "We never left one alive, if one was wounded, we would run our bayonets through him."

The Person Sitting in Darkness is aware of all this, and if we are to save the Business, we must explain these facts to him. Twain then proceeds to do this, saying:

There have been lies, yes, but they were told in a good cause. We have been treacherous, but that was only in order that real good might come out of apparent evil. True, we have crushed a deceived and confiding people; we have turned against the weak and the friendless who trusted us; we have stabbed an ally in the back and slapped the face of a guest; we have bought a Shadow from an enemy that hadn't it to sell; we have robbed a trusting friend of his land and his liberty; we have invited our clean young men to shoulder a discredited musket and do bandits' work under a flag which bandits have been accustomed to fear, not to follow; we have debauched America's honor and blackened her face before the world; but each detail was for the best.... Give yourself no uneasiness; it is all right.

This will give the Person a splendid new start. But, although everything is going well just now, the Americans are still a little troubled about their uniform and their flag being there. Twain has a simple solution for this problem:

They are not needed there; we can manage in some other way. England manages, as regards the uniform, and so can we. We have to send soldiers — we can't get out of that — but we can disguise them. It is the way England does in South Africa. Even Mr. Chamberlain himself takes pride in England's honorable uniform, and makes the army down there wear an ugly and odious and appropriate disguise, of yellow stuff such as quarantine flags are made of, and which are hoisted to warn the healthy away from unclean disease and repulsive death. This cloth is called khaki. We could adopt it. It is light, comfortable, grotesque, and deceives the enemy, for he cannot conceive of a soldier being concealed in it.

And as for a flag for the Philippine Province, it is easily managed. We can have a special one — our States do it; we can have just our usual flag, with the white stripes painted black and the stars replaced by the skull and cross-bones.

And Twain concludes his scathing satire: "By help of these suggested amendments, Progress and Civilization in that country can have a boom, and it will take in the Persons who are Sitting in Darkness, and we can resume business at the old stand."

Actually, there was little in Twain's essay of a factual nature that had not already appeared in contemporary anti-imperialist writings. What made "To the Person Sitting in Darkness" the greatest literary contribution to the anti-imperialist movement was its irony and grim humor. Through biting satire, puns, colloquial twists, understatement, and especially through vivid metaphors (the head-studded monument to Reverend Mr. Ament; Civilization as a bale of goods for export; the personification of Russia "with its banner of the Prince of Peace in one hand and its loot-basket and its butcher-knife in the other," etc.), Twain ripped the masks off the imperialist warmakers.

The case has doubtless been put as vigorously before by others [Dr. W. A. Croffut, Secretary of the Washington, D. C. Anti-Imperialist League wrote to Twain], but the splendid satire and blistering irony will give your words a momentum which nothing else could. And hundreds will read this because you wrote it who could not be got to taste of such truths from any other source. . . . When a man having the public ear as you have dares to come out with such an unlimited roasting of the powers that be, it gives us great hope. . . . Though I am an old-fashioned Republican I have been greatly dispirited since the election. But your trumpet-blast sounds the pulses again and sounds like the beginning of a new campaign.

From Edwin Burritt Smith, Chairman, Executive Committee of the American Anti-Imperialist League, came the comment: "I can say, as one familiar with the literature on the subject, that it is the strongest indictment of imperialism with all its cant and humbug that has yet appeared." Erving Winslow, Secretary of the New England Anti-Imperialist League, wrote: "Will you permit me to thank you for your pungent article in the 'North American' and to welcome you into the front ranks of the leaders of the Anti-Imperialist cause? Probably no one shot will tell with such effect as yours and I much doubt if all of them put together will do so." A leading official of the Canadian Anti-Imperialist League assured Twain that his article "will . . . be effective here in Canada where there is also an Imperial question; we have been sending our young men to South Africa to slay the Dutch farmers, who at all events have never done us any wrong; we too have our mouths full of the pious hypocrisy of the civilization Trust."

Many newspapers and magazines reprinted Twain's article in part, and most publications in the United States and England commented editorially. The Springfield (Mass.) *Republican*, a leading anti-imperialist daily, announced that with the publication of the article, "Mark Twain, the master satirist, has suddenly become the most influential anti-imperialist and the most dreaded critic of the sacrosanct person in the White House that the country contains." *The Nation* was effusive in its praise: "His satirical weapons were never keener, or played about the heads of Imperialists with a more merciless swish. In one long burst of sarcasm he exposes the weariful hypocrisy of the American policy in the Philippines, and covers it with ridicule mountain-high. Mark Twain was never a respecter of persons, and in this grim satire of his he flies straight at the highest." The periodical further pointed out that Twain's courage was as great as his writing skill. Where other satirists had attacked only the dead, Twain had boldly struck out at living targets. "Not counting the risk to his personal popularity, he has let us see the flame of his honest anger burning against shame and cheating in the highest matters of national policy. He is a man to be reckoned with in this business." In London, the *Review of Reviews* editorialized: "Mark Twain has contributed much to the gaiety of nations. He also has time and again touched with unerring finger the weak points in our civilisation, but he has never combined in a single article so much mordant humour and such merciless truth as are to be found in the inimitable essay which he contributed to the *North American Review* for February. This article is a masterpiece in its way, and as a contribution to current political controversy there is nothing like it printed in the English language. It is a thousand pities that so admirable a contribution to the great controversy of the day should not be reprinted and circulated by the million throughout the United States and the United Kingdom."

The article did receive a wide circulation after it was published in pamphlet form by the New York Anti-Imperialist League. One hundred and twenty five thousand copies were distributed, according to the League's Secretary, making it the organization's most popular piece of literature.

"To the Person Sitting in Darkness" enraged the imperialists. But, knowing Twain's popularity, some thought it wiser to deal with the article as a temporary mental aberration. One had to expect that prolonged absence from his native land would cause the humorist "to get out of touch with things American," so he should be excused for having fallen prey to the un-American propaganda of the Anti-Imperialist League. It only showed that "he is, after all, merely human, and not the demigod some of us had begun to think him. There is positive comfort in the thought that even Mark Twain is not infallible." Others, in the same vein, argued that "he is a humorist and is not to be taken seriously when he discourses on serious subjects." It was nothing to get unduly concerned about, for soon enough "the great purveyor of sunshine to his fellowmen" would return to humor, the field to which he belonged. The New York *Sun* remarked, in answering a request for comment on Twain's article: "We are sorry to say that *Mark* is on a spree. Don't mention it. For the moment he is in a state of mortifying intoxication from an overdraught of seriousness, something to which his head has not been hardened. Wait, and welcome the prodigal as of old on his return. He will be along again in time." But many in the imperialist camp minced no words in expressing their rage. One wrote furiously: "Exactly why a professional 'funny man,' whose life-work has been the construction of amusing absurdities, should consider himself or be considered by others qualified to seriously discuss grave questions of statesmanship that he has never studied, we don't know." Another urged Twain's friends to advise him that "as a moralist he is clearly a failure," and that unless "he quietly ... withdraws from the field," his name would soon be forgotten. An anonymous pro-imperialist critic predicted: "A hundred years from now it is very likely that *The Jumping Frog* alone will be remembered."

Criticizing these sneering diatribes, the Rochester *Union-Advertiser* declared on February 5, 1901: "The life-work of Mark Twain has not consisted altogether in the construction of amusing absurdities. His best work has been done in the satirical treatment of absurdities already existing. Our contemporary thinks that a humorist should not deal with important questions, and that he should not be taken seriously when he deals with them. Well, why not? A large sense of the incongruous is what makes a humorist. It is because Mark Twain has this sense very highly developed that he is better able than most people to see the weak points in our position in relation to the inhabitants of the Philippines."

The charge of "treason" was also hurled. "Mark Twain a Traitor," read a headline in a pro-imperialist paper. Had an article like "To the Person Sitting in Darkness" appeared in any other way, raged the *Army and Navy Journal*, the author would have been convicted as a "traitor" to his country. A clergyman, quoting the editorial with approval, gave as further proof of Twain's "treason" the fact that the humorist had not gone to fight in the Philippines.

Twain replied in a speech before the Lotos Club, and accused his clerical critic of confusing the issue. Acting when the country's life was in danger was a different thing from supporting a war of aggression in an arena far removed from its boundaries. As he pointed out several times during the winter and spring of 1901, true patriotism consisted of opposing the government sending "young fellows . . . to the Philippines on a land-stealing and liberty-crucifying crusade." The men who were being hailed as "patriots" by the imperialist press were simple people who had "turned Traitor to keep from being called Traitor." The real "patriot" was the Filipino who resisted the invasion of his country by "bandits" in American uniforms. On February 14, 1901, Twain inscribed the following in a book for a friend:

I have rearranged the "Battle Hymn of the Republic" this afternoon and brought it down to date — sample stanza:

I have read this bandit gospel writ in burnished rows of steel,
As ye deal with my pretentions, so with you my wrath shall deal,
Let the faithless sons of freedom, crush the patriot with his heel
  Lo, Greed is marching on.

The other stanzas read:

*Mine eyes have seen the orgy of the launching of the
Sword;*
*He is searching out the hoardings where the stranger's
wealth is stored;*
*He has loosed his fateful lightning, & with woe & death
has scored;*
His lust is marching on.

*I have seen him in the watch-fires of a hundred circling
camps;*
*They have builded him an altar in the Eastern dews &
damps;*
*I have read his doomful mission by the dim & flaring
lamps —*
His might is marching on.

*We have legalized the Strumpet & are guarding her re-
treat;*
*Greed is seeking out commercial souls before his judg-
ment seat;*
Oh, be swift, ye clods, to answer him! be jubilant my feet!
Our god is marching on!

*In a sordid slime harmonious, Greed was born in yonder
ditch;*
With a longing in his bosom — for other's goods an itch;
Christ died to make men holy, let men die to make us rich;
Our god is marching on.

"To the Person Sitting in Darkness" brought Mark Twain
much abuse, but it won countless supporters for the anti-
imperialist cause. "He is getting some hard knocks now
from the blackguards and hypocrites for his righteous fun

with McKinley's attempt to colonize the Philippines," Howells wrote to his sister on February 24, "but he is making hosts of friends too." Anti-imperialism in the United States was stirred as never before as many Americans, heretofore, indifferent to the issue, began to see the full consequences of the administration's policies. "During the past four months," wrote Rev. Thomas B. Payne, "I have said many of the same things to a young man, an ex-soldier of the Spanish War who has been bewitched by McKinley's course in [the] Philippines, but could not change him. He read your article, and arose from it converted."

Small wonder a leader of the Anti-Imperialist League exulted: "Praise to the Eternal! A voice has been found."

"To My Missionary Critics"

The clergyman who called Mark Twain a "traitor" was only one of scores of ministers who attacked him following the publication of "To the Person Sitting in Darkness." What particularly rankled the clergy were his satirical thrusts at the missionaries' role in imperialism.

At one time, as we have seen, the missionaries benefited from favorable publicity in Twain's writings. In his letters from the Sandwich Islands, in 1866, and in his early lectures, he had cited approvingly their part in the development of civilization in the Islands. Yet, even at that time, his praise was not unqualified, and he censured them privately in his notebook for "insincerity and hypocrisy." As the years passed, Twain became more and more convinced that the whole idea of trying to convert a man to another religion was immoral and unethical. Invited in 1893 to attend a meeting and say a few words in behalf of foreign missions, he bluntly refused. "I have no sympathy with such things & take no interest in them," he informed his correspondent. Three years later, he wrote in his notebook:

It is a most strange vocation, the missionary's. There is no other reputable occupation that resembles it — unless party politics may be called reputation. In all lands the religious deserter ranks with the military deserter; it is considered that he has done a base thing & shameful. It is the mish's trade to make religious deserters.

Whatever may have remained of Twain's earlier appreciative attitude toward the missionaries vanished during his travels in the Orient and Africa. He saw with his own eyes how the missionaries used the banner of Christianity to uphold and advance the cause of imperialism, the robbery of territory, and the exploitation of the people there. Realizing that the missionary had become the tool of the imperialists, he was revolted by the use of religion to maintain an evil system.

He expressed his revulsion in several unpublished pieces even before it was made crystal clear to all in his essay in the *North American Review*. In one of his unpublished comments he accused the missionary of having "loaded vast China onto the concert of Christian Birds of Prey," and voiced the hope "that the missionary's industries will be restricted to his native land for all time to come." But it was in "To the Person Sitting in Darkness" that he treated the matter fully, using the conduct of Reverend Mr. Ament to drive home the point that the missionary movement served as a front for imperialism.

This precipitated a deluge of condemnatory letters. "You have looted pure and Christian character," wrote an indignant correspondent. "You join those hooting at your Savior on the cross, when you set the rabble hooting at those who have taken their lives in their hands." Another wrote: "Truly I had always thought you to be a Christian! ... Were you ever judged insane? Be honest, truly how much money does the Devil give you for arraigning Christianity and missionary causes?"

The public attack opened with a letter from the Reverend Dr. Judson S. Smith, Secretary of the American Board of Commissioners for Foreign Missions. Smith's letter, published in the New York *Tribune* of February 15, 1901, defended Ament, praised his character and his contributions to Christianity over many years in China, questioned the authenticity of the *Sun* dispatch quoted in Twain's introductory paragraphs, and demanded an apology from Mark Twain. Replying in a letter to the *Tribune*, Twain insisted that Ament had arraigned himself and not he Ament. Quoting at length from the dispatch from China, published in the *Sun*, he concluded:

Whenever he can produce from the Rev. Mr. Ament an assertion that the *Sun's* character-blasting dispatch was not authorized by him; and whenever Dr. Smith, can buttress Mr. Ament's disclaimer with a confession from Mr. Chamberlain, the head of the Laffan News Service in China, that that dispatch was a false invention and unauthorized, the case against Mr. Ament will fall at once to the ground. There has been some time to get these absolutely essential documents by cable — fifty-one days — Why not get them now? Does Dr. Smith believe that with loose and wandering arguments and irrelevant excursions all around and outside of the real matter in hand he can pull Mr. Ament out of the unspeakable scrape he is in?

Dr. Smith was not satisfied. He wrote again, a few weeks later, and again demanded that Twain apologize. He reported that Ament, in reply to a request for comment on the *Sun* dispatch, explained that "fines thirteen times the indemnity" was a cable error for "fines one third the indemnity."

All this time, Twain himself had been carefully checking into the authenticity of the charge against Ament. He had written to China and asked for "the plain, straight facts." On the basis of the evidence submitted, he was convinced that everything he had written was correct. "I hope you will not retract or explain or do anything except rub it in harder," E. L. Godkin, editor of *The Nation*, wrote to Twain as soon as he heard that he was preparing a detailed answer to Dr. Smith. Twain obliged in "To My Missionary Critics," published in the *North American Review* of April, 1901.

Most of the article is a recapitulation of the charges

leveled at Ament in the previous essay. It made adroit use of the fact that only one of the charges — the exact amount of fines collected — no longer held true. Twain thus placed the American Board in the un-Christian position of justifying the morality of Ament's action on the ground that he had not collected fines from the Chinese thirteen times the indemnity, but had demanded *only* one and one-third the correct amount. The extra one-third, Twain insisted, was theft and exortion quite as much as thirteen times the amount. And he made powerfully ironical use of the Board's argument that Ament's "whole procedure is in accordance with a custom among the *Chinese*, of holding a village responsible for wrongs suffered in that village, and especially making the head man of the village accountable for wrongs committed there." "Is there no way, then," he asked, "to justify these thefts and extortions and make them clean and fair and honorable?" And he answered:

Yes, there is. It can be done; it has been done; it continues to be done — by revising the Ten Commandments and bringing them down to date: for use in pagan lands. For example:

Thou shalt not steal — except when it is the custom of the country.

This way out is recognized and *approved* by all the best authorities, including the Board. . . .

The American Board had asked for it so it could hardly complain of the manner in which its case had been demolished. Indeed, one paper had even warned the Board not to tangle with Mark Twain. "He will apologize to Mr. Ament," it wrote before the publication of "To My Missionary Critics," "in a way that Mr. Ament and his friends will remember."

With the publication of "To My Missionary Critics," the rout of the American Board was complete. While some of the orthodox religious publications continued to denounce Twain vehemently, "a vast following of liberal-minded readers, both in and out of the Church" upheld him. Said the London *Review of Reviews*:

Now, Mark Twain is the last man in the world to write a word reflecting upon the self-sacrificing labours of missionaries who are missionaries indeed, to whose labours and martyrdom the world owes many of the best things which it possesses. But of that modern type of missionary who in the name of the Prince of Peace acts often as the precursor of war and conquest, and who insists upon the defence of the Gospel by gunboats and Maxims, excites in Mark Twain somewhat of the same stern and scathing indignation which it would have excited in the Founder of our faith.

Edward S. Martin, the noted reformer, spoke for all progressive Americans when he said: "How great it is to feel that we have a man among us who understands the rarity of plain truth, and who delights to utter it, and has the gift of doing so without cant."

Twain's criticism of missionaries and the attention it received forced the missionary movement to take some steps to divest itself of some of the more blatant aspects of its services to imperialism. Twain, however, had little faith in the ability of the missionary movement, particularly as represented by "its reverend bandits of the American Board," to cleanse itself of the "stain" of imperialism. In July, 1901, Yang Wing, a Chinese educator whom he had earlier befriended, wrote to Twain for help in making a Chinese relief appeal to the United States government. Twain explained to Twichell why he could not comply with the request: "For me to assist in an appeal to that Congress of land-thieves and liars would be to bring derision on it; and for me to assist in an appeal for cash to pass through the hands of those missionaries out there, of any denomination, Catholic or Protestant, wouldn't do at all. They wouldn't handle money which I soiled, and I wouldn't trust them with it anyway."

About the same time, in "The United States of Lyncherdom," Twain urged the missionaries to leave China, where they could do no good, and return to the United States to reform the mobs who were lynching Negroes: "O kind missionary, o compassionate missionary, leave China! come home and convert these Christians."

In all the support Twain received for his criticism of the missionary movement, nothing pleased him more than the knowledge that Howells stood "shoulder to shoulder" with him on the issue. The two men had not seen eye-to-eye about the justice and desirability of the Cuban campaign; but after Twain returned to the United States, they were in close agreement on every current issue related to imperialism. "We agree perfectly about the Boer War, and the Filipino War, and war generally," Howells wrote to his sister on February 24, 1901, informing her at the same time that he was seeing "a great deal of Mark Twain nowadays."

Twain and Howells joined in endorsing the American Anti-Imperialist League, signing the Independence Day manifesto it issued in 1901 which urged "all lovers of freedom to organize in defense of human rights, now threatened by the greatest free government in history," and specifically called for independence for the Philippines. Again in February, 1902, Twain's and Howells' names were listed among the signers of another document distributed by the anti-imperialist movement. They were among a large group of notable American citizens who presented (through Senator George F. Hoar of Massachusetts) a "Petition from Sundry Citizens of the United States Favoring the Suspension of Hostilities in the Philippine Islands and a Discussion of the Situation between the Government and the Filipino Leaders."

The petition opened with quotations from the late President McKinley's protests against the concentration camp policy practiced by Spain in Cuba; it then cited newspaper clippings, private letters from American soldiers, official records, and press correspondents' reports to show that the administration was pursuing in the Philippines the same "inhuman methods" that Spain had been guilty of. For example, the Manila *Times*, an American daily reported on November 4, 1901, that "General Smith had threatened to shoot all Filipinos in Samar who were found outside of the coast towns to which they were ordered," and it added that "General Smith was as good as his word."

The petition concluded.

We respectfully petition — First, That an investigation be made in regard to the practice of our army in the Philippine Islands, by a committee of the Senate, and that the exact truth be laid before the people of the United States. Second, That, if these reports are true, steps be taken at once to stop reconcentration, the killing of prisoners, the shooting without trial of suspected persons, the use of torture, the employment of savage allies, the wanton destruction of private property, and every other barbarous method of waging war, which this nation from its infancy has ever condemned. Third, That appropriate steps be taken at once, by treating with the representatives of the Filipinos in arms, to secure a suspension of hostilities in order that an opportunity be given for a discussion of the situation between the Government and the Filipino leaders, who would be permitted to visit this country for this purpose. Fourth, That pending the negotiations strict orders be given to the officers in command of our troops to deal with the inhabitants of the Philippine Islands as with persons whom one day we hope to make our friends.

The names of the petitioners followed and included, "W. D. Howells, New York City," and "Mark Twain, New York City."

Congress took no action on the petition; and the only step the administration took was to deliver a mild reprimand to General Smith. The latter coolly admitted that he had given instructions to "kill and burn" and "to make Samar a howling wilderness," and had seen to it that his instructions were followed.

Miscellaneous Anti-Imperialist Writings

Twain's decision to affix his name to the petition came after a long and careful study of well substantiated reports of outrages perpetrated upon the Filipinos by American troops. Enraged both by these reports and by the indifference of Congress to the petition, he expressed his fury in scores of anti-imperialist writings. Nearly all, however, remained unpublished, probably because of Mrs. Clemens' objections.

Although they remained unpublished, Twain's anti-imperialist writings of this period are significant of his thinking on this issue. Press reports of the announcement by General Arthur MacArthur, in charge of American troops in the Philippines, that "the Philippine incident is closed — substantially," drew from Twain this evaluation of what had been accomplished by the entire "incident":

... we may now take an account of stock and find out how much we have made by the speculation — or lost. The Government went into the speculation on certain definite grounds which it believed from the viewpoint of statesmanship, to be good & sufficient. To wit: 1, for the sake of the money supposed to be in it; 2, in order to become a World Power and get a back seat in the Family of Nations.

We have scored on number 2. We have secured a back seat in the Family of Nations. We have scored it & [are] trying to enjoy the tacks that are in it. We are a World Power, no one can deny it, a brass-gilt one, a tuppence, ha'penny one, but a World Power just the same. We have bought some islands from a party that did not own them; with real smartness & a good counterfeit of disinterested friendliness, we coaxed a weak nation into a trap, & closed it upon them; we went back on our honored guest of the stars & stripes when we had no further use for him, & chased him into the mountains; we are as indisputably in possession of a widespreading archipelago as if it were our property; we have pacified some thousands of the islanders & buried them; destroyed their fields; burned their villages & turned their widows & orphans out of doors; furnished heart-breaking exile to dozens of disagreeable patriots & subjugated the remaining millions by Benevolent Assimilation which is the pious new name of the musket; we have acquired property in the three hundred concubines & other slaves of our business-partner, the Sultan of Sulu, & hoisted our protecting swag over that flag.

And so, by these providences of God — the phrase is the Government's, not mine — we are a World Power; & are glad & proud, & have a Back Seat in the Family. With tacks in it. At least we are letting on to be glad & proud; & it is the best way. Indeed, it is the only way. We must maintain our dignity for people are looking. . . .

Though he put it first, Twain failed to deal with the other reason for our Philippine policy — "the money supposed to be in it." But this does not detract from the damning indictment he presents of the policy. Even this was mild, however, compared with the lengthy piece he penned on the anniversary of the "Greeting from the Nineteenth Century to the Twentieth." Entitled, "The Stupendous Procession," it purports to be a description of the successive floats of a mammoth parade.

At the appointed hour it ["The Stupendous Procession"] moved across the world in the following order:

The Twentieth Century

A fair young creature, drunk and disorderly, borne in the arms of Satan. Banner with motto, "Get What You can, Keep What You Get."

Guard of Honor — Monarchs, Presidents, Tammany Bosses, Burglars, Land Thieves, Convicts, etc., appropriately clothed and bearing the symbols of their several trades.

Christendom

A majestic matron in flowing robes drenched with blood. On her head a golden crown of thorns; impaled on its spine the bleeding heads of patriots who died for their country — Boers, Boxers, Filipinos; in one hand a slingshot in the other a Bible, open at the text — "Do unto others," etc. Protruding from pocket, bottle labeled, "We bring you the blessings of civilization." Necklace — handcuffs and a burglar's jimmy.

Supporters — At one elbow Slaughter, at the other Hypocrisy.

Banner with motto — "Love your Neighbor's Goods as Yourself."

Ensign — The Black Flag.

Guard of Honor — Missionaries, and German, French, Russian and British soldiers laden with loot.

To the music of the "Spheres (of Influence)," each imperialist power, "Christendom's favorite children," passes by with its "purchases" and "Other Acquisitions." England heads the procession:

Supporters — Mr. Chamberlain and Mr. Cecil Rhodes. Followed by Mutilated Figure in Chains, labeled, "Transvaal Republic," and Mutilated Figure in Chains, labeled, "Orange Free State."
Ensign — The Black Flag; in its Union, a Gold Brick.

Spain comes next, "attended by the Head of the Holy Office and subordinates bearing the broken and rusty torture-tools of the Inquisition."
Then comes Russia, "a crowned & mitred Polar Bear," followed by:

Weary Column of Exiles — Women, Children, Students, Statesmen, Patriots, stumbling along in the snow:
Mutilated Figure in Chains, labeled, "Finland."
Floats piled with bloated corpses — Massacred Manchurian peasants.
Ensign — The Black Flag.
Banner — "In his Name."

The float representing France carries a guillotine with Zola under the axe, and other patriots "gagged and awaiting their turn." Following on foot are:

Mutilated Figure, labeled, "Dreyfus."
Mutilated Figure in Chains, labeled, "Madagascar";
Mutilated Figure in Chains, labeled, "Tonquin";
Guard of Honor — Detachment of French Army, bearing Chinese "heads" and loot.
Ensign — the Black Flag.
Banner, with motto — "France, the light of the World."

Germany is next:

A Helmeted Figure with Mailed Fist holding Bible aloft — followed by

Mutilated Figure in Chains, labeled, "Shantung";

Property on a Float, labeled, "A Province," three tons of Gold coin, a Monument, and a Memorial Church — price of two slain missionaries.

Guard of Honor — column of German missionaries bearing their exacted tribute — famous now, in the world, of "680 Chinese heads." As per unrepudiated statement of Rev. Mr. Ament.

Ensign — The Black Flag.

Banner, with motto — "For God and S —."

The remainder of "The Stupendous Procession," by far the major portion — is devoted to the United States and its imperialist aggressions during and after the Spanish-American War. Twain describes his own country as:

A noble Dame in Grecian costume, crying, her head bare, her wrists manacled. At her feet her cap of liberty.

Supporters — On the one hand Greed; on the other, Treason. Followed by

Mutilated Figure in Chains, labeled, "Filipino Independence," and an allegorical Figure of the administration, caressing it with one hand, and stabbing it in the back with the other.

Banner, with motto — "Help us take Manila and you shall be free — in a horn."

The American procession includes 12,000 Filipinos bribed by the United States Army to betray their own people, "and murder their fathers and brothers and neighbors." An American Adjutant General justifies the use of such traitors by declaring: "England does it in India and in China, and what Christian England does, cannot we as equals — imitate? Moreover, we did it in the Civil War — made soldiers of the negroes." The General is interrupted by "A Frivolous Stranger" who observes that the Negroes "didn't fight their own race and blood, they fought only their hated white enslavers and oppressors." He is promptly ordered out of the procession.

Bringing up the rear of "The Stupendous Procession" is a float representing the flag and thus described in the bitterest of Twain's satirical inventories:

The American Flag

Waving from a Float piled high with property — the whole marked with Boodle. To wit:

1,200 Islands — when we get them.

Filipino Independence.

Crowd of slaughtered patriots — called "rebels."

Filipino Republic — annihilated.

Crowd of deported patriots — called "rebels."

A Crowned Sultan — in business with the United States and officially-recognized Member of the Firm.

2,000 slaves — joint property of the Firm.

800 concubines — joint property of the Firm.

Motto on the Flag — "To what base uses have I come at last."

The Pirate Flag. Inscribed, "Oh, you will get used to it, Brother. I had sentimental scruples at first, myself."

Banners — scattered at intervals down the long procession, and glinting distantly in the sunlight; some of them bearing inscriptions of this sort:

"All white men are born free and equal." Declaration of Independence.

"All white men are and of right ought to be free and independent." Ibid.

14th Amendment: "White slavery shall no longer exist where the American flag floats."

"Christ died to make men holy,

He died to make white men free."

(Battle Hymn of the Republic. "He" is Abraham Lincoln.)

"Governments derive their just powers from the consent of the governed white men." Declaration of Independence.

Statue of Liberty

Enlightening the World. Torch extinguished and reversed. Followed by

The American Flag

furled, and draped with crepe.

Shade of Lincoln,

towering vast and dim toward the sky, brooding with pained and indignant aspect over the far-reaching pageant.

"The Stupendous Procession" closes with a stirring statement by Lincoln's shade: "These pigmy traitors will pass & perish & be forgotten. They & their treasons. And I will say again with the hope & conviction of that other day of darkness & peril. 'This nation, under God, shall have a new birth of freedom!'".

Albert Bigelow Paine, who published a few extracts from it in his biography of Twain, called "The Stupendous Procession" a "fearful document, too fearful, we may believe, for Mrs. Clemens ever to consent to its publication." She, it appears, was particularly upset by its treatment of the American flag. Actually, Twain himself thought it too strong, and took back the statement that it had been "polluted" when it "was sent out to the Philippines to float over a wanton war and robbing expedition." Apologizing to the flag, he concedes that "it was only the Government that sent it on such an errand that was polluted. Let us compromise on that, I am glad to have it that way. For our flag could not well stand pollution, never having been used to it, but it is different with the Administration."

What makes "The Stupendous Procession" a "fearful document" is not merely its description of evil and gruesome figures, representing imperialism and its deeds. Such representations were common in anti-imperialist writings of the period. But Twain used this device much more effectively. For one thing, by linking all imperialist powers together he was able to show their common brutalities and their common resort to sanctimonious hypocrisies. Note, for example, how each imperialist power invoked religion in its behalf, and condemned those who fought oppression as "traitors."

Although the satire in "The Stupendous Procession" is cruder than in "To the Person Sitting in Darkness," and therefore could not have been as effective an exposure of imperialism had it been published, it had a new factor which was absent in the earlier essay. In "The Stupendous Procession," Twain, unlike most anti-imperialist writers, stresses the connection between oppression at home and imperialism abroad. Imperialist Russia exiles its own advocates of freedom for Russians; imperialist France frames Dreyfus and persecutes Zola and other friends of

373

freedom; imperialist America deprives its own Negro population of the democratic rights promised to all in the Declaration of Independence and the Constitution. It follows logically that the friends of freedom in one's own country must support the struggle for freedom of the colonial people, for both struggles are intertwined.

Clearly, Twain recognized the connection between imperialism and white chauvinism. His understanding of this connection was probably influenced by his correspondence with Kelly Miller and other Negro leaders of the period. Miller, Professor of Mathematics at Howard University and a Negro leader in Washington, D. C., corresponded with Twain, praised him for "pointing out, in your fine inimitable way, the evils of the policy of imperialism," and sent him leaflets and pamphlets which bore out "its [imperialism's] special bearing upon a class of American citizens upon whom these evils will ultimately fall most heavily."

Another example of Twain's understanding of the connection between imperialism and the problems of the Negro people is to be found in his unpublished review of Edwin Wildman's biography of Aguinaldo, the Filipino insurgent leader. He compares Aguinaldo's early life as a boy in the Philippines under Spanish rule with that of a Negro boy in an Alabama town in the United States who "has already climbed to a high civic post in his (say) Alabama town — *and by consent of the whites.*" That Aguinaldo could obtain an education and later a government post proved the Spaniards better than our white Southerners. With the United States Army dominated by Southerners, the likelihood was that Filipino children would have as few opportunities to advance in life under American domination as did the Negro children in the South. Discussing Wildman's description of the Katipunan, a patriotic organization which fought for Filipino independence and which Aguinaldo joined, as composed of men who tortured and murdered their opponents, Twain emphasizes that "they were not worse than our Christian Ku-

Klux gangs of former times, nor than are our church-going, negro-burners of to-day. And these native-American torturers and assassins have not the Katipunan's excuse: for they had no teachers, they invented their brutalities themselves." The Katipunans were taught torture and murder by the Spanish suppressors of the Filipino independence movement.

All too few anti-imperialist writers saw as clearly as did Mark Twain the relationship between the suppression of freedom for the Filipino and for the Negro in the United States.

"In Defense of General Funston"

Frederick Funston, Brigadier-General of Volunteers in the American Army, returned from the Philippines late in 1901 to be hailed as a hero in the imperialist press. A year before, the General had captured Aguinaldo. This achievement had been accomplished after intercepting and deciphering a message from Aguinaldo. The message disclosed Aguinaldo's hiding place and that he was expecting reinforcements. Disguising his men as Americans held prisoners by a band of Filipino reinforcements, General Funston seized the leader of the Filipino independence movement.

On March 8, 1902, General Funston spoke at the Lotos Club in New York City, reminiscing about his experiences in the Philippines, and proudly and in detail describing Aguinaldo's capture. He disclosed all the ruses he had used. These included bribing a courier to betray his trust, disguising his men in enemy uniforms, and — the crowning *coup* — wheedling food for the famished Americans from Aguinaldo. The food was supplied under the impression that the Americans were prisoners of the Filipinos who pretended to be the reinforcements Aguinaldo expected, but had been bribed by the Americans to betray him. It was this food, Funston coolly admitted, that made it possible for the Americans to carry out their treacherous mission. While greeting Aguinaldo in friendly fashion, their concealed riflemen mowed down his bodyguards.

Funston called Aguinaldo a "cold-blooded murderer," "an assassin," and "a dictator," vilified those in the United States who compared him and other insurgent Filipino leaders "with the men who won the independence of the United States more than a hundred years ago." He called "perfectly ridiculous" the idea that the Filipinos, whom he described as "a drunken, uncontrollable mob" with the mentality of four-year-old children, were fit for self-government. Indeed, he charged that the Filipinos did not really desire independence, but were being incited against the "benevolent policies" of the U.S. government "by a lot of misinformed and misguided people here in the United States." In particular, he singled out for condemnation the writers in the Anti-Imperialist League who had protested "outrages" in the Philippines. "I say," Funston declared vehemently, to the delight of his wealthy audience, "that I would rather see any of these men hanged — hanged for treason, hanged for giving aid and comfort to the enemy — than see the humblest soldier in the United States Army lying dead on the field of battle." In passing, Funston admitted that some abuses might have crept into the conduct of American soldiers in the Philippines, but he called them inconsequential. "I believe it is safe to say that there has never been a war in the world where the people have shown such patience as have the United States troops in the Philippine Islands."

"Bravo! Gen. Funston" ran the headline with which the New York *Sun* captioned its full report of the Lotos Club speech. As Mark Twain read it his blood boiled. Although he was withholding from publication other comments on American policy in the Philippines, he decided to make an exception with General Funston.

In his unpublished review of the biography of Aguinaldo by Edwin Wildman, Twain had already characterized the Filipino leader as one motivated by the same love for freedom that had influenced "Washington, Tell, Joan of Arc, the Boers, and certain other persons whose ideals are held in reverence by the best men and women of all nations." When one considered that Aguinaldo had started life "with only such chances as a Southern negro lad has to-day, and climbed up, step by step, to the Rulership of a nation and the unshared authority of its armed-forces," one had to place this man among the truly great figures in history, one whose name would be remembered long after the generals who led the imperialist war of conquest against him and his people would be forgotten.

Aguinaldo and the men he led, Twain insisted, "were patriots; they were fighting for their country's independence, the highest and noblest of all causes, and that is an inspiration which is able to lift up even little people and make them great." Yet these were the people whom General Funston described as "assassins," and "a drunken, uncontrollable mob" incapable of self-government. In the margin of his copy of the New York *Sun's* text of Funston's speech, Twain wrote: "Funston says it is ridiculous to regard the F[ilipino]'s as sufficiently civilized for self-government. If he had any sagacity he would keep these innocent sarcasms to himself, not bray them out in public. In these days Civ[ilization] has enough to bear, without the added burden of F[unston]'s approval & championship. . . ."

In the margin next to Funston's condemnation of anti-imperialist writers as traitors who should be hung for treason, Twain wrote:

If I were in the Phil[ippines] I could be imprisoned for a year for publicly expressing the opinion that we ought to withdraw & give those people their independence – an opinion which I desire to express now. What is treason in one part of our States & stealings is doubtless law everywhere under the flag. If so, I am now committing treason — by the provisions of that imperial act & if I were out there I would hire a hall & do it again. On these terms I would rather be a traitor than an archangel. On these terms I am quite willing to be called a traitor — quite willing to wear that honorable badge — & not willing to be affronted with the title of

Patriot & classified with the Funstons when so help me God I have not done anything to deserve it.

"Let us keep silent," General Funston had advised, warning the critics of the Philippine policy that if they continued to speak out, they would risk being treated as traitors as well as being called traitors. Mark Twain refused to keep silent. Instead he published one of his bitterest and most effective attacks on the policy, ironically titling it "In Defense of General Funston." It appeared in the *North American Review* of May, 1902.

Although Twain blasted Funston, he used him as a springboard for a general condemnation of imperialism in the Philippines. He dwelt on the deceptions Funston practiced in capturing Aguinaldo, and then excoriated the general's behavior and through it, the policy he was upholding. General Funston, Twain argued with ingenious irony, could not be blamed, because his behavior was customary in imperialist war. Funston's disposition was "born with him"; it was the "It," over which the General could have no control:

It had a native predilection for unsavory conduct, but it would be in the last degree unfair to hold Funston to blame for the outcome of his infirmity, as unfair as it would be to blame him because his conscience leaked out through one of his pores when he was little — a thing which he could not help, and he couldn't have raised it, anyway; It was able to say to an enemy, "Have pity on me, I am starving; I am too weak to move, give me food; I am your friend, I am your fellow-patriot, your fellow-Filipino, and am fighting for our dear country's liberties, like you — have pity, give me food, save my life, there is no other help!" and It was able to refresh and restore Its marionette with the food, and then shoot down the giver of it while his hand was stretched out in welcome.

Imperialism condoned all acts of treachery in its behalf, hence Funston could consider it perfectly normal to accept food and guidance from Aguinaldo, when he and his party, eight miles from the rebel leader's camp, were unable to move from exhaustion, and then turn around and shoot down the Filipinos who saved them and capture Aguinaldo himself. This, Twain labels, "hospitality repaid in a brand-new, up-to-date, Modern Civilization fashion." Mixed with Twain's irony is his deep concern lest Funston's brand of patriotism might supersede Washington's and Lincoln's with the youth of America. Funston, "a weak-headed and weak-principled" officer, he warns, was already being hailed as a great American hero, and "there are now public-school teachers and superintendents who are holding up Funston as a model hero and Patriot in the schools."

Compared to the "Funstian Patriots," Twain admits that he and other anti-imperialists were "Traitors." But to be called "Traitors" by the "Funstian Patriots" did not disturb him. "They are always doing us little compliments like that; they are just born flatterers, these boys." For what did Funstonism mean? It meant "the torturing of Filipinos by the awful 'water-cure'"; it meant General Smith's notorious order to "kill and burn" and "make Samar a howling wilderness." If this was patriotism, then Twain was proud to be called a "traitor" by such "patriots."

Twain closes the "Defense" with a plea that Aguinaldo should be freed: "He is entitled to his freedom. If he were a king of a Great Power, or an ex-president of our republic, instead of an ex-president of a destroyed and abolished little republic, Civilization (with a large C) would criticise and complain until he got it."

"The War Prayer"

Following "In Defense of General Funston," Twain published nothing on imperialism for almost three years, although he continued to write much on the subject, which he withheld from publication. Among these writings was his bitter condemnation of war and the war makers in *The Mysterious Stranger*. Never has the process by which a nation may be seduced into supporting an unjust war been more brilliantly described than in the following passage:

The loud little handful — as usual — will shout for the war. The pulpit will — warily and cautiously — object — at first; the great, big dull bulk of the nation will rub its sleepy eyes and try to make out why there should be a war, and will say, earnestly and indignantly, "It is unjust and dishonorable, and there is no necessity for it."

Then the handful will shout louder. A few fair men on the other side will argue and reason against the war with speech and pen, and at first will have a hearing and be applauded; but it will not last long; those others will outshout them, and presently the anti-war audience will thin out and lose popularity.

Before long you will see this curious thing: the speakers stoned from the platform, and free speech strangled by hordes of furious men who in their secret hearts are still at one with those stoned speakers — as earlier — but do not dare to say so. And now the whole nation — pulpit and all — will take up the war-cry, and shout itself hoarse, and mob any honest man who ventures to open his mouth; and presently such mouths will cease to open.

Next the statesmen will invent cheap lies, putting the blame upon the nation that is attacked, and every man will be glad of those conscience-soothing falsities, and will diligently study them, and refuse to examine any refutations of them; and thus he will by and by convince himself that the war is just, and will thank God for the better sleep he enjoys after this process of grotesque self-deception.

It is indeed ironical that this passage should have been published first in *Harper's Monthly* of November, 1916. Soon Americans who opposed their country's entrance into the First World War and spoke out against it were to be stoned and imprisoned.

It was in the same spirit that in 1904-05 Twain wrote "The War Prayer," a terrible indictment of war. It opens with a description of the wartime atmosphere. In every breast "burned the holy fire of patriotism... in the churches the pastors preached devotion to flag and country, and invoked the God of Battles, beseeching His aid in our good cause in outpourings of fervid eloquence which moved every listener." There was no room for doubt, no room for disapproval of the proceedings: "and the half dozen rash spirits that ventured to disapprove of the war and cast a doubt upon its righteousness straightway got such a stern and angry warning that for their personal safety's sake they quickly shrank out of sight and offended no more in that way."

On a Sunday morning, the volunteers assemble in church. Twain describes their dreams of glory gained in battle, the pride of their relatives and friends, and the envy of those "who had no sons and brothers to send forth to the field of honor, there to win for the flag, or failing, die the noblest of deaths." The service begins, and the preacher and congregation pray that the "ever-merciful and benignant Father of us all would watch over our noble young soldiers, and aid, comfort, and encourage them in their patriotic work; bless them, shield them in the day of battle and the hour of peril, bear them in His mighty hand, make them strong and confident, invincible in the bloody onset, help them to crush the foe, grant to them and to their flag and country imperishable honor and glory."

A tall, aged, white-robed stranger ascends to the preacher's side, and stands there waiting. The preacher, unaware of his presence, concludes the prayer with the fervent appeal, "Bless our arms, grant us the victory, O Lord, our God, Father and Protector of our land and flag." The stranger motions the preacher aside, and announces that he is a messenger from God. He informs the startled congregation that God has heard their prayer and will grant it if, after his messenger has explained its full import, they still desire it. He has been commissioned by God to put into words the unspoken part of the prayer, "the other part of it — that part which the pastor — and also you in your hearts — fervently prayed silently." The messenger bids the congregation hear the unspoken implications of the prayer for victory, and "the many unmentioned results which follow victory — *must* follow it, cannot help but follow it."

The unuttered prayer goes:

"O Lord, our Father, our young patriots, idols of our hearts, go forth to battle — be Thou near them! With them — in spirit — we also go forth from the sweet peace of our beloved firesides to smite the foe. O Lord, our God, help us to tear their soldiers to bloody shreds with our shells; help us to cover their smiling fields with the pale forms of their patriot dead; help us to drown the thunder of the guns with the shrieks of their wounded, writhing in pain; help us to lay waste their humble homes with a hurricane of fire; help us to wring the hearts of their unoffending widows with unavailing grief; help us to turn them out roofless with their little children to wander unfriended the wastes of the desolated land in rags and hunger and thirst, sports of the sun-flames of summer and the icy winds of winter, broken in spirit, worn with travail, imploring Thee for the refuge of the grave and denied it — for our sakes who adore Thee, Lord, blast their hopes, blight their lives, protract their bitter pilgrimage, make heavy their steps, water their way with their tears, stain the white snow with the blood of their wounded feet! We ask it, in the spirit of love, of Him Who is the Source of Love, and Who is the ever-faithful refuge and friend of all that are sore beset and seek His aid with humble and contrite hearts. Amen."

(After a pause.) "Ye have prayed it; if ye still desire it, speak! The messenger of the Most High waits."

The piece ends with the ironical sentence: "It was believed afterwards, that the man was a lunatic, because there was no sense in what he said."

"I have told the truth in that," Twain said in adding "The War Prayer" to the pile of manuscripts that were not to be submitted for publication, "and only dead men can tell the truth in this world. It can be published after I am dead."

KING LEOPOLD'S SOLILOQUY

Mark Twain did not specify that he must be dead before his indictment of Belgium's imperialist exploitation of the Congo could be published. In 1905 it appeared under the title, *King Leopold's Soliloquy: A Defense of His Congo Rule.*

In 1876, Leopold II of Belgium organized and assumed the presidency of the International Association for the Exploration and Civilization of Central Africa. When the African explorer, Henry M. Stanley, failed to interest British capital or officialdom in the lower Congo, he turned to Leopold who sent him back to Africa to stake claims for the Association. In 1884, the United States recognized the Association as an "independent state." The Berlin Conference of 1885, summoned to settle European conflicts in Africa, admitted Leopold's claims but called for free trade, the "moral well-being" of the native population, and suppression of the slave trade. King Leopold's "exclusive mission," it declared, was "to introduce civilization and trade into the center of Africa." The Congo Free State was established as a sovereign state under the personal suzerainty of Leopold. The Belgian parliament sanctioned Leopold's "exclusively" personal ownership of the Congo.

Thus Leopold secured possession of one million miles of territory occupied by some twenty million Africans. The most brutal imperialist exploitation developed in the so-called Congo Free State. Leopold declared "all vacant lands" in this vast country state property (or his own personal property), likewise all the produce of these lands. The dispossessed people were driven into slave labor, to collect such "state property" as rubber and ivory. By 1904 Leopold's "exclusive mission" had cost between five and eight million lives. Others had survived only as cripples, for amputation of hands and feet as punishment for trifling offenses was the common practice of Leopold's agents.

Protests were voiced during the 1890's and early 1900's by explorers, missionaries and reformers. But the stories they told were so horrible that they were disbelieved. Then in February, 1904, the British Foreign Office released the report of Roger Casement, its consul at Boma, Belgian

383

Congo. This fearful document revealed the fiendish exploitation of the African people. Casement described the forced labor — a virtual state of slavery — by which European fortunes were made. The Africans had to gather their quotas of rubber from the wild vines or have their hands chopped off, their genitals severed, their villages burned down, their children mutilated and murdered. Bosses of labor gangs brought their superiors baskets full of hands; smoked, to preserve them in the humid climate. African women were tortured, murdered, raped and driven into brothels for King Leopold's soldiers or agents. The iniquitous tax system forced the African workers to return to Leopold the miserable pay they earned for their incredibly hard labor. Whole villages were wiped out, the land expropriated, and the communal society destroyed. Leopold's Congo rule, which had made him one of the richest men in the world, was revealed as imperialism at its worst.

In England these disclosures led to the formation of the vigorous Congo Reform organization, headed by E. D. Morel. The movement spread to the United States. Its most notable publication was Twain's *King Leopold's Soliloquy*.

This brilliant denunciation of the Leopoldian system was not the result of a sudden inspiration. Twain had, for years, expressed his hatred for "the pirate king of Belgium" in private correspondence. In 1903 he wrote a friend that all the horrors described in massacres from the beginning of recorded history "are the merest trifles compared with King Leopold's bloody doings in the Congo State to-day. I have been arranging for Leopold with St. Peter." He would see to it that St. Peter would register as Leopold's trademark, "the photograph of a little black boy with a hand & foot cut off," and force the king "to wear it in hell." Thanking the author of *The Crime of the Congo* for a copy of his booklet, Twain noted: "It seems curious that for about thirty years Leopold & the Belgians have been daily & nightly committing upon the helpless Congo natives all the hundred kinds of atrocious crimes known to the heathen savage & the pious inquisitor without rousing Christendom to a fury of generous indignation; *all* Christendom: statesmen, journalists, philanthropists, women, children, even religious people, even the Church, even the pulpit."

Twain felt that Americans bore a large share of the responsibility for the establishment and continuance of the Leopoldian system, the United States having been the first power to ratify the arrangement under which Leopold obtained "exclusive" ownership of the Congo. In an unpublished piece, written on Thanksgiving Day, 1904 and entitled "A Thanksgiving Sentiment," Twain wrote:

We have much to be thankful for. Our free Republic being the official godfather of the Congo Graveyard; first of the Powers to recognize its pirate flag & become responsible through silence for the prodigious depredations & multitudinous murders committed under it upon the helpless natives by King Leopold of Belgium in the past twenty years: now therefore let us be humbly thankful that this last twelvemonth has seen the King's usual annual myriad of murders reduced by nearly one & one half per cent; let us be humbly grateful that the good King, our pet & protege, due in hell these sixty-five years, is still spared to us to continue his work & ours among the friendless & the forsaken; & finally let us live in the blessed hope that when in the Last Great Day he is confronted with his unoffending millions upon millions of robbed, mutilated & massacred men, women & children, & required to explain, he will be as politely silent about us as we have been about him.

In the fall of 1904, Twain was asked by E. D. Morel, head of the Congo Reform Association, to use his pen "for the cause of the Congo natives." Twain set to work immediately. Probably because he was satisfied with "The Czar's Soliloquy," which he had just finished, he chose the same form for the article on Leopold. He completed it early in 1905.

King Leopold's Soliloquy opens with a picture of Leopold deeply disturbed: "Throws down pamphlets which he has been reading. Excitedly combs his flowing spread of whiskers with his fingers; pounds the table with his fists, lets off brisk volleys of unsanctified language at brief intervals, repentantly drooping his head, between volleys, and kissing the Louis XI crucifix hanging from his neck, accompanying the kisses with mumbled apologies; presently rises, flushed and perspiring, and walks the floor, gesticulating."

Leopold is distressed because at last the truth of his exploitation of the Congo is being made public. "In these twenty years," he rages, "I have spent millions to keep the press of the two hemispheres quiet, and still these leaks keep on occurring. I have spent other millions on religion and art, and what do I get for it? Nothing. Not a compliment. These generosities are studiedly ignored, in print. In print I get nothing but slanders — and slanders again — and still slanders, and slanders on top of slanders!... Miscreants they are telling *everything*!"

He then describes in detail, with excerpts from various reports, the terrible conditions in the Congo, after which he observes bitterly:

Yes, they go on telling everything, these chatterers! They tell how I levy incredibly burdensome taxes upon the natives — taxes which are a pure theft; taxes which they must satisfy by gathering rubber under hard and constantly harder conditions, and by raising and furnishing food supplies gratis — and it all comes out that when they fall short of their tasks through hunger, sickness, despair, and ceaseless and exhausting labor without rest, and forsake their homes and flee to the woods to escape punishment, my black soldiers, drawn from unfriendly tribes, and instigated and directed by my Belgians, hunt them down and butcher them and burn their villages — reserving some of the girls. They tell it all: how I am wiping a nation of friendless creatures out of existence by every form of murder for my private pocket's sake.

All this and more is true, Leopold agrees, but what annoys him is that the reporters fail to tell what is really important: "But they never say, although they know it, that

I have labored in the cause of religion at the same time and all the time, and have sent missionaries there (of a 'convenient stripe' as they phrase it), to teach them the errors of their ways and bring them to Him who is all mercy and love, and who is the sleepless guardian and friend of all who suffer. They tell only what is against me, they will not tell what is in my favor."

Leopold cites as a glaring example of such bias the report that he provides nothing for the Congo and its people in return for robbing the land of its great wealth "*but hunger, terror, grief, shame, captivity, mutilation and massacre.*"

That is their style! I furnish "nothing"! I send the gospel to the survivors, these censure-mongers know it, but they would rather have their tongues cut out than mention it. I have several times required my [slave] raiders to give the dying an opportunity to kiss the sacred emblem; and if they obeyed me I have without doubt been the humble means of saving many souls. None of my traducers have had the fairness to mention this; but let it pass; there is One who has not overlooked it, and that is my solace, that is my consolation.

As Leopold reads the gruesome reports of the savagery inflicted upon the Congo people, he remains undisturbed until he comes upon the statement: "The crucifying of sixty women!" Now he is upset.

How stupid, how tactless! Christendom's goose flesh will rise with horror at the news. "Profanation of the sacred emblem." That is what Christendom will shout. Yes, Christendom will buzz. It can hear me charged with half a million murders a year for twenty years and keep its composure, but to profane the Symbol is quite another matter. It will regard this as serious. It will wake up and want to look into my record. Buzz? Indeed it will; I seem to hear the distant hum already.... It was wrong to crucify the women, clearly wrong, manifestly wrong. I can see it now, myself, and am sorry it happened, sincerely sorry. I believe it would have answered just as well to skin them... (With a sigh). But none of us thought of that; one cannot think of everything; and after all it is but human to err.

Leopold consoles himself with the knowledge that, regardless of the reports, his tenure is secure. He congratulates himself for having the United States behind him, it having been the first nation to grant him the wardenship of the Congo Free State. He observes gleefully that the "self-appointed Champion and Promoter of the Liberties of the World, is the only democracy in history that has lent its power and influence to the establishing of an *absolute monarchy*." Since the other nations also sanction the grant, Leopold feels secure, because "neither nations nor governments can afford to confess a blunder."

Twain submitted the *Soliloquy* to the magazines, but none dared to touch it. He then gave it to the American Congo Reform Association, which had it published as a pamphlet under the imprint of the P. R. Warren Company of Boston. At Twain's advice, it included drawings and photographs of mutilated Negroes — men, women, and children. Under the title on the cover was a drawing of a cross and knife with the slogan: "By this Sign We Prosper." The pamphlet was also issued in England, with a preface by E. D. Morel. An edition of the pamphlet, dated January 1, 1906, carried this note: "The publishers desire to state that Mr. Clemens declines to accept any pecuniary return from this booklet, as it is his wish that all proceeds of sales above the cost of publication shall be used in furthering effort for the relief of the people of the Congo State." It sold for twenty-five cents per copy.

From England Twain received the heart-felt thanks of the Congo Reformers. "I thank you most deeply for having written it," wrote E. D. Morel, "and for placing it so generously at the disposal of the American Congo Reform Association." The British press was almost unanimous in its praise. *The Athenaeum* hailed it as "a trenchant satire," and praised Twain as "a serious writer of remarkable courage as well as a humorist." "We are glad to see Mark

Twain taking part in a campaign against the owner of the Congo Free State," declared *Punch*. *The Bookman* called the *Soliloquy* a "remarkable book" and concluded its review: "There has not in our time been a fiercer satire or a finer instance of the value of humour as an instrument of reform. The book is a terrible indictment. . . ."

In the United States, readers of the *Soliloquy* also expressed their gratitude to the author. A typical letter was from W. W. Morrison of Lexington, Kentucky, which read: "I am writing ,not only in my own name, but I venture to assert also in the names of the millions in the Congo Free State, to thank you for your little book, 'King Leopold's Soliloquy'! I believe it has done and will do more good than anything that has yet been written on this gruesome theme. People are reading it and they are talking."

They were doing more than "talking." In December, 1905, Henry I. Kowalsky, an agent employed by the Belgian government, frantically notified King Leopold that as a result of Twain's pamphlet, a strong anti-Leopold movement was developing in the United States: "Mark Twain, or Samuel Clemens (which is his proper name), must certainly have a retainer from the English people. The fight here [in the United States] is organized as it has never been before. Monster petitions have been circulated and signed; the industry of the opposition is very manifest, and I can asure you that you cannot afford to turn a deaf ear to what I am saying."

In America, unlike England, the *Soliloquy* was not reviewed in the press, though scattered comments appeared in articles discussing the Congo Free State. A writer in the *American Journal of Theology* commented in an article, entitled "Fresh Light on the Dark Continent": "Several succinct statements of the case against the Congo State are available in this country. But the brochure which is likely to do the most popular execution is *King Leopold's Soliloquy*. The great humorist never wielded his pen more pointedly in behalf of honesty and humanity."

"I think there is no question that an adverse influence is

holding back editorial comment on the pamphlet," wrote Thomas B. Barbour, Secretary of the Congo Reform Association, to Twain. The leaders of the Association were convinced that the absence of editorial comment pointed to deliberate conspiracy to suppress criticism of the Leopoldian system; and that the forces which had exerted pressure on the magazines not to publish the *Soliloquy,* were applying similar pressure on distributors not to push sales of the pamphlet.

It soon became clear who was applying the pressure. Negotiations had been concluded between Leopold and J. P. Morgan, John D. Rockefeller, Thomas Fortune Ryan and Daniel Guggenheim, representing American finance capital, for an arrangement under which the American capitalists would cut into the profit derived from exploitation of the Congo. The group of capitalists announced publicly that they were interested only in the "business character" of the deal, and had "absolutely nothing to do with King Leopold's management of Congo affairs in the past, or what he may do in an administrative way in the future." But it was revealed in the New York *American* that, together with Leopold's agents in the United States, they spent money lavishly to restrict the circulation of the Congo Reform Association's publications, and hired professors and clergymen — including Cardinal Gibbons, who later recanted — to justify Leopold's rule over the Congo. Wide circulation was given to a pamphlet entitled, *An Answer to Mark Twain,* which accused the author of *King Leopold's Soliloquy* of "an infamous libel against the Congo State" and of having lent his name to a "filthy work."

When Twain had agreed to write his *Soliloquy* he had made it clear that he would "stop there," and would under no circumstances become involved in the Congo Reform movement, organizationally or otherwise. But for several months following publication of the booklet, he did precisely the opposite. He became its first Vice President, and, in this capacity, used his influence with government officials in Washington and London in behalf of the proposal that the United States and England join in demanding a Commission of Inquiry to investigate atrocities in the Congo Free State. But, when the Congo Reform Association planned a nation-wide lecture tour for Twain to rouse public opinion behind the proposal, he called the whole thing off. "I have retired from the Congo," he wrote to Thomas Barbour on January 8, 1906:

> I shall not make a second step in the Congo matter, because that would compel a third, in spite of one — & a fourth & a fifth, & so on. I mean a *deliberate* second step; what I may do upon sudden *impulse* is another matter — *they* are out of my control.
>
> If I had Morel's splendid equipment of energy, brains, diligence, concentration, persistence — but I haven't; he is a "mobile," I am a "wheelbarrow."

To an appeal in June, 1906 for "further aid in the work of this [Congo Reform] Association," Twain replied that he was "heart and soul" in any movement to rescue the Congo from Leopold, and he would contribute financially. But he could not speak or write any more. As his final contribution to the subject, he proposed an epitaph for Leopold: "Here under this gilded tomb lies the rotting body of one the smell of whose name will still offend the nostrils of men ages and ages after the Caesars and Washingtons & Napoleons shall have ceased to be praised or blamed & been forgotten — Leopold of Belgium."

Twain's booklet long continued to rally public opinion behind the movement for Congo Reform. "In 1908," writes Basil Davidson in *The Reporter* of January 27, 1955, "under great international pressure — Mark Twain was foremost in bringing that to bear — and the pressure of its own conscience, the Belgian Parliament brought the Leopoldian system to an end." The Congo Free State was annexed to Belgium; the atrocities ceased, and other reforms were put into force. But imperialism and its evils remained. Forced labor continued in the Congo for many years. Today, as in the days of Leopold, the wealth of the Congo flows into foreign coffers — Belgian corporations and American and British bankers who are big investors in the Belgian Congo firms.

In a large advertisement in the New York *Herald Tribune* of March 20, 1957, the Belgian government boasted of its role in the history of the Congo. "... *All the Congolese have, first and foremost,*" the advertisement emphasized, "a feeling of gratitude toward the nation which, sparing neither pain nor blood, brought them the blessings of civilization." All who wish to know what these "blessings of civilization" consisted of, would do well to read Mark Twain's great work, *King Leopold's Soliloquy*.

The Fruits of Imperialism

The published reports revealing that the American financiers, Morgan, Rockefeller, and Ryan, had negotiated with King Leopold to share in the loot from the Congo, did not come as a surprise to Mark Twain. For a number of years he had felt that the American imperialists were prepared to wipe out every aspect of the country's democratic heritage in their lust for profits. That such men should collaborate with the bestial monarch was both logical and consistent. Twain believed that the United States had reached a turning point in 1896 and 1897; thereafter imperialism had been eroding the nation's democratic heritage. By 1901 he was convinced that the imperialists had gone a long way towards their goal, and that the country itself had "gone to hell." Indeed, he predicted to Howells the ultimate triumph of a dictatorship of wealth in the United States. Howells reported the conversation in his "Editor's Easy Chair" column in *Harper's Monthly* in the course of a discussion of the desirability of a hall of fame:

A friend of this seat of ordinarily hopeful contemplation, to whom it had imparted the doubts of the hall of fame hitherto set down, held that it was altogether wrong to have them. He is not himself one of the fatly satisfied Americans who fancy the fulfillment of our mission to mankind in our present welter of wealth and corpulent expansion. Rather he finds that the true American life has been wellnigh choked in it, and that we stand gasping in a tide of glory and affluance that may soon or late close over the old America forever. He speaks darkly of a dying republic, and of a nascent monarchy or oligarchy.

Yet, even while he was predicting the doom of the Republic, Twain clung to the hope that the "golden patriotism" of "Washington, and Franklin, of Jefferson and Lincoln" would replace the "false patriotism" imported along with imperialism "from monarchial Europe." For a while, he took heart from the questioning public attitude toward the treatment of the Filipinos. Thus he wrote in the concluding portion of "To the Person Sitting in Darkness": "Conviction will follow doubt. The nation will speak . . . and in that day we shall right such unfairness as we have done. We shall let go . . . of the sceptered land-thieves of Europe, and be what we were before, a *real* World Power . . . by right of the only . . . hands guiltless of the sordid plunder of any helpless people's stolen liberties."

But, as Twain saw the "Juggernaut car" of imperialism roll over the anti-imperialist forces, hope gave way to pessimism. He knew why imperialism was victorious. In his "Defense of General Funston," he pointed out that Funstonism was the logical result of the increasing dominance of the "Robber Barons": "The swiftly-enriched wrecker and robber of railway systems lowers the commercial morals of a whole nation for three generations." Imperialism had ushered in "a sordid and commercialized age, and few can live in such an atmosphere and remain unaffected by it." Money was the "symbol" of civilization; it was behind all of the atrocities of imperialism. Take Leopold, for example: "His cold-blooded murders mount into the millions! And all *for money*, simply for money, solely for money. None of his countless atrocities in Africa has ever

393

had any but the one object — the acquirement of money which did not belong to him; unearned money, stolen money."

Money, too, had corroded American democracy to the point where it was almost impossible to redeem it. "Money is the supreme idea," Twain wrote to Twichell. "Money-lust has always existed, but not in the history of the world was it ever a craze, a madness, until your time and mine." This "lust" had "rotted" America (as well as Europe), and made it "hard, sordid, ungentle, dishonest, oppressive." It had corrupted the nation's moral values to such a degree that it had kept "America [from] rising against the infamy of the Philippine War."

Twain's pessimism deepened in 1906 with the news of a new "infamy of the Philippine War" — the massacre of the Moros, a Philippine tribe, at the order of the American governor of the Philippines, General Leonard Wood. General Wood and his subordinates had trapped the entire tribe in the crater of an extinct volcano, near Jolo. There six hundred men, women, and children were exterminated. For this achievement, Wood and his officers and men received a congratulatory message from President Theodore Roosevelt lauding their "brave feat of arms wherein you and they so well upheld the honor of the American flag."

Helen Keller recalls Twain's lecture on the incident before a distinguished company at Princeton, including University President, Woodrow Wilson. Twain "poured out a volume of invective and ridicule" on these "military exploits," assailed President Roosevelt, and paid tribute to the Moro people, massacred "because we have been trying for eight years to take their liberties away from them." He also blamed the American people for having done nothing to prevent it. It seemed to him that a people that tolerated such atrocities by its government was destined to lose its own liberty.

In 1906 or 1907, Twain wrote two chapters of a projected work, called variously "Glances at History" and

"Outlines of History." This purported to be versions of the fall of the Great Republic. They were not published, along with other sketches written on the same idea.

The Great Republic is shown on the eve of launching a war of conquest against a small country seeking independence. A wise man warns the people not to support the war. The Republic, he reminds them, is a world-wide symbol of freedom, particularly to people who live in monarchies. While that symbol endures, "the Republic is safe, her greatness is secure, and against them the powers of the earth cannot prevail." But if war is launched, the picture will change. "I pray you to pause and consider," he pleads. "Against our traditions we are entering upon an unjust and trivial war, a war against a helpless people and for a base object — robbery."

The wise man's words are ignored. Those who agree with him and speak out against the war, are silenced by the politicians' cry, "Our Country, right or wrong." The wise man answers:

"In a Republic, who is 'the Country?' Is it the Government which is for the moment in the saddle? Why, the Government is merely a servant — merely a temporary servant; it cannot be its prerogative to determine what is right and what is wrong, and decide who is a patriot and who isn't. Its function is to obey orders, not originate them. Who, then, is 'the Country?' Is it the newspapers? Is it the pulpit? Is it the school superintendent? Why, these are mere parts of the country, not the whole of it; they have not command, they have only their little share in the command. They are but one in the thousands; it is in the thousand that command is lodged; they must determine what is right and what is wrong; they must decide who is a patriot and who isn't.

"Who are the thousand — that is to say, who are 'the Country?' In a monarchy, the King and his family are the country; in a republic it is the common voice of the people. Each of you, for himself, by himself and on his own responsibility, must speak. And it is a solemn and mighty responsibility, and not lightly to be flung aside at the bullying of pulpit, press, government, or the empty catch-phrases of politicians. Each man must for himself alone decide what is right and what is wrong, which course is patriotic and which isn't. You cannot shirk this and be a man. To decide against your convictions is to be an unqualified and inexcusable traitor, both to yourself and to your country, let men label you as they may....

"Only when a republic's life is in danger should a man uphold his government when it is in the wrong. There is no other time.

"This republic's life is not in peril. The nation has sold its honor for a phrase."

These words also went unheeded and the next chapter shows the Republic as having become rotten to the core. "Lust of conquest had... done its work... trampling upon the helpless abroad had taught her, by a natural process, to endure with apathy the like at home; multitudes who had applauded the crushing of other peoples' liberties, lived to suffer for their mistake in their own persons. The government was irrevocably in the hands of the prodigiously rich and their hangers-on, the suffrage had become a mere machine, which they used as they chose. There was no principle but commercialism, no patriotism but of the pocket."

The plutocrats, envying the aristocracies of Europe, were vying with each other to gain titles of nobility. The drift toward monarchy was gaining momentum. At this moment, a mysterious "Prodigy" arose in the far South, a shoemaker who led his armies northward. "Army after army, sovereignty after sovereignty went down under the mighty tread of the shoemaker, and still he held his conquering way — North, always North."

The "sleeping Republic" awoke to its danger. "It drove the money-changers from the temple, and put the government into clean hands." But the change had come too late. The money-changers had long before secured their power by buying up the allegiance of half the country and the armed forces with soldier-pensions, "and turned a measure which had originally been a righteous one into a machine for the manufacture of bond-slaves." The common people armed themselves to defend the reforms introduced by the shoemakers and destroy the power of the money-changers.

"A civilian army, officered by civilians, rose brimming with the patriotism of an old forgotten day and rushed multitudinously to the front, armed with sporting guns and pitchforks." But again the people were too late. For the money-changers and the shoemaker had made a deal to replace the Republic with a monarchy. "He conferred titles of nobility upon the money-changers, and mounted the republic's throne without firing a shot."

Twain concludes: "It was thus that Popoatahualtapetl [the name of the new monarch] became our master; whose mastership descended in a little while to the Second of that name, who still holds it by his Viceroy this day."

Thus did Mark Twain, depressed over the victory of the imperialists, predict the end of the American Republic — unless the masses swept aside the money-changers and restored the foundations of justice upon which the Republic had rested before the ambitions of imperialism had tempted them to injustice toward weaker peoples.

Twain expected little from the men of his generation, "corrupted by money-lust," but he still had hope that the youth of America would redeem its democratic heritage — provided, of course, they were educated in the true meaning of patriotism and loyalty. He called upon all mothers to teach their children day in and day out the following lesson: "Remember this, take it to heart, live by it, die for it if necessary; that our patriotism is medieval, outworn, obsolete; that the modern patriotism, the true patriotism, the only rational patriotism, is *loyalty to the Nation* ALL the time, loyalty to the Government when it deserves it."

It had all been summed up by the Connecticut Yankee:

My kind of loyalty was loyalty to one's country, not to its institutions or its office-holders. The country is the real thing . . . to watch over. . . . Institutions are extraneous, they are its mere clothing, and clothing can wear out, become ragged. . . . To be loyal to rags . . . that is a loyalty to unreason, it is pure animal; it belongs to monarchy, was invented by monarchy. . . . The citizen who thinks he sees that the commonwealth's political clothes are worn out, and yet holds his peace and does not agitate for a new suit, is disloyal; he is a traitor. That he may be the only one who thinks he sees this decay, does not excuse him; it is his duty to agitate anyway.

Chapter Eight
CONCLUSION

It has always been dangerous to be a comic writer. Throughout history the respectable critics, the genteel reviewers have written off the popular humorists as low, perverse, coarse, squalid or depressing, and have dismissed them as caricaturists and portrayers of "the worst" or "the less attractive side of human nature." Humor has always been treated by such critics as the "lighter side" of serious literature.

Mark Twain, like other great humorists, had to pay the high price of being a comic writer, the penalty of humor. Paine reports a conversation in which Twain said: "I shall never be accepted seriously over my signature. People always want to laugh over what I write and are disappointed if they don't find a joke in it."

This attitude has persisted down to the present day. Scholars have taken Twain to pieces and hardly a facet of his life and work has not been examined critically. Yet the fact remains that Twain is still regarded by most Americans either as a humorist or a writer of books for children.

Humor certainly needs no apology, and I do not wish to imply that the common attitude to Mark Twain means that his greatness as a writer is diminished by his being classified as a humorist. It is wise, in this connection, to repeat Howells' warning. For despite his determination to convince his contemporaries that Twain was more than a mere "funny fellow," Howells warned the twentieth century audience against renouncing the humor that endeared him to mankind. He told the younger generation to beware of reversing "the error of the elder, and taking everything in earnest, as these once took nothing in earnest from him."

This danger may exist. But more prevalent is the critical tendency to regard Mark Twain as being only a great writer when he wrote as a humorist, and to view his attempts to be anything but a humorist as generally disastrous. By fastening only on his humor, these interpreters have shorn Twain of much of what was most meaningful in his outlook both for his own day and ours.

We owe thanks to Mark Twain for his humor, but we owe much to him for the recurrent serious strains which gave staying power to his humor, and that Twain himself in later years regarded as "the gravity which is the foundation and of real value." Of course, it is hardly news now to say that Mark Twain had his serious weaknesses as a social satirist. He was often superficial, slapdash, and inaccurate. He himself conceded that he lacked stability in pursuing a cause: "I scatter from one interest to another, lingering nowhere. I am not a bee, I am a lightning bug." He was wrong-headed on many issues, and at times his prejudices made his interpretations absurd. He could be amazingly bad at predicting. He contradicted himself many times. A foolish consistency, he correctly pointed out, is the hobgoblin of little minds, but some of his inconsistencies were not the fruit of wisdom. His faith in the correctness of his thinking was sometimes overbearing. No one can deny that potboiling tarnished, and hasty conclusions blemished his astonishing gift as a satirist.

Yet when all this has been said, the main drift of his social criticism remains valid and meaningful. For Mark Twain, despite these weaknesses, took his role as a social critic with seriousness and responsibility. From the beginning, he took the side of the defenseless or oppressed, and fought corruption, privilege and abuse wherever he found them with a fierce humor.

There are many varied strains running through Twain's social criticism, expressed in his very crude early sketches, his travel books, his recreation of the Mississippi River country, his novels, letters, notebooks and pamphlets. But the dominant one is a burning hatred of all forms of intolerance, tyranny and injustice, an abhorrence of cant and pretension, a passion for human freedom, a fierce pride in human dignity, a love for people and for life ,a frank and open contempt for the mean, the cruel, the selfish, the small and petty. Despite all hesitations and contradictions, he was true to the precept that the man of letters must with all his force oppose every form of tyranny. "Satirize all human grandeurs & vanities," he wrote in his notebook. This he did with the weapons of caricature, burlesque, irony, biting sarcasm and humor, and with a style that represented a high point in the craftmanship of satire.

Mark Twain had a cold, sharp eye for facts, and a passion for exactly observed detail in his writing. Yet he consciously and deliberately exaggerated by the use of the technique of burlesque. He was convinced that the best way to fight evil, dogmatism and bigotry was by exaggerating their excesses and painting them in colors of lurid absurdity — a technique used by the great satirists throughout history. The pen "warmed up in hell" shed divine comedy, and Twain could slip a knife into the side of his readers as though it had been buttered because he kept them laughing so hard. He could also say angry things, and he aroused the nation to anger and shame by exposing greed and hypocrisy in society.

But whatever technique or form he used, Twain was never dull. Howells, then editor of *The Atlantic*, paid what he intended as a supreme compliment to one of Twain's books when he reported that he had begun the book and for the first time in many years found himself reading as a reader rather than as an editor. To be sure, Twain disdained structure, sprawled in his writing, reveled in diffusion. "Formal schemes," he said, "are about as appealing as a tight collar." But the American people did not mind. He spoke to them in their own spoken language with power and simplicity, but also with beauty, grace and rhythm. Hemingway was right in declaring that in Mark Twain all American writing begins.

But the critics have repeatedly asserted that even the best of Mark Twain's work contains many faults. Of course it does! Every worth-while piece of literature contains many faults, and every worth-while writer commits them. But what makes the writer worth-while is that he has something to say for his time that is meaningful and remains meaningful for generations to come.

It has been said that Twain took a forthright stand only "on minor and safe things, like Christian Science and Foreign Missions." But it is necessary only to read him to see that he was a critic of the major bigotries and oppressions of his time. He was sharply concerned with the corruption of the processes of representative government by the business elements who were, as he showed in *The Gilded Age*, the real but hidden rulers of the nation; with the role of the Church hierarchy and the press as agencies of the privileged classes; with the distortion by these agencies of the aims of organized labor, whose objectives he defended as being in the best interest of the entire nation; with the destructive influences of racism, especially anti-Negro, anti-Jewish, and anti-Chinese prejudice; with the cruelty of the imperialist masters of the colonial dominions — and with a host of other important issues. There is no field that he neglects — he covers the government and politics, the Church, women's rights, the economy, the press, organized labor, the rights of minorities, and, of course, war and imperialism. On most of these issues, as Owen Wister so well put it, "he saw straight, thought straight, and spoke out."

Probably the first novel most Americans ever read which treated a Negro with respect and sympathy was *Huckleberry Finn* with its warm portrayal of the indomitable, great-hearted Jim. And the second must have been *Pudd'nhead Wilson* in which Roxana, the young Negro woman slave emerges as the most believable, the most honored character of all. In both novels he showed that the Negro slave, though brutalized, was as human and as lovable and as admirable as any man. Twain never presses this point, never pleads for this recognition, but his portraits convey with extraordinary convictions a lasting impression of individual character and personality.

In these two works, Twain went back into the past, but he did so not for nostalgia or escape, but for demonstration that slavery could not destroy the Negro people's desire for freedom and to point up their right to enjoy the freedom that finally came. Likewise, in his great works, *A Connecticut Yankee in King Arthur's Court* and *The Prince and the Pauper,* he used the technique of historical fiction to demonstrate the superiority of democracy to monarchy, republicanism to aristocracy, reason to superstition, and organized labor to servile workers dependent upon their employers' whims. He was not content merely to rail against ancient evils in his books set in medieval times. Nor did he beat a dead dog in these novels. The evils he exposed had their counterparts in the 1880's, and he sought to make the connection crystal clear. The very fact that these novels became ammunition in the contemporary struggles for greater political and economic democracy is proof of his success.

Twain never gave up exposing the evils he saw in American society, but neither did he cease to assert his conviction that America was the best society the world had yet known. But this was a true patriotism, a thing not of oratorical words and flag-waving, but of substance and quality. He called on the American people to understand that the true patriot rejects a narrow chauvinism, and he pleaded with them to abandon wars of imperialist domination as wicked, evil and cruel, and thus to restore America as a moral and political influence in the molding of world democracy. It was this truly patriotic love of America which fanned to white heat the bitterness he revealed in "The United States of Lyncherdom" and in his slashing attack on imperialism in "To the Person Sitting in Darkness." If any one still doubts that Mark Twain was a social satirist of the first rank, let him read these essays, and along with them his "War Prayer," that trenchant satire on war and the warmongers. There is scarcely a sentence which is not a gem.

These masterpieces of social criticism were written at a time when we have been led to believe that the dominant strain in Mark Twain was one of cynicism and pessimism, and when he had lost all hope and sympathy for the human race. To say only this is to pen a senseless libel on a great man.

There was indeed a pessimistic strain in Mark Twain which increased as he grew older. Yet the older he grew the more effective social criticism he wrote. At no time was he more critical of the shortcomings of American democracy and, at the same time, more concerned with its preservation and extension than at the turn of the century when he attacked imperialism. He was not at all sure that the American people could be awakened to seize upon their opportunities, and he came almost to mock at them for being so supine before their betrayers. But this doubt never sapped the strength of his faith in the ideas and ideals of democracy, nor in the real spirit of the American people — a spirit which he so frequently described as resilient, independent and kindly, with a saving salt of humor and scepticism.

Twain's frequent protestations of disgust with all mankind were belied by a shining compassion, an infinite capacity for love. This dominated everything he wrote, even *The Mysterious Stranger*, which is certainly the most pessimistic of his work. In spite of the gathering clouds of personal misery that shadowed his later years, in spite of all the things he found wrong with "the damned human race," he remained the sensitive, remarkable man who, far from believing in nothing, was profoundly committed to the struggle for human freedom, and who continued to use all his great talents, his phenomenal mastery of words, to advance that struggle.

"All his life," writes Helen Keller, "he fought injustice wherever he saw it in the relations between man and man, in politics, and in war. I loved his views on public affairs; perhaps because they were so often the same as my own.

"He thought he was a cynic, but his cynicism did not make him indifferent to the right of cruelty, unkindness, meanness, or pretentiousness. He would often say, 'Helen, the world is full of staring, soulless eyes.' He would work himself into a frenzy over dull acquiesence in any evil that could be remedied."

No American writer has ever been more dedicated to the welfare of mankind, and no one more grievously wounded by its follies.

In 1916 Sherwood Anderson wrote to Waldo Frank: "What you say about Mark Twain interests me. I have long wondered why he, with Whitman, has not been placed where I have always believed he belonged — among the two or three really great American artists." He was that certainly. But he was more too. His social criticism, expressed in novels, stories, essays, and pamphlets, ranks with that of Milton, Swift, Defoe, Junius, Voltaire, Tom Paine, and Bernard Shaw, both in terms of literary quality and their influence on public opinion. His humor tipped a sword's point. It cuts through social and political pretenses, defended and enriched the democratic heritage of the American people, and helped Americans understand themselves and the world.

Mark Twain was our greatest social critic. As such he speaks to us with an immediacy that surmounts the barriers of time.

EXPLANATORY NOTES

MTP refers to Mark Twain Papers, Bancroft Library, University of California.

DV refers to manuscripts in this collection arranged by Bernard De Voto and Paine to those arranged by Albert Bigelow Paine.

The first number in square brackets refers to the page in the text, the second number to the line on that page.

[26, 28] The Mark Twain byline probably first appeared in print in the Virginia City *Territorial Enterprise* for February 3, 1863, affixed to a "Letter from Carson City." Henry Nash Smith, literary editor of the Mark Twain Estate, admits that the evidence is not conclusive; the name may have been used earlier, but it definitely was used on the date assigned. (*Mark Twain of the "Enterprise."*)

[40, 1] According to contemporary accounts, Twain formed his own publishing firm because of his battle with the American Publishing Company over royalties. He was reported to have demanded sixty percent of the proceeds from his new book — *The Adventures of Huckleberry Finn* — and when he was turned down, he formed his own concern. (*Literary Life*, II, Jan. 1885, 178.)

[52, 38] Arthur L. Scott, editor of *Mark Twain: Selected Criticism*, contends that the fact that Harte and Howells so early recognized Twain as more than "a buffoon" disproves the theory that his real genius was not generally acknowledged. Scott, however, ignores the fact that for many years the Harte-Howells' viewpoint found little support among other serious critics.

[55, 33] The first firm to sell Twain's books was the American Publishing Company of Hartford, Connecticut, one of the important subscription book publishers. Later, Twain's works were distributed by Osgood of Boston, and finally by his own firm of Charles L. Webster and Company. Not until the firm of Harper and Brothers became his publisher in 1896 did Twain abandon the subscription method of marketing his books — and even then not entirely. *Following the Equator*, published in 1897, was sold through subscription.

[70, 27] Shaw was also quoted as saying: "Of course ... Mark Twain is in much the same position as myself: he has to put matters

in such a way as to make people who would otherwise hang him believe he is joking."

[78, 15] Van Wyck Brooks, however, immediately tempered his statement by expressing the conviction that Twain's popularity has been kept alive by the "oxygen of advertising," and that by 1950, his memoirs would seem to publishers a doubtful risk. In *The Times of Melville and Whitman,* published in 1947, Brooks although still regarding Twain as a split personality, calls him a great folk artist and a "serio-comic Homer." Still later, in *Days of the Phoenix: The Nineteen-Twenties I Remember,* published in 1957, Brooks conceded that Twain "was perhaps more centrally the champion of justice, the hater of shams and the generous lovable genius than the man I had pictured, as Mark Twain's humour had a positive value that I had all but entirely failed to suggest." Yet he went on to insist that he was still convinced that Twain "had made the great refusal and that *The Ordeal of Mark Twain* was substantially just."

[90, 28] The allusions in the text to Hall are to A. Oakley Hall, Mayor of New York and a leader of the Tweed Ring; Connolly is Richard B. Connolly, the City Controller, another leader of the Tweed Ring; Fisk is James Fisk, Jr.; Gould is Jay Gould; Barnard is Judge Barnard, a tool of the Tweed Ring; Winans is a member of the Ring. The Holy Crusade of the Forty Thieves refers to the corrupt Common Council of New York City in the 1850's of which Tweed was a member.

[118, 4] On May 3, 1883, Isabella Beecher Hooker wrote to Twain thanking him for consenting to speak at a mass meeting on women's rights, and asking him to contribute to help finance the meetings. "I will ask you to help me pay expenses of other speakers from New York & Boston & the hall — all of which I have assumed in order to make the sessions free." (Isabella to Twain, May 3, 1883, MTP.) Twain not only spoke at the meeting, but contributed towards the expenses.

[140, 1] Evidently Twain anticipated this reaction, for he wrote in his notebook in 1888: "Everytime in a book I happen to speak of a king differently from the way one speaks of a God, or of a noble differently from the way one speaks of the Son of God, it is stricken out of the European reprints. Seems to give the (poor) (?) proofreader the (cold shudders) dry grips." (Unpublished Notebooks, No. 23 [I], 1888, 11 MTP.)

[151, 3] Twain set down his own opinion of Shaw in his unpub-

lished autobiography, on August 23, 1907: "Bernard Shaw has not completed his fifty-second year yet, and therefore is merely a lad. The vague and far-off rumble which he began to make five or six years ago is near-by now, and is recognizable as thunder. The editorial world lightly laughed at him during four or five of those years, but it takes him seriously now; he has become a force, and it is conceded that he must be reckoned with. Shaw is a pleasant man; simple, direct, sincere, animated; but self-possessed, sane, and evenly poised, acute, engaging, companionable, and quite destitute of affectations. I liked him. He shows no disposition to talk about himself or his work, or his high and growing prosperities in reputation and the materialities — but mainly — and affectionately and admiringly — devoted his talk to William Morris, whose close friend he had been and whose memory he deeply reveres." (2183-84, MTP.)

[156, 25] In the original manuscript, Twain was even more vehement in his call for assassination of the Czar than in the published version. In the latter, he calls upon the Russian mothers to teach their children "that our patriotism is medieval, outworn, obsolete; ... the only rational patriotism is *loyalty to the Nation ALL* the time, loyalty to the Government when it deserves it." In the original manuscript, he has the same mothers tell their children: "When you grow up, knife a Romanoff wherever you find him, loyalty to these cobras is treason to the nation; be a patriot, not a prig — set the people free." (No. 173, MTP.)

[159, 14] De Leon called Twain's message to the Boston *Globe* humor of the keenest, but said that Twain had failed to understand that the basic reason for the treaty of peace was the fear on the part of the world bourgeoisie, including the capitalists of Japan, that continuation of the war would result in the Czar being overthrown, and that this, in turn, would stimulate revolutionary upheavals the world over. "Peace was dictated at Portsmouth by Roosevelt who acted as the representative of the world's labor oppressors." (*Daily People*, Sept. 7, 1905.)

[163, 34] In his letter to Twain, March 20, 1907, Arthur Bullard, Secretary of the Friends of Russian Freedom, noted: "The object of this Society may be briefly stated as follows: To further in every way in its power the movement for a representative government in Russia as understood by the Russian people and expressed in their Duma." (MTP.) It is clear that the Society did not call for the removal of the Czar.

409

[199, 1]   For a different interpretation of Twain's attitude towards Mary Baker Eddy, *see* Clara Clemens, *Awake to a Perfect Day,* (New York, 1956, 15-19.) Basically, however, Twain contended that Mary Baker Eddy's great contribution was the addition of the one word, "Christian," to an established method of healing, which never had made much headway. "But Mrs. Eddy devised the name, & hitched the business to an old, time-tested, sound, prosperous religion — & look at the results. . . ." ("The International Lightning Trust," DV No. 374, 1909, MTP.)

In an unpublished fragment, "The Slave Trade," Twain noted that the early English slave-trading companies attached the word "Christian" to their names, and observed ironically that this was quite logical "as the newly revived [slave trading] industry was thenceforth to be a Christian monopoly, legalized and helped by Christian English parliaments, and to number two Christian English kings in the membership of a couple of its greatest slave-trading companies. . . ." Under these circumstances, it was quite fitting that the name of the ship of England's "first regular slaver, John Hawkins . . . was the 'Jesus.'" (Paine, No. 200, Box 4a, MTP.)

[211, 16]   In 1885, Twain met Jay Gould at his Western Union headquarters and lunched with his son. "Damned insignificant people," he wrote in his notebook afterwards, (No. 19, May 28, 1885, MTP.)

[220, 19]   Prior to its discovery in the Mark Twain Papers, it had been impossible to locate the full text of Twain's speech. It did not appear in the Hartford *Courant* for the dates following March 22, 1886. A search of all historical societies and leading libraries in Connecticut reveals that they do not possess a copy. Nor does "The Monday Evening Club."

[227, 11]   Twain sent his essay to Howells on March 31, 1888. "It was written in the biggest days of the Knights of Labor," he wrote in the accompanying letter. (William Dean Howells Papers, Harvard College Library.)

[234, 26]   Twain was particularly concerned by the opposition that would develop in the Typographical Union to the Paige typesetter, should it prove successful and displace the linotypist, and in an appeal "To the Printers," he wrote in his notebook in 1888: "You will make as much as you did before. . . . There will (be) more & bigger papers, & more men required." (No. 22 [I], May 5, '88, MTP.)

[237, 4]   Twain did not specify the nationality that was the one

exception, but it is clear that it was the French he had in mind. The passage quoted is followed by a slur on French judicial procedure as practiced in the Dreyfus case. Next to the Dreyfus affair, the event that seems most to have turned Twain against the French was the reception accorded the Czar of Russia in 1896. He wrote in his notebook on September 2, 1896: "The French have gone mad over the approaching visit of the Czar. Such an exhibition of boot-licking adulation has never been seen before. The wife of the Pres(ident) of the Republic is not good enough to take part in the reception — by Russian command — & those lickspittles accept it & are not insulted. Is there anything that can insult a Frenchman?" (Unpublished Notebooks, No. 31 [I], MTP.) Despite this criticism, Twain had the highest admiration and respect for France's revolutionary traditions.

[253, 19]   The incident referred to took place in 1851, and was known as the "Jerry Rescue." It resulted in the rescue of the fugitive slave, William Henry, commonly known throughout the city of Syracuse as Jerry, by a crowd of abolitionists who took him to Canada.

[254, 21]   Some Twain scholars have stated flatly that his rebel sympathies are clearly set forth in ten letters published in the New Orleans *Crescent* during the first three months of 1861 which were signed by Quintus Curtius Snodgrass. However, Twain nowhere claimed authorship of the letters, and the evidence for their authenticity is so dubious that I am convinced that they should not be included in any examination of Twain's thinking on the eve of the Civil War. A number of leading Twain scholars with whom I have discussed the matter, including Professor Henry Nash Smith and Professor Arthur L. Vogelback, feel as I do.

[262, 8]   A recent writer, however, notes that Twain "may have gone too far . . . but not much too far" in attributing the Civil War to Scott's influence. (Marshall Fiswick in *The Saturday Review*, April 16, 1956, 9.) For further evidence of how intensely Twain disliked Scott's novels, *see* his letter to Brander Matthews, May 4, 1903, in the Brander Matthews Papers, Columbia University Library.

[263, 2]   Years later, Twain called the story a "shameful tale of wrong & hardships." (Unpublished Notebooks, No. 28 (I), 1895, 8, MTP.)

[272, 12]   The degree to which Cable influenced Twain's thinking on the Negro question is difficult to determine accurately. In his

study of the relationship between Twain and Cable, Guy A. Cardwell argues that Cable's forceful stand in favor of civil rights for the Negro may well have had great influence on Twain. (*Twins of Genius*, 75-76.) The only evidence on this point that we have from Twain himself is the following sentences from a letter he wrote to William Dean Howells in November, 1882: "... Cable has been here, creating worshipers on all hand. He is a marvelous talker on a deep subject. ..." (William Dean Howells Papers, Harvard College Library.) Twain does not specify what the "deep subject" was, but it is not conjecturing too much to conclude that Cable talked about civil rights for the Negro.

[286, 24]   In Twain's original manuscript text of the essay, he includes an additional comment on clergymen. "Observe the Talmages," he writes, referring to a popular Brooklyn clergyman, "how daringly they assault the saloon, the dance, the theatre. It is popular, and not dangerous. But there are no Talmages at the lynchings. ..." (MTP.)

[299, 17]   Twain, however, was aware that his essay was "'timely' (in the sense of fresh & new *and* of immediate & large interest) because of the Dreyfus matter. ..." (Twain to Mr. Rogers, Nov. 2, '98, MTP.)

In his study, *Mark Twain in Germany* (New York, 1939), Edgar H. Hemminghaus lists the German translations of Mark Twain's works through 1936, and the essay "Concerning the Jews" is not among them. Dixon Wecter points out that Twain's books were banned by the Nazis, but this must have occurred after 1936. It was probably hastened by the anti-Nazi activity of Clara Clemens. Twain's daughter was shocked by the vicious campaign against the Jews under the Nazis. In March, 1938, she wrote to her daughter Nina Gabrilowitsch, expressing her horror over the arrest of her Jewish friends in Vienna: "Something must happen to stem the force of that hypermonster!! (Hitler). Gladly would I take a hand in a war against such a menace to the rights of individuals. ... I believe that some of us may succeed in starting a fiery ball that will roll right into the oratorical throats of the Hitlerites. I am praying for it. ..." She did what she could to start the "fiery ball" rolling. In November, 1938, aroused by the horrors against the Jews which took place on "black Thursday" in Germany, she began to publish denunciations of the Nazis, and urged the United States government to launch a campaign to expose the whole Hitler regime. (*See* Caroline Thomas Harnsberger, "The Remaining

Twain: A Life of Clara Clemens," unpublished *Ms.*, in possession of author.)

[327, 14] The "Boxers" were members of a secret society in China, "The Righteous Harmony Fists," but since they kept in training by gymnastics, they were called "Boxers." Their goal was to eject all foreigners from their country.

[333, 3] On June 1, 1896, Twain wrote in his notebook: "Boers say, if the Uitlanders don't like our laws (tyrannies) let them leave; we didn't ask them to come, & we don't want them. Did the nigger ask the *Boer* to come?" (No. 30 [1], 24-25, MTP.)

[344, 31] In the original manuscript, the words, "her halo battered," are included after "besmirched and dishonored." (MTP.)

[351, 2] It is somewhat ironical in view of the reference to "Maxims" in the essay that one of the most effusive letters in its praise should come from Sir Hiram Maxim, inventor of the Maxim gun, who wrote to Twain from England: "What you have done is of very great value to the civilization of the world. . . . Every word that you write is eagerly sought after and read by countless millions on both sides of the Atlantic." (May 8, 1901, MTP.)

[357, 33] The pamphlet omitted entirely the whole first section of the article dealing with Rev. Mr. William Ament. Published sometime in the spring of 1901, the cost of printing and distributing the pamphlet seems to have been paid for by Andrew Carnegie. "Just tell me you are willing," Carnegie wrote to Twain on February 8, 1901, "& many thousands of the holy little Missal (*sic*) will go forth. This inimitable satire is to become a classic. I count among my privileges in life that I know you the author." (MTP.)

[363, 35] Writing to Twichell, Twain referred to Ament as an "idiot Christian pirate," and to Rev. Smith as a "hypocrite and liar." (June, 1901, MTP.) Several years later, again in a letter to Twichell, he referred to the missionary movement as "that criminal industry." He added: "Joe, where is the fairness in the missionary's trade? His prey is the children; he cannot convert adults. He beguiles the little children to forsake their parents' religion & break their hearts. Would you be willing to have a Mohammedan missionary do that with your children or grandchildren? Would you be able to keep your temper if your own government *forced* you to let that Mohammedan work his will with those little chaps? You can't answer anything but NO to these questions. Very well, it closes your mouth. You haven't a shadow of right to uphold & bid Godspeed to the Christian missionary who intrudes his deprave(d)

trade upon foreign people who do not want him. 'Do unto others, etc.' is a Christian sarcasm, as long as Christian missionaries exist." (Twain to Twichell, April 19, 1909, MTP.)

[365, 38]   In a letter to Twichell, June, 1901, Twain noted that "there is plenty for them [the missionaries] to do at home." (MTP.)

[388, 34]   In the preface to the British edition, Morel praised Twain for "placing the manuscript unreservedly in the hands of the leaders of the [Congo Reform] movement in the United States and England and declining to accept a penny piece from the proceeds of the publication."

[390, 21]   In November, 1906, Thomas Fortune Ryan's and Daniel Guggenheim's American Congo Company obtained a ninety-nine-year option to collect rubber and other vegetable products over 4,000 square miles in the Congo, plus a ten-year option to buy 2,000 square miles of territory. The *Société Internationale Forestière et Minère du Congo* was organized by American financiers, and obtained a ninety-nine year monopoly on all mines discovered within six years in a district covering half the Congo Free State. King Leopold and his Belgian banking collaborators cut themselves in for a big slice in every cession and option. (New York *American*, Dec. 10-14, 1906.)

[390, 28]   Kowalsky was probably the author of the anonymous pamphlet, *An Answer to Mark Twain,* which sought unsuccessfully to refute some of the arguments in *King Leopold's Soliloquy.* (no date, Copy in British Museum.)

SOURCES OF QUOTATIONS FROM UNPUBLISHED MANUSCRIPTS

Unless otherwise indicated all references are to the Mark Twain Papers, Bancroft Library, University of California. DV refers to manuscripts arranged by Bernard De Voto when he was literary trustee of the Mark Twain Papers, and Paine to manuscripts arranged by Albert Bigelow Paine when he was literary trustee.

Abbreviations of other references cited:

A.F. of L. — American Federation of Labor Archives, Washington, D.C.

AJC — American Jewish Archives, Cincinnati, Ohio.

BC — Albert A. Berg Collection, New York Public Library.

BM — British Museum.

FC — Fairbanks Collection, Huntington Library, San Marino, California.

HCL — Harvard College Library.

Harnsberger — Caroline Thomas Harnsberger, "The Remaining Twain: A Life of Clara Clemens," unpublished Ms., in possession of author.

L of C — Library of Congress.

MC — Willard S. Morse Collection, Yale University Library.

The first number refers to page in the text and the second number to line on that page.

24, 18	Twain to "Dear Sir," June 24, 1874.
35, 26	Twain to Mrs. Fairbanks, Feb. 6, 1869, FC.
45, 23	Notebooks, No. 32 (b) (I), 1898, 20.
48, 7	Lord Curzon to Twain, May 27, 1907.
93, 24	Twain to Dr. John Brown, Feb. 28, (1874), MC.
117, 38	Autobiography, March 1, 1907, 1880–81.
119, 3	Notebooks, No. 25, 1891, 47.
119, 9	*Ibid.*, No. 28 (I) Oct. 5, 1895, 57.
120, 31	"Skeleton Plan of a Proposed Casting Vote Party."
121, 15	*Ibid.*
122, 27	Twain to Orion Clemens, March 27, 1895.
128, 4	Notebooks, No. 33, Aug. 29, 1900, 25.
128, 15	Notebooks, No. 28, Oct. 19, 1885, 117.
128, 25	Autobiography, dictated July 16, 1908, 2596.
128, 28	Notebooks, No. 32 (a) (I), 1879, 30.

128, 35 Autobiography, 1907, 2278.

129, 12 "Free Silver," DV No. 341.

130, 20 *Ibid.*

131, 11 "The Stupendous Procession," 1901.

133, 6 Notebooks, No. 36, Oct. 31, 1907; Autobiography, dictated July 16, 1908, 2596.

134, 10 "On Professor Mahaffy," DV No. 128, No. 6.

136, 29 Notebooks, No. 18, 11.

137, 32 Notebooks, No. 23 (I), 1888, 13–14.

137, 33 *Ibid.*, 25.

137, 35 *Ibid.*, 9.

137, 38 *Ibid.*, 12.

138, 2 *Ibid.*, No. 24, Sept. 1889, 27.

138, 6 *Ibid.*, No. 25, Dec. 1889, 38.

138, 38 Twain to Howells, Aug. 5, 1889, William Dean Howells Papers, HCL.

156, 4 Notebooks, No. 24, Feb. 1890, 38–39.

156, 18 *Ibid.*, No. 27, Sept. 9, 1891, 4.

157, 12 Twain to Joe Twichell, June 1, 1905.

157, 17 Twain to Clara Clemens, Sept. 2, 1905.

157, 24 Undated Ms.

158, 11 Ms., 1905.

158, 19 A. J. Roberts to Twain, Aug. 31, 1905.

158, 34 Original Ms., dated Tuesday Sept. 5, 1905.

159, 8 *Ibid.*

160, 28 "A Cloud-Burst of Calamaties," DV No. 246, April 1906.

161, 30 Twain to Rev. Joseph Twichell, April 18, 1906.

163, 2 "The Gorky Incident," April 28.

163, 37 Twain's penciled note on letter of Arthur Bullard, March 20, 1907.

171, 27 Unpublished letter, Jan. 2, 1869, Harnsberger, 63.

177, 28 Notebooks, No. 23 (I), 1888, 10.

180, 18 "Letter From the Recording Angel."

180, 29 Folder marked, "Material from typescript of Autobiography omitted in published text."

181, 34 "The International Lightning Trust; A Love Story," DV No. 374.

185, 16 "Letter From the Recording Angel."

185, 21 Notebooks, No. 31 (II), 1896–97, 31.

196, 22 Notebooks, No. 32 (b) (II), 38.

196, 27 *Ibid.*, Feb. 1, 1898, 55.

199, 2   Twain to Mrs. Day, March 21, (1901 or after).

202, 3   Notebooks, No. 32 (b) (II), 1899, 62.

208, 20   Unpublished fragment, DV No. 128, 1900.

211, 9   "Notes for a social history of the United States from 1850 to 1900," DV No. 31.

211, 26   Autobiography, 1907, 2278.

212, 29   Notebooks, No. 31 (II), 1896–97.

213, 4   Ms., Sept. 6, DV No. 372.

216, 5   Notebooks, No. 24, Feb. 1890, 38.

226, 18   "Knights of Labor — The New Dynasty."

227, 19   W. D. Howells to Twain, April 18, 1888.

232, 32   Notebooks, No. 24, Dec. 1889, 54.

234, 26   Notebooks, No. 23 (II), 1888–89, 37.

234, 29   *Ibid.*, No. 32b (II), Sept. 1897, 41.

235, 6   Ibid., No. 31 (II), Dec. 1896, 31.

235, 35   Dictated July 24 & 25, 1907, Autobiography, 2067–68.

236, 11   Notebooks, No. 28, Jan. 5, 1896, 18.

236, 26   Notebooks, No. 28, Jan. 4, 1896, 18.

236, 28   Unpublished papers, DV No. 31.

238, 23   Twain to Frank E. Burrough, Dec. 15, (19)00.

238, 38   Notebooks, No. 39 (b) (II), 1899, 66.

259, 30   "Miscellaneous Piece," DV No. 128.

260, 11   "River Notes, 1882," 27, in Notebooks.

260, 34   Notebooks, No. 16, 1882, 32.

260, 36   *Ibid.*, No. 23 (II), 1888–89, 60.

269, 19   *Ibid.*, No. 28 (I), 1895, 35-36.

280, 38   Clara Marshall to Twain, Feb. 27, 1901.

283, 7   Twain to James A. Garfield, Jan. 12, 1881, Garfield Papers, L of C.

287, 31   Twain to "Dear Bliss," Aug. 26, 1901.

288, 22   Notebooks, No. 23 (II), 1888–89, 39.

288, 35   *Ibid.*, No. 32 (a) (II), 1897, 59.

292, 4   "Newhouse's Jew Story," DV No. 44.

292, 24   "Mr. Randall's Jew Story," DV No. 44.

293, 3   Notebooks, No. 14, 1879, 11.

299, 4   Twain to Simon Wolf, Sept. 15, 1899, AJC.

317, 17   Notebooks, No. 28, 1895, 51.

319, 2   *Ibid.*, No. 28 (I), Jan. 4, 1896, 16.

325, 20   David G. Haskins Jr. to Samuel Gompers, Dec. 7, 1898, A. F. of L.

328, 26   Mark Twain to Dean Howells, Aug. 30, 1898, HCL.

332, 24   Joe (Twichell) to Twain, June 1, 1898.

333, 5   Notebooks, No. 30 (II), June 1896, 42.

333, 25   *Ibid.*, No. 32 (a) (II), 1897, 24.

336, 14   "The Missionary in World Politics," Summer, 1900.

336, 24   Joe (Twichell) to Twain, June 1, 1898, Aug. 24, 1900.

340, 26   Twain to J. Y. MacAlister, Dec. 31, 1900, Item 82,
          Parke-Benet Galleries, Sale No. 855, April 1–2, 1947.

341, 18   Twain to Laurence Hutton, Dec. 3, 1900.

344, 5   Twain to J. Y. MacAlister, Dec. 31, 1900, *op. cit.*

345, 4   Printed card in William Augustus Croffut Papers, L of C.

356, 11   Dr. W. A. Croffut to Twain, Feb. 5, 1901.

356, 17   Edwin Burritt Smith to Twain, Feb. 21, 1901.

356, 23   Erving Winslow to Twain, Feb. 5, 1901.

356, 30   Gordon Waldron to Twain, Toronto, Feb. 9, 1901.

359, 27   "As Regards Patriotism," No. 240.

360, 29   "Battle Hymn of the Republic (Brought Down to Date),"
          DV No. 744.

361, 11   Rev. Thomas B. Payne to Twain, Feb. 12, 1901.

361, 13   Edwin A. Berenholtz to Twain, March 5, 1901.

361, 32   Letter copied in Notebooks, No. 27, 1893.

362, 3   Notebooks, No. 29 (I), 1896, 16.

362, 19   "The Missionary in World Politics," Summer, 1900.

362, 28   A Sister to Twain, April 25, 1901.

362, 32   A. S. Buchanan to Twain, March 26, 1901.

363, 29   Twain to Joe (Twichell), March 10, (1901).

363, 32   E. L. Godkin to Twain, March 22, (1901).

369, 5   DV No. 358, Philippines.

373, 3   "The Stupendous Procession," 1901.

373, 17   DV No. 128, 1903.

374, 18   Kelly Miller to Twain, Feb. 2, 1901.

375, 5   Paine No. 89aa.

377, 15   *Ibid.*

378, 2   Twain's handwritten "Notes on Funston's Speech,"
          Paine No. 89b.

382, 27   "The War Prayer," dictated 1904–05, Paine No. 118.

384, 35   Twain to Mary Rogers, (1903).

385, 6   Twain to "Dear Sir", (1900's).

385, 28   "King Leopold, 1904, A Thanksgiving Sentiment."

385, 31   Twain to Dr. Barbour, Feb. 10, 1906, BC.

388, 34   E. D. Morel to Twain, Nov. 7 and Dec. 1905.

389, 15   W. W. Morrison to Twain, Feb. 13, 1906.

389, 27   Henry I. Kowalsky to King Leopold, Dec. 7, 1905, BM.

390, 1   Thomas B. Barbour to Twain, Sept. 7, Oct. 9, 11, 1905.

390, 31   Henry I. Kowalsky to King Leopold, Dec. 7, 1905, BM.

391, 15   Twain to Dr. Barbour, Jan. 8, 1906, BC.

391, 18   John Daniels, Corr. Sec'y, Congo Reform Assoc., to Twain June 7, 1906, and Twain's penciled note on it.

393, 33   Autobiography, March 26, 1907, 1910.

394, 3   "On Leopold, About 1906," DV No. 1370 and 3709.

396, 8   "Passages from Glances at History," No. 168.

397, 12   "Outline of History."

397, 20   "Dialogue on the Philippines, 1902–03," DV No. 357.

400, 9   Notebooks, No. 31 (I), 1896, 48.

401, 5   Notebooks, No. 32 (II), 1898, 52.

BIBLIOGRAPHY

I. BIBLIOGRAPHIES

Articles on American Literature Appearing in Current Periodicals 1920-1945, Durham, N. Car., 1947.

Asselineau, Roger, *The Literary Reputation of Mark Twain From 1910 to 1950. A Critical Essay and a Bibliography*, Paris, Librairie Marcel Didier, 1954.

Branch, Edgar M., "A Chronological Bibliography of the Writings of Samuel Clemens to June 8, 1867," *American Literature*, May, 1946, pp. 109-59.

Johnson, Merle, *A Bibliography of the Works of Mark Twain*, N.Y., 1910; revised edition, N.Y., 1935.

II. MANUSCRIPTS

American Federation of Labor Correspondence, American Federation of Labor.

Archives, Washington, D. C.

American Jewish Archives, Cincinnati, Ohio.

Albert A. Berg Collection, New York Public Library.

William Augustus Croffut Papers, Library of Congress.

Fairbanks Collection, Huntington Library, San Marino, California.

William Dean Howells Papers, Harvard College Library.

Thomas L. Leeming Collection, Princeton University Library.

Brander Matthews Papers, Columbia University Library.

Willard S. Morse Collection, Yale University Library.

Mark Twain Papers, Huntington Library, San Marino, California.

Mark Twain Papers, Bancroft Library, University of California.

III. UNPUBLISHED STUDIES

Burnham, Thomas Bond, "Mark Twain and the Gilded Age," M.A., University of Idaho, 1937.

Burnham, Thomas Bond, "Mark Twain and the Machine," Ph.D., University of Washington, 1949.

Buxton, Teresa, "A Study of the Relationship of William Dean

Howells and Samuel Clemens," Ph.D., Bucknell University, 1930.

Carter, Paul, Jr., "The Social and Political Ideas of Mark Twain," Ph.D., University of Cincinnati, 1939.

da Ponte, Durant, "American Periodical Criticism of Mark Twain, 1869-1917," Ph.D., University of Maryland, 1953.

Dozer, Donald Marquand, "Anti-Imperialism in the United States, 1865-1895," Ph.D., Harvard University, 1947.

Flowers, Frank C., "Mark Twain's Theory of Morality," Ph.D., University of Louisiana, 1941.

Gibson, William Merriam, "Mark Twain and William Dean Howells, Anti-Imperialists," Ph.D., University of Chicago, 1940.

Harnsberger, Caroline Thomas, "The Remaining Twain: A Life of Clara Clemens," unpublished *Ms.*, in possession of author.

Hays, John Q., "The Serious Elements in the Writings of Mark Twain," Ph.D., University of California, 1942.

Jonas, Alexander E., "Mark Twain and Religion," Ph.D., University of Minnesota, 1950.

Rodney, Robert M., "Mark Twain in England: A Study of English Criticism of and Attitude Toward Mark Twain: 1867-1940," Ph.D., University of Wisconsin, 1945.

Schmidt, Paul G., "Mark Twain's Use of the Vernacular," Ph.D., University of Illinois, 1953.

Scott, Arthur Lincoln, "Mark Twain as a Critic of Europe," Ph.D., University of Illinois, 1953.

Smalley, Webster L., "Critical Reception of Mark Twain in England, 1870-1910," M.A., Columbia University, 1948.

Smith, Sister M. Brigetta, "American Opinion of the Dreyfus Affair," M.A., Catholic University of America, 1946.

Vogelback, Arthur Laurence, "The Literary Reputation of Mark Twain in America, 1869-1885," Ph.D., University of Chicago, 1939.

Wiggins, Robert Alonzo, "Mark Twain's Novels: Principles and Practice of Realism," Ph.D., University of California, 1953.

IV. PUBLISHED BOOKS BY MARK TWAIN AND THOSE CONTAINING WRITINGS OF MARK TWAIN USED IN THIS STUDY.

The Collected Works of Mark Twain, "Author's National Edition," N. Y., 1899.

A Connecticut Yankee in King Arthur's Court; A Tramp Abroad;

Christian Science; Following the Equator; Literary Essays; Life on the Mississippi; Personal Recollections of Joan of Arc; Puddn'head Wilson; Roughing It; Sketches, New and Old; The American Claimant, Etc.; The Adventures of Huckleberry Finn; The Adventures of Tom Sawyer; The Gilded Age; The Innocents Abroad; The Man That Corrupted Hadleyburg, Etc.; The $30,000 Bequest; Tom Sawyer Abroad; The Prince and the Pauper.

Curious Dream and Other Sketches, London, 1872.

Europe and Elsewhere, intro. by Albert Bigelow Paine, N. Y. 1923.

Extract from Captain Stormfield's Visit to Heaven, N. Y., 1909.

Is Shakespeare Dead?, N. Y. 1909.

Letters from Honolulu written for the "Sacramento Union" by Mark Twain, intro. by John W. Vandercock, Honolulu, 1939.

Letters from the Sandwich Islands written for the "Sacramento Union," intro. and conclusion by G. Ezra Dane, San Francisco, 1937.

Mark Twain's (Burlesque) Autobiography and First Romance, London, 1871.

Mark Twain's Autobiography, edited by Albert Bigelow Paine, N. Y., 1924.

Mark Twain in Eruption, edited by Bernard De Voto, N. Y., 1940.

Mark Twain's Letters, edited by Albert Bigelow Paine, N. Y., 1917.

Mark Twain's Letters in the "Muscatine Journal," edited by Edgar M. Branch, Chicago, 1942.

Mark Twain's Letters to Will Bowen, edited by Theodore Hornberger, Austin, Texas, 1941.

Mark Twain to Mrs. Fairbanks, edited by Dixon Wecter, San Marino, Calif., 1949.

Mark Twain's Notebook, edited by Albert Bigelow Paine, N. Y., 1935.

Mark Twain of the "Enterprise," edited by Henry Nash Smith and Frederick Anderson, Berkeley, Calif., 1957.

Mark Twain's Speeches, edited by Albert Bigelow Paine, N. Y., 1923.

Merry Tales, N. Y., 1892.

Number One, Mark Twain's Sketches, N. Y., 1874.

Report from Paradise, intro. by Dixon Wecter, N. Y., 1952.

Screamers, London, 1871.

Sketches of the Sixties, edited by John Howell, San Francisco, 1927.

The Celebrated Jumping Frog of Calaveras County, and other Sketches, N. Y., 1867.

The Complete Short Stories of Mark Twain, edited by Charles Neider, N. Y. 1957.

The Curious Republic of Gondour and Other Whimsical Sketches, N. Y., 1919.

The Love Letters of Mark Twain, edited by Dixon Wecter, N. Y. 1949.

The Mysterious Stranger, N. Y., 1916.

The Washoe Giant in San Francisco, edited by Franklin Walker, San Francisco, 1938. *Traveling With The Innocents Abroad: Mark Twain's Original Reports from Europe and the Holy Land,* edited by Daniel Morley McKlithan, Norman, Okla., 1958.

Washington in 1868, edited by Cyril Clemens, Webster Groves, Mo., 1943.

What is Man? and other Essays, N. Y., 1917.

V. MARK TWAIN ITEMS REFERRED TO IN TEXT AND REPRINTED IN BOOKS

"A Double-Barreled Detective," *The Man That Corrupted Hadleyburg, Etc.*

"A New Beecher Church," *Curious Dream and Other Sketches.*

"A Tribute," *Mark Twain's Speeches.*

"A True Story," *Sketches New and Old.*

"A Word of Encouragement for Our Blushing Exiles," *Europe and Elsewhere.*

"Concerning the Jews," *Literary Essays.*

"Consistency," *Mark Twain's Speeches.*

"Corn-Pone Opinions," *Europe and Elsewhere.*

"Daniel in the Lion's Den — and Out Again All Right," *Sketches of the Sixties.*

"Esquimau's Maiden's Romance," *The Man That Corrupted Hadleyburg, Etc.*

"Fenimore Cooper's Literary Offenses," *Literary Essays.*

"Important Correspondence. Between Mr. Mark Twain of San Francisco, and Rev. Bishop Hawks, D.D., of New York, Rev. Phillips Brooks of Philadelphia, and Rev. Dr. Cummings of Chicago, Concerning the Occupancy of Grace Cathedral," and "Further of Mr. Mark Twain's Important Correspondence," *Sketches of the Sixties.*

"Independence Day Speech in England, July 4, 1907," *Mark Twain's Speeches.*

"License of the Press," *Mark Twain's Speeches.*

"My First Lie and How I Got Out of It," *The Man That Corrupted Hadleyburg, Etc.*

"Niagara," *Sketches New and Old.*

"Reflections on the Sabbath," *The Washoe Giant in San Francisco.*

"Running for Governor," *Screamers.*

"Skeleton Plan of a Proposed Casting Vote Party," *Europe and Elsewhere.*

"Temperance and Women's Rights," *Europe and Elsewhere.*

"The German Chicago," *Literary Essays.*

"The Great Prize Fight," *The Washoe Giant in San Francisco.*

"The Late Benjamin Franklin," *Sketches New and Old.*

"The Latest Sensation," *The Washoe Giant in San Francisco.*

"The New Wildcat Religion," *The Washoe Giant in San Francisco.*

"The Private History of A Campaign That Failed," *Merry Tales.*

"The Savage Club Dinner," *Mark Twain's Speeches.*

"The Story of the Good Little Boy Who Did Not Prosper," *Sketches New and Old.*

"The Turning Point of My Life," *What is Man? and Other Essays.*

"$30,000 Bequest," *The Man That Corrupted Hadleyburg, Etc.*

"To the Person Sitting in Darkness," *Europe and Elsewhere.*

"What Have the Police Been Doing?" *The Washoe Giant in San Francisco.*

"What Paul Bourget Thinks of Us," *Literary Essays.*

VI. MARK TWAIN ITEMS REFERRED TO IN TEXT AND NOT PUBLISHED IN BOOKS

"About Smells," *Galaxy*, May, 1870, pp. 721-22.

"Female Suffrage," *Alta California*, May 19, 1867.

"Female Suffrage. Views of Mark Twain," St. Louis *Daily Missouri Democrat*, March 12, 13, 15, 1867.

"Female Suffrage," New York *Sunday Mercury*, April 7, 1867.

"Fenimore Cooper's Further Literary Offenses," *New England Quarterly*, Sept. 1946, p. 299.

"In Defense of General Funston," *North American Review*, May, 1902, pp. 614-24. *King Leopold's Soliloquy: A Defense of His Congo Rule by Mark Twain*, Boston, 1905, London, 1906.

"Let's Look at the Record: An Open Letter to his Countrymen by Mark Twain," Kansas City *Journal*, June 15, 1879.

"Mark Twain Says Not I," New York *Tribune*, Feb. 15, 1901.

"Open Letter to Col. Vanderbilt," *Packard's Monthly*, March, 1869, pp. 89-91.

"Stirring Times in Austria," *Harper's Monthly*, March, 1898, pp. 530-40.

"The Czar's Soliloquy," *North American Review*, March, 1905, pp. 321-22.

"The Facts in the Case of the Great Beef Contract," *Galaxy*, May, 1870, pp. 718-21 and Sept. 1870, pp. 42-43.

"The Revised Catechism," New York *Tribune*, Feb. 1, 1874.

"The Treaty with China," New York *Tribune*, Aug. 4, 1868.

"Those Blasted Children," New York *Sunday Mercury*, Feb. 21, 1864.

"To My Missionary Critics," *North American Review*, April, 1901, pp. 520-34.

"Ye Cuban Patriot: A Calm Inspection of Him," Buffalo *Express*, Dec. 25, 1869.

It is impossible to list all the material read in connection with the present study — books about Mark Twain, biographies, autobiographies and specialized studies, newspaper and magazine articles dealing with Mark Twain or giving the background of his times. The following is a list only of the more important works.

VII. BOOKS

Allen, Jerry, *The Adventures of Mark Twain*, Boston, 1954.

Andrews, Kenneth R., *Nook Farm — Mark Twain's Hartford Circle*, Cambridge, Mass., 1950.

Beard, Charles A. and Mary R., *The Rise of American Civilization*, N. Y., 1924.

Bellamy, Gladys Carmen, *Mark Twain as a Literary Artist*, Norman, Oklahoma, 1950.

Benson, Ivan, *Mark Twain's Western Years*, Palo Alto, Calif., 1938.

Blair, Walter, *Native American Humor*, N. Y., 1937.

Bobrova, M., *Mark Twain*, Moscow, 1954. (In Russian)

Branch, Edgar M., *The Literary Apprenticeship of Mark Twain*, Urbana, Ill., 1950.

Brashear, Minnie M., *Mark Twain: Son of Missouri*, Chapel Hill, N. Car., 1934.

Brooks, Van Wyck, *The Ordeal of Mark Twain*, N. Y., 1920; revised edition, N. Y., 1935.

Brooks, Van Wyck, *The Times of Melville and Whitman*, N. Y., 1947.

Brooks, Van Wyck, *Days of the Phoenix: The Nineteen-Twenties I Remember*, N. Y., 1957.

Brown, Sterling, *The Negro in American Fiction*, Washington, 1937.

Canby, Henry Seidel, *Turn West, Turn East: Mark Twain and Henry James*, N. Y., 1951.

Cardwell, Guy A., *Twins of Genius: Twain and Cable*, Lansing, Mich., 1953.

Carter, Everett, *Howells and the Age of Realism*, Phila., 1955.

Churchill, Winston S., *A Roving Commission: My Early Life*, N. Y., 1930.

Clemens, Clara, *My Father, Mark Twain*, N. Y. 1931.

Clemens, Clara, *My Husband: Gabrilowitsch*, N. Y. 1936.

De Voto, Bernard, *Mark Twain's America*, Boston, 1932.

De Voto, Bernard, *Mark Twain at Work*, Cambridge, Mass., 1942.

De Wolfe, M. A., *Memories of a Hostess: A Chronicle of Eminent Friendships Drawn Chiefly from the Diaries of Mrs. James T. Fields*, Boston, 1920.

Elderkin, John, etc., *After Dinner Speeches at the Lotos Club, Arranged by John Elderkin, Chester S. Lord, Charles W. Price*, N. Y., 1911.

Ferguson, John De Lancey, *Mark Twain: Man and Legend*, Indianapolis, 1943.

Foner, Philip S., *History of the Labor Movement in the United States*, vol. II, N. Y., 1955.

Foner, Philip S., *Life and Writings of Frederick Douglass*, vol. IV., N. Y., 1955.

Forbes, W. Cameron, *The Philippine Islands*, Boston, 1928.

Frank, Waldo, *Our America*, N. Y., 1919.

Frear, Walter Francis, *Mark Twain and Hawaii*, Chicago, 1947.

Garraty, John A., *Henry Cabot Lodge: A Biography*, N. Y., 1953.

Gilder, Rosamond, editor, *Letters of Richard Watson Gilder*, N. Y., 1916.

Gillis, William R., *Gold Rush Days with Mark Twain*, N. Y., 1930.

Harnsberger, Caroline Thomas, *Mark Twain at Your Fingertips*, N. Y., 1948.

Heller, Otto, *The Seriousness of Mark Twain*, Address at the Annual Dinner of the State Historical Society at Hannibal, Missouri, May 19, 1935. Hannibal, 1935.

Hemminghaus, Edgar H., *Mark Twain in Germany,* N. Y., 1939.

Henderson, Archibald, *Bernard Shaw, Playboy and Prophet,* N. Y., 1932.

Henderson, Archibald, *Mark Twain,* N. Y., 1910.

Hicks, Granville, *The Great Tradition,* N. Y., 1933.

Howells, William Dean, *My Mark Twain: Reminiscences and Criticism,* N. Y., 1910.

Jones, Howard Mumford, editor, *The Letters of Sherwood Anderson,* Boston, 1953.

Kazin, Alfred, *On Native Grounds,* N. Y., 1942.

Keller, Helen, *The Story of My Life,* N. Y., 1905.

Langdon, Jarvis, *Samuel Langhorne Clemens, Some Reminiscences and Some Excerpts from Unpublished Manuscripts,* n.p., n.d.

Lawton, Mary, *A Lifetime with Mark Twain: The Memoirs of Katy Leary, for Thirty Years His Faithful Servant,* N. Y., 1925.

Liljegren, Sven B., *The Revolt Against Romanticism in America As Evidenced in the Works of Samuel L. Clemens,* Pub. American Institute of University of Upsala, 1947.

Logan, Rayford W., *The Negro in American Life and Thought, The Nadir,* N. Y., 1932.

Lyman, George D., *Sage of the Comstock Lode,* N. Y., 1934.

Mack, Effie Mona, *Mark Twain in Nevada,* N. Y., 1947.

Matthews, Brander, *Inquiries and Opinions,* N. Y., 1907.

Macy, John Albert, *The Spirit of American Literature,* N. Y., 1913.

May, Henry F., *Protestant Churches and Industrial America,* N. Y., 1949.

McElroy, Robert, *Grover Cleveland, The Man and the Statesman,* N. Y., 1923.

Mencken, H. L., *Happy Days, 1880-1892,* N. Y., 1940.

Mendelson, M., *Mark Twain,* Moscow, 1939. (In Russian)

Millis, Walter, *The Martial Spirit,* Boston, 1931.

Moehle, Dr. Günter, *Das Europabild Mark Twains,* Berlin, 1940.

Mott, Frank Luther, *Golden Multitudes,* N. Y., 1947.

Mumford, Lewis, *The Golden Day: A Study in American Experience and Culture,* N. Y., 1926.

Nichol, John, *American Literature, An Historical Sketch, 1620-1880,* Edinburgh, 1882.

Paine, Albert Bigelow, *Mark Twain: A Biography. The Personal and Literary Life of Samuel Langhorne Clemens,* N. Y., 1912.

Parrington, Vernon L., *Main Currents in American Thought*, vol. III, N. Y., 1930.

Pattee, F. L., *A History of American Literature Since 1870*, N. Y., 1911.

Perlo, Victor, *American Imperialism*, N. Y., 1951.

Perry, Bliss, *The American Mind*, Boston, 1912.

Phillips, Catherine Coffin, *Cornelius Cole, California Pioneer and United States Senator*, San Francisco, 1924.

Pond, James Burton, *Eccentricities of Genius. Memories of famous men and women of platform and stage*, N. Y., 1900.

Pratt, Julius W., *America's Colonial Experiment*, N. Y., 1951.

Pratt, Julius W., *The Expansionists of 1898*, Baltimore, 1936.

Rutter, John P., *A Thirty Years View of Marion County*, 1861.

Schönemann, Friederich, *Mark Twain als literarische Persönlichkeit*, Jena, 1925.

Scott, Arthur L., editor, *Mark Twain: Selected Criticism*, Dallas, 1955.

Sherman, Stuart P., *On Contemporary Literature*, N. Y., 1917.

Spiller, Thorp, Johnson, Canby, *Literary History of the United States*, N. Y., 1948.

Storey, Moorfield and Lichauco, Marcial P., *The Conquest of the Philippines by the United States*, N. Y., 1926.

Taylor, Colin B., *Mark Twain's Margins on Thackeray's 'Swift,'* N. Y., 1935.

Taylor, Walter Fuller, *The Economic Novel in America*, Chapel Hill, N. Car., 1942.

Trilling, Lionel, *The Liberal Imagination: Essays on Literature and Society*, N. Y., 1950.

Van Doren, Carl, *The American Novel*, N. Y., 1921.

Vedder, Henry C., *American Writers of To-Day*, N. Y., 1894.

Wagenknecht, Edward, *Mark Twain: the Man and His Work*, New Haven, 1935.

Webster, Samuel C., *Mark Twain, Business Man*, Boston, 1946.

Wecter, Dixon, *Mark Twain in Three Moods*, San Marino, Cal., 1948.

Wecter, Dixon, *Sam Clemens of Hannibal*, N. Y., 1953.

West, Victor Royce, *Folklore in the Works of Mark Twain*, Lincoln, Nebraska, 1930.

Wilson, Edmund, *The Shores of Light*, N. Y., 1952.

Wolf, Simon, *The Presidents I Have Known*, N. Y., 1918.

Altick, Richard D., "Mark Twain's Despair: An Explanation in Terms of His Humanity," *South Atlantic Quarterly*, Oct., 1935, 359-67.

Anonymous, "Saving of Mark Twain," *Literary Digest*, Nov. 24, 1917, 54-59.

Anonymous, "Mark Twain Orates on Death of Democratic Party in 1880," *Twainian*, Jan-Feb. 1947, 2-3.

Anonymous, "Mark Twain as a Serious Force in Literature," *Current Literature*, June, 1910, 663-67.

Anonymous, "Mark Twain's Investments," *Colliers*, Nov. 12, 1910, 32.

Anonymous, "Mark Twain as a Publisher," *Bookman*, Jan. 1913, 489-94.

Anonymous, "Gorky Incident: An Unpublished Fragment by Mark Twain," *Slavonic Review*, Aug. 1944, 37-38.

Anonymous, "Tributes to Mark Twain," *North American Review*, June, 1910, 381*ff*.

Anonymous, "Mark Twain, Radical," *Saturday Review of Literature*, Nov. 1, 1924, 241.

Anonymous, "Mark Twain's New Deal: Connecticut Yankee at King Arthur's Court," *Ibid.*, Dec. 16, 1933, 352.

Anonymous, "Mark Twain's Introductory Remarks at the Time of Churchill's First American Lecture," *American Notes & Queries*, Jan. 1946, 47-48.

Armstrong, K. J., "Mark Twain's Early Writings Discovered," *Missouri Historical Review*, 1930, 485-501.

Barnes, F. L., "Fresh Light on the Dark Continent," *American Journal of Theology*, Jan. 1906, 198.

Blair, Walter, "Mark Twain, New York Correspondent," *American Literature*, 1939, 247-59.

Brown, Herbert R., "The Great American Novel," *Ibid.*, March 1935, 1-14.

Brown, Sterling A., "Negro Characters as Seen by White Authors," *Journal of Negro Education*, Jan. 1933, 180-201.

Burnam, Tom, "Mark Twain and the Paige Typesetter: A Background of Despair," *Western Humanities Review*, Winter, 1951-52, 29-36.

Carter, Paul Jr., "Mark Twain and the American Labor Movement," *New England Quarterly*, Sept. 1957, 352-58.

Carter, Paul Jr., "Mark Twain and War," *Twainian*, March, 1942, 1-3.

Clemens, Susy, "Biography of Mark Twain," *North American Review*, May 17, 1907, 1-3.

Colby, F. M., "Mark Twain's Illuminating Blunder," *Bookman*, Dec. 1910, 355-57.

Compton, Charles H., "Who Reads Mark Twain?" *American Mercury*, April, 1934, 465-71.

De Leon, Daniel, "An Irrepressible Humorist," *Daily People*, Sept. 7, 1905.

De Voto, Bernard, "Mark Twain About the Jews," *Jewish Frontier*, May 1939, 7-9.

De Voto, Bernard, "Mark Twain Papers: with excerpts from Twain's unpublished 'Outlines of History,'" *Saturday Review of Literature*, Dec. 10, 1938, 3-4, 14-15.

Dickinson, Leon Townsend, "Mark Twain's Revisions in writing *The Innocents Abroad*," *American Literature*, May, 1947, 139-57.

Douglas, Robert, "The Pessimism of Mark Twain," *Mark Twain Quarterly*, Winter, 1941, 1-4.

Eastman, Max, "Mark Twain's Elmira," *Harper's*, May, 1938, 620-32.

Edwards, Peter G., "The Political Economy of Mark Twain's *Connecticut Yankee*," *Mark Twain Quarterly*, 1950, 2, 18.

Ferguson, De Lancey, "The Case for Mark Twain's Wife," *University of Toronto Quarterly*, Oct. 1939, 9-21.

Guest, Boyd, "Twains Concept of Woman's Sphere," *Mark Twain Quarterly*, Winter-Spring, 1945-46, 1-4.

Gibson, William M., "Twain and Howells: Anti-Imperialists," *New England Quarterly*, Dec. 1947, 435-70.

Hamada, Masajiro, "Mark Twain's Conception of Social Justice," *Studies in English Literature* (Japan), Oct. 1936, 593-616.

Hoben, John B., "Mark Twain's *A Connecticut Yankee*: A Genetic Study," *American Literature*, Nov. 1946, 197-218.

Howells, William Dean, "Our Spanish Prisoners at Portsmouth," *Harper's Weekly*, Aug. 20, 1898, 826-29.

Jones, Alexander, "Heterodox Thought in Mark Twain's Hannibal," *Arkansas Historical Quarterly*, 1951, 244-57.

Keller, Helen, "Mark Twain as He Revealed Himself to Helen Keller," *American Magazine*, July 1929, 50-51.

Lang, Arthur, "The Art of Mark Twain," *Illustrated News of the World*, Feb. 14, 1891, 222.

Lanzar, Maria C., "The Anti-Imperialist League," *Philippine Social Science Review*, Aug. 1930, 1-13.

Leavis, F. R., "Mark Twain's Neglected Classic: The Moral Astringency of *Pudd'nhead Wilson*," *Commentary*, Feb. 1956, 128-29.

Leisy, Ernest E., "Mark Twain's Part in *The Gilded Age*," *American Literature*, Jan. 1937, 445-47.

Lorch, Fred W., "Mark Twain and the Campaign That Failed," *Ibid.*, Jan. 1941, 454-60.

Mendelson, M., "Mark Twain Accuses," *Soviet Literature*, May, 1948, 151-61.

Oliver, R. T., "Mark Twain's Views on Education," *Education*, Oct. 1940, 112-15.

Orians, G. Harrison, "Walter Scott, Mark Twain and the Civil War," *South Atlantic Quarterly*, Oct. 1941, 342-59.

Parsons, Coleman O., "The Devil and Samuel Clemens," *Virginia Quarterly Review*, Autumn, 1947, 582-602.

Pattee, Fred Lewis, "On the Rating of Mark Twain," *American Mercury*, June. 1928, 183-91.

Remes, Carol, "The Heart of Huckleberry Finn," *Masses & Mainstream*, Nov. 1955, 8-16.

Rosenberger, Edward G., "An Agnostic Hagiographer," *Catholic World*, Sept. 1928, 717-23.

Schmidt, Paul, "Mark Twain's Satire on Republicanism," *American Quarterly*, Vol. 5, Winter, 1953, 344-56.

Shuster, G. N., "The Tragedy of Mark Twain," *Ibid.*, March, 1917, 731-37.

Sillen, Samuel, "Dooley, Twain and Imperialism," *Masses & Mainstream*, Dec. 1948, 6-14.

Stewart, G. R., "Bret Harte upon Mark Twain in 1866," *American Literature*, Nov. 1941, 263-64.

Stewart, H. L., "Mark Twain on the Jewish Problem," *Dalhousie Review*, Jan. 1935, 455-58.

Taylor, Walter F., "Mark Twain and the Machine Age," *South Atlantic Quarterly*, Oct. 1938, 384-96.

Thompson, C. M., "Mark Twain as an interpreter of American Character," *Atlantic Monthly*, April, 1897, 243-50.

Tidwell, J. N., "Mark Twain's Representation of Negro Speech," *American Speech*, Oct. 1942, 174-76.

Van Doren, Carl, "Mark Twain and Bernard Shaw," *Century*. March, 1925, 705-10.

Vogelback, Arthur L., "Mark Twain: Newspaper Contributor," *American Literature*, May, 1948, 111-28.

Vogelback, Arthur L., "The Publication and Reception of *Huckleberry Finn* in America," *Ibid.*, Nov. 1939, 260-72.

Vogelback, Arthur L., *"The Prince and the Pauper:* A Study in Critical Standards," *Ibid.*, March, 1942, 48-54.

Vogelback, Arthur L., "Mark Twain and the Tammany Ring," *Publications of the Modern Language Society of America*, March, 1955, 69-77.

Walker, Franklin, "An Influence from San Francisco on Mark Twain's *The Gilded Age*," *American Literature*, March, 1936, 63-66.

Webster, Samuel and Doris, "Whitewashing Jane Clemens," *Bookman*, 1925, 531-35.

Williams, March McCullock, "In Re 'Pudd'nhead Wilson,'" *Southern Magazine*, Feb. 1894, 99-102.

Wister, Owen, "In Homage to Mark Twain," *Harper's Monthly*, Oct. 1935, 547-56.

Wright, Conrad, "The Sources of Mr. Howells' Socialism," *Science & Society*, Autumn, 1938, 514-17.

INDEX

439